Handbook of
Latin American
Popular Culture

Handbook of Latin American Popular Culture

EDITED BY
Harold E. Hinds, Jr.
AND
Charles M. Tatum

Greenwood Press
Westport, Connecticut • London, England

Library of Congress Cataloging in Publication Data

Main entry under title:

Handbook of Latin American popular culture.

  Bibliography: p.
  Includes index.
  1. Latin America—Popular culture.   I. Hinds,
Harold E.   II. Tatum, Charles M.
F1408.3.H316   1985   306′.4′098   84-22558
ISBN 0-313-23293-8 (lib. bdg.)

Library of Congress Catalog Card Number: 84-22558
ISBN 0-313-23293-8

First published in 1985

Greenwood Press
A division of Congressional Information Service, Inc.
88 Post Road West
Westport, Connecticut 06881

Printed in the United States of America

♾™

The paper used in this book complies with the
Permanent Paper Standard issued by the National
Information Standards Organization (Z39.48-1984).

10   9   8   7   6   5   4   3   2   1

To Elizabeth

Contents

Acknowledgments

We gratefully thank the people who have supported this project: M. Thomas Inge, for suggesting that we submit a proposal to Greenwood Press to edit a volume on Latin American popular culture; Marilyn Brownstein and Cynthia Harris, editors at Greenwood Press, who exhibited much confidence in us throughout the lengthy process of putting together this volume; Dr. Elizabeth Blake (Academic Dean, University of Minnesota, Morris), Dr. Ted Underwood (Head, Division of Social Sciences, University of Minnesota, Morris), and Dr. Thomas Gale (Dean, Arts and Sciences, New Mexico State University), for their encouragement and financial backing; and Barbara McGinnis, Reference Librarian, University of Minnesota, Morris, for her willing assistance in obtaining reference works that often seemed to require the training of an experienced sleuth.

Preface

When we were approached by Greenwood Press to coedit a handbook on the popular culture of Spanish and Portuguese Latin America, our initial response was a mixture of excitement and apprehension. We were excited because, as active scholars in the field, we were keenly aware of the paucity of reliable research tools in general and the absence of a broadly conceived panoramic work in particular. We knew that such a work could make a solid contribution to the understanding and appreciation of popular culture in Latin America. At the same time, while we were reasonably confident that there were scholars with sufficient breadth and sophistication to write some of the chapters, we were apprehensive that we would not find individuals willing to contribute in other less established areas of research. Another factor contributing to our initial "pre-game" jitters was the impressive three-volume *Handbook of American Popular Culture* edited by M. Thomas Inge.[1] While it was to serve as our model, we naturally asked ourselves if we could produce a work worthy of the prototype in the field.

The present volume represents a modest, yet sound, beginning. We believe that our contributors have given us solid overviews of ten areas of popular culture in Latin America. All were faced with the dilemma of having to deal with many countries, an imposing problem. While most Latin American countries share, in a very general sense, a common history and culture, the evolution of their diverse forms of popular culture is often not at all uniform. This is due to many factors, such as the rate of economic development, which in some countries has had a direct bearing on the establishment and development of popular culture industries. To cite one example, the more industrialized countries such as Mexico, Brazil, and Argentina have active and artistically sophisticated popular film industries, while such industries are practically nonexistent in the poorer countries of Paraguay, Ecuador, or El Salvador. Our contributors were thus faced with the difficult task of using their expertise in one aspect of one country's popular culture to research, make intelligent observations, and draw well-thought-out conclusions about other countries. In a sense, every Latin Americanist, whatever his/her discipline, who sets out to give a global view of the region is faced with the same problem. We believe our contributors have handled it quite ably.

Popular culture scholarship in Latin America is in its infancy. This is neither unique nor surprising considering that popular culture in general is a relatively new field in which scholars began to examine, conceptualize, and research in a methodical way only as recently as twenty years ago. Russell B. Nye's seminal work, *The Unembarrassed Muse: The Popular Arts in America*, appeared in 1970.[2] The *Journal of Popular Culture*, the first and still the most important journal devoted to the serious study of popular culture, only began in the late 1960s; and the only journal with a Latin American focus, *Studies in Latin American Popular Culture*, was established in 1981. While—as Inge points out in the preface to his handbook—some established disciplines such as sociology and film studies were many years ahead of their time in the examination of popular culture, its serious, scholarly study is a recent phenomenon in the United States. However, when we compare the state of scholarship in this country to that in Latin America, we can begin to develop a deep appreciation for the basic research obstacles encountered by our contributors.

To illustrate this, let us briefly compare a couple of areas of popular culture in the United States included in Inge's handbook with their counterparts in Latin America covered in this volume. Film studies, for example, appear to be fairly advanced in this country in terms of general reference works, encyclopedias of film, works listing the location of films, bibliographic guides, annual indexes, and journals. By contrast, John Mosier observes that there is no general work on Latin American film and with one exception, there is no reliable work on a national cinema that lives up to its title. Further, there is a great need for standard critical texts on the various aspects of films within the region. Much of the study of Latin American film—most of which is recent—has been done by journalists who are, by and large, self-taught and generally lacking in critical sophistication.

While the five centers for early films and film-related material in this country are not totally adequate, Latin American film scholars are faced with doing work in centers of individual countries, none of which is well supplied with research materials. In terms of recent films, one has a greater opportunity to see Latin American films at European film festivals than in Latin America. In the United States recent films are readily available for viewing in large cities and distributors regularly cooperate with researchers.

Comic art research in the United States and Latin America can be similarly contrasted. Although, according to Inge, it "has been the most generally neglected area of popular culture [in the United States] until very recently," and lacks sound bibliographical and reference works, researchers have available to them several standard panoramic treatments, encyclopedias, and checklists.[3] When viewed regionally, the situation for scholars working in the area of comic art in Latin America is far worse. The lack of collections of basic source material can be depressing. No Latin American country has the equivalent of the San Francisco Academy of Comic Art, the Popular Culture Library at Bowling Green State University, or other centers; rather, researchers must rely on transient second-hand book stores or an occasional lucky contact with one of a handful of private collectors.

In general, the situation described above also prevails in the areas of popular music, sports, television, photonovels, cartoons, and festivals and carnivals in Latin America.

In addition to the physical and logistical problems of doing adequate research, our contributors were forced to deal with the conceptual dilemma of defining popular culture within a Latin American context. *Cultura popular* in Spanish does not translate directly as "popular culture"; rather, it connotes "folk culture," which is still to be found thriving, particularly in rural areas. What, then, to do with "folk culture" and on what basis to separate it from "popular culture"? The answers vary.[4] Robert Lavenda, for example, while excluding purely Indian festivals and carnivals because they were not present in "popular" contexts, nevertheless feels that the distinction between them and festivals and carnivals that are integrated into the national popular culture is somewhat artificial. Gerard Béhague finds popular music synonymous with urban commercial music but notes that musicologists and others, prior to the 1950s, also included folk and traditional music under the general rubric of *música popular*.

Naomi Lindstrom reflects this more sophisticated definition of "popular" as an urban commercial phenomenon in her comments that the spread of cartoons is linked to technology and increased numbers of readers. Joseph Straubhaar's observation that television dominates other mass media and forms of popular culture in a number of more urbanized and industrialized countries also supports this definition. It is also implicit in several other chapters and coincides with Russell Nye's conclusion that popular culture is the "child of modern technology, wholly dependent for its extension on modern techniques of duplicating and multiplying materials along with much more effective and less costly methods of production and distribution."[5] Urbanization, at times accompanied by significant industrialization, provided a large audience for popular culture. It is not mere chance, then, that popular culture thrives in Latin America's largest urban centers.

A cursory examination of the *Journal of Popular Culture* (*JPC*) reveals that many of its contributors have relied heavily on the critical-methodological approaches prevalent in their own disciplines, be they literature, cultural anthropology, sociology, philosophy, music, mass communications, or history. Articles and in-depth sections of the *JPC* have been devoted to exploring and calling for the development of critical-methodological approaches that are uniquely suited to the study of popular culture as a new discipline.[6] The surveys of critical works in the following chapters on Latin America also reveal many approaches, but two emerge with surprising regularity: (1) the cultural imperialism approach, and (2) the semiological approach based mainly on the works of the Italian theorist Umberto Eco.

The first approach is based on a Marxist theory of economic dependency: that is, that the world is divided into economically advanced, capitalist, exploiting countries, which constitute a metropolitan center; and the rest of the countries, known as peripheral or satellite countries. The latter are economically dependent on and exploited by the former. This dependency "is an embodiment of the neo-colonial relation between the strong and the weak, the rich and the poor, and the exploiting and the exploited."[7] While there is no distinct or coherent theory of cultural imperialism, the theory draws heavily on the theoretical analogues of economic dependence.[8] Thus economically dominant nations culturally exploit and control weaker ones by manipulating the means of production, distribution, and even the content of mass media and popular culture, such as movies, television, radio, comics, and photonovels. This approach is alluded to in the chapters by Harold Hinds, Jr., Cornelia Butler Flora, Joseph Straubhaar, and John Mosier. The major work that popularized this approach is probably Ariel Dorfman and Armand Mattelart's *How to Read Donald Duck: Imperialist Ideology in the Disney Comic.*[9]

Umberto Eco's collection of essays, *Apocalípticos e integrados ante la cultura de masas* [*Attitudes of the Doomsayers and the Well-Adjusted toward Mass Culture*] is the single most important semiological work preferred by critics of diverse forms of Latin American popular culture.[10] Eco's thesis is that "forms of high culture such as literature and art organize their signs according to a non-habitual code which requires interpretative work by the receiver. Mass culture, in contrast, relies on easily learned formulas, denying the receiver an active participation in the production of the message."[11] Like Roland Barthes and other semioticians, Eco believes that semiotic analysis offers "a metalanguage that enables the critic to unmask the mythic language of mass culture."[12] Eco views mass culture as "anti-culture" produced by the powerful and forced upon the defenseless mass consumer. It conveys a sense of false security by holding out the promise that the consumer may redeem himself socially and economically and be saved from an impending apocalypse by emulating the super-beings of films, comics, and television. The message underlying this process is ultimately alienating and self-destructive.

Concerning future research needs, our contributors make many valuable suggestions while displaying varying degrees of dissatisfaction with the state of research in their respective areas. Some believe that virtually nothing has been adequately researched. For example, John Mosier states that hardly anything substantive has been written on film. Naomi Lindstrom feels that everything needs to be done on cartoons, and Harold Hinds, Jr., only slightly more optimistic, writes that nearly everything needs to be done on comics. In general, our contributors point to a serious lack of basic research tools such as bibliographies, collections, guides to collections, catalogues, descriptive surveys and monographic studies. They also call for content analyses of specific genres; the critical evaluation of sources; interviews; in-depth studies of popular culture industries including their finances, distribution, and legal constraints; consumer impact and response studies; and studies focusing on the contextual relationship between society and popular culture.

The possibilities for research in Latin American popular culture are thus immense. We hope that this handbook will go far in stimulating interest and serious scholarly attention in this new and exciting field.

NOTES

1. M. Thomas Inge, ed., *Handbook of American Popular Culture,* 3 vols. (Westport, Conn.: Greenwood Press, 1978–1981).

2. Russell B. Nye, *The Unembarrassed Muse: The Popular Arts in America* (New York: The Dial Press, 1970).

3. Inge, *Handbook of American Popular Culture*, vol. 1, p. 77.

4. For succinct discussions on the definition of popular culture and the differences between popular and folk culture, see Ray B. Browne, "Popular Culture: The World around Us," in *The Popular Culture Reader*, ed. Jack Nachbar, Deborah Weiser, and John L. Wright (Bowling Green, Ohio: Popular Press, 1978), pp. 12–18; Russell B. Nye, "Notes on a Rationale for Popular Culture," in *The Popular Culture Reader*, pp. 19–27; Tom Kando, "Popular Culture and Its Sociology: Two Controversies," *Journal of Popular Culture* 9, no. 2 (Fall 1975): 438/86–455/103; Ray B. Browne, "Popular Culture: Notes toward a Definition," in *Popular Culture and Curricula*, ed. Ray B. Browne and Ronald J. Ambroselli (Bowling Green, Ohio: Popular Press, 1972), pp. 1–13.

5. Nye, "Notes," p. 20.

6. See *Journal of Popular Culture* 9, no. 2 (Fall 1975):349–508, an in-depth section on "Theories and Methodologies in Popular Culture"; *Journal of Popular Culture* 11, no. 2 (Fall 1977): 379–513, an in-depth section on "Sociology and Popular Culture"; John Cawelti, "The Concept of Formula in the Study of Popular Culture," *Journal of Popular Culture* 3 (1969):381–90; Hayden White, "Structuralism and Popular Culture," *Journal of Popular Culture* 7 (1974):759–75; *Journal of Popular Culture* 9, no. 2 (1975):139–289, in-depth section on "History and Popular Culture."

7. Chin-Chuan Lee, "Economic Dependency and Cultural Imperialism," in *Mass Communication Review Yearbook*, vol. 3, ed. D. Charles Whitney, Ellen Wartella, and Sven Windahl (Beverly Hills, London, and New Delhi: Sage Publications, 1982), p. 295.

8. Chin-Chuan Lee persuasively argues this point in his *Media Imperialism*

Reconsidered. The Homogenizing of Television Culture (Beverly Hills and London: Sage Publications, 1980). See particularly chapter two, "Economic Dependency and Cultural Imperialism: Theoretical Perspectives," pp. 29–65.

9. Ariel Dorfman and Armand Mattelart, *How to Read Donald Duck: Imperialist Ideology in the Disney Comic*, translated and introduction by David Kunzle (New York: International General, 1975).

10. Umberto Eco, *Apocalípticos e integrados ante la cultura de masas,* translated by Andrés Boglar (Barcelona: Editorial Lumen, 1968).

11. Ellen McCracken, "Toward an Interdisciplinary Semiotics: Michele Mattelart's *La cultura de la opresión femenina,*" *Studies in Latin American Popular Culture* 1 (1982):241.

12. Ibid. p. 238.

Handbook of
Latin American
Popular Culture

Gerard Béhague

1 Popular Music

The term *música popular* in both Spanish and Portuguese has denoted traditionally the generic sense of music of the people, encompassing what folklorists and ethnomusicologists call folk and traditional music as well as urban music. Only since the 1950s do we see a more frequent differentiation between folk and popular music, when the term *folklore musical* or simply *folklore* became common, and *música popular* gradually assumed the contemporary sense of urban popular, commercial music. It is to this sense of popular music that the present chapter addresses itself. Urban popular music represents musical repertories, genres, and behaviors specific to urban areas. Such music corpora are generally disseminated through commercial outlets such as the publication of sheet music collections, radio and television broadcasts, and the recording industry and reflect the social stratification of a particular area, whether social strata are conceived in socioeconomic, generational, or ethnic terms. In addition, certain Latin American popular music movements, genres, and styles have often resulted from sociopolitical participation and criticism.

Latin American folklorists and sociologists have studied urban popular music from their respective disciplinary vantage points to illustrate other domains of popular culture, to point out the stylistic preference of certain social groups within a given society, or to identify symbols expressed through music by such groups. Other social scientists, assuming a materialistic philosophical stance, have attempted to relate popular music trends to ideologies and social struggles. While these approaches have contributed substantially to the understanding of certain aspects of popular music phenomena, they failed to elucidate the processes of creation and consumption and ultimately the meanings of specific musics primarily because music is conceived as an artifact or a product and because the potential relationships of music as a sound phenomenon and as a vehicle of cultural communication are generally neglected. Music historians in Latin America since the beginning of the twentieth century have generally given some attention to the popular music of their individual countries but, most frequently, in conjunction with parallel folk music genres or in dealing with the sources of musical nationalism drawn upon by art-music composers. Musicologists have tended to ignore popular music altogether because of their rather limited perception of its esthetic worth and because of historical musicology's "elitist idealism" to use an expression of John Shepherd (Shepherd 1982:148). It was only in the 1960s that popular music emerged as worthy of serious study.

HISTORIC OUTLINE

Historical and sociological data relating to popular music trends and productions in Latin America are very incomplete. There has been no systematic compilation of sheet music collections and anthologies of popular music, no gathering of historical documents dealing with early recordings and radio broadcasts, and no systematic musicological analysis of the very extensive repertories produced in the various republics since about 1850, the approximate time at which urban music had developed a distinctive, cohesive identity. In the twentieth century, individual Latin American countries have not developed consistently bibliographical tools that provide precise figures to measure the popularity of specific pieces at a given time among specific segments of society. The ready access to information provided for in American popular music, for example, by "Your Hit Parade" broadcasts (1935–1958) and since 1940 by *Billboard* weekly charts simply is unavailable in Latin America. The following summary of the historical development of popular music is of necessity sketchy and emphasizes those geographical areas of Latin America for which readily available data exist.

As an urban phenomenon Latin American popular music first developed in the early nineteenth century, primarily as an upper-class activity involving semipopular theatrical genres and salon music and as a parallel to art-music traditions. It is impossible, however, to attempt to trace a homogeneous, unbroken tradition of urban music because of insufficient documentary sources. Independence and later the abolition of slavery facilitated the interaction between urban and rural areas, although in many cities and towns the interpenetration of folk and urban cultures remained quite dynamic well into the period of World War II. In general, the first characteristic popular music genres emerged in the last quarter of the nineteenth century. Frequently urban renditions of folk music genres prevailed, and since only a handful of popular music genres originated in cities before the mid-1910s, a clear distinction between folk and popular music at that time is difficult to establish. In most cases performing characteristics rather than the structural contents of urban popular forms represent the distinguishing feature of that music.

Since approximately the 1920s (and particularly after about 1945), urban growth in most Latin American countries has resulted in a massive development of urban cultures. In some of the largest cities, this growth and the consequent cultural diversity have been phenomenal. Urban popular music has expressly reflected the cultural, ethnic and socioeconomic diversity of the cities. Fashionable European and other foreign species of popular music have always been present in the major cities in which some segments of society tended to emulate their European counterpart. Thus, the main nineteenth-century ballroom dances such as the waltz, mazurka, polka, schottische, contredanse, and others were readily adopted in all cities and towns and with time suffered the process of "creolization," that is, transformation into local, national genres. The waltz, for example, served as a forerunner to a large number of popular dances in the whole continent, with different names such as *pasillo* (*vals del país* [country waltz]), *vals criollo* [creole waltz], *vals melopeya* [melodic or lyric waltz], and *valsa-choro* [Brazillian popular dance form]. The great European salon music tradition left also a strong imprint on Latin American urban music and provided an important source for numerous popular genres of the early twentieth century. In addition, the prevailing romantic character of many popular song types originated in that tradition whose gentility came to be happily combined with the *criollo* tradition of Latin American cities.

In the twentieth century the influence of North American Tin Pan Alley and other popular genres had its obvious repercussions in the hybrid forms that developed in the 1920s and 1930s (for example, the *rumba-fox*, the *Inca-fox* and the *samba-fox*). The big jazz band era of the 1930s and 1940s also left its imprint on the performing media of many classical Latin American urban popular forms. In the 1950s, several attempts were made, particularly in Cuba, Puerto Rico, and Brazil, to develop Latin expressions of jazz, and the 1960s and 1970s have seen assimilations of rock 'n' roll and rock music often fused with local folk-urban traditions, which gave rise to substantial innovations. Concurrently *música folklórica* in urban contexts became part of the *peña* [rock] fashion established in the 1960s and was the point of departure of a new style associated with political movements, a style that in a short period of time took on a pan Hispanic American character.

Mexico and the Spanish Caribbean

Much Mexican popular music of the nineteenth century was influenced by European salon music. One of the best examples of that influence comes from the set of waltzes *Sobre las olas* [*On the Waves*, 1891] by Juventino Rosas (1868–1894), one of the first Mexican popular composers to win international fame.

The most national popular genres of nineteenth-century Mexico were the *jarabe* [old Mexican Indian folk dance] and the *danza mexicana* [Mexican Dance]. Dating from the late colonial period, the *jarabe*, as dance and song genre, enjoyed wide popularity during the war of independence and since then has been practiced by most popular musicians. Although late nineteenth-century *jarabe* pieces were generally published in solo piano versions, in practice they were performed by various popular bands or ensembles, including *mariachis* [Mexican street musicians]. Those *jarabes* in 3/4 metre were often easily transformed into fast-tempo waltzes, as was the case in the famous *Cielito lindo* [*Pretty Little Honey*], believed to have been written by a Quirino F. Mendoza during the 1910 Mexican Revolution. The *danza mexicana* stemmed from the Cuban *contradanza* [contradance], itself transformed by the Andalusian tango and the Cuban *habanera* [dance typical of Havana], which stressed the duple metre structure and the basic dotted rhythm and the feeling of disjunction between duple and triple divisions of the beat that came to epitomize many Latin American and Caribbean popular dances. In Mexico, the *danza* was cultivated by composers such as Ernesto Elorduy (1853–1912), Felipe Villanueva (1862–1893) in the salon music tradition, and later by Miguel Lerdo de Tejada (1869–1941). Lerdo de Tejada was the first major popular composer of the twentieth century who made the *danza* into a vocal genre. Many popular pieces originally written as simple songs were performed as *danzas* or *habaneras*, such as *La Paloma* [*The Dove*] and the well-known *La Cucaracha* [*The Cockroach*], popularized during the Mexican Revolution.

Despite the variety of dance music genres since the beginning of the twentieth century, the *canción mexicana* [Mexican song] (and particularly the *canción romántica mexicana* [romantic Mexican song]) came to epitomize the whole domain of Mexican popular music. The modern history of the romantic *canción* begins with the publication in 1901 of Lerdo de Tejada's *Perjura* [*Perjury*]. The history of the *canción* is one of catchy melodies that have remained in the collective memory of the Mexican people. Besides its obvious kinship with Italian opera, the *canción* has been influenced by other popular song genres, especially the Cuban *bolero* [dance characterized by sharp turns and stamping of the feet]. The special type of *canción* known as *ranchera* [ranch song] is more distinctively Mexican in that it originated from folk-song tradition and retained specific performance characteristics of that tradition. As an urban genre, it appeared in the 1920s, at first primarily to accompany sound films, and was popularized in the 1930s.

Canciones and *boleros* have been written by the hundreds since the 1920s. By far the most popular composer of his generation was Agustín Lara (1897–1970), whose song *Granada* was an international hit. Other famous composers of *canciones* and other genres were Tato Nacho (Ignacio Fernández Esperón, 1894–1968), author of some two hundred songs, and Guty Cárdenas (1905–1932), immortalized among his countrymen by his songs

Rayito de sol [*Little Sunray*], *Nunca* [*Never*], and *Caminante del Mayab* [*Mayab Wayfarer*]. The 1930s also saw the further development of urban popular music with the establishment of the first regular recording companies, the Victor Talking Machine Company, which opened its Mexican factory in 1935, and several years later Columbia Records. Likewise, the first radio station to pay attention to popular music was XEW Radio in Mexico City (*La Voz de la América Latina* [The Voice of Latin America]), which began broadcasting in 1930 and maintained its leadership role until about the mid-1950s, when television took over.

In the 1940s, urban composers began to pay attention to the *corrido*, the folk ballad of Mexico. In the process of urbanization, the *corrido* underwent a few changes, that is, predominantly duple metre, *copla* [quatrain] literary form, vocal duet and trio performance in harmonized fashion, and *mariachi* and *norteña* [northern border] ensemble accompaniment. The best example of the phenomenal popularity of a modern *corrido* is *Juan Charrasqueado*, written by Victor Cordero. José Alfredo Jiménez (1926–1973) has been very successful with his *corridos* evoking historical events or the beauty of the Mexican provinces.

Cuba has exerted the widest sphere of influence in the development of numerous Latin American popular musical forms throughout this continent. From the *habanera*, the *son cubano* [Cuban sound], the *danza cubana* [Cuban dance], and the *bolero* to the *mambo, rumba, conga,* and *chachachá*, Cuban music has either shaped the *criollo* music genres in other countries of the continent or been adopted in toto at various periods as fashionable dance music. Of the many popular forms, the *habanera* and the *son* first characterized Spanish Caribbean music. A typical example of a composed *habanera* was Eduardo Sánchez de Fuentes's piece entitled *Tú* [*You*], published in 1894. The *son*, which became urbanized during the 1910s, has a strongly syncopated rhythmic accompaniment, resulting in the folk version in a typically Afro-Cuban polyrhythmic texture. As opposed to its Spanish counterpart, the Cuban *bolero* as a dance stresses a duple metre and the same rhythmic patterns of the early *habanera*. Since the 1920s, the *bolero* has been essentially a vocal genre of highly romantic and sentimental character whose lyrics stress love themes of the most varied types. One of the most popular composers of *boleros* was Ernesto Lecuona (1896–1963), whose songs *Malagueña* [*Woman from Malaga*], *María la O*, and *Siboney*, among many others, immortalized him.

The traditional *rumba* has three recognized subtypes, the *guaguancó*, the *colombia*, and the *yambú*. Musically and choreographically, the first of these was the forerunner of the urban *rumba* that developed around the 1920s. As a dance, the *rumba* deals with courtship and the male domination over the female and involves extensive hip and shoulder movements and a pelvic thrust movement known as *vacunao*. The urbanization of the dance retained the hip and shoulder movement, but the *vacunao* was made less obvious or disappeared altogether. This urbanization was also due to numerous dance bands that developed in the 1930s, the first to gain popularity being the Havana Casino Orchestra of Don Azpiazu. The most commercialized of all in the United States was that of Xavier Cugat.

The specific new Cuban song known as *nueva trova* [new song] reflects the ideals, the history, and the struggles of the Cuban Revolution. This musical movement, which gave rise to protest music in several South American countries in the 1960s, was not one of protest as such but rather of expression and promotion of the revolution's ideology. The movement started and grew spontaneously among young people who wanted to express through song their experience and feelings within the revolution.

Among the numerous Caribbean dances, the *merengue* [meringue], which originated in the Dominican Republic, has enjoyed popularity throughout the Caribbean and South America, particularly in the Central American countries, Puerto Rico, Venezuela, and Colombia. The Haitian *méringue* developed its own *créole* character but is related to the Dominican genre.

Venezuelan popular music shares common musical characteristics with both the Caribbean and the Andean-Colombian areas. The most popular genres, however, the *joropo*, the *valse*, and the *merengue*, are typical native (*criollo*) expressions. As a music and literary genre, the *joropo* has been cultivated by popular composers since the latter part of the nineteenth century and has remained the most characteristic national dance of Venezuelan popular music. In the 1910s, it was associated with light theatrical pieces, the most successful of which was the *joropo* of the *zarzuela* [comic opera] *Alma Llanera* ["Soul of the Plains"] written in 1914 by Pedro Elías Gutiérrez.

The Andean Countries

Since the beginning of the twentieth century, Andean urban popular music of clear national derivation has frequently consisted of urbanized renditions and therefore transformations of folk songs and folk dances. In Colombia the most popular forms have been the *bambuco*, the *porro*, the *cumbia*, and the *pasillo*. The vocal part of the urban *bambuco* involves a duet of male voices singing in parallel thirds, although originally it was a serenading song for solo voice. No dance form has had the lasting popularity in Latin America of the *cumbia*, originally an Afro-Panamanian and Colombian (Atlantic coastal area) folk dance. In its urbanization the *cumbia* lost some of its choreographic figures, such as the typical hip movement and the zig-zag motion of the male dancer, but the musical characteristics are similar. The *pasillo*, another widespread popular dance-song, also known in the nineteenth century as the *vals del país*, is a moderately slow waltz-like dance whose rhythm does not stress the downbeat as in its European counterpart. Sung by either solo voice or duet in parallel thirds, it is accompanied by either piano (in the salon context), the *tiple* [treble guitar] and guitar supported by tambourines and "spoons" (used like Spanish castanets), or an *estudiantina* [string ensemble].

The popular music of Ecuador includes the *sanjuanito*, the *pasillo*, and the *cachullapi*. Much like the Peruvian *huayno*, the *sanjuanito* is a dance in duple metre, strictly instrumental with syncopated melodies frequently in the minor mode, with a regularly and strongly accented accompaniment. The Ecuadorian *pasillo* enjoys popularity both in the *sierra* [highland] mestizo communities and in the coastal area, particularly the city of Guayaquil.

Popular music in the various Peruvian cities and towns reflects to a large extent local musical traditions. Thus, cities like Cuzco, Ayacucho, and Arequipa exhibit a popular musical style akin to the mestizo folk music tradition of the highland region. The popular *huayno*, similar to its folk counterpart but performed by urban bands with an instrumentation foreign to the folk tradition, has maintained its strong status among highland urban communities. Coastal cities such as Trujillo, Chiclayo, or Piura in the north and Pisco and Ica in the south have popular musical expressions related to *criollo* tradition, for example, the popular *marinera* and the *vals criollo*. The Lima population at large favors the *criollo* music genres, and especially the *vals criollo*. Originated in Lima between 1900 and 1910, the *vals* became the main musical expression of the urban working class throughout the 1920s and 1930s. Cultivated by composers such as Felipe Pinglo Alva, Laureano Martínez, Carlos Saco, Filomeno Ormeño, Chabuca Granda, and Alicia Maguiña, the *vals* lyrics reflect in general the psychology of the Peruvian people at different times, their cultural personality, and their conflicts, attitudes, and value systems resulting from their reaction to social conditions.

Bolivian popular composers have also cultivated the *huayño popular*, the *cueca*, the *yaravi*, and the *taquirari*. The stylized *cuecas* for piano written by Simeón Roncal (1870–1953) continue to enjoy a great popularity among Bolivian pianists. As in the other highland Andean areas, the Bolivian *yaravi* is a melancholy love song. The *taquirari*, a sung dance, originated in the eastern provinces of Beni and Santa Cruz; the singing almost invariably calls for parallel thirds or sixths. In the cities and towns of the Bolivian plateau, the *bailecito*, similar to the *cueca*, has been extensively cultivated. The *carnavalito*, spread throughout the country, is a characteristic popular dance in which the rhythmic hemiola prevails.

Since the 1960s, festivals of *música folklórica* in urban settings have given rise to the development of a new style and sound of popular music recreating and stylizing aspects of indigenous and mestizo music. As a strictly urban phenomenon this trend toward folk music revival and *música criolla* rested primarily in the hands of members of the upper and middle classes. These musicians became highly proficient performers on indigenous musical instruments and adopted truly traditional and folk music genres, albeit in a more or less free style. In 1965, the La Paz *Peña Naira* opened as an urban cultural center. This is where the group *Los Jairas* began, at first under the direction of the famous *charango* [small, Indian 10–string guitar-like instrument] player, Ernesto Cavour. In the 1970s, the most popular and influential group was *Savia Andina* [*Andean Vigor*], made up of four highly professional musicians consisting of a guitar player/singer, a percussionist, a *charango* virtuoso, and a player of *quena* [flute], *zampoña* [pan pipe], and occasionally *tarka* [vertical flute] or *mohoceño* [large flute].

In addition to the adaptations of international forms of popular music, Chilean urban music consists of such popular forms as the *cueca* and urban versions of *tonadas, tristes, carnaval,* and *tiranas*. The Chilean *cueca*, a dance with song, alternates rhythmic figures in 6/8 and 3/4 metres. The singing is done by one or two voices, accompanied by guitar, *charango,* flute (*quena* or *pincullo*), and *bombo*. The *Nueva Canción* [New Song] movement, which spread to the whole of Latin America in the 1960s, originated in Chile. This movement, following the example of the Cuban model, was associated with social protest, labor movements and reform, and the strongly revolutionary sentiment of the period. The New Song movement centered around a group of talented musicians-poets of whom the main figures were Violeta Parra (Sandoval); her children, Angel and Isabel Parra; Patricio Castillo; Patricio Manns; and Victor Jara.

Argentina, Uruguay, and Brazil

Among the various popular music genres of Argentina and Uruguay since the beginning of the twentieth century none epitomizes as deeply the social and cultural history of those countries as the tango. For this reason alone, the tango has remained by far the most important popular form that originated in both countries. In the Río de la Plata area, the tango came to symbolize the hopes, successes, and failures of the millions of European immigrants who hoped to work in the farms but who settled in the *arrabal* or ghettos of Buenos Aires and Montevideo. The *milonga*, a dance of Afro-Argentine and Uruguayan folk tradition in duple metre and syncopated rhythm, probably contributed to the development of the tango in the area. Choreographically, the tango is in part a local adaptation of the Andalusian tango, of the Cuban *danzón* and *habanera*, and, to a lesser extent, of the European polka and schottische. Essentially three types of tango developed: the strongly rhythmic instrumental *tango milonga* for popular orchestras, the instrumental or vocal *tango-romanza* with a more melodic and romantic character, and the accompanied *tango-canción*, which is strongly lyric and sentimental. It is in the *tango-canción* that the major themes characteristically associated with the tango as popular culture appear. Carlos Gardel (1887–1935), a popular idol who continued to fascinate most Argentines well into the 1970s, was particularly important in making the tango fashionable in Europe and the Western Hemisphere, and his major contribution was to transform it into a song genre of social and cultural significance.

Perhaps the most successful tango ever composed was *La Cumparsita* [*Little Masquerade*, 1917], written by Gerardo Matos Rodríguez in Montevideo. Other representative popular pieces were Julio César Sanders's *Adiós Muchachos* [*Good-bye Boys*, 1928], Enrique Santos Discépolo's *Yira, yira* (1930), Angel Villoldo's *El choclo* [*Ear of Corn*], Juan Carlos Cobián's *Nostalgias* [*Nostalgia*], Francisco Camaro's *Adiós, pampa mía [Good-bye, My Plain]*, and Edgardo Donati's *A media luz* [*Half-Light*]. While the tango lost some of its earlier popularity in the 1950s, it was revived in the 1960s and 1970s. Innovations affected it, particularly the so-called new tango movement, whose leading exponent was Astor Piazzolla (b. 1921), who wrote tango suites transformed into ballets. The "new tango," although controversial, penetrated the elitist night clubs of Buenos Aires in the 1960s.

The popular music of Brazil began to acquire stylistic originality during the last thirty years of the nineteenth century. The sentimental love song, *modinha*, and the song-dance *lundu*, cultivated in the salons since the period of Independence, began to be popularized among urban musicians in the 1870s. Local adaptations of European urban dances, particularly the polka, gave rise to new genres such as the *maxixe*, the *tango brasileiro* [Brazilian tango], and the *choro*, whose most successful composers were Joaquim Antonio da Silva Callado, Francisca Gonzaga, and Ernesto Nazareth. The *choro* of the 1920s to the 1940s stressed virtuoso improvisation of instrumental variations and the consequent counterpoint of remarkable imagination as in the pieces of the Velha Guarda band of Pixinguinha (Alfredo da Rocha Viana).

Carnival, first organized on a regular basis in the late 1890s in Rio de Janeiro, stimulated the development of urban popular music. At first simple marches, polkas, and waltzes were used, but the most typical carnival genre, the urban samba, emerged during the second decade of the twentieth century. The first recognized samba to be recorded was *Pelo telefone* [*By Phone*], by Ernesto dos Santos, nicknamed Donga, in 1917. From that date, the samba became standardized as an urban genre. Several species of the form appeared from the 1920s to the 1940s, including the folk-like dance known as *partido-alto* and the previously mentioned *samba de morro* (sometimes referred to as *batucada*) cultivated by people of the *favelas* [hillside slums] and the first *escolas de samba* [samba schools] of Rio de Janeiro. Its accompaniment was provided primarily by percussion instruments. Around 1928 two significant new developments affected the samba: the creation of the "samba schools" and the advent of the genre *samba-canção* [samba song]. Both epitomized the dichotomy that separated the music of the lower economic classes and that of the middle and upper classes.

The *samba-canção* was meant for middle- and upper-class consumption. Melodically and textually it was strongly reminiscent of the older *modinhas*, while harmonically and rhythmically it was influenced in the 1940s and 1950s by the Cuban *bolero* and the "fox-blues." Together with other hybrid forms such as *samba-choro* and *samba-fox*, the *samba-canção* dealt with love and unhappiness often in melodramatic terms. One of Brazil's popular idols, Francisco Alves (1898–1952), was a singer of *samba-canções*. Among the most important composers of urban sambas were José Luiz de Morais (1883–1961), nicknamed Caninha; Alfredo da Rocha Viana, nicknamed Pixinguinha (1898–1973); Ary Barroso (1907–1964), who won international acclaim; Noel Rosa (1910–1937); and Carlos Ferreira Braga (b. 1907), nicknamed João de Barro.

In the 1950s, the urban samba in its ballroom context suffered the influence of the big band with stereotyped arrangements seeking to emulate the American big jazz band sound of about ten years earlier. The reaction to such arrangements led to the development in the mid-1950s of the samba jazz phenomenon (influenced by the cool sound of Miles Davis) and, in turn, to the *bossa nova* movement of the late 1950s, which provided Brazilian popular music with new currents and a dynamic vitalization that brought about in the 1960s and 1970s highly sophisticated musicians.

Around the mid-1960s, a group of musician-poet-performers known as *Tropicália*, mostly from Bahia, emerged on the Brazilian scene and included such different personalities as Caetano Veloso, Gilberto Gil, Gal Costa, José Carlos Capinam, Torquato Neto, Tom Zé, the *bossa nova* singer Nara Leão, and the composer-arranger Rogério Duprat. Sociopolitically, *tropicalismo* [tropicalism] was meant to awaken the consciousness of the middle class to the Brazilian tragedy of poverty, exploitation, and oppression and to point out the true nature of the modern Brazilian reality. Musically, the *Tropicália* movement brought about drastic innovations by widening the Brazilian musical horizon through adherence to and adaptation of the most relevant musical trends of the 1960s, for example, the rock-Beatles phenomenon and the experimental new musics of the electronic age.

Because recordings constitute the primary source of study of popular music of the twentieth century, the history of recorded music represents an essential aspect of the development of the medium but can hardly be sketched at the present time with any degree of completeness and accuracy, except for the recording careers of some of the famous musicians.

REFERENCE WORKS

The best general guide to Latin American music remains Gilbert Chase's *A Guide to the Music of Latin America* (2d edition), a thoroughly annotated bibliography organized by country, with subheadings for folk and popular music. The guide covers materials published up to about 1960. More recent material can be found in the music section of the *Handbook of Latin American Studies*. Examination of such standard references immediately reveals the scant attention that urban popular music has received and the consequent paucity of critical studies. *América Latina en su música* [*Latin America in Its Music*], edited by Isabel Aretz, supplies, however, excellent insights into the place and status of popular music and musicians from diachronic and synchronic perspectives. Particularly relevant are Alejo Carpentier's chapter on "América Latina en la confluencia de coordenadas históricas y su repercusión en la música" ["Latin America in the Confluence of Historical Coordinates and Its Repercussion on Music"], Rafael José de Menezes Bastos's "Situación de la música en la sociedad" ["The Status of Music in Society"], Luis Felipe Ramón y Rivera's "El artista popular" ["The Popular Artist"], Argeliers León's "La música como mercancía" ["Music as Merchandise"], and Isabel Aretz's "La música como tradición" ["Music as Tradition"]. Although limited in scope, Martha Ellen Davis's *Music and Dance in Latin American Urban Contexts: A Selective Bibliography* provides a useful model for the sort of bibliographic compilation that is so crucial for the study of Latin American music in urban areas. Also informative in dealing with music in urban contexts is Luiz Heitor Corrêa de Azevedo's "The Present State and Potential of Music Research in Latin America." The very comprehensive bibliography on Colombian music, Carmen Ortega Ricaurte's "Contribución a la bibliografía de la música en Colombia" ["A Bibliographic Contribution to the Music of Colombia"] lists all pertinent items on popular music published up to about 1972, including sheet music or scores reproduced in periodicals and books.

Various music encyclopedias and dictionaries provide factual data on popular music genres and history and bibliographical information on popular composers and musicians. The main and most updated dictionary is *The New Grove Dictionary of Music and Musicians*, which includes entries on each country of the Latin American continent and numerous articles on popular composers, on specific forms of popular song and dance, and on the main popular musical instruments. For Argentine music, Rodolfo Arizaga's *Enciclopedia de la música argentina* [*Encyclopedia of Argentine Music*] gives brief references to and definitions of the major folk-popular dances and instruments of the *criollo* tradition. In Brazil, the best general reference work is Marcos Marcondes, ed., *Enciclopédia da música brasileira: erudita, folclórica, popular* [*Encyclopedia of Brazilian Music: Artdite, Folk, Popular*], which provides more coverage of popular music than any other music tradition. The most comprehensive bibliography is Luiz Augusto Milanesi and Antonio Fernando Corrêa Barone, *Bibliografia da música popular brasileira* [*Biography of Popular Brazilian Music*]. Biographical data on Peruvian popular musicians and institutions are found in Rodolfo Barbacci's "Apuntes para un diccionario biográfico musical peruano" ["Notes toward a Bibliographical Dictionary of Peruvian Music"] and Carlos Raygada's "Guía musical del Perú" ["Musical Guide to Peru"]. Although out of date, Otto Mayer-Serra's two-volume dictionary *Música y músicos de Latinoamérica* [*Music and Musicians of Latin America*] includes valuable information on popular music throughout the continent, and particularly in Mexico. The *Diccionario de la música cubana, biográfico y técnico* [*Dictionary of Cuban Music, Biographical and Technical*] by Helio Orovio has numerous entries on Cuban popular musicians. Although Robert Stevenson's *A Guide to Caribbean Music History* stresses bibliographical items dealing primarily with pre-1900 aspects of Caribbean music, it includes valuable annotations on entries directly or indirectly related to popular music. Angelina Pollak-Eltz includes musical entries on Venezuelan music in her *Bibliografía afrovenezolana* [*Afrovenezuelan Bibliography*].

HISTORICAL AND CRITICAL WORKS

The numerous national music histories published since the early twentieth century treat in varying degrees the subject of popular music. Popular songs and dances of Mexico retain the attention of Miguel Galindo in his *Nociones de historia de la música mejicana* [*Some Thoughts on the History of Mexican Music*]. Gabriel Saldívar's *Historia de la música en México* [*History of Music in Mexico*] does not concern itself with the twentieth century, but the third part discusses folk music types related to popular songs and dances. A good historical treatment of colonial folk-music development is offered by Robert Stevenson in *Music in Aztec and Inca Territory*. Although it treats primarily the historical development of art music, Otto Mayer-Serra's *Panorama de la música mexicana desde la independencia hasta la actualidad* [*Panorama of Mexican Music from Independence to the Present*] provides useful comments on some aspects of nineteenth-century Mexican popular music. Popular songs of Guatemala occupy a small portion of Victor Miguel Díaz's *Las bellas artes en Guatemala* [*Fine Arts in Guatemala*]. Given the close relationship of folk and popular music in Guatemala, *Folklore musical de Guatemala* [*Musical Folklore in Guatemala*] by L. Paret-Limardo de Vela provides a very useful overview. The most updated historical account of Costa Rican music is Bernal Flores's *La música en Costa Rica* [*Music in Costa Rica*], which gives basic information on aspects of popular music in that country. The historical development of Cuban popular music is still best treated in Alejo Carpentier's *La música en Cuba* [*Music in Cuba*]. It is somewhat updated in José Ardévol's *Introducción a Cuba: la música* [*Introduction to Cuba: Music*]. In his "Visión musical de nuestra historia" ["Musical Vision of Our History"] (in *La Enciclopedia de Cuba*] [*Encyclopedia of Cuba*) Natalio Galán Sariol only touches upon popular music. The main types of Dominican folk and popular musical forms are discussed in Julio Arzeno's *Del folk-lore musical dominicano* [*About Dominican Musical Folklore*], and popular music and musicians are the subject of part of the bilingual monograph *Music and Musicians of the Dominican Republic. Música y músicos de la República Dominicana* by Jacob Maurice Coopersmith. The best historical overview of the various traditions of Puerto Rican music is found in the volume *La música* [*Music*] (of *La Gran Enciclopedia de Puerto Rico* [*The Great Encyclopedia of Puerto Rico*]) written by Héctor Campos Parsi, who discusses popular music in two phases, up to the end of the nineteenth century and then in the twentieth century. Anna Figueroa de Thompson's *An Annotated Bibliography of Writings about Music in Puerto Rico* is professionally done, but urban popular music receives scant attention. The growth of Venezuelan popular music especially in Caracas is sketched in José Antonio Calcaño's *La ciudad y su música: Crónica musical de Caracas* [*The City and Its Music: Musical Chronicle of Caracas*]. The two major historical introductions to the music of Colombia are José Ignacio Perdomo Escobar's *Historia de la música en Colombia* [*History of Music in Colombia*] and Andrés Pardo Tovar's *La cultura musical en Colombia* [*Musical Culture in Colombia*]. Urban popular music in Ecuador has not been the subject of special treatment. Segundo Luis Moreno's *Historia de la música en el Ecuador* [*History of Music in Ecuador*], a compilation of his numerous writings, provides a good general treatment of the country's regional folk expressions strongly influential in the development of urban popular forms. Although Peruvian folk music has been studied in considerable detail, there is, to date, no general history of music in Peru that would provide an introduction to folk and popular music in major Peruvian cities. The same situation exists in Bolivia, where the attention to mestizo, Indian, and art-music traditions has almost obliterated the study of urban popular music. Although quite old and full of inaccuracies, the work *La musique des Incas et ses survivances* [*The Music of the Incas and its Survivals*] by the French, Raoul and Marguerite d'Harcourt still provides a good foundation for the folk music of Bolivia, Peru, and Ecuador. Chilean music historiography has been copious. First is *Los orígenes del arte musical en Chile* [*The Origins of Musical Art in Chile*] by Eugenio Pereira Salas, who offers in chapter seventeen a good introduction to the historical development of dance and popular music, particularly in the nineteenth century. More recently, popular music is treated in *Historia de la música en Chile* [*History of Music in Chile*] by Samuel Claro and Jorge Urrutia Blondel and in very general terms in Samuel Claro's *Oyendo a Chile* [*Listening to Chile*]. The best single-volume treatment of Argentine folk music is Isabel Aretz's *El folklore musical argentino* [*Argentine Musical Folklore*], indispensable for a basic understanding of many aspects of urban music. Vicente Gesualdo's two-volume *Historia de la música en la Argentina* [*History of Music in Argentina*] provides the most comprehensive coverage of urban popular music in the late nineteenth and early twentieth century. Lauro Ayestarán's work *La música en el Uruguay* [*The Music of Uruguay*] contains an excellent discussion and thorough documentation of the origins of popular music in that country. Brazilian music history has dealt traditionally with the whole range of the country's musical expressions. Part I of Renato Almeida's *História da música brasileira* [*History of Brazilian Music*] deals with *música popular* [popular music] broadly conceived. Biographical data on urban popular musicians are methodically given in *Panorama da música popular brasileira* [*Panorama of Brazilian Popular Music*] by Ary Vasconcelos.

Specialized studies on popular ·music in the various Latin American republics abound, although the level of serious criticism is quite uneven. For Mexican music, Juan S. Garrido's *Historia de la música popular en México (1896–1973)* [*History of Popular Music in Mexico (1896–1973)*] provides interesting insights from an important personality in the field, although it does not truly represent a historical treatment of the subject. Claes af Geijerstam's *Popular Music in Mexico*, one of the very few studies in English, is based on limited first-hand knowledge and experience and should be used with great caution. *La música popular de México (Origen e historia de la música que canta y toca el pueblo mexicano)* [*Popular Music of Mexico (Origin and History of Music that the Mexican People Sing and Play)*] by Jas Reuter is a general discussion of the subject and far too ambitious in its coverage. In addition, the word "popular" is here taken in the broadest sense. The writings of Vicente T. Mendoza represent the best attempt to deal with folk and popular music. Particularly important is his *Panorama de la música tradicional de México* [*Panorama of Traditional Music in Mexico*], *El corrido mexicano* [*The Mexican Corrido*], and *La canción mexicana* [*The Mexican Song*], to name but a few. Rubén M. Campos's *El folklore musical de las ciudades* [*The Musical Folklore of the Cities*] remains a model of historical and musical documentation of late nineteenth century Mexican urban music. Studies of regional expressions of popular songs include the well-known *La canción popular de Yucatán* [*The Popular Song of Yucatán*] by Gerónimo Baqueira Foster, *Monografías y cantares huastecos* [*Huastecan Monographs and Songs*] by Hilario Menéndez Peña, Jesús C. Romero's *La música en Zacatecas y los músicos zacatecanos* [*Music in Zacatecas and Zacatecan Musicians*] and Eloisa Ruiz Cavalho de Baqueiro's *Tradiciones, folklore, música y músicos de Campeche* [*Traditions, Folklore, Music and Musicians of Campeche*]. Biographies of specific composers/performers are numerous. Particularly important are Daniel Castañeda's *Balance de Agustín Lara* [*An overview of Agustín Lara*] and Mario Talavera's *Miguel Lerdo de Tejada* [*Miguel Lerdo of Tejada*]. Hugo de Grial's *Músicos mexicanos* [*Mexican Musicians*] is a useful source of biographic information as well. Los Hermanos Márquez provides *25 biografías de compositores populares* [*25 Biographies of Pop-*

ular Composers], a work that includes some of the best-known figures. Quite revealing as an example of Mexican disk jockeys' concerns about their activities and the type of information they sought to convey in the late 1950s and early 1960s is Roberto Ayala's *Musicosas: manual del comentarista de radio y televisión* [*Music Things: A Commentator's Manual for Radio and Television*]. Through his magazine *Audiomúsica* [*Audiomusic*], Otto Mayer-Serra rendered an invaluable service to popular music in Mexico by publishing informative articles, such as his own "La industria mexicana del disco" ["The Mexican Record Industry"], and an annual assessment of activities and releases in "Panorama 1964 de la música popular" ["1964 Panorama of Popular Music"], "Panorama de la música popular (1965–66)" ["Panorama of Popular Music (1965–66)"], and "Panorama de la música popular (1966–67)" ["Panorama of Popular Music (1966–67)"]. Statistical and miscellaneous data on popular musicians and the media are available in part in *Sociedad de Autores y Compositores de México: XXV años de la SACM* [*Society of Authors and Composers of Mexico: XXV Years of SACM*], whose history is intimately connected to the popular musical scene since the mid–1950s. The gradual assimilation of international pop styles into Mexican music has not been studied very seriously. The rock music phenomenon in Mexico suffered from a virtually total lack of recognition by scholars of popular culture. *Música tropical* [tropical music], the general label applied to Afro-Caribbean music, has likewise received attention disproportionate to its importance. David K. Stigberg's "*Jarocho, Tropical*, and 'Pop': Aspects of Musical Life in Veracruz, 1971–72" is, for this reason alone, a welcome study of the various popular musical traditions in the city, the socio-historical-economic determinants of styles, and the social profiles of the music makers and consumers of such musics. The fully ethnomusicological treatment provided in this study is only too rare in the publications on Mexican popular music. The "New Song" in Mexico has been the subject of a few studies. Anthar López Tirado gives us a general but perceptive overview in "La Nueva Canción en México" ["The New Song in Mexico"].

Despite its enormous influence throughout the hemisphere, Cuban popular music has not been studied with the seriousness that it deserves. A good general introduction in English is Emilio Grenet's *Popular Cuban Music*, which includes eighty pieces by such well-known composers as Sánchez de Fuentes, Sindo Garay, and Ernesto Lecuona and an essay on the evolution of music in Cuba, with special attention to the major popular genres, that is, the *contradanza, habanera,* the *son, canción, conga,* and *rumba.* The Afro-Cuban folk music elements have been so pervasive in urban popular music that a knowledge of Afro-Cuban folk music literature is essential. Fernando Ortiz's seven-volume work on the subject remains the basic foundation although not all seven volumes are directly relevant to urban music. These volumes are *La africanía de la música folklórica de*

Cuba [*African Elements in Cuban Folk Music*], *Los bailes y el teatro negros en el folklore de Cuba* [*Black Dances and Theater in Cuban Folklore*], and five volumes on *Los instrumentos de la música afrocubana* [*Afrocuban Musical Instruments*]. Harold Courlander also wrote on "Musical Instruments of Cuba." Argeliers León provides a historical and stylistic discussion of Cuban folk and popular music in *Música folklórica cubana* [*Cuban Folk Music*], while María Teresa Linares offers general comments on popular music and musicians in *La música popular* [*Popular Music*]. The short essay, "El son, exclusividad de Cuba" ["The *Son*, A Cuban Exclusive"] by Carlos Borbolla gives some pertinent insight into the unique musical nature (particularly in terms of melodic and rhythmic organization) of Cuban popular music. The only truly musical analysis of the rumba is provided by Larry Crook in "A Musical Analysis of the Cuban Rumba." The compilation of Alejo Carpentier's newspaper articles entitled *Ese músico que llevo dentro* [*That Musician Inside of Me*] (3 vols.) contains some relevant items. Individual biographies of popular music figures in Cuba are not very numerous. Marino Gómez Santos wrote on Xavier Cugat, while Desi Arnaz in *A Book* offers autobiographical and other informative materials. Given the strong Cuban involvement in the development of *salsa* music in the 1960s, an overview of the *salsa* literature is appropriate. Chapter eight of John Storm Roberts's *The Latin Tinge, The Impact of Latin American Music on the United States* deals specifically with the origin and development of *salsa* in New York. Although a valuable attempt at gathering a staggering amount of information, this book is full of factual errors and misconceptions. Joseph Blum delineates some "Problems of *Salsa* Research" such as musical exploitation and racial or ethnic prejudice, and Jorge Duany places popular musical development in Puerto Rico in the context of socio-economic trends in "Popular Music in Puerto Rico: Toward an Anthropology of *Salsa*." Particularly interesting for its all-encompassing coverage of *salsa* is César Miguel Rondón's *El libro de la salsa: crónica de la música del caribe urbano* [*The* Salsa *Book: A Chronicle of Caribbean Urban Music*], which offers the most comprehensive history of that style and movement not only in New York but in the Caribbean and Venezuela. The book also provides significant illustrations (photos of musicians, composers, and record jackets) and a good discography.

The music of Puerto Rico is sketched historically and analytically in *La música en Puerto Rico: panorama histórico-cultural* [*Music in Puerto Rico: Historical-Cultural Panorama*], by María Luisa Muñoz, and folk music is the subject of Francisco López Cruz's study entitled *La música folklórica de Puerto Rico* [*Folk Music in Puerto Rico*]. However, the history of urban popular music in Puerto Rico remains to be written. The Afro-Puerto Rican song and dance genres that have had the greatest impact on popular music are the *bomba* and the *plena*, which, however, have not been studied in depth. Although E. Figueroa Berríos's "Los sones de la bomba en la tradición popular de la costa sur de Puerto Rico" ["The Sounds of the *Bomba* in the Popular Tradition of the Southern Coast of Puerto Rico"] reveals an important music repertory, the question of the form's urbanization is not addressed. The *plena*, in its urban renditions, has, to my knowledge, not been the subject of any special study. The most detailed description is found in Héctor Campos Parsi's volume *La música* mentioned previously.

Folk and popular music in the Dominican Republic is well analyzed in the previously mentioned *Del folk-lore musical dominicano* [*About Dominican Musical Folklore*], by Julio Arzeno. Special attention is given to the *merengue* with numerous musical examples. This study is somewhat updated in Coopersmith's monograph previously mentioned, including a brief analysis of the rhythmic patterns of the *merengue*. The third part of Jorge Bernarda's *La música dominicana, Siglos XIX-XX [Dominican Music, XIX-XXth Centuries]* treats popular music in two parts, dance music and music for singing. Besides the *merengue*, such dances as the *yuca*, *saranduga* and *carabiné* are discussed. Popular ensembles and the history of dance bands and their repertories are treated in Luis Alberti Mieses's *De música y orquestas bailables dominicanas, 1910–1959* [*On Dominican Music and Dance Orchestras, 1919–1959*], including a number of *merengues* for the piano by the author. Emilio Rodríguez Demorizi's *Música y baile en Santo Domingo* [*Music and Dance in Santo Domingo*] presents various newspaper columns published over the years, among which are some specific historical descriptions of popular genres, particularly the *merengue*.

The well-known Venezuelan folklorist and ethnomusicologist Luis Felipe Ramón y Rivera has been very prolific on all aspects of his country's oral musical traditions. His book *La música popular de Venezuela* [*Venezuelan Popular Music*] is a very useful historical and analytic study on urban popular music conceived solely in its national dimensions, that is, foreign modern influences and imitations are deliberately omitted. Thus, he offers pertinent discussion on such popular genres as the *vals, pasillo, bambuco, merengue, canción, canción-bambuco, tonada, bolero,* and *joropo.* The book includes wonderful reproductions of nineteenth- and twentieth-century sheet music pieces and an appropriate list of local newspapers consulted for this study. An earlier publication by Ramón y Rivera, *El joropo: baile nacional de Venezuela* [*The Joropo: The Venezuelan National Dance*], should be consulted for the study of the urban versions of the *joropo*.

The urban musical expressions of the Central American republics have heretofore been neglected in favor of their folk and traditional musics. Panamanian folk music is well documented in Narciso Garay's *Tradiciones y cantares de Panamá* [*Panamanian Traditions and Songs*] and updated in Lila R. Cheville and Richard A. Cheville's *Festivals and Dances of Panama*, which gives some attention to the urban manifestations of such genres as *mejorana, punto, cumbia,* and *tamborito.*

Colombian music has been studied rather comprehensively, with the exception of urban popular music. Since the major national genres of urban music have their origin in the folk tradition, the following publications represent a logical first step in the study of urban music. Guillermo Abadía wrote extensively on folk music and dances. Particularly relevant are his "Panorama de las músicas folklórica y popular" ["Panorama of Folk and Popular Music"] and *La música folklórica colombiana* [*Colombian Folk Music*]. Manuel Zapata Olivella gives us specific information on the major genres of popular music in "Los ritmos populares" ["Popular Rhythms"], "Comparsas y teatro callejero en los carnavales colombianos" ["*Comparsas* and Street Theater in Colombian Carnivals"], and "Los pasos del folklore colombiano: la cumbia" ["The Course of Colombian Folklore: The *Cumbia*"]. A historical and choreographic survey of the *cumbia* is provided in "La cumbia, síntesis musical de la nación colombiana" ["The *Cumbia*, Musical Synthesis of Colombia"], by Delia Zapata Olivella. Various aspects of the *bambuco* have retained the attention of numerous writers, among them Bernardo Arias Trujillo's "Elogio del bambuco" ["In Praise of the *Bambuco*"], Lorenzo Marroquín's "El bambuco" ["The *Bambuco*"], Milina Muñoz's "El IV reinado del bambuco" ["The Fourth Reign of the *Bambuco*"], Alfonso María Rojas's "El bambuco de Colombia" ["The *Bambuco* of Colombia"], and Daniel Zamudio's chapter 3, "El Bambuco," of his *El folklore musical en Colombia* [*Musical Folklore in Colombia*]. A fairly comprehensive study of the *bambuco* is *Orígenes históricos del bambuco, teoría musical y cronología de autores y compositores colombianos* [*Historical Origins of the Bambuco, Musical Theory and a Chronology of Authors and Composers*] by Lubín E. Mazuera M. A thoroughly documented study on Colombian musical instruments, folk and popular music, and dances is Harry C. Davidson's *Diccionario folklórico de Colombia* [*Colombian Folkloric Dictionary*]. In his *Canciones y recuerdos* [*Songs and Memories*] Jorge Añez offers numerous biographies of popular musicians and the scores and texts of some of the most popular songs of the repertory. Heriberto Zapata Cuéncar provides alphabetical entries of biographies of composers of art and popular music from Antioquia in his *Compositores antioqueños* [*Antiochian Composers*]. Although journalistic, the chronicles on popular songs by Alvaro Ruiz Hernández (*Personajes y episodios de la canción popular* [*Figures and Episodes of Popular Song*]) are worth reading.

Although urban music of Ecuador as such as been virtually overlooked, a few small anthologies are available, among them *Album de música nativa* [*An Album of Native Music*] and *Música ecuatoriana* [*Ecuadorian Music*] which include a total of twenty-two pieces of popular music of the coastal area in the 1930s. The *pasillo* of both coastal and highland cities makes up Alberto Morlaz Gutiérrez's *Florilegio del pasillo ecuatoriano* [*An Anthology of the Ecuadorian Pasillo*], essentially an anthology of *pasillo* texts with biographical data on some seventy-six popular composers.

In Peru there has been no attempt to present an overall assessment of popular music. Specific genres, however, have received some attention. The *sayno* (*huayno*)is studied in great detail in Josafat Roel Pineda's "El wayno del Cuzco" ["The *Wayno* of Cuzco"], with the transcription of some 151 *waynos* from that region. The anthropologist Paul Doughty provides substantial insights on the place of the *huayno* in Lima among migrants from the highland in "Behind the Back of the City: 'Provincial' Life in Lima, Peru," and in "Peruvian Migrant Identity in the Urban Milieu." The *vals peruano* [Peruvian waltz] or *criollo* is treated in historical terms by César Santa Cruz Gamarra in *El waltz y el valse criollo* [*The Waltz and the Creole Waltz*]. Sergio Zapata Agurto's "Psicoanálisis del vals peruano: contribución al estudio de la personalidad básica del hombre peruano" ["A Psychoanalysis of the Peruvian Waltz: A Contribution to the Study of the Basic Personality of the Peruvian"] follows a particularly effective approach stressing psychoanalytic and sociological interpretation of the various subjects of the lyrics. An equally fruitful study is provided by Steve Stein in "El vals criollo y los valores de la clase trabajadora en la Lima de comienzos del siglo XX" ["The Creole Waltz and the Values of the Lima Working Class at the Beginning of the XXth Century"], emphasizing a socio-historical treatment of the subject.

Historical and critical studies of popular music in Bolivia and Chile are not numerous. Of all phases of that music in the twentieth century the "Nueva Canción" movement has received the most attention. In *La Nueva Canción en América Latina* [*The New Song in Latin America*], Eduard Carrasco gives an overview of the Chilean case. More specific studies on Chilean music of the 1960s and 1970s are "El canto nuevo en Chile (1973–1980)" ["The New Song in Chile (1973–1980)"] by Bernardo Subercaseaux and "La Nueva Canción Chilena" ["The Chilean New Song"] by Stu Cohen. The main studies of the life and works of Violeta Parra and Victor Jara are *Victor Jara: His Life and Songs*, edited by Ted Dicks; *Victor Jara*, by Galvarino Plaza; *Violeta Parra* by Patricio Manns; and *Yo canto la diferencia: canciones de Violeta Parra* [*I Sing Differences: Violeta Parra's Songs*], by Parra herself. For Bolivian urban music, Gilka Wara Céspedes discusses "New Currents in 'Música folklórica' in La Paz, Bolivia," stressing the relationship of music in La Paz since the 1950s to indigenous music, with special attention to such renowned groups as Los Jairas and later Savia Andina.

The literature on the Argentine tango is extensive. It has been studied from the choreographic, literary, folkloric, and musical points of view. Strictly musical studies, however, are far less numerous. One of the most comprehensive references on the tango is *El libro del tango. Historias e imágenes* [*The Book of the Tango. Histories and Images*], by Horacio Ferrer, organized by alphabetical entries on all pertinent subjects (composers, pieces, orchestras, instruments, and others). In *La sociología del tango*

[*Sociology of the Tango*], Julio Mafud places the genre in its proper socio-historical context. The most thorough discussion on the origins of the tango is still provided by Vicente Rossi in his *Cosas de negros* [*Of Concern to Blacks*] and on its historical evolution by Horacio Ferrer in *El tango: su historia y su evolución* [*The Tango: Its History and Evolution*]. Ernesto Sábato gives us a vivid picture of the relevance of the form for the Argentine in *El tango: discusión y clave* [*The Tango: A Discussion and Key*], and Julie M. Taylor's "Tango: Theme of Class and Nation" examines the interrelated elements of tango as folklore, song, and dance and discusses the most important themes surrounding the tango and its manifestations in everyday life. The literature on Carlos Gardel abounds. The most significant biographies and interpretations are *Carlos Gardel* by Blas Matamoro, which includes a discography and filmography; *El tango y su mundo* [*The Tango and Its World*] by Daniel Vidart, who dedicates a substantial portion of this socio-anthropological study to Gardel; and "El mundo de los tangos de Gardel" ["The World of Gardel's Tangos"] by Darío Cantón. The latter analyzes a selected group of tango lyrics from Gardel's repertoire as a means of examining the socio-cultural background of the first period of the tango-song, best represented by Gardel's career. The Instituto Nacional de Musicología "Carlos Vega" ["Carlos Vega" National Institute of Musicology] began issuing in 1980 a substantial *Antología del tango rioplatense* [*Anthology of River Plate Tango*] (vol. 1, from its beginnings to 1920), dividing the subject into "Historico-Musical Aspects" and "Musicological Aspects," the latter being the most detailed analysis of the tango's musical and choreographic structures known to me. Particularly important for some aspects of the history of popular music in Argentina is Jesús Martínez Moirón's *El mundo de los autores* [*The World of the Authors*], which provides a detailed history of SADAIC (Sociedad Argentina de Autores y Compositores de Música) [Argentine Society of Writers and Composers of Music].

In the 1960s Brazil saw a virtual explosion of renewed interest in urban popular music, as a result of new currents, generically referred to as *Moderna música popular brasileira* [*Modern Popular Brazilian Music*]. Perhaps because of the controversies surrounding the appearance of innovating trends, such as *bossa nova* and *tropicalismo*, studies of popular music of the past and present multiplied at an unusual pace. Up to the late 1950s, the major overview of folk and popular music was Oneyda Alvarenga's *Música popular brasileira* [*Popular Brazilian Music*], originally published in Spanish in 1947. Only one chapter in this book deals with urban popular music, viewed in a rather narrow perspective. The second edition of the book (1982) is hardly a new edition since it only adds a few notes and does not take into account any other study on the subject since the first edition. *Música popular brasileira* [*Popular Brazilian Music*] by José Eduardo Homem de Mello has been the only attempt at tracing a general history of Brazil's popular music, based on first-hand information for the contemporary portion of his survey. In the 1960s and 1970s, the sociologist José Ramos Tinhorão wrote extensively on the subject of *MPB* (*Música Popular Brasileira*). His *Pequena história da música popular—Da modinha à canção de protesto* [*A Short History of Popular Music—From the Modinha to the Protest Song*] focuses on the historical development of some of the main genres, such as *modinha, lundu, maxixe, tango, choro*, and various types of *samba*. Interesting interpretations despite strong personal judgments and bias pervade in his other studies, particularly *Música popular—de índios, negros e mestiços* [*Popular Music—Concerning Indians, Blacks, and Mestizos*], *O samba agora vai* . . . —a farsa da música popular no exterior [*The Samba goes on* . . . —The Farce of Popular Music in Foreign Countries*], *Música popular—teatro e cinema* [*Popular Music—Theatre and Cinema*], and *Música popular—os sons que vêm da rua* [*Popular Music—Sounds From the Street*]. Tinhorão unearths excellent documentation that provides a thorough basis for his sociological insights, but unfortunately he lacks stylistic understanding and the intrinsic musical aspects of the repertoires he studies are, for the most part, ignored. He excels, however, in tracing, for the first time in Brazil, the history of the modern technological means of sound reproduction, examining in the process the influence on popular music of the record industry, radio, and television in his book *Música Popular—do gramofone ao rádio e TV* [*Popular Music—From the Gramophone to the Radio and TV*]. His somewhat debatable thesis in this study is that as the technological means become more sophisticated, the cultural expressions of the large urban masses are less represented in radio and TV programs. Ary Vasconcelos gives a very sketchy and trivial account of popular music history and short biographies in *Raízes da música popular brasileira (1500–1889)* [*The Roots of Brazilian Popular Music (1500–1889)*]. Among the various publications on popular music brought out by FUNARTE (Fundação Nacional de Arte) [National Art Foundation] in the 1970s, Jota Efegê's *Figuras e coisas da música popular brasileira* [*Figures and Matters about Brazilian Popular Culture*] is an informative series of newspaper and periodical articles reporting on various events and personalities from 1940 to 1978. Important biographies are also part of that collection, among them Mário de Moraes's *Recordações de Ary Barroso* [*Memories of Ary Barroso*], Sérgio Cabral's *Pixinguinha, vida e obra* [*The Life and Work of Pixinguinha*] and *Filho de Ogum Bexinguento* [*The Devotee of Ogum Bexinguento*], also on Pixinguinha, by Marilia T. Barboza da Silva and Arthur L. de Oliveira Filho. Carmen Miranda's career is comprehensively described by Abel Cardoso Junior in *Carmen Miranda, a cantora do Brasil* [*Carmen Miranda, Brazil's Singer*]. The best accounts on the golden period of the classical urban *samba* are provided by Almirante in his *No tempo de Noel Rosa* [*In Noel Rosa's Era*] and Lúcio Rangel in *Sambistas e chorões* [*Samba Dancer and New Samba Rhythms*]. Francisco

Guimarães (d. 1947), nicknamed Vagalume, was in the 1930s and 1940s one of the best known journalists who followed closely the popular musical scene (especially Carnival) of the period. His book *Na roda do samba* [*On the Samba's Trail*] (1933), re-edited in a second edition in 1978, offers first-hand insights and information of fundamental importance for an under-standing of the popular milieu in which the urban *samba* developed. Li-kewise, *O Chôro* [*The Choro*], by Alexandre Gonçalves Pinto, originally published in 1936, is a well-informed chronicle of the *chorões* [popular strolling, serenading musicians] of Rio de Janeiro. Carnival and samba schools have been the subjects of only a few serious studies. Sérgio Cabral in *História das escolas de samba* [*The History of Samba Schools*] and *As escolas de samba* [*Samba Schools*] reviews the history of the major samba schools and the annual parades and their music numbers up to the 1970s. More impressionistic accounts are given by Ari Araújo and Erika Herd in *Expressões da cultura popular: as escolas de samba do Rio de Janeiro e o amigo da madrugada* [*Expressions of Popular Culture: Samba Schools of Rio de Janeiro and the Morning Friend*] and Antônio Candeia Filho and Isnard Araújo in *Escolas de samba—árvore que esqueceu a razi* [*Samba Schools: The Tree That Forgot Its Roots*]. The most penetrating histories of carnival music, however, are *O carnaval carioca através da música* [*The Rio Carnival Seen through Its Music*], by Edigar de Alencar and *História do carnaval carioca* [*A History of Rio Carnival*] by Eneida de Morais. Paulo da Portela (1901–1949), one of Brazil's foremost samba school lead-ers and composers, is the subject of an excellent study, *Paulo da Portela: traço de união entre duas culturas* [*Paulo de Portela: A Hyphen Between Two Cultures*] by Marília T. Barboza da Silva and Lygia Santos. This study provides not only detailed information on the composer's career and an assessment of his contributions but also a detailed discography and a list of unpublished works.

The *bossa nova, jovem guarda,* and *tropicália* movements of the 1960s and 1970s gave rise to numerous studies, at first in rather polemic terms. Tinhorão's *Música popular—um tema em debate* [*Popular Music—A Po-lemical Theme*] is a reactionary review of *bossa nova*. The chronicle of Gumercindo Saraiva in *A canção popular brasileira* [*The Brazilian Popular Song*] is somewhat more objective in dealing with *bossa nova* and *jovem guarda* [young guard] (also known as "iê, iê, iê"). *Balanço da bossa: antologia crítica da moderna música popular brasileira* [*Bossa Inven-tory:Critical Anthology of Modern Popular Brazilian Music*], by Augusto de Campos and others, is made up of a series of articles arranged chron-ologically since the advent of *bossa nova* (1958). Most of them are in-depth studies of the various facets of *bossa nova*, including some pertinent stylistic comparative comments with the "classical" samba. This anthology also deals with the *Tropicália* musicians, and interviews with such personalities as Caetano Veloso and Gilberto Gil are reprinted for their historical value.

For English readers, Béhague's "Bossa and Bossas: Recent Changes in Brazilian Urban Popular Music" and "Brazilian Musical Values of the 1960s and 1970s: Popular Urban Music from Bossa Nova to Tropicalia" offer an interpretive review of the currents and a musical and textual analysis of representative pieces with translation into English of the various song texts. Various interpretations of the ideologies involved in the innovative currents of popular music are provided by Walnice Galvão in "MPB: uma análise ideológica" ["MPB: An Ideological Analysis"], by Roberto Schwarz in "Remarques sur la culture et la politique au Brésil, 1964–1968" ["Remarks on Culture and Politics in Brazil, 1964–1968"], and *Tropicália: alegoria, alegria* [*Tropicalia: Allegory, Joy*] by Celso F. Favaretto. This latter study is an interesting cultural analysis of the *tropicália* movement within the Brazilian cultural context of the late 1960s, with special attention to the technique of textual construction in *tropicália* songs. First-hand data from the major figures of that movement are found in *Alegria, alegria* by Caetano Veloso and in *Gilberto Gil: Expresso 2222*, an anthology of interviews and short articles organized by Antonio Risério. The close relationship of Brazilian modern poetry with popular music since *bossa nova* is the subject of the excellent study *Música popular e moderna poesia brasileira* [*Popular Music and Modern Brazilian Poetry*] by Affonso Romano de Sant'Anna.

A special mention should be made of the protest song movement in Latin America. Besides the items already mentioned, the anthology ¡*Basta! Canciones de testimonio y rebeldía de América latina* [*Enough! Songs of Testimony and Revolt from Latin America*] compiled by Meri Franco-Lao presents a fairly comprehensive collection of songs from virtually all Latin American countries dealing with socio-historical questions or simply social protest. Rina Benmayor gives a good historical overview of the influential Cuban protest song in "La 'Nueva Trova': New Cuban Song," and Nicolás Cossio and Félix Soloni, respectively, in "Encuentro de la canción protesta, Cuba 1967" ["The Protest Song Meeting, Cuba 1967"] and "La canción protesta, tradición cubana de más de un siglo" ["The Protest Song, A Cuban Tradition for More Than a Century"] include full texts of protest songs.

CENTERS AND RESEARCH COLLECTIONS

All of the national libraries of the Latin American nations contain rich holdings on urban popular music in the form of sheet music, newspapers, periodicals, and books. Unfortunately there is no systematic description of such holdings dealing specifically with popular music. The following library and research collections should be consulted in order to gain access to primary and secondary source materials.

In Mexico, besides the National Library, the Centro Nacional de Investigación, Documentación e Información Musical [National Center for Musical Research, Documentation and Information] (Liverpool 16, Mexico 6 DF) holds substantial materials on Mexican music in general and can provide assistance for popular music research. This is also true for Guatemala at the Centro de Estudios Folklóricos [Center for Folklore Studies] at the Universidad de San Carlos de Guatemala (Av. de la Reforma 0-09, Zona 10, Guatemala). In Cuba, the Biblioteca Nacional José Martí's [José Martí National Library] music division and the Centro para la Investigación y Desarrollo de la Música Cubana [Center for the Research and Development of Cuban Music] are good centers of information. In Puerto Rico the Instituto de Cultura Puertorriqueña [Institute of Puerto Rican Culture] founded in 1955 has a musical archive of printed and manuscript music and has issued a series of recordings of Puerto Rican popular music. The music libraries at the University of Puerto Rico, Río Piedras, and the Inter-American University of Puerto Rica, San Germán, hold materials on Puerto Rican popular music. In 1983, the branch of the University of Puerto Rico at Cayey founded the Centro Iberoamericano de Documentación Musical [Iberoamerican Center for Musical Documentation] (whose first *Boletín Informativo* [*Bulletin of Information*] was published at the end of 1983), which intends to become an efficiently modern documentation and information center on all aspects of Hispanic music (CIBDOM, Colegio Universitario de Cayey, Cayey PR 00633).

The Venezuelan capital has three main centers of music documentation: the División de Fonología [Phonology Division] of the National Library (Instituto Autónomo Biblioteca Nacional y de Servicios de Bibliotecas [National Library and Library Services Autonomous Institute], Carmelitas, Apartado 6525, Caracas 1010); the Instituto Interamericano de Etnomusicología y Folklore [Interamerican Institute of Ethnomusicology and Folklore] (Charallavito, Calle Miranda, Qta. San José, Apartado 81015, Caracas); and the Instituto Latinoamericano de Investigaciones y Estudios Musicales "Vicente Emilio Sojo" ["Vicente Emilio Soto" Latin American Institute for Research and Musical Studies] (Calle Los Mangos, Quinta No. 9, Apartado 70537, Caracas 1071). In Colombia, besides the National Library and the music library of the National Conservatory, the Instituto Colombiano de Cultura [Colombian Institute of Culture] has created a Centro de Documentación Musical [Musical Documentation Center] (Calle 11 no. 5–51, Bogotá) whose archive includes printed and manuscript music, newspaper articles, and recorded Colombian music (see José L. Arbena's "Centro de Documentación Musical of Bogota" ["Musical Documentation Center of Bogotá"]). For Ecuadorian popular music, the Benson Latin American Collection at The University of Texas at Austin holds Professor Johannes Riedel's papers related to music of the 1940s. The core of the collection is ten volumes of manuscript transcriptions of various genres of popular music written by numerous composers of the period. These volumes are supplemented by printed music, books, journals, and concert programs. In Lima the National Library has a Centro de Documentación [Documentation Center] (Instituto Nacional de Cultura [National Institute of Culture], Ancash 390, Lima) that includes substantial musical materials. More specialized is the Escuela Nacional de Música [National School of Music] of the Instituto Nacional de Cultura [National Institute of Culture] (Av. Emancipación, 180, Lima), which holds good materials on all aspects of Peruvian music. The Centro de Documentación of Chilean music is part of the Facultad de Artes [Arts Faculty] of the University of Chile (Casilla 2100, Santiago), which includes various archives of manuscripts, printed scores, and of recordings of Chilean music.

In Argentina, both the Instituto Nacional de Musicología [National Institute of Musicology] (Piedras 1260 A, 1140 Buenos Aires) and the Instituto de Investigaciones Musicológicas "Carlos Vega" ["Carlos Vega" Institute of Musicological Research] of the Universidad Católica Argentina [Argentine Catholic University] (Humberto 1°, 656, 1103 Buenos Aires) are major resource centers on any aspect of Argentine music. In Montevideo the best research collection on popular music is undoubtedly the archive of SODRE (Servicio Oficial de Difusión Radio Elétrica [Radio Electric Broadcasting Official Service]), founded in 1931. To my knowledge, however, this archive has not been catalogued. Since Dr. Francisco Curt Lange (Casilla 540, Montevideo) acted as librarian of SODRE and supervised its musical library, he is an excellent resource person.

Brazilian musical institutions are numerous, but only a few have paid attention to urban popular music collection development. In addition to the Music Division of the National Library (Palácio da Cultura 3°, and, Rua Pedro Leça, Rio de Janeiro), which contains the most comprehensive music collection in the country, the Centro de Documentação [Documentation Center] of FUNARTE (Rua Araújo Porto Alegre, 80 Rio de Janeiro 20030) and the Biblioteca FUNARTE [FUNARTE Library] have substantial materials on popular music in the form of books, newspaper and periodical articles, and recordings. FUNARTE has issued over the years important phono-discs on *Monumentos da música popular brasileira* [*Monuments of Brazilian Popular Music*] (six albums), *Meio século de carnaval carioca (1915–1965)* [*A Half Century of Rio Carnival (1915–1965)*] (four albums), and *Brazilian Popular Music* (ten albums).

FUTURE RESEARCH

It becomes clear that the gathering of collections of research materials is the most pressing first step in any serious, long-range research in Latin American urban popular music. Much remains to be done but, considering the inordinate amount of materials and the number of questions to be investigated, a monographic approach would seem wiser, whether in dealing with a specific historical period, a given style or urban tradition, a group of musicians, or specific genres. Overviews of Latin American popular music taken as a holistic category will not likely be satisfactory at this particular time. Yet, questions of an inter-American nature need to be addressed urgently, such as, for example, the so-called pan-Hispanic American popular music since the 1960s, or the *salsa* movement throughout the hemisphere. Most importantly, future research in the field of popular music needs to reflect the ideal but attainable balance and integration of strictly musicological analyses and ethnological inquiries. Questions of origin and influence remain important, to be sure, but issues of paramount import pertain to music and its cultural dynamics, to music as the driving symbol of ethnicity or group identity. The current theories and methods of popular music research can stand a good testing in the specific cases of Latin American societies. Future research will of necessity confront the matter of commercialization whose mechanism needs to be reassessed and whose influence on the musical end-product demands an objective analysis. Ultimately, however, the understanding of the processes of creation and consumption of Latin American popular music, and the meanings assigned by Latin American to that music, will be achieved through direct involvement and participation, not through library work alone.

BIBLIOGRAPHY

Books and Articles

Abadía, Guillermo. *La música folklórica colombiana* (Bogotá: Universidad Nacional de Colombia, 1973).
————. "Panorama de las músicas folklórica y popular," *Revista Espiral* nos. 116–117 (Sept.–Dec. 1970).
Alberti Mieses, Luis. *De música y orquestas bailables dominicanas, 1910–1959* (Santo Domingo: Taller, 1975).
Alencar, Edigar de. *O carnaval carioca através da música*. 2 vols. (Rio de Janeiro: Livraria Freitas Bastos, 1965).
————. *Nosso Sinhô do samba* (Rio de Janeiro: Civilização Brasileira Editôra, 1968).
Almeida, Renato de. *História da música brasileira*. 2d ed. (Rio de Janeiro: F. Briguiet & Cia., 1942).
Almirante. *No tempo de Noel Rosa*. 2d ed. (Rio de Janeiro: Francisco Alves, 1977).
Alvarenga, Oneyda. *Música popular brasileira*. 2d ed. (São Paulo: Livraria Duas Cidades, 1982).
Alves, Henrique L. *Sua excelência o samba* (Palermo, Brazil: E.i.l.A. Palma, 1968).
Añez, Jorge. *Canciones y recuerdos* (Bogotá: Ediciones Mundial, 1968).
Araújo, Ari, and Herd, Erika. *Expressões da cultura popular: as escolas de samba do Rio de Janeiro e o amigo da madrugada* (Petrópolis: Editôra Vozes, 1978).

Arbena, Joseph C. "Centro de Documentación Musical of Bogotá." *Latin American Music Review* 1, no. 1 (Spring/Summer 1980):128–29.

Ardévol, José. *Introducción a Cuba: la música* (Havana: Instituto del Libro, 1969).

Aretz, Isabel, ed. *América Latina en su música* (México: Siglo XXI, 1977).

———. *El folklore musical argentino* (Buenos Aires: Ricordi Americana, 1952).

Arias Trujillo, Bernardo. "Elogio del bambuco." *Hojas de cultura popular colombiana* (Bogotá) 2 (February 1947).

Arizaga, Rodolfo. *Enciclopedia de la música argentina* (Buenos Aires: Fondo Nacional de las Artes, 1971).

Arnaz, Desi. *A Book* (New York: William Morrow, 1976).

Arzeno, Julio. *Del folk-lore musical dominicano* (Santo Domingo: La Cuna de América, 1927).

Ayala, Roberto. *Musicosas: manual del comentarista de radio y televisión*, vol. 1 (México: Editorial Selecciones Musicales S.A., 1971).

Ayestarán, Lauro. *La música en el Uruguay*. Vol. 1 (Montevideo: SODRE, 1953).

Azevedo, Luiz Heitor Corrêa de. "The Present State and Potential of Music Research in Latin America." In *Perspectives in Musicology*, edited by Barry S. Brook, Edward O.D. Downes, and Sherman Van Solkema, 249–69 (New York: W.W. Norton, 1972).

Ballonoff, Paul A. "Origen de la cumbia: breve estudio de la influencia intercultural en Colombia." *América Indígena* 31, no. 1 (January 1971):45–49.

Baqueiro, Eloisa Ruiz Cavalho de. *Tradiciones, folklore, música y músicos de Campeche* (Campeche: Publicaciones de Gobierno del Estado de Campeche, 1970).

Baqueiro Foster, Gerónimo. *La canción popular de Yucatán* (México: Editorial del Magisterio, 1970).

Barbacci, Rodolfo. "Apuntes para un diccionario biográfico musical peruano." *Fénix* 6 (1949):414–510.

Béhague, Gerard. "Bossa and Bossas: Recent Changes in Brazilian Urban Popular Music." *Ethnomusicology* 17, no. 2 (May 1973):209–33.

———. "Brazilian Musical Values of the 1960s and 1970s: Popular Urban Music from Bossa Nova to Tropicália." *Journal of Popular Culture* 14, no. 3 (Winter 1980):437–52.

Benmayor, Rina. "La 'Nueva Trova': New Cuban Song." *Latin American Music Review* 2, no. 1 (Spring/Summer 1981):11–44.

Bernarda, Jorge. *La música dominicana. Siglos XIX-XX* (Santo Domingo: Editora de la Universidad Autónoma de Santo Domingo, 1982).

Blum, Joseph. "Problems of *Salsa* Research." *Ethnomusicology* 22, no. 1 (January 1978):137–49.

Borbolla, Carlos. "El son, exclusividad de Cuba." *Yearbook for Inter-American Musical Research* 11 (1975): 152–56.

Cabral, Sérgio. *As escolas de samba. O quê, quem, como, quando e por quê* (Rio de Janeiro: Editora Fontana, 1974).

———. *História das escolas de samba* (Rio de Janeiro: Rio Gráfica Editora, n.d.).

———. *Pixinguinha, vida e obra* (Rio de Janeiro: FUNARTE, 1978).

Calcaño, José Antonio. *La ciudad y su música. Crónica musical de Caracas* (Caracas: Edición y distribución "Conservatorio Teresa Carreño," 1958).

Campos, Augusto de, et al. *Balanço da bossa: Antología crítica da moderna musica popular brasileira.* 2d ed. (São Paulo: Editora Perspectiva, 1974).

Campos, Rubén M. *El folklore musical de las ciudades* (Mexico: Secretaría de Educación Pública, 1930).

Campos Parsi, Héctor. *La música. La Gran Enciclopedia de Puerto Rico.* Vol. 7, ed. Vicente Báez (Madrid: Ediciones Madrid, 1976).

Candeia Filho, Antônio, and Araújo, Isnard. *Escola de samba—árvore que esqueceu a raiz* (Rio de Janeiro: Editora Lidador, 1978).

Cantón, Darío. "El mundo de los tangos de Gardel." *Revista Latinoamericana de Sociología* (Buenos Aires) 4, no. 3 (November 1968): 341–61.

Cardoso Junior, Abel. *Carmen Miranda, a cantora do Brasil* (São Paulo: Edição particular do autor, 1978).

Carpentier, Alejo. *Ese músico que llevo dentro* (selección de Zaila Gómez) 3 vols. (Havana: Editorial Letras Cubanas, 1980).

———. *La música en Cuba* (México: Fondo de Cultura Económica, 1946).

———. "La música popular cubana." *Signos* (Consejo Nacional de Cultura, Biblioteca José Martí) 2, no. 3 (May–August 1971): 7–12.

Carrasco, Eduard. *La Nueva Canción en América Latina* (Santiago: CENECA, 1982).

Castañeda, Daniel. *Balance de Agustín Lara* (México: Ediciones Libres, 1941).

Céspedes, Gilka Wara. "New Currents in 'Música Folklórica' in La Paz, Bolivia." *Latin American Music Review* 5, no. 2 (Fall/Winter, 1984): 217–42.

Chase, Gilbert. *A Guide to the Music of Latin America.* 2d ed. (Washington, D. C.: Pan American Union, 1962).

Cheville, Lila R., and Cheville, Richard A. *Festivals and Dances of Panama* (Panama: published by the authors, 1977).

Claro, Samuel. *Oyendo a Chile* (Santiago, Chile: Editorial Andrés Bello, 1979).

———, and Urrutia Blondel, Jorge. *Historia de la música en Chile* (Santiago, Chile: Editorial Orbe, 1974).

Cohen, Stu. "La Nueva Canción Chilena." Notes to *Chile Vencerá: An Anthology of Chilean New Song* (Somerville, Mass.: Rounder Records 4009–4010, n.d.).

Coopersmith, Jacob Maurice. *Music and Musicians of the Dominican Republic. Música y músicos de la República Dominicana* (Washington, D.C.: Pan American Union, 1949).

Cossio, Nicolás. "Encuentro de la canción protesta. Cuba 1967." *Bohemia* (Havana) 59, no. 27 (July 1967): 46–51.

Courlander, Harold. "Musical Instruments of Cuba." *The Musical Quarterly* 28, no. 2 (April 1942): 227–40.

Crook, Larry. "A Musical Analysis of the Cuban Rumba." *Latin American Music Review* 3, no. 1 (Spring/Summer 1982): 92–123.

Davidson, Harry C. *Diccionario folklórico de Colombia.* 3 vols. (Bogotá: Banco de la República, 1970).

Davis, Martha Ellen. *Music and Dance in Latin American Urban Contexts: A Selective Bibliography* (Brockport, N.Y.: SUNY Department of Anthropology, 1973).

Díaz, Victor Miguel. *Las bellas artes en Guatemala* (Guatemala: Tipografía Nacional, 1934).

Dicks, Ted, ed. *Victor Jara: His Life and Songs* (London: Elm Tree Books, Ltd. [Essex Music International Ltd.], 1976).

Diniz, Jaime C. *Nazareth: estudos analíticos* (Recife, Brazil: DECA, 1963).

Doughty, Paul L. "Behind the Back of the City: 'Provincial' Life in Lima, Peru." In *Peasants in Cities*, edited by William Mangin, 30–45 (Boston: Houghton Mifflin Co., 1970).

———. "Peruvian Migrant Identity in the Urban Milieu." In *The Anthropology of Urban Environments*, edited by Thomas Weaver, 39–50 (Washington, D.C.: The Society for Applied Anthropology, 1972).

Duany, Jorge. "Popular Music in Puerto Rico: Toward an Anthropology of *Salsa.*" *Latin American Music Review* 5, no. 2 (Fall/Winter 1984): 186–216.

Efegê, Jota (pseud. of João Ferreira Gomes). *Ameno Resedá: o rancho que foi escola* (Rio de Janeiro: Editora Letras e Artes, 1965).

———. *Figuras e coisas da música popular brasileira.* 2 vols. (Rio de Janeiro: FUNARTE, 1978–1979).

Favaretto, Celso F. *Tropicália: alegoria, alegria* (São Paulo: Kairós Livraria e Editora, 1979).

Ferrer, Horacio. *El libro del tango. Historias e imágenes.* 2 vols. (Buenos Aires: Ediciones Ossorio-Vargas, 1970).

———. *El tango: su historia y su evolución* (Buenos Aires: Colección La Siringa, 1960).

Figueroa Berríos, Edwin. "Los sones de la bomba en la tradición popular de la costa sur de Puerto Rico." *Revista del Instituto de Cultura Puertorriqueña* 5 (1963): 46–48.

Flores, Bernal. *La música en Costa Rica* (San José: Editorial Costa Rica, 1978).

Fonfrías, Ernesto Juan. *Apuntes sobre la danza puertorriqueña* (San Juan: Instituto de Cultura Puertorriqueña, 1970).

Franco-Lao, Meri. *¡Basta! Canciones de testimonio y rebeldía de América Latina* (México: Ediciones ERA, 1970).

Galán Sariol, Natalio. "Visión musical de nuestra historia." *La Enciclopedia de Cuba.* Vol. 7, ed. Vicente Báez (Madrid: Playor S.A., 1974).

Galindo, Miguel. *Nociones de historia de la música mejicana.* Vol. 1 (Colima: Tipografía de "El Dragón," 1933).

Galvão, Walnice Nogueira. "MMPB: uma análise ideológica." *Aparte* 2 (1968).

———. *Saco de gato, ensaios críticos* (São Paulo: Livraria Duas Cidades, 1976).

Garay, Narciso. *Tradiciones y cantares de Panamá* (Brussels: Presses de l'Expansion, 1930).

Garrido, Juan S. *Historia de la música popular en México: 1896–1973* (México: Editorial Extemporáneos, 1974).

———. *Historia moderna de la música popular mexicana* (booklet). RCA Records, Vol. 3, MKLA 117, 1976.

Geijerstam, Claes af. *Popular Music in Mexico* (Albuquerque: University of New Mexico Press, 1976).

Gesualdo, Vicente. *Historia de la música en la Argentina.* 2 vols. (Buenos Aires: Editorial Beta, 1961).

Gómez Santos, Marino. *Xavier Cugat* (Barcelona: Ediciones Clipper, 1958).

Gradante, William. " 'El Hijo del Pueblo': José Alfredo Jiménez and the Mexican

Canción Ranchera." *Latin American Music Review* 3, no. 1 (Spring/Summer 1982): 36–59.

Grenet, Emilio. *Popular Cuban Music* (Havana: Carasa & Cia., 1939).

Grial, Hugo de. *Músicos mexicanos.* 4th ed. (México: Editorial Diana, 1971).

Guimarães, Francisco. *Na roda do samba.* 2d ed. (Rio de Janeiro: FUNARTE, 1978).

Handbook of Latin American Studies. Humanities (Austin: University of Texas Press, 1983).

d'Harcourt, Raoul, and d'Harcourt, Marguerite. *La musique des Incas et ses survivances* (Paris: P. Geuthner, 1925).

Hollanda, Chico Buarque de. *A banda: manuscritos de* . . . (Rio de Janeiro: Editôra Paulo de Azevedo, 1966).

León, Argeliers. *Música folklórica de Cuba* (Havana: Biblioteca Nacional José Martí, Departamento de Música, 1964).

Linares, María Teresa. *La música popular* (Havana: Instituto del Libro, 1970).

Lopes, J., and Peres, M., "La música popular brasileña." *Música* (Havana, Casa de las Américas) 18 (1971): 1–5.

López Cruz, Francisco. *La música folklórica en Puerto Rico* (Sharon, Conn.: Troutman Press, 1967).

López Tirado, Anthar. "La Nueva Canción en México." *IMC* (Organo de Difusión del Instituto Michoacano de Cultura, Morelia, Michoacán) (August–November 1982): 3–6.

Mafud, Julio. *La sociología del tango* (Buenos Aires: Editorial Americalee, 1966).

Manns, Patricio. *Violeta Parra* (Madrid: Ediciones Jucar, 1977).

Marcondes, Marcos, ed. *Enciclopédia da música brasileira: Erudita, folclórica, popular* (São Paulo: Editôra Art, 1977).

Márquez, Los Hermanos. *25 biografías de compositores populares* (México: n.p., 1966).

Marroquín, Lorenzo. "El bambuco." *Boletín de Programas* (Radio-televisora Nacional, Bogotá) 226 (April 1966).

Martínez Moirón, Jesús. *El mundo de los autores* (Buenos Aires: Sampedro Ediciones, 1971).

Matamoro, Blas. *Carlos Gardel* (Buenos Aires: Centro Editor de América Latina, 1971).

———. *Historia del tango* (Buenos Aires: Centro Editor de América Latina, 1971).

Mayer-Serra, Otto. "La industria mexicana del disco." *Audiomúsica* 42 (1961).

———. *Música y músicos de Latinoamérica.* 2 vols. (México: Editorial Atlante, S.A., 1947).

———. *Panorama de la música mexicana desde la independencia hasta la actualidad* (México: El Colegio de México, 1941).

Mazuera M., Lubín E. *Orígenes históricos del bambuco, teoría musical y cronología de autores y compositores colombianos.* 2d ed. (Cali: Imprenta Departamental, 1972).

Mello, José Eduardo Homem de. *Música popular brasileira* (São Paulo: Edições Melhoramentos, 1976).

Mendoza, Vicente T. *La canción mexicana: ensayo de clasificación y antología* (México: Universidad Nacional Autónoma de México, 1961).

————. *El corrido mexicano, antología, introducción y notas* (México: Fondo de Cultura Económica, 1954).

————. *Panorama de la música tradicional de México* (México: Imprenta Universitaria, 1956).

Menéndez Peña, Hilario. *Monografías y cantares huastecos* (México: Compañía General Editora, 1944).

Milanesi, Luiz Augusto, and Barone, Antonio Fernando Corrêa. *Bibliografía de música popular brasileira* (São Paulo: n.p., 1978).

Moraes, Mário de. *Recordações de Ary Barroso* (Rio de Janeiro: FUNARTE, 1979).

Morais, Eneida de. *História do carnaval carioca* (Rio de Janeiro: Editora Civilização Brasileira, 1958).

Moreno, Segundo Luis. *Historia de la música en el Ecuador.* Vol. 1 (Quito: Casa de la Cultura Ecuatoriana, 1972).

Morláz Gutiérrez, Alberto, comp. *Florilegio del pasillo ecuatoriano* (Quito: Editorial "Fray Jodoco Ricke," 1961).

Muñoz, María Luisa. *La música en Puerto Rico* (Sharon, Conn.: Troutman Press, 1966).

Muñoz, Milina. "El IV Reinado del bambuco." *Revista Colombiana de Folklore* 9 (1964–1965): 235–57.

Orovio, Helio. *Diccionario de la música cubana, biográfico y técnico* (Havana: Editorial Letras Cubanas, 1981).

Ortega, Jesús. "Canciones de Sindo Garay." *Signos* (Biblioteca Nacional José Martí) 1, no. 1 (November 1969): 304–27.

Ortega Ricaurte, Carmen. "Contribución a la bibliografía de la música en Colombia." *Revista de la Dirección de Divulgación Cultural* (Universidad Nacional de Colombia) 12 (August 1973): 83–255.

Ortiz, Fernando. *La africanía de la música folklórica de Cuba* (Havana: Publicaciones del Ministerio de Educación, 1950).

————. *Los bailes y el teatro de los negros en el folklore de Cuba* (Havana: Publicaciones del Ministerio de Educación, 1951).

————. *Los instrumentos de la música afrocubana.* 5 vols. (Havana: Publicaciones del Ministerio de Educación and Cárdenas y Cia., 1952–1955).

"Panorama 1964 de la música popular." *Audiomúsica* 126 (1964): 9.

"Panorama de la música popular (1965–66)." *Audiomúsica* 151 (1966): 8–9.

"Panorama de la música popular (1966–1967)." *Audiomúsica* 175 (1967): 9, 26.

Pardo Tovar, Andrés. *La cultura musical en Colombia (Historia Extensa de Colombia)* 20, no. 6 (Bogotá: Ediciones Lerner, 1966).

Parra (Sandoval), Violeta. *Yo canto la diferencia: canciones de Violeta Parra* (Buenos Aires: Lagos, 1976).

Perdomo Escobar, José Ignacio. *Historia de la música en Colombia.* 5th ed. (Bogotá: Plaza & Janes Editores Colombia Ltda., 1980).

Pereira, João Baptista Borges. "O negro e a comercialização da música popular brasileira." *Revista do Instituto de Estudos Brasileiros* (Universidade de São Paulo) 8 (1970): 7–15.

Pereira Salas, Eugenio. *Historia de la música en Chile (1850–1900)* (Santiago: Editorial del Pacífico, S.A., 1957).

Pinto, Alexandre Gonçalves. *O Chôro*. Facsimile ed. (Rio de Janeiro: FUNARTE, 1978).

Plaza, Galvarino. *Victor Jara* (Madrid: Ediciones Jucar, 1976).

Pollak-Eltz, Angelina. *Bibliografía afrovenezolana* (Caracas: Universidad Católica "Andrés Bello," 1976).

Pulido, Esperanza. "Música popular de México." *Heterofonía* 36 (1974): 12–16.

Ramalho Neto, A. *Historinha do desafinado: bossa nova* (Rio de Janeiro: Casa Editora Vecchi, 1965).

Ramón y Rivera, Luis Felipe. *El joropo: baile nacional de Venezuela* (Caracas: Dirección de Cultura y Bellas Artes, 1953).

———. *La música popular de Venezuela* (Caracas: Ernesto Armitano Editor, 1976).

Rangel, Lúcio. *Sambistas e chorões: aspectos e figuras da música popular brasileira* (Rio de Janeiro: Francisco Alves, 1962).

Raygada, Carlos. "Guía musical del Perú." *Fénix* (Lima) 12 (1956–1957): 3–77; 13 (1963): 1–82; 14 (1964): 3–95.

Restrepo Duque, Hernán. *Lo que cuentan las canciones: cronicón musical* (Bogotá: Editorial Tercer Mundo, 1971).

Reuter, Jas. *La música popular de México. Origen e historia de la música que canta y toca el pueblo mexicano*. 2d ed. (México: Panorama Editorial, S.A., 1981).

Risério, Antonio, comp. *Gilberto Gil: Expresso 2222* (Salvador, Bahia: Editora Corrupio, 1982).

Roberts, John Storm. *The Latin Tinge. The Impact of Latin American Music on the United States* (New York, Oxford: Oxford University Press, 1979).

Rodríguez Demorizi, Emilio. *Música y baile en Santo Domingo* (Santo Domingo: Librería Hispaniola, 1971).

Roel Pineda, Josafat. "El wayno del Cuzco." *Folklore Americano* (Lima) 6–7 (1959): 129–246.

Rojas, Alfonso María. "El bambuco de Colombia." *Revista "Huila"* (Neiva, Colombia) 2, no. 11 (1958): 23–25.

Romero, Jesús C. *La música en Zacatecas y los músicos zacatecanos* (México: Universidad Nacional Autónoma de México, 1963).

Rondón, César Miguel. *El libro de la salsa: crónica de la música del caribe urbano* (Caracas: Editorial Arte, 1980).

Rossi, Vicente. *Cosas de negros* (Buenos Aires: Librería Hachette, 1926).

Ruiz Hernández, Alvaro. *Personajes y episodios de la canción popular* (Barranquilla: Luz Negra, 1983).

Sábato, Ernesto. *El tango: discusión y clave*. 2d ed. (Buenos Aires: Biblioteca Clásica y Contemporánea, 1965).

Sadie, Stanley, ed. *The New Grove Dictionary of Music and Musicians*. 20 vols. (London: Macmillan, 1980).

Saldívar, Gabriel. *Historia de la música en México* (México: Editorial "Cvltvra," 1934).

Santa Cruz Gamarra, César. *El waltz y el valse criolla* (Lima: Instituto Nacional de Cultura, 1977).

Sant'Anna, Affonso Romano de. *Música popular e moderna poesia brasileira* (Petrópolis: Editora Vozes, 1978).

Saraiva, Gumercindo. *A canção popular brasileira em três tempos* (São Paulo: Gráfica Saraiva, 1968).

Schwarz, Roberto. "Remarques sur la culture et la politique au Brésil, 1964–1968." *Les Temps Modernes* 288 (1970).

Shepherd, John. "A Theoretical Model for the Sociomusicological Analysis of Popular Music." *Popular Music* 2 (1982): 148.

Silva, Marilia T. Barboza da, and Oliveira Filho, Arthur L. de. *Filho de Ogum Bexiguento* (Rio de Janeiro: FUNARTE, 1979).

―――, and Santos, Lygia. *Paulo da Portela: traço de união entre duas culturas* (Rio de Janeiro: FUNARTE, 1980).

Signos (Biblioteca Nacional José Martí) 2, no. 3 (May–August 1971). Special issue on Cuban popular music.

Sierra, Luis Adolfo. *Historia de la orquesta típica: evolución instrumental del tango* (Buenos Aires: A. Peña Lillo Editor, 1966).

Siqueira, Baptista. *Ernesto Nazareth na música brasileira: ensaio histórico-científico* (Rio de Janeiro: Gráfica Editôra Aurora, 1966).

Sociedad de Autores y Compositores de México: XXV años de la SACM (México: SACM, 1971).

Soloni, Félix. "La canción protesta, tradición cubana de más de un siglo." *Bohemia* (Havana) 59, no. 30 (Junc 1967): 18–21.

Stein, Steve. "El vals criollo y los valores de la clase trabajadora en la Lima de comienzos del siglo XX." *Socialismo y Participación* 7 (March 1982): 43–50.

Stevenson, Robert. *A Guide to Caribbean Music History* (Lima: Ediciones "CVLTVRA," 1975).

―――. *Music in Aztec and Inca Territory*. 2d ed. (Berkeley: University of California Press, 1976).

Stigberg, David K. "*Jarocho, Tropical*, and 'Pop': Aspects of Musical Life in Veracruz, 1971–72." In *Eight Urban Musical Cultures. Tradition and Change*, edited by Bruno Nettl, 260–95 (Urbana, Chicago, London: University of Illinois Press, 1978).

Subercaseaux, Bernardo. "El canto nuevo en Chile (1973–1980)." *Cuadernos Americanos* 39 (September 1980): 88–95.

Talavera, Mario. *Miguel Lerdo de Tejada: su vida pintoresca y anecdótica* (México: Editorial "Compas" [194?]).

Tati, Miécio. "Elementos de uma escola de samba." *Revista Brasileira de Folclore* 10, no. 26 (January–April 1970): 85–92.

Taylor, Julie M. "Tango: Theme of Class and Nation." *Ethnomusicology* 20, no. 2 (May 1976): 273–91.

Thompson, Anna Figueroa de, comp. *An Annotated Bibliography of Writings about Music in Puerto Rico* (Ann Arbor: Music Library Association, 1974).

Tinhorão, José Ramos. *Música popular—de índios, negros e mestiços* (Petrópolis: Editora Vozes, 1972).

―――. *Música popular—do gramofone ao rádio e TV* (São Paulo: Editora Ática, 1981).

―――. *Música popular—os sons que vêm da rua* (Rio de Janeiro: Edições Tinhorão, 1976).

―――. *Música popular—teatro e cinema* (Petrópolis: Editora Vozes, 1972).

―――. *Música popular—um tema em debate*. 2d ed. (Rio de Janeiro: JCM Editores, 1969).

―――. *Pequena história de música popular—Da modinha à canção de protesto*. 2d ed. (Petrópolis: Editora Vozes, 1975).

―――. *O samba agora vai...―a farsa da música popular no exterior* (Rio de Janeiro: JCM Editores, 1969).

Vasconcellos, Ary. *Panorama da música popular brasileira*. 2 vols. (São Paulo: Livraria Martins Editora, 1964).

―――. *Raízes da música popular brasileira (1500–1889)* (São Paulo: Livraria Martins Editora and Brasília: Instituto Nacional do Livro, 1977).

Vela, Lise Paret-Limardo de. *Folklore musical de Guatemala* (Buenos Aires: n.p., 1960). Document no. 176 of the International Congress of Folklore held in Buenos Aires, December 1960.

Veloso, Caetano. *Alegria, alegria* (Rio de Janeiro: A Pedra Q Ronca, 1977).

Vidart, Daniel. *El tango y su mundo* (Montevideo: Ediciones Tauro, 1967).

Zamudio, Daniel. "El Bambuco," *El folklore musical en Colombia* (Boletín de Programas) (Radiotelevisora Nacional de Colombia), no. 202 (June 1961).

Zapata Agurto, Sergio. "Psicoanálisis del vals peruano: contribución al estudio de la personalidad básica del hombre peruano." *Revista de Ciencias Psicológicas y neurológicas* (Universidad Mayor de San Marcos, Lima) 5, nos. 1–2 (March–June 1968): 5–61.

Zapata Cuéncar, Heriberto. *Compositores Antioqueños* (Medellín: Editorial Carpel, 1962).

―――. *Centenario de Pelón Santamarta, 1867–1967: vida, andanzas y canciones del autor de "Antioqueñita"* (Medellín: Editorial Granamérica, 1967).

Zapata Olivella, Delia. "La cumbia, síntesis musical de la nación colombiana." *Revista del Folklore* 3, no. 7 (Bogotá, 1962): 187–204.

Zapata Olivella, Manuel. "Comparsas y teatro callejero en los carnavales colombianos." *Boletín Cultural y Bibliográfico* (Biblioteca Luis-Angel Arango, Bogotá) 6, no. 11 (1963): 1763–65.

―――. "Los pasos del folklore colombiano: la cumbia." *Vínculo Shell* (Bogotá) (1962).

―――. "Los ritmos populares." *Boletín Cultural y Bibliográfico* (Biblioteca Luis-Angel Arango, Bogotá) 5, no. 11 (1962): 1498–99.

Anthologies (Selective list, collections of texts omitted)

Album de música nativa. No. 1 (Guayaquil, Ecuador, 1933).

Album de música cubana, Sindo Garay. (Havana 1941).

Andrade, Mário de, comp. *Modinhas Imperiais* (São Paulo: Casa Chiarato, 1930).

Antología del Tango Rioplatense. Vol. 1. (Buenos Aires: Instituto Nacional de Musicología "Carlos Vega," 1980).

Canciones Panamericanas. Songs of the Americas (New York, Chicago, San Francisco: Silver, Burdett Co., 1942).

Cardenal A., Salvador. *Nicaragua: música y canto*. 2d ed. (Managua: Fondo de Promoción Cultural del Banco de América, 1977).

Caymi, Dorival. *Cancioneiro da Bahia*. 4th ed. (São Paulo: Livraria Martins Editôra, 1967).

Cugat, Xavier, ed. *Collection of Pan American Songs* (New York: Robbins Music Corp., 1942).

————. *The Other Americas: An Album of Typical Central and South American Songs and Dances* (New York: E. B. Marks Music Corp., 1938).

Gallet, Luciano, comp. *Canções populares brasileiras* (Rio de Janeiro: Carlos Wehrs e Cia., n.d.).

Grenet, Emilio, ed. *Popular Cuban Music; 80 revised and corrected compositions* (Havana: Carasa & Cia., 1939).

Hague, Eleanor, comp. *Spanish-American Folksongs* (Lancaster, Pa.; New York: The American Folklore Society, 1917).

d'Harcourt, Marguerite Béclard. *Mélodies populaires indiennes; Equateur, Pérou, Bolivie* (Milan: G. Ricordi & C., 1923).

The Latin-American Songbook (Boston, New York: Ginn and Co., 1942).

Mendes, Julia de Brito, comp. *Canções populares do Brazil* (Rio de Janeiro: J. Ribeiro dos Santos, 1911).

Monumentos da música popular brasileira (six albums) (Rio de Janeiro: FUN-ARTE, n.d.)

Música ecuatoriana. No. 2. (Guayaquil, Ecuador, 1935).

Música popular brasileira. Brazilian Popular Music (ten albums) (Rio de Janeiro: FUNARTE, n.d.).

Péret, Elsie Houston, comp. *Chants populaires du Brésil* (Paris: P. Geuthner, 1930).

Piñeros Corpas, Joaquín. *El cancionero noble de Colombia* (three discs, 36-p. booklet, English-Spanish edition) (Bogotá: Editorial Antares-Fonotón, 1962).

Ríos Toledano, Miguel, comp. *Al pueblo mexicano. Única y auténtica colección de treinta jarabes, sones principales y más populares aires nacionales* (México: H. Nagel, ca. 1885).

Robledo González, Carlos, ed. *Colección de danzas y bailes regionales mexicanos, recopilados y arreglados para piano* (México: n.p., n.d.).

Serrano Redonnet, Ana., ed. *Cancionero musical argentino* (Buenos Aires: Ediciones Culturales Argentinas, 1964).

Sojo, Vicente Emilio, ed. *Primer cuaderno de canciones populares venezolanas* (Caracas: Ministerio de Educación Nacional, 1940).

————. *Segundo cuaderno de canciones populares venezolanas* (Caracas: Radio Caracas, 1942).

Toor, Frances. *A Treasury of Mexican Folkways* (New York: Crown Publishers, 1947).

Zúñiga, J. Daniel, comp. *Colección de bailes típicos de la provincia de Guanacaste* (San José, Costa Rica: Imprenta Nacional, 1929).

Periodicals and Magazines

(Note: For dates and locations of Music Periodicals, refer to *The New Grove Dictionary*, Vol. 14, entry "Periodicals.")

América Indígena (Mexico City)
American Music (Sonneck Society)
Audiomúsica (Mexico City)
Boletín Interamericano de Música (*Inter-American Music Bulletin*) (Washington, D.C.)

Boletín Latino-Americano de Música (Montevideo: Instituto Interamericano de Musicología)
Buenos Aires Musical (Buenos Aires)
Caribbean Studies (University of Puerto Rico, Río Piedras)
Ethnomusicology (Society for Ethnomusicology, Inc.)
Folklore Americano (Lima, Peru)
Guatemala Indígena (Guatemala City)
Heterofonía (Mexico City)
Inter-American Music Review (Los Angeles)
Journal of American Folklore (The American Folklore Society)
Journal de la Société des Américanistes
Latin American Music Review–Revista de Música Latinoamericana (University of Texas, Austin)
Latin New York (New York City)
Música (Havana, Casa de las Américas)
Nuestra Música (Mexico City)
Revista Brasileira de Folclore (Rio de Janeiro)
Revista Brasileira de Música (Rio de Janeiro)
Revista Colombiana de Folclor (Bogotá)
Revista de Estudios Musicales (Mendoza, Argentina)
Revista del Instituto de Cultura Puertorriqueña (San Juan, Puerto Rico)
Revista del Instituto de Investigaciones Musicológicas "Carlos Vega" (Buenos Aires)
Revista Musical Chilena (Santiago, Chile)
Revista Musical de Venezuela (Caracas)
Revista Nacional de Cultura (Caracas)
Revista Venezolana de Folklore (Caracas)

Kent Maynard

2 Popular Religion

> Popular religion might be defined as religion which reflects the beliefs
> of a broad spectrum of the populace. In some cases popular religion
> may be no more than a set of ideas upon which a large number of
> persons tend to agree. In other cases it may be formalized into specific
> doctrines and practices exhibited by organized groups. But formalized
> religion can be classified as popular only if there is acceptance of its
> basic beliefs by many persons beyond the boundary of the group (Potter
> 1970:712).

There is a long tradition of writing about "popular religion" by Latin
Americans and Latin American specialists, though more often than not
utilizing another name. In some cases it may be taken or mistaken for a
religiosity representing the pre-Columbian religious heritage of Latin
America (Cf. Friedlander 1975). It may be identified implicitly or explicitly
with a presumed "folk" tradition (e.g., Redfield 1941) or seen as part and
parcel of a wider national consciousness (e.g., Paz 1961). Popular religion
has been vilified by representatives of orthodoxy (e.g., Arriaga 1968), as
well as held up as worthy of respect and a basis for a critical awareness of
society (Arevas 1974). An analogous example of ambivalence is found in
the social scientific literature, where some view popular religiosity as in-
ducing and perpetuating a false awareness about the nature of class society
(e.g., de Kadt 1967), while others note its ability to give voice to feelings
of oppression (e.g., Fallas 1970) or even to serve as the basis or medium
of rebellions and revolts (e.g., Reed 1964; Wachtel 1977).

There are additional dimensions, of course, to the discussions and debates surrounding popular religion. Pursuing such issues, however, is premised on understanding the very ambiguity in defining popular religion itself.
An initial difficulty comes in distinguishing between popular religion and
religion per se. Richard Potter's (1970) definition found in the epigraph, for

example, would seem to differentiate between them initially on the basis of widely shared beliefs versus beliefs found in organized groups. To limit popular religion to mere belief, however, seems both empirically and theoretically problematic. Potter does allow for the inclusion of organized religious groups if their beliefs are more widely shared, yet this would not seem to exclude church bodies such as the Vatican from popular religion.

Potter, however, implies a resolution to this difficulty in his remark that popular religion is both popular and of the populace (1970:712). "Popular" derives from the Latin *popularis*, "of the people," while "populace" is from the Italian word *popolaccio*, a derogatory reference to "the rabble," denoting "the common people," those without special rank or wealth (Cf. *Webster's International Unabridged Dictionary*, Third Edition). Popular religion, therefore, signifies a religion distinct, not from organized worship, but from "official" doctrine and practice. It points to a difference in the power between such groups and their relative ability to assert their religious system as orthodoxy, definitive of reality for the entire society. The subordinate position of popular religion refers to the ease with which it is called into question by dominant members of society, rather than to the sheer number of individuals who ardently believe in it. A religion may be popular, even of the majority, yet remain without control over the principal sources of power in a society.

Popular religion, thus, implies a rank- or class-based society, where neither the distribution of knowledge nor access to power is egalitarian. This is suggested by Harold Hinds's definition of popular culture in general as "those aspects of culture which are widely disseminated and consumed by large numbers of people in a national culture, often through mass media" (1980:410f). It seems possible, however, to include within such a definition subordinate popular religions from rank and class societies that are not nation-states, such as local beliefs and practices flourishing in the Inca Empire, along side of the royal religion (Rowe 1946). If the latter is admitted, it is important to include in the "mass media" that disseminate popular religion such sources as oral tradition, dance, or drama (e.g., Kurath 1967; Movote Best 1953).

If popular religion is inherently tied to wider issues of class, rank, and ethnic relations in a stratified society, it becomes an ideological element crucial in portraying the linkage between symbolic structures and power. The extent to which writers on Latin American popular religion conceive of it as ideology or the way in which the latter is defined will be equally important to explore. The notion of popular religion as ideological, however, raises the prospect that the study of popular religion, and popular culture generally, is essential to any analysis of the origins and workings of stratified societies. Popular culture and religion are, like magic in Michael Taussig's words, "poetic echoes of the cadences that guide the innermost course of the world" (Taussig 1980:15). They stand at the core of the social reproduction of stratified societies and those cataclysmic historical moments when new definitions of reality and a new social order come to the fore. Popular culture and religion are, therefore, no longer popular but official.

HISTORICAL OUTLINE AND REVIEW OF THE LITERATURE

To summarize the origins and history of popular religion in Latin America first requires attention to the types of popular religion and the characteristics of their theology and practice. Popular religion clearly derives in the main from the Spanish and Portuguese conquests and the arrival of European Catholicism. As many authors point out, however, it draws to varying degrees on other religious traditions, such as the indigenous Indian religions and African beliefs and practices from the period of slavery (W. Madsen 1957; Bastide 1978). Such a popular Catholicism, with all of its local variations, falls on a continuum from groups that remain essentially Indian or African in their orientation, though reflecting the conditions of the conquest or of slavery, to those that involve a genuine syncretism. These latter groups are often unaware of the disparate elements in their past (Cf. Herskovits 1943; Thompson 1954; and Friedlander 1975). Popular Catholicism is complemented by two other popular religious systems in Latin America, those of spiritism or spiritualism and Protestantism (Cf. Camargo 1961; Damboriena 1962).

The literature on popular religion in Latin America, with the partial exception of that for Protestantism, contains few general surveys or analyses and a relative lack of comprehensive bibliographical materials. Numerous articles, however, are to be found in the increasing number of excellent Latin American journals, such as *América Indigena* [*Indigenous America*], *América Latina* [*Latin America*], and *Allpanchis Phuturinqa* (Cuzco), as well as other journals including *Latin American Perspectives, Studies in Latin American Popular Culture,* the *Journal of American Folklore,* and the *Journal of Latin American Lore.*

Discussions of Latin American popular religion may appear in general surveys of Latin American society, culture, or history. Emilio Willems (1975:64), for example, notes that "[t]he cult of the saints, monasticism, mysticism, religious fiestas, and a proliferation of religious brotherhoods are usually cited to characterize Latin American Catholicism." Julius Rivera (1978) includes a section entitled "Some Popular Beliefs," in which he discusses the import of *Marianismo* [the cult of the Virgin Mary], the role of Satan, and the importance of the dead found in All Saints Day and All Souls Day observances. Other general studies or summaries may be from a more theological perspective. José Arevas reports on some of the findings of a social scientific conference on popular religion, entitled *Encuentro*

Latinamericano de Religiosidad Popular [*Latin American Conference on Popular Religiosity*] held in December 1973 at the Universidad Católica [Catholic University] in Santiago de Chile (1974). Arevas notes the pejorative views toward popular Catholicism of many in the church hierarchy in the past, but suggests that the church must respect such religiosity, though not uncritically, as a reflection of the actual social conditions of its adherents. Felipe Berryman (1971), a North American priest in Panama, and J. M. Bonino (1976), an Argentine Protestant theologian, present similar views (Cf. Marzal 1973; Zalles 1976). The report of the Instituto de Teología do Recife [Theological Institute of Recife] (1974) on "popular faith" in the Brazilian northeast also reflects the church's interest in acquiring greater knowledge of lay thought and practice and has the advantage of quoting extensively from informants about their beliefs.[1]

Descriptions and analyses abound that discuss popular religion in light of the history or character of particular nations and the development of nationalism. The literature on popular Catholicism and religion in this genre for Brazil is probably more extensive than for any other region or country in Latin America. Pedro Assis Ribeiro de Oliveira (1976b, 1977) has published two bibliographies on popular Catholicism. Oliveira (1970, 1976a) also provides more general descriptions of popular religiosity, as does Charles Wagley (1971) in his chapter on "Church and State," for *An Introduction to Brazil*. Both join René Ribeiro (1956) in his classic study *Religião e relações raciais* [*Religion and Racial Relations*] in pointing to the independence of *catolicismo de bairro* [neighborhood Catholicism] from the church and its linkage to racial, ethnic, and class factors.

Popular religion has been widely studied in Mexico, though certainly other areas in Latin America are represented as well (Cf. Millas 1962). For its moving portrait of Mexican identity, Octavio Paz's (1961) *The Labyrinth of Solitude* relies in good measure on its analysis of *guadalupanismo* (the central place of the Virgin, "Our Lady of Guadalupe") in Mexican national religious life, the importance of the spirits of the dead, and particularly the underlying meanings of the fiesta complex. More general surveys of Mexican popular religion are found in the works of Anita Brenner (1929) and Robert E. Quirk (1973).

In addition to these studies focusing on particular countries, there is a plethora of analyses dealing with specific aspects of popular religion that may be either local to one area or found throughout Latin America. The literature on "Our Lady of Guadalupe" illustrates the former, whereas discussions of *Marianismo* [the cult of the Virgin] per se apply to the entire continent. One of the most pertinent accounts of the role of Guadalupe in Mexico remains Francisco de La Maza's (1953) *El guadalupanismo mexicano* [*Mexican Guadalupeism*], which so vividly documents both the history of the cult and its relationship to a rising creole identity and Mexican nationalism (Cf. Demarest and Taylor 1957; Turner and Turner 1978; and

Wolf 1958). After the Virgin of Guadalupe was declared the Patroness of New Spain by Pope Benedict XIV in 1756, it was no accident that Father Hidalgo should lead the rebels against Spain under her banner (Stevens 1973:94).[2]

That "Our Lady of Guadalupe" was to be named patroness of all Latin America by Pope Pius X denotes not only her own position but the importance of Mary as the mother of God in popular Catholicism. Evelyn Stevens (1973) underscores the importance of the Virgin as a role model for women.[3] While Stevens and others rightly point out the popular imagery of Mary as humble, passive, sexually neutral, and ascetically spiritual, Fredrick Pike (1978:242) suggests that this view is most typical of the working classes. In upper-class thought the Virgin is associated with courtly love, almost erotic in nature, and inspirational of heroic deeds. In this connection, Rivera (1978:99) notes that in many countries of Latin America the Virgin of Mount Carmel is patroness of the armed forces.

Other themes in popular religion in Latin America, in addition to *Marianismo*, have also received special attention. Though not pretending to be exhaustive, topics such as the civil-religious hierarchies of many communities, popular religious festivals, dances and dramas, as well as the widespread involvement of religion in healing, are found frequently in the literature.

Civil-religious hierarchies are present particularly in Indian communities throughout Spanish Latin America, though absent in Brazil (Forman 1975:276f). Such hierarchies have been described in particular detail for the many groups in Mesoamerica (Cf. Cancian 1967; Carrasco 1961; and M. Nash 1958), though other areas such as the Andean region have also been systematically described (INDICEP 1973). Though regarded as one system, civil-religious hierarchies involve a gradated series of religious and civil offices for many areas, with the individual alternating between each type of office. Participation in this system is viewed as a *cargo*, a burden, as it involves great expense to carry out all of the duties of office and the fiestas associated with the saints, Holy Week, and other religious observances. This ritual structure may have as one effect the leveling of wealth and reinforcement of egalitarian ties, as Gonzalo Aguirre Beltrán (1967) suggests in his study of mestizo communities. Office holders, however, also receive the esteem of fellow villagers and constitute not only the central religious figures in many communities, but their political leaders as well.[4]

In considering cargo systems one is inevitably drawn to the wider fiesta complex to which they are related. Festivals, of course, occur in many contexts, such as fiestas for patron saints, Carnival, or other orthodox religious holidays including All Saints Day, Christmas, and Easter. They occur throughout Spanish and Portuguese Latin America in both Indian and *ladino* [non-Indian part of the dominant society] communities. They cut across the class structure, albeit with well-defined variations (Cf. González Sol 1947; Reina 1967; and Sánchez García 1956). Of central importance to any description of popular Catholicism, a thorough analysis of Latin American festivals by Robert H. Lavenda is presented in this volume.

Of related importance are the many forms of popular religious art, such as drama, dance, oral humor, and narrative, associated with festivals and other religious contexts (Cf. Bedregal 1976; Carvalho-Neto 1977; Correa, Cannon, Hunter, and Bode 1961; and Kurath 1967). Marilyn Ravicz (1970) notes that religious plays and other performing arts were used by the earliest Catholic missionaries in proselytizing in Mexico, a fact quite evident for other areas of Latin America as well (e.g., Wachtel 1977). Dramas such as the *posadas* describing the search for lodging in Bethlehem by Mary and Joseph (W. Madsen 1960), the Passion play (J. Nash 1967/68), the Dance of the Conquest (Correa, et al. 1961), and "Moors and Christians" (Ricard 1966) are found especially in peasant Indian communities in Latin America. Frequently bound up with such dramas, though also found independently, are dances (e.g., Kurath 1967; Lekis 1958), mythology (e.g., Mendelson 1967) and oral narratives (e.g., Chilcote 1979; Edmunson 1967b; Falla 1970; and Movote Best 1953).

Not all of these artistic expressions of popular religiosity are part of oral tradition. Increasingly, for example, dramas such as "Moors and Christians" may be scripted and involve troops of actors (Friedlander 1975:105–6). Similarly, Shepard Forman (1975:211) notes that many ideas found in Brazilian peasant religion are learned through the *literatura de cordel* [cord literature], "troubadour songs that are now printed in pamphlet form" and sold at local markets (Cf. Casa de Rui Barbosa 1964).

Songs in other areas may also be associated with games, which often have a religious content, as Munro Edmunson (1967a) points out for the Mesoamerican area. The same can be said for ritual humor, where joking may instruct in proper morality while also conveying a different sense of the appropriate relationship between the human and supernatural spheres than is often found in orthodox Christianity (Cf. Bricker 1973; Edmunson 1967a).

In the increasing consideration being given to the role of the arts in popular religion, an emerging theme is their potential for expressing an awareness of ethnic or class boundaries. Nathan Wachtel (1977) argues persuasively that in the folklore, dramas, and dances of Latin American peasant communities, the importance given to reenactments of the conquest reflects an abiding awareness of discrimination and oppression. Through such images as the devil and his symbolic ties with the conquerors, a *patrón* [patron], or a capitalist economic system, anathema to the values characteristic of indigenous economies, popular religion critically comments on and proscribes the dominant social system (J. Nash 1979; Taussig 1980; and K. Warren 1978). Falla (1970), however, introduces a cautionary note. In his study of Juan Noj, a common mythological figure in Guatamala and highland Chiapas, Falla suggests that such themes do not express an awareness of exploitation.[5] Yet portraying such conditions as inevitable limits the prospect for political action based on a consciousness of subordination.

The involvement of popular religiosity with illness and healing has also received special attention. Many authors have suggested the preoccupation of popular religion with sickness and death (e.g., Leacock and Leacock 1972; Reichel-Dolmatoff and Reichel-Dolmatoff 1961). This parallels the import of matters of life and death in religion generally. Whatever else religion may be, it functions to assert a meaningful universe. Since both death and illness make precarious the meaning of that universe for the individual and community, they introduce the radical threat of anomie into society. Religion, then, is universally concerned certainly with curing illness, but at a more fundamental level with explaining death and sickness through theodicy (Berger 1967). Popular religion in Latin America is no exception, and a good deal has been written on its relation to Hippocratic conceptions of medicine, the concern with hot and cold, the concern with dry and wet, and the notion of *mal aire* [evil air] (Cf. Currier 1966; Foster 1953b; and Kelly 1965). Other influences such as magical forms of medicine and spiritist conceptions are also present (Cf. Kelly 1965; C. Madsen 1968). Illness and death are related as well to other magical beliefs widespread in *ladino* and Indian communities, such as the notions of *susto* [magical fright], *envidia* [envy], and the "evil eye," and conceptions of *brujería* [witchcraft] (Cf. Rubel 1964; Gillin 1945, 1951; and Kearney 1972).[6] Summaries and discussions of conceptions of disease, etiology, and therapy have been undertaken particularly for Mesoamerica (e.g., Adam and Rubel 1967; Aguirre Beltrán 1963; and Holland 1963) and the Andean region (e.g., Homero Palma 1973; Valdivia Ponce 1975).

The plethora of material on Mesoamerica and the Andean area is repeated in any perusal of monographs or ethnographies of particular communities or ethnic groups, a principal source for information on popular religion. This is due in part to the early and intensive Catholic missionary presence in both geographical areas, but also because of the continuing vitality of the non-Christian indigenous religious traditions that remain in much of the Maya, Quechua, and Aymara cultural regions. Original anthropological interest in these and other regions certainly was precipitated by a wider preoccupation with questions about acculturation, the "retention" of pre-conquest elements, and syncretism.

Given the long history, especially within anthropology, of ethnographic community studies, a survey of Latin American monographs must necessarily be selective. Here attention will be paid to those that devote significant discussion to religion.

With the traditional anthropological emphasis on the study of small-scale communities, much of the research has been carried out in rural peasant and Indian areas, although a growing corpus exists for towns and larger urban areas. Much of the former research, again, is especially rich for the Maya areas of Guatemala, Yucatán, and highland Chiapas. The Harvard Chiapas Project alone, conducted in the *Tzotzil*-speaking community of Zinacantan and neighboring areas, has produced an extraordinary amount of information on their complex ritual and belief structure (Vogt 1976), religious change (Wasserstrom 1978), myth (Hunt 1977), oral tradition (Blaffer 1972; Gossen 1974; and Laughlin 1977), dreams (Laughlin 1976), ritual humor (Bricker 1973), shamanism (Fabrega and Silver 1973) and the civil-religious hierarchy (Cancian 1965), among other topics.[7]

As James Greenberg (1981:1) says, recent excursions into these more cognitively oriented and structuralist analyses represent a new departure from earlier functionalist studies often concerned with assessing the degree of syncretism and acculturation in Mesoamerica (Cf. La Farge 1947; Parsons 1936; Redfield and Villa Rojas 1934; and Wagley 1949). Other more recent studies have dealt with the important issues of the changes that are occurring in the old closed corporate community structure, as the national economic, political, and religious orders increasingly penetrate rural areas (e.g., Brintnall 1979; Greenberg 1981), and with the involvement of popular religion in contending with those wider structures (e.g., J. Nash 1970; K. Warren 1978).

A similar array of issues is reflected in the literature from the Andean region, as well as other areas in Spanish America and Brazil. Much of the early research in the Andean area on the Quechua and Aymara groups was ethnohistorical in character (e.g., Kubler 1946). These and other accounts often focused on the question of acculturation, as did the early work on Afro-Brazilian religious traditions (e.g., Carneiro 1948; Eduardo 1966). John Gillin's (1951) study of a coastal community in Peru was an early effort to set out what he referred to as "creole culture," a common Peruvian cultural system blending together Indian and Spanish elements in a national tradition. He, as so many others of that period, thus, draws on a structural-functionalist approach to emphasize the unifying aspects of popular Catholicism (e.g., Falls-Borda 1955; Pierson 1951; and Service and Service 1954). Certainly, as Marvin Harris (1956) notes, popular Catholicism and other aspects of rural and small-town society and culture do share many elements with urban areas; the old notion of a folk-urban continuum has long been shown problematic. Certainly, also, popular Catholicism can be a fundamental basis of social organization, as Eduardo Galvão (1955) demonstrated in his study of Itá in Brazil. Yet just as surely one must not forget the profound differences within popular Catholicism, not least of which are those relating to different classes and ethnic groups. Richard N. Adams (1959), in his study of the Peruvian highlands community of Muquiyauyo, was one of the first to recognize the class and ethnic character of religion, as it can be used both to downplay such differences and reassert class boundaries.[8]

The analysis of the class and/or ethnic basis of popular religion has received real impetus from current studies such as Billie Jean Isbell's (1978) *To Defend Ourselves: Ecology and Ritual in an Andean Village*. Isbell argues that religion acts as a barrier against outside intrusions from the national society, while mitigating the effects of change that have already occurred. In the mining communities of Bolivia, popular religion likewise serves to reassert ethnic and class solidarity, satirizing and censuring the nationally and internationally based socioeconomic and political forces that dominate these communities (Iriarte 1972; J. Nash 1979).

These and other recent studies, while recognizing the European and Christian influences on indigenous societies, also demonstrate the extent to which the Catholic and non-Christian aspects of their religious life remain, in June Nash's (1979:122) words, "co-existent and apparently contradictory world views" (Cf. Wachtel 1977:156). Manuel Marzal (1971) and Taussig (1980), for example, both point out the basic incompatibility between Catholic and Andean conceptions of the world, and the world's relationship with supernatural forces. Others, such as Joseph Bastien (1978), have provided detailed structural analyses of the Aymara world view, while José Gushiken (1977) and Douglas Sharon (1978) discuss Andean ritual and shamanism.[9]

Having reviewed sundry analyses of popular religion in Latin America with regard to particular countries, topical areas of interest, and monographs on specific ethnic groups and communities, the potential for diversity within popular religion seems all too apparent. Though most authors stress the complex variety even within popular Catholicism alone, George Foster (1960), at least, argues for its relative homogeneity: "From the Rio Grande to Patagonia the cult of the Virgin Mary is the core of religious loyalty, the same saints are honored on the same days and in essentially the same fashion and the same mass draws the faithful each Sunday" (cited by W. Madsen 1967:369).

Clearly, there *are* real similarities in Latin American popular Catholicism; yet, to underemphasize the equally essential differences is to risk not understanding the complex interplay of international and national, as well as local historical circumstances that produce popular belief and practice. It is not simply a matter of proper recognition for all of the locally defined saints not officially recognized by the church (Cf. Service and Service 1954) or of assessing the differences in the centrality of religiosity for group life (e.g., Harris 1956; Reichel-Dolmatoff and Reichel-Dolmatoff 1961). It is rather that a consideration of the "great variation" produced in popular Catholicism and religion by class and ethnic variables and local historical factors is crucial for appreciating the origins and present character of Latin American religion (Willems 1975:66ff).

To understand the causes of the variation in popular religion requires attention to its origins. Berryman (1971:286) argues that the very idea of a dichotomy between popular and official Catholicism corresponds to the rise of the bourgeoisie and expansion of capitalism; those often referred to as "good" Catholics who "practice" official doctrine are the middle and upper classes. Willems (1975), however, introduces a proper note of caution in pointing out that both the middle and upper classes may also engage in popular practices departing from official doctrine. The *irmandades* (in Spanish, *hermandad, cofradía,* or *mayordomía*), or religious brotherhoods, in Brazil offer a clear example. Originally introduced as an extension of monasticism for lay participation in prayer and devotionals for the souls of the dead, they became organizations promoting public worship, particularly in the fiesta complex and invocation of saints. With their accumulated wealth, they frequently took on an array of social services for their members, in some cases even building hospitals, and, at least among the upper classes, became powerful enough to act contrary to ecclesiastical wishes (Willems 1975:71ff; Wagley 1971).[10]

Nevertheless, Berryman's point is well taken that the presence of popular Catholicism is often correlated with areas where the bourgeois classes have not penetrated. He suggests that low attendance at mass, the low number of church marriages, high number of free unions, and low percentage of an indigenous priesthood be used as signs of the prevalence of popular Catholicism, particularly in the Caribbean, Central America, Brazil, and the coastal areas of Mexico, Venezuela, Colombia, and Ecuador. Official Catholicism, on the other hand, is said to have entered popular culture "to some degree" in Central Mexico and Andean Ecuador (Berryman 1971:286).

Support for the negative correlation between popular religion and the presence of the bourgeois classes comes indirectly from many authors who stress that the growth of popular religion has been due historically to the lack of control exercised by the hierarchy in many rural areas of Latin America (Cf. Hoornaert 1974). Since the clergy have tended to locate in urban areas amongst the middle and upper classes, rural religion has often developed in virtual isolation. A partial exception to this, of course, would be the early Spanish missionary interest in the large populations of Indians found in central and southern Mexico, Guatemala, and the Andean areas (Cf. Braden 1930; Duviols 1971; and Ricard 1966).

Yet this too led to a lack of missionary interest in other regions. The Services (1954:239), for example, argue for Paraguay that,

[m]uch of the lore of the Paraguayan rural people is that of the general ideological system of Catholicism, in part actually taught by the church and in part traditionalized folk Catholicism. But, as in most of southern South America, the official church has never been as strong, either in colonial times or at present, as in Mexico or Peru, so that up-to-date official church teachings have not been particularly influential. Spain never was very interested in its southern colonies, and there were

no great concentrations of Indians to attract the attention of either the church or the state.

Unlike elsewhere in Latin America, thus, Paraguay and the south were not as affected by the Inquisition and the attempt to impose official doctrine (Cf. Duviols 1971; Wachtel 1977).

The relationship between the lack of clergy and the rise of popular religion seems certain in Latin America: as Rivera (1978:109) remarks, even at present there is only one priest for every 5,000 Catholics, in comparison with a 1:800 ratio in Europe. Priests themselves often lacked a thorough grounding in church doctrine. Yet as Willems (1975:66) argues, explanations that focus only on the lack in numbers or qualifications of the clergy fail to reckon with another factor in the rise of popular religion— that of the active presence of competing religious systems in indigenous and African belief. Gilberto Freyre (1966), for example, chronicles the early fusion that occurred in Brazil between the cultures of the conquerors and various Indian groups. This amalgamation of beliefs and practices was repeated across all of Latin America, as has been noted, and is well-documented in an extensive literature on syncretism and acculturation (Cf. Herskovits 1943; W. Madsen 1967; and Edmonson, et al. 1960).

One of the difficulties with much of the acculturation literature has been that the framework may mask the fact that most acculturation is not voluntary, but a coercive process that can and has resulted in genocide and ethnocide (Bodley 1982). Yet the early Catholic missionaries also served to perpetuate indigenous belief and practices, as well as syncretisms, through their methods of proselytization (Cf. Braden 1930; Ricard 1966; and Wachtel 1977). By correlating the Christian pantheon and calendar with indigenous deities and ritual cycles, for example, the church virtually assured the development of a popular religiosity that departed from orthodox teachings.

It must also be remembered that the Spanish and Portuguese Catholicism of the conquerors itself contained many elements of Iberian folk religion (Willems 1975:67; cf. Ribeiro 1956).[11] Certainly the early Spanish and Portuguese settlers shared with indigenous groups a profound acceptance, though a differing interpretation, of the power of magic and an array of supernatural beings that further promoted the inclusion and creation of new religious elements (Taussig 1980). Thomas Bruneau (1982) and Willems (1975) also refer to the medieval character of Iberian Catholicism of the time, with its marked affinity with monasticism. Such tendencies were in no small part responsible for features of Latin American Catholicism, like the religious brotherhoods, or the *beatos* [holy men] of Brazil, which may incorrectly be assumed to be autochthonous (Cf. Kubler 1946; S. Gross 1968). Much of rural Catholicism in both Brazil and elsewhere in Latin

America remains wedded to the even older medieval elements of sixteenth-and seventeenth-century Iberian Catholicism (Cf. Wagley 1971).[12]

A crucial issue beyond simply the number or even location of the clergy and their effect on the rise of popular religious variants to church doctrine, is that of the fundamental interests and attitudes of the clergy in regard to both indigenous and peasant societies. In describing the growth of religious elites in Latin America, Ivan Vallier (1967) suggests that the church was almost always most attentive to the interests and welfare of the upper classes. Riolando Azzi (1976) implies that the similarity of church and elite interests is due, in part, to the status of Catholicism as the official religion of the state. Forman (1975:219) concludes for Brazil that, "[a] negligent clergy which primarily serves the upper classes, the constant demand for payment for services rendered, and a lack of sympathy for the peasant belief system have all alienated a sizable segment of the flock."

Evidence of this "lack of sympathy" is found very early in accounts of the evangelization of the Indians (e.g., Kubler 1946). Distrust of missionary motives and skepticism about the veracity of their beliefs is nicely expressed in a quote from a confessional manual for the Quechua by Diego de Torres (ca. 1584), cited by Wachtel (1977:153–54):

They sometimes say that God is not a good God, that he does not care for the poor, and that the Indians turn to him in vain. . . . Just as Christians have images and worship them, so they can worship Huacas, idols and stones, for images are the Christians' idols. . . . One may well worship both Our Lord Jesus Christ and the Devil, since both work together and are related. The Indians are reluctant to accept, and express doubt at, certain articles of faith: above all the mystery of the Holy Trinity, the unity of God, the passion and death of Jesus Christ, the virginity of Our Lady, holy communion, universal resurrection.

The identity of the church with the interests of the state and elite classes, thus, has contributed in many parts of Latin America to either a persistent anticlericalism or certainly a reserve concerning the priest as a person (Cf. Quirk 1973; Harris 1956). Such an association between the formal church and social elites was often symbolized eloquently in rural Brazil, for example, with the local church frequently being essentially the private chapel of a local elite family, with the church built adjacent to the house. Bruneau (1982:22) suggests that a pattern developed for clergy in Brazil, culminating in the late nineteenth century, in which they were either political "strong-men" ensuring votes for the local elite or concerned with more personalistic forms of religion such as devotional groups. In either case they were not in a position to exercise much influence over local religious patterns, except through coercive measures. Indeed, Oliveira (1976a) has suggested that many of the changes in the Brazilian church were adopted at the national level, often influenced by the current European trends, but with little impact at the local rural level.

One continues to find in the literature critical accounts of the breach between the official church and popular Catholicism, though clearly numerous changes have occurred at all levels in the church, particularly since the second Vatican Council. Pertinent sources for these changes include Frank Salomon's (1982:100–101) review in his larger examination of work on Andean societies, and the expanding literature on the post-Vatican II church and politics, and liberation theology. In contemplating the prospects, in particular for the inclusion of the religious beliefs and practices of the Quechua and Aymara within the church, Salomon (1982:100–101) concludes the following:

The degree to which Andean ritual could be accommodated remained controversial because of dogmatic strictures on "syncretism." Responses ranged from proposals of stringent tests (Combin 1972) through the contemplation of an "iglesia indígena en el Perú" ["an indigenous church in Peru"] (Marzal 1973) to a call for a fundamental self-examination of Western relations with the sphere of sacred experience (Kusch 1972). In practice, innovative priests seem often to have felt themselves in a dilemma insofar as their aspirations for a church respectful of Andean culture clashed with their disapproval of some Andean cultural demands (e.g., use of ritual as a vehicle for upward mobility; Zalles 1976). Zalles notes, too, that the church, because of its international structure, has special possibilities for transcending the artificial dismemberment of the Andean cultural orbit into national minorities.

Having discussed the variations and origins of popular Catholicism, to what degree are we able to spell out its characteristics and theology, as well as those for the other popular religions of Latin America? This review should have demonstrated the extent to which discussions have been dominated by close analysis of the many national, regional, and local variants, that is, the rich diversity of popular religion in Latin America. Diversity in popular religion is not merely geographical or by class or ethnic group, but over time as well. One should be careful to avoid any implication that popular religion is a static system. On the contrary, contemporary popular beliefs are not simply identical with sixteenth-century Catholicism. Berryman (1971) and Douglas Brintnall (1979) with others, have pointed out, moreover, that it is continuing to change with the growth in urbanism and the breakdown in the rural closed corporate community structure, among other factors.

Nevertheless, there have been a number of significant attempts to set out common patterns in the structural characteristics and beliefs of popular Catholicism. Popular Catholicism is an on-going system of beliefs and practices virtually independent of the church, a fact confirmed by both numerous field studies and attitudinal surveys (e.g., Azevedo 1966). As Berryman observes,

In Latin America, *the masses of people never accepted official* (Tridentine) *Catholicism*. They never accepted the Church as mediator of salvation in the sense intended by Tridentine theology and pastoral practice. As is well known, popular Catholicism centers on a number of preoccupations, such as death, health, and immediate temporal concerns, that give rise to a number of practices: prayer to favorite saints, holy water, *mandas* (promises made to God in order to gain some favor) (1971:285; emphasis original).

John Gillin also has set out characteristics of popular Catholicism based on his observations in San Carlos, a *ladino* and Indian community in Guatamala. He notes that in San Carlos, (1) religious beliefs are considered Catholic; there is no explicit awareness of non-Christian, preconquest elements; (2) priests and other official representatives of the church are viewed only as administrators of the sacraments and play only a peripheral role in the actual ritual life of the community; (3) the latter complex is officiated by lay officials, such as those participating in the *cargo* system common throughout Spanish America; (4) at the center of this system is the "Cult of Images," the fiesta complex surrounding the community's and individual's ties with the saints and the *cofradía* religious brotherhoods that organize it. Important also are community agricultural ceremonies and official religious holidays such as All Saints Day, Christmas and Easter. (5) Most orthodox aspects of the church, however, are of small import, since they require the priest and he is seldom in the community, a pattern repeated throughout rural Latin America. And (6) there is little inclination to convert to other religious systems, such as the more "puritanical" Protestantism (Gillin 1951:77–78).

Since Gillin completed his work in the 1940s, of course, the likelihood of conversion to Protestantism in Guatemala and elsewhere has increased (Cf. J. Nash 1960; Roberts 1967; and Reina and Schwartz 1974). Nevertheless, Gillin's description points out a number of common themes widely distributed in Latin America, including Brazil. Thales de Azevedo constructs a similar list of traits for Brazilian popular Catholicism. Azevedo considers five basic dimensions in his distinction between "folk" and official Catholicism. The former (1) lacks a conception of salvation; and (2) a conception of sin; (3) the sacraments receive little emphasis, and the priest is viewed principally as a functionary of the church, not as a mediator with God; (4) folk Catholicism is centrally involved with the cult of the saints; and (5) it makes use of domestic liturgies rather than the formal rites of the Church (Azevedo 1963; cited by Forman 1975:275f). For Azevedo folk Catholicism is distinguished by its concern for worldly needs such as health and economic well-being. While Shepard Forman (1975:211) does not disregard this element, he also argues that folk Catholicism is in reality "a mixture of this-worldly manipulation and mystical asceticism." There is a profound "spirituality" to Brazilian popular belief, as with any religious system, which always is about the world, in relationship with it, but not reducible to a purely pragmatic exercise (Forman 1975:211; Taussig

1980:14ff). The fiesta may be utilitarian, but as Paz (1961:51) makes clear, it is also sacred, liminal; not just an excess, protective against the envy of the gods, but a revolt, "a sudden immersion in the formless."

This issue is reflected in discussions about the nature of the social relationship between the believer and the saints. Numerous authors have pointed out the frequent identification of saints, or even God, with the elite classes as *patrón* or *patrão* [patron], with the paternalistic image of the parent (e.g., Leers 1967). There is the semblance of a patron-client relationship between believer and saint that centers on the *promesa* [religious vow] which is made by believers to honor a saint in some way, whether burning candles, going on a pilgrimage, or other devotional act, if some request is granted. This relationship has been viewed as essentially an exchange relationship on the order of the secular, self-interested ideal of economic liberalism. Credence is lent on occasion to this model when the devout, having not received a wish, may chastize the saint in different ways (Cf. Pierson 1951). Even this, however, is not the simple equivalent of economic self-interest. Forman (1975:206, 217ff) argues, in an insightful analysis of Brazilian popular religion, that unlike economic relationships, one's ties with a patron saint are rarely broken, embedded as they are in deep complex social relationships in all areas of life.

Yet as Forman (1975:218) himself remarks, popular Catholicism, though "premised on personal salvation has become characterized by community involvement and the strengthening of inter-personal bonds, which reinforce those notions of submissiveness and obligation that mark Brazilian peasant ideology." This emphasis on corporate public worship is located especially in the importance of the saints. The formal rites and sacraments of the church, such as the Eucharist, confirmation, or even baptism and last rites, may receive less emphasis than does the on-going personal and social relationship with the saints (Cf. Forman 1975; Gillin 1951; Rivera 1978; and Vogt 1976). Robert Quirk (1973:5) remarks for Mexico that,

[f]or the majority of Mexicans, religion is bound up in these extra-sacramental rituals—making a pilgrimage; praying to a favorite saint, in a church, at home, or at a roadside shrine; carrying the saint's image into the fields to bring rain or to ensure fertility; taking food to the cemetery on the Day of the Dead.

Both Paz (1961) and Elsie Clews Parsons (1936) underscore the special importance in Mexico of *las ánimas*, the departed souls of the dead, though certainly they are prominent throughout Latin America, as they are propitiated and honored in their active influence on the living, in the course of All Souls and All Saints days, as well as wakes, funerals, and novenas.

In addition to the souls of the dead, which in some areas are essentially synonymous with companion spirits (Cf. Hartmann 1973), there are numerous beings in the popular pantheon. These include the devil and among many others, *duendes*, dwarfs or trolls (Cf. Gillin 1951; Millones 1975; and Taussig 1980). Yet the saints are most actively appealed to in remedying misfortune and the search for a better future. This is confirmed, for example, by Bruneau's (1982) attitudinal survey for Brazil, in which he reports the most widespread characteristics of popular Catholicism as the making of promises to saints, belief in miracles, and, to a lesser degree, praying to saints. Their importance is seen in the fact that in Latin America both Jesus Christ and Mary, in all of their local manifestations, are often considered to be saints, albeit frequently at the head of a hierarchy of saints. Further, each Virgin, local Christ, or saint is felt to have a distinct personality (Cf. Service and Service 1954).

Willems, in his general discussion of Latin American culture, refers to three principal reasons for the supplication of saints: their involvement in matters of an individual's life cycle, their contending with vicissitudes induced by natural forces, and their importance as advocates or mediators with the wider supernatural realm (1975:69). The proliferation of local saints, of which many are not recognized officially by the church, has occurred for local reasons. Most communities, whether villages or large cities, have patron saints. For example, Andean cities, such as Lima and Cuzco, venerate El Señor de los Temblores [the Lord of the Earthquakes] due to very understandable regional concerns (Willems 1975:71).

The presence of favorite and famous saints, Christs, and Virgins occurs in many areas. Guadalupe is a case in point for Mexico. Others include Our Lady of Juchitán, San Juan de Lagos, Our Lord of the Maize in Michoacán, and especially the "Black Christ," Our Lord of Chalma (Quirk 1973:4; Brenner 1929; Turner and Turner 1978). Analogous lists have been compiled for other areas, such as Brazil. Wagley (1971:218–19) comments on the predominance of shrines and pilgrimages in rural Brazil, especially Nossa Senhora da Aparecida, near Guaratinguetá in the state of São Paulo and the shrine of Bom Jesús da Lapa in Bahia, where as many as 30,000 make a pilgrimage to attend the annual day of celebration (Cf. D. Gross 1971; Medina 1972; and Oliveira 1970). Bernardo Leers (1967) provides a detailed discussion of local manifestations of the Virgin, while Forman (1975:277f) considers the significance of São João in Brazil and Iemanjá, the Goddess of the Sea, important in Afro-Brazilian groups.

The importance of the saints cannot be appreciated without the larger corporate forms of worship and organization of which they are a part. Civil-religious hierarchies, *hermandades*, and the fiesta complex itself all provide important vehicles helping to define the social structure of both rural and urban areas. The importance of religious ritual as a source of social organization is found in other institutions as well, such as *compadrazgo*, or godparenthood. Modeled on the orthodox practice of spiritual parents at the "rebirth" of baptism, godparenthood has undergone considerable elaboration, particularly in Indian communities. One may find a host of godparents for occasions such as first communion, marriage, first hair-cutting or nail-cutting, and so forth. Moreover, the emphasis on the godparent-godchild tie or that of the coparents, as well as the type of obligations incurred by such relationships, show a good deal of variation. For summaries and bibliographies on *compadrazgo* see especially Mario Dávila (1971), George Foster (1953a), Sidney Mintz and Eric Wolf (1950), and Robert Ravicz (1967).

That popular Catholicism is a principal basis of social organization in Latin American communities, that it contains a rich array of ritual activities, should not preclude taking note of its personal aspects for the believer, as well as its theological characteristics (Cf. Sánchez-Arjona 1974). Far too many studies, as Forman (1975:211) trenchantly observes, have focused on the practices of popular religion without analyzing its meaning for participants. There is a theological stance inherent in ritual life; essential to this theology for Brazilian peasants is "a fundamental and deep belief in an all-powerful God who is at the center of all occurrences, good and bad, and to whose will each individual must submit completely and unquestioningly" (Forman 1975:212).

This perspective is reminiscent of other accounts for Spanish America, such as Michael Kearney's (1972) discussion of a Zapotec world view where God is the arbiter of destiny. God, however, is often thought of as being remote or even harsh. William Madsen (1960:31), for example, describes the Aztec-speakers of San Francisco Tecospa as accepting a view of life in which God is not gentle, but "a harsh creator who, in the Aztec tradition of multiple creations, periodically destroys the world and remakes it" (1960:31). Madsen (1960:31) argues that Tecospans "accepted Catholic rites, but rejected [the] Christian doctrine" of free will, because it denies Aztec fatalism in which life was predetermined at birth. Tecospans remain fatalistic and express this fatalism in their belief that destiny is determined by a Manichaean battle between the devil and God. Similar statements on the fatalism of Latin American peasants are common in the literature but cannot be explained with reference to syncretism for all areas (Cf. Bruneau 1982:30). Nor is fatalism complete. Among Brazilian peasants the very importance of the *promesa*, intervention of saints, and miracles bespeaks the possibility of altering apparent circumstances (Forman 1975:213).

The notion of fatalism is bound up with ideas about destiny; it may also be related to other conceptions of the world, such as the Zapotec emphasis on uncertainty and the everpresent danger of *engaño* [deception] (Kearney 1972:59ff). It is also related to the widespread emphasis on death and suffering found in Mexico (Kearney 1972:91). A similar emphasis is found generally in Latin America. Gerardo and Alicia Reichel-Dolmatoff, for example, suggest for Aritama in Colombia that "[a]t present, man's sinfulness, man's suffering, and man's certainty of death form the great common foundations of the religious system" (1961:340). Unlike Tecospan belief or that which Gillin (1951) or Azevedo (1963) suggests is typical for popular Catholicism, this view rests on a conception of sin. Humans express their inherently evil natures by making others suffer (Reichel-Dolmatoff and Reichel-Dolmatoff 1961:340).

The emphasis in popular Catholicism on the constancy of suffering and death is reflected in its conception of the Christ figure. Both Orlando Fals-Borda (1955) and Miles Richardson (1970) characterize Colombian conceptions of Jesus as emphasizing a long-suffering Christ, not the risen Lord of the resurrection. In Latin America, it is Good Friday, not Easter, which is the center of ritual significance, with the stations of the cross and the agony of the crucifixion dramatically portrayed. It is common to find images or paintings of Jesus only as an infant or adult man in the midst of the Passion. In Ixtepeji, Zapotec images never represent Christ with a halo (Kearney 1972:91). In an instructive article on "The Image of Christ in Spanish America as a Model for Suffering," Miles Richardson, Marta Pardo, and Barbara Bode (1971) set out how the image of Jesus is associated with the concepts of patience, respect, faith, formality, conformity, and resignation. The role of Christ is to teach one how to control his or her own response to suffering, to emulate his patience in an inhuman world (1971:251). The authors point out that other figures, such as the Virgin of Guadalupe, may be more important in this regard for some areas of Latin America. They also suggest that this image of Jesus may be less important to Afro-Brazilian religions. Yet clearly the role of Christ and his relationship with the saints in the fiesta complex are central to much of popular Catholicism.

That Afro-Brazilian religions are not simply to be assessed as popular Catholicism, per se, is well taken. It, thus, remains to discuss these traditions along with two other major currents in Latin American popular religion, that of spiritism and Protestantism.

Afro-American religion is exceptionally rich and varied in its tradition, with by far the majority of research conducted in Brazil. Yet as Roger Bastide's (1974) important review article on Afro-American research makes clear, there are other Afro-American traditions beyond Brazil in need of study (Cf. Aguirre Beltrán 1958; Pollak 1966, 1972; and Whitten 1974).

Afro-Brazilian religions involve the creative reworking of African, Catholic, and Amerindian elements. The history of these new religions is discussed in detail by Roger Bastide (1978) as part of his comprehensive study of *The African Religions of Brazil*. Bastide (1978:109ff) notes the very early separation of the Catholicism of the black slaves from that of the owners. As early as 1711 there were celebrations for both São Benedito and the Virgin of the Rosary, both of special import among Afro-Brazilians. Similarly, black religious brotherhoods grew up around the saints and were present in Rio by 1753 (Karasch 1979). The adoration of black saints and Virgins, as Bastide (1978:113) remarks, "was initially imposed upon the

Africans from outside, as a step toward their Christianization, and . . . the white masters regarded it as a means of social control to promote subservience in their slaves." As elsewhere, however, blacks transformed this adoration into "an instrument of ethnic solidarity and social justice" (1978:114).

In observing Afro-Brazilian religions, their great heterogeneity emerges. The most conservative groups are the Yoruba and Dahomean-derived religions of the northeast, such as Candomblé of Bahia. Yet there exist different groups such as the Batuque of Belém or Umbanda present in many of the southern urban centers in particular (Leacock and Leacock 1972; Ortiz 1978). Ruth and Seth Leacock (1972:317) argue that much of the diversity of Afro-Brazilian religion has been understated due to predominant study of the conservative groups such as Candomblé, the Casa das Minas, and the Xangô (e.g., Carneiro 1948; Herskovits 1943; and Ribeiro 1952). Even Bastide (1958) focuses especially on Candomblé, though clearly Bastide (1978) and Eduardo (1966) include major discussions of a range of groups.

The focus on groups like Candomblé is due in part to the influence of the interest in acculturation evident for many of the early researchers (e.g., Herskovits 1937; Eduardo 1966). Bastide (1978) himself is interested in exploring the "interpenetration of civilizations" and draws on acculturation models, albeit in a critical manner, always with reference to the ethnic and class factors of the contact situation.

The coherent ritual and cosmological elements and strong corporate orientation of the conservative groups have been noted by many authors. They express an ethnically distinct Afro-Brazilian community. Newer religious groups, such as the Batuque in Belém, are more individualistic, with more emphasis on individual consultation with leaders, who act as mediums for a pantheon of spirits of African, Amerindian, and other origins (Leacock and Leacock 1972:319). Bastide (1978:379) suggests that such religions reflect the "proletarianization of Blacks," where increased industrialization and urbanism have resulted in the gradual disintegration of the old ethnic enclaves and the formation of a new Brazilian national consciousness.

Recent growth in Umbanda, often referred to as a distinctively "Brazilian" religion, illustrates these changes (Cf. Pressel 1974). By 1968 Umbanda, located principally in urban centers such as São Paulo, had already reached 256,603 members (Monteiro 1978:xxvii). Early work on Umbanda focused on its special appeal to the urban lower classes, who were often rural migrants (Cf. Camargo 1961).[13] Diana Brown's (1979) research especially has shown how Umbanda cuts across class lines in popular participation as it continues to grow.

Umbanda contains elements of both Afro-Brazilian religions and spiritism, another important popular tradition in Brazil. Candido Camargo

(1961) argues that there is a continuum with Umbanda at one end and Kardecismo at the other; what links them is their common emphasis on spirits of the dead, possession by mediums, and the importance of "spiritual fluids" in achieving spiritual well-being. The spiritism of Kardecismo derives from the writings of Alan Kardec (1976), a nineteenth-century French medium whose doctrine has been accepted elsewhere in Latin America, including Mexico (Kelly 1961). Kardec viewed his system as a science based on sensory data. While Kardecismo in Brazil may be highly intellectualistic with an emphasis on parapsychology, particularly in middle- and upper-class centers, Brazilians generally have emphasized its more religous elements, such as the parallel between saints and spirits in the devotion of believers (D. Warren 1968). Indeed, it was not until the 1920s and particularly the 1930s, when Francisco Candido Xavier, a well-known medium, reinterpreted Kardecismo in a nationalistic vein, that spiritism became a mass movement in Brazil (Willems 1975:371).

Bruneau (1982:27) estimates that from 20 to 30 percent of all Brazilians are involved in spiritism, with over 32,000 centers in São Paulo alone. Any such estimates must be tempered, however, with the realization that many spiritists, and especially Umbandists, will also list themselves as Catholics. Esther Pressel (1974) attributes the rapid growth of Umbanda in part to this very willingness to permit members to hold on to their Catholic identity, unlike, say, Pentecostalism or Kardecismo. Other factors are its individualistic emphasis on consultation, its concern with a broader Brazilian national identity than the older Afro-Brazilian groups, its link with Kardecismo giving it appeal to the middle classes, yet its emphasis on emotional and religious elements rather than on intellectualism (1974:224–25).

Spiritism, then, often represents a fusion of Afro-Brazilian elements and Kardecismo with a very real sense of Brazilian nationalism. Yet spiritists also have erected a parallel set of institutions to those of the state, such as orphanages, clinics, food dispensaries, and schools, to meet social needs of the public at large. "Spiritists, once primly anti-Marxists, seem to have lost faith in the capacity of either free enterprise or the nation-state to bring distributive justice to Brazil" (D. Warren 1968:402).

Umbanda, in this light, appears to have an ambivalent relationship with emerging class and ethnic factors in Brazilian urban society. Bastide (1978:380) expresses this in regard to Afro-Brazilian participation in Umbanda, by arguing that it asserts their new sense of Brazilian identity while protesting against racial discrimination. Leacock and Leacock (1972:323) question any extension of this interpretation to all new Brazilian religions or to members of the working class generally. Bastide, in their view, has overemphasized the racial aspect of contemporary Brazilian religions like Umbanda and the Batuque. For the Batuque, they found instead of social protest, an identification of important spirits with the upper classes. Batuque does not promise its mostly working-class members to change their social world, but "help[s] them to survive in that world" (1972:326; cf. D. Warren 1968:405).

In considering the link between a growing industrial, urban society and religion, Protestantism, as another expanding popular religious movement in Latin America, deserves attention. It would seem no accident that the more industrialized countries, such as Brazil, Chile, Mexico, and Argentina, also have the largest Protestant populations (Read, Monterroso, and Johnson 1969:50). By 1970 Brazil alone recorded over 4.8 million Protestants, of which 2.9 million were in various Pentecostal groups (Monteiro 1978:xxvii; cf. De Moura 1972).

A considerable amount of work has been done on Latin American Protestantism. Much of it has been carried out from Protestant and Catholic perspectives, but a growing body of historical and social scientific literature exists. The best bibliography on Latin American Protestantism is by John H. Sinclair (1976). Sinclair has assembled an impressive catalogue of sources, with annotations, including general works, bibliographies, conference reports, periodicals, and literature by and about Protestants for each country in Latin America.

General works on Latin American Protestantism are frequently from a religious perspective dealing with evangelical strategies for "church growth" (e.g., Read and Ineson 1973). Historical works also exist, both for Latin America generally (e.g., Goslin 1956) and for Protestantism in particular, on countries or regions, such as Mexico (Helms 1955; Penton 1965), Peru (Bahamonde 1952), Argentina (Ehms 1971), or the Rio de la Plata area (Monti 1969). A number of ethnographies and monographs have been done for both urban churches and movements (e.g., Flora 1976; Maynard 1981; and Roberts 1967) and for rural groups (e.g., Curry 1968; Miller 1970, 1971, 1975). More specialized analyses have also been done on religious phenomena like *glossolalia* (e.g., Goodman 1972, 1974).

The early Protestant population of Latin America in the nineteenth century consisted mostly of European immigrants like the Moravians, who settled in areas such as Brazil. Much of the more recent growth in Protestantism, however, began initially with the proselytization of North American and European missionaries toward the latter end of the nineteenth century. This was often correlated with the political ascendency of the liberal movement, which saw in separation of the church and state one means of political advantage (Cf. Mecham 1966). Prior to the 1916 "Congress on Christian Work in Latin America" in Panama, most evangelical work was carried out by fundamentalist mission boards and a few historical churches like the Methodists (Cf. Missionary Educational Movement 1917; Kessler 1967). Following World War I historical churches expanded their mission activities; yet it was the new pentecostal churches that grew most quickly in many areas (Cf. Flora 1976; Lalive d'Epinay 1969; Willems 1967; and Vergara 1962). The result has been that in Latin America, including

Andean countries such as Ecuador with small Protestant populations, Protestantism is a heterogeneous phenomenon in terms of theology, social organization, and the social class or ethnic background of the constituency of its many denominations and independent churches. Even without including groups such as the Seventh-Day Adventists, Mormons, and Jehovah's Witnesses, the internal differences between the historical, fundamentalist, and pentecostal denominations are significant and real sources for distinctions in social identity (Maynard 1981).

The majority of analyses on Latin American Protestantism, as one might expect, has concerned its phenomenal growth in the 1970s. Most explanations center on socioeconomic changes in Latin American society, though others recognize the significance of broader political and economic dependence on Europe and especially the United States (Cesar 1968, 1973). Many authors have observed the correlation between Protestant growth and urbanism and industrialization (e.g., Lalive d'Epinay 1969; Nida 1958; and Willems 1967), though clearly Protestantism is also growing among some Indian communities and in areas of colonization (e.g., Casagrande 1978; Willems 1967).

Ignacio Vergara (1962) points out that much of the rapid urban growth of Chilean Protestantism has occurred principally among the lower working classes, a fact found in many other areas as well. He suggests that this is due, in part, to their particular ability to form voluntary associations, though this would seem to be only a necessary, not a sufficient, explanation. John Saunders (1960) emphasizes the egalitarian structure of many Protestant groups and the high status enjoyed by women (Cf. Curry 1968). Cornelia Flora's (1975) work on Pentecostal women is particularly informative here in its even-handed assessment of their position especially in the United Pentecostal Church of Colombia.

Willems (1967:250), in his major study of Protestantism in Brazil and Chile, *Followers of the New Faith*, acknowledges the importance of the close-knit social ties and egalitarian style of the Pentecostals in particular. Yet he and Cristián Lalive d'Epinay (1969) both also emphasize a rising "secularism" as a result of urban growth. With the breakdown of old structures and values, Protestantism provides new answers in a situation of rapid social change. With its emphasis on the Weberian Protestant ethic, it also leads to greater social mobility and a rise in the middle class. While Protestantism is adaptive to a situation not met adequately by folk Catholicism as a rural religion, the latter nevertheless encouraged Protestant growth through its tradition of religious experimentation (Willems 1967:249).

One should be careful of portraying "folk" Catholicism as only a rural religion or of implying that its rural variant is not equally capable of adaptation to urban settings. Yet Willems's point is well taken on the correlation of Protestantism with urban growth and the emphasis by believers on social mobility (Cf. Denton 1971). Others, such as Jean Pierre Bombart

(1969) and especially Bryan Roberts (1967), have reached similar conclusions. Roberts (1967), for example, in his study of a neighborhood in Guatemala City, shows how Protestant churches can serve as way stations on the road to social mobility; once a new class status is achieved, members often leave the church. A similar incentive for joining such churches has been that of improved education or standard of living. This has been describe for rural Indian communities (Lewellen 1978; J. Nash 1960).

Ted Lewellen (1978:6) and Willems (1967:256), among others, thus argue for a positive adaptive function of Protestantism, in which it eases the transition to incorporation in the wider, expanding national economy. One should, however, point out the ambivalent and disruptive features of such changes. Lalive d'Epinay (1969) "considers the potential of Pentecostalism in Chile, for reinforcing socioeconomic and class differences, and accepting the political *status quo*." In regard to Indian groups, Elmer Miller (1970, 1975) has studied the secularizing tendencies of Protestant conversion and its incursions on traditional Toba belief. Joseph Casagrande (1978) has analyzed its destruction of the old fiesta system for an Ecuadorian Quechua community. Blanca Muratorio (1981), in particular, has discussed the "ambiguous" consequences of Protestantism for the Ecuadorian Quechua in the Colta area. Protestant conversion does not instill new values of the Protestant ethic, since such values are already part of peasant life. While it may raise the standard of living marginally for converts, it does so through their rejection of the redistributive values of the fiesta system (1981:525). Furthermore, by accepting the predominant ideology of fundamentalist mission groups, which presents a benevolent image of the state, Quechua converts may actually become more "docile," less likely to mount organized protests about the entrenched ethnic and class inequalities of Ecuadorian society (1981:526). Yet Muratorio also points out that Protestantism has become paradoxically a vehicle for a renewed ethnic pride in Quechua identity. In some cases this may mask the incorporation of new patterns that actually reflect the exchange values of the wider capitalist structure; in others, however, Protestant Quechua leaders are critically aware of their exploitation due to both their ethnic and class position in society (1981:529–530).[14]

THEORETICAL PERSPECTIVES

Questions such as those about the consequences of Protestant conversion are one example of much wider theoretical discussions about the nature of popular religion in Latin America. As is evident from the previous discussion, much of that debate has centered on popular Catholicism as the predominant form of popular religiosity. It is clear from the present review that many analytic styles and explanatory modes have been used in the study of popular religion. Yet, much of the literature focuses on an issue raised by Muratorio; to wit, is popular religion fundamentally supportive of the existing structures of society, or does it lend itself to protest and change? Any such question, of course, must be asked of specific religions in specific historical contexts. There is a significant difference, for example, between asking this of a long-standing majority religion such as popular Catholicism and the growth experienced in a minority religion such as Protestantism. Even in regard to Protestantism, however, while most analysts link it directly to change, some view it essentially as functioning to smooth transitions in society (e.g., Willems 1967), while others, like Muratorio (1981), raise the prospect of Protestantism's growth to a more fundamental criticism of society itself.

In regard to popular Catholicism, the issue of change has been addressed from two different perspectives. The first essentially derives from functionalist positions in which institutions like the fiesta complex are said to promote social integration while psychologically placating individual uncertainties and fears (e.g., Gillin 1951; Fals-Borda 1955; and Service and Service 1954). Others, equally in a structural-functional vein, agree that folk Catholicism, in its millenarian forms, for example, can lead to change, but only in the absence of other, more secular possibilities for protest (Cf. S. Gross 1968; Perreira de Queiroz 1960).

A second position is more Marxist or conflict oriented. Popular Catholicism does not so much integrate society as justify existing social inequalities (Vessuri 1971). It diverts attention from the need for change (de Kadt 1967), in part because of its emphasis on fatalism and supporting the patron-client relationship through its image of the saints (Leers 1967).

There is another dimension to this latter concern with religion and protest. In more recent Marxist influenced work, religion is not simply equated with false consciousness; it is also revelatory, portraying the contradictions in the conditions under which we live (Taussig 1980). In June Nash's (1979) work on Bolivian tin miners, she spells out how religious rituals "schedule protest."

It is during these rituals that the spirit of rebellion comes to the surface. Resistance takes many forms, but it is always strengthened by the self-determination of a people who have not yet lost their self-identity. The rituals and belief combine to reinforce the myths which encompass their history, and the celebrations of carnival, the *ch'alla* and the earth-warming ceremonies prepare the people for a time when they can shape their own destiny. Sectarian leaders usually reject ritual protest as deviance. However, if one thinks of it as a rehearsal that keeps alive the sentiment of rebellion until a historically appropriate moment, it may reinforce political movements (1979:169).

Taussig (1980) makes very clear that religious protest is not merely a last resort when it is the only culturally appropriate form of rebellion or when no secular means of protest exist. The plantation workers of the Cauca region in Colombia and the tin miners of Bolivia analyzed by Taussig (1980:14) are two of the most politically conscious groups in Latin America, yet they also express protest in religious terms.[15]

It has been suggested that some forms of popular religion, such as spiritism, are less revolutionary than engaged in the building of alternative institutions, a parallel vision of society (D. Warren 1968). Many authors, however, are now suggesting that popular religion is capable of being both apologetic for existing structures and a vehicle for criticism (Cf. Bastide 1978; Forman 1975; and Pessar 1981). In James Greenberg's (1981:191) analysis of the Chatino civil-religious hierarchy, he argues that the fiesta system is an "instrument of colonial exploitation," reinforcing economic dependency, yet it is also a defense of a distinctive way of life.

This debate about popular religion and change is particularly characteristic of the literature on Brazilian messianic and millenarian movements. René Ribeiro (1970) notes the long history of such movements and their derivation from Amerindian sources, from the millennialist strain of popular Catholicism, and from the medieval Portuguese belief in the return of King Sebastian, killed in a battle with the Moors. Maria Isaura de Perreira de Queiroz (1960, 1963, 1965) has provided reviews of the many movements throughout Brazilian history and includes an excellent bibliography (1965).

For Perreira de Queiroz (1963, 1965) such movements are essentially transitory. They do reinforce local social ties, while also easing the shift from subsistence to commercial agriculture. Forman (1975:281–82f) agrees that while movements attempt to solidify local ties, they also reject the expansion of capitalist economic ties in agriculture. Rui Facó (1972) pushes this further to argue that millennialism is disguised rebellion against the elite classes. Pessar (1981) rejects such an interpretation because although they are protests, they are inspired as much by religious motivations about apocalyptic fears and hopes for salvation as by political issues (Cf. Ribeiro 1970). She also agrees with Forman's (1975:206) argument that the immediate cause of such movements is the inability of local elites to fulfill properly their traditional patron-client relationships. This is due to their diminishing power with increased governmental centralization and the growth of capitalist forms of agricultural production. The protests of millennialist movements, then, are not against the elite classes as such, but only against particular patrons unable to carry out their moral obligations (Pessar 1981:265). Theirs is a reactionary-revolutionary character, more concerned with establishing the new Jerusalem in the wilderness than undertaking a change in the system at large (Pessar 1981:273; Forman 1975:238).

Other political movements involving the Brazilian peasantry, however, have also included an effective appeal to religious symbols (Forman 1975:240). This is most evident in the involvement of the Catholic church since the 1950s, and especially since the Second Vatican Council, in movements promoting political participation and socioeconomic reform.[16] This has included the organization of Christian Democratic Parties (Williams 1967), as well as agricultural and community development through such programs as peasant rural unions and the *Movimento de Educação de Base* [Base Educational Movement] in Brazil (de Kadt 1970). Latin American priests have participated in a wide variety of popular movements, including the involvement of Camilo Torres with Colombian guerrilla forces (Torres Restrepo 1966). Individual priests and often substantial segments of the church hierarchy have become increasingly active on issues of human rights and social justice in many countries including Brazil, Guatemala, El Salvador, and Nicaragua (Lernoux 1980; Cabestrero 1982). Much of this has been conducted in the context of a growing Latin American "liberation theology" that derives its theological exegesis from the popular concerns of the peasantry and working classes (e.g., Gutiérrez 1973; Segundo 1976).

Many of these movements represent joint efforts by the church hierarchy and the lower classes. As such they have attempted to build indigenous leadership, but may also reflect the influence of middle- and upper-class leaders as well (Smith 1982). Efforts have also been made by conservative members of the elite to make use of religion in espousing their own causes. In Brazil the Family Marches with God for Liberty, the Family Rosary Crusade, and the Brazilian Society for the Defense of Tradition, Family and Property are all examples of conservative groups (Antoine 1973).

Certainly popular religion has been used to promote upper-class interests in many other areas as well. Robert Lavenda (1980), for example, demonstrates how Venezuelan elites changed Carnival in Caracas in order to enunciate new values consistent with their greater incorporation in the international capitalist economy.

In concluding this review therefore, one should not forget that Catholicism itself in Latin America and certainly many aspects of popular Catholicism today were imposed originally on the communities of Indians and black slaves with one aim: to justify racism and class exploitation (Bastide 1978; Greenberg 1981). There can be no doubt that popular religion, whether arising from the peasant and working classes themselves or influenced by elites, can also lead to protest. Such religion has been "reecologized," in Greenberg's (1981:193) terms, to fit their political economy, to express their own world view and "resentment" of oppression (Pessar 1981:262).

Popular religion, thus, *is* inherently ideological in the sense that it is always tied to social interests. It is only through being related to real concerns in actual historical circumstances that religious symbols or any symbols acquire meaning. That the symbols of popular religiosity can be reinterpreted and manipulated in a variety of ways, that they can both call to arms and calm with assurances of the rightful privileges of hierarchy returns us to that ambivalence of religion remarked upon by Blanca Muratorio (1981). The consequences of that ambivalance remain unclear for the future directions of Latin American popular religion and for the lives of the faithful. With this in mind, studies of popular religiosity take on special importance and urgency.

RESEARCH CENTERS

While a good argument can be made for studying popular religion in Latin America, there is a lack of research centers specifically concerned with its analysis. Most efforts in this area, as with Latin American popular culture generally, have occurred through special issues of journals or individual articles and monographs, as well as more inclusive efforts such as *Studies in Latin American Popular Culture*.

FUTURE DIRECTIONS IN RESEARCH

The ambivalence of the role of popular religiosity in Latin America reflects an analogous diversity in existing research on Latin American religious life. It is true, certainly, as has been seen, that there are several clearly expressed themes in the literature. The bearing of religion on social change and popular movements is an obvious example; one that is far more in evidence for Latin America than for North American analyses of popular religion.[17] Yet even in the analysis of popular religion and change, research is hindered by the lack of a common terminology and analytical structure. This is reflected in this chapter in the phrase that refers to a literature on "popular religiosity," a label not recognized by many of the authors in the field.

The concern about terminology is more than simply an arcane definitional issue. How one approaches the analysis of religiosity, as "folk," ethnic, or class-based, for example, immediately shapes the questions and results of research. To perpetuate such terminological and theoretical congeries, therefore, is to restrict efforts at comparative analysis and ensure a parochial understanding of the significance of research in popular religion.

By making use of a common analytical framework such as that provided by "popular culture," we can begin to develop a set of fundamental assumptions and concepts. One advantage of pursuing this direction is that the study of popular culture, with its connotation of the mass packaging of culture, can subsume the study of class or ethnic enclaves under a broader analysis of the nation-state and supranational economic structures and processes. The majority of research at present has focused on the religious systems of particular ethnic groups or the religious aspects of national identity, at times without any explicit recognition of how such religious elements are conditioned by the underlying economic and class structure.

Consider, for example, the excellent body of literature that exists on the religiosity of Indian groups or even on the contrasts or similarities in Indian and rural *ladino* religion. Yet there is a severe lack of materials discussing the origins and development of urban working-class Catholicism in contrast to upper-class religion. Accounts of middle-class forms of religion, with the partial exception of some Protestant and spiritist groups, are also virtually absent in the literature. There is no question but that the emerging Latin American middle classes are much influenced by bourgeois, upper-class notions of religiosity. Yet as the case of spiritism and Protestantism in Brazil demonstrates, they are also open to other forms of religious experience shared more broadly with the working and lower classes. Studies of popular religion, therefore, need to address the relationship between religion and *both* class and ethnic factors as separate variables.

Only by analyzing popular religion in light of ethnic and class variables can one then begin to make a connection between religiosity and ideology more generally. Casting research on popular religion in terms of its dynamic relationship with issues like urbanization, industrialization, and the increasing penetration of the capitalist mode of production in peasant and Indian communities will help in understanding how popular ideologies are more than false consciousness or blueprints for rebellion. It will point the way toward a critique of cultural forms that presumes their essential status as human products, revelatory of that which we take to be meaningful, while also functioning to produce social realities beyond our ken or masking one layer of significant relationships from another. Popular religiosity, as any ideology, can be manipulated to screen the middle and lower classes from being cognizant of powerful structures and forces produced by upper-class activity. Yet screens, of course, are not opaque; they only dim or distort. To reconstruct theoretically, thus, how we depend upon ideology while being constrained by it is prerequisite to the very appreciation of how society is produced and reproduces itself anew.

Such studies in popular religion, indeed in popular culture as a whole, are not to be trivialized. To do so implies a class-based scholarship concerned with a cannon that excludes "mass culture." Scholarship is here essentially replicating the pejorative connotation of popular as being "of the populace," a culture presumed to be shallow, artificial, or crassly imitative of upper class, and therefore, more "genuine" culture. To learn how popular imagery can recapture derivative symbols, or assert entirely different images, creative of reality, suggests the seriousness of research in popular culture. The study of popular religion, in particular, by addressing a realm of culture that lays claim to being pre-cultural, descriptive of the really real, is central to the task of setting out that popular view of reality.

NOTES

1. For a more personal account by a Brazilian lay Catholic and social scientist, see Thales de Azevedo (1953).

2. Jacques Lafaye's (1976) important study of *Quetzalcóatl and Guadalupe* should also be mentioned here. Lafaye demonstrates how Guadalupe was utilized by the Spanish Catholic authorities to substitute for Tonantzín, an Aztec goddess associated with the moon; Quetzalcóatl was viewed as St. Thomas by "creole apologists" to point to the prior Christianization of the Indians and, thus, the superfluous character of the Spanish conquest.

3. Consider Eugene Nida's (1957) use of the term *mariology*.

4. Frank Cancian (1965) illustrates the variation that can occur in civil-religious hierarchies. Note also James Greenberg's (1981) work on Chatino religion and economics for its bibliography and contribution to the debate on interpreting cargo systems. Frank Salomon (1982) also provides an excellent bibliography and discussion, not only on Andean civil-religious systems and their hierarchical and egalitarian variations, but for Andean ethnography of the 1970s in general.

5. June Nash's (1967/68) analysis of the Passion Play also clarifies how figures in the dramas and rituals of peasant Indian communities may be identified with *ladino* culture, an allusion to the play's role in the subordination of Indian society.

6. For the related topic of nagualism, the widespread belief in the power of humans to transform themselves into animals, see George Foster (1944).

7. Similar topics, of course, have been investigated for other ethnic groups in Mesoamerica, such as the social functions of civil-religious hierarchies (e.g., Dow 1974; Greenberg 1981), cognitive studies of world view (e.g., Kearney 1972), religious and other dimensions of social identity (e.g., Friedlander 1975; Iwánska 1971), as well as more holistic accounts of the social and religious life of the community (e.g., Aguirre Beltrán 1958; Carrasco 1952; Crumrine 1977; and Spicer 1980).

8. Also see Gerardo and Alicia Reichel-Dolmatoff's (1961) account of the Colombian highlands town of Aritama for their similar awareness of the involvement of popular religion in class and ethnic distinctions.

9. Compare also Faron's (1964) work on Mapuche morality and ritual.

10. An analogous departure from orthodoxy has occurred among some elements of the middle and upper classes in regard to their participation in Umbanda and spiritism in Brazil and elsewhere (Brown 1979).

11. For a contrasting view, as has been discussed, see Foster's (1960) argument that Spanish missionaries brought a relatively uniform Catholicism to Latin America, with few European folk traditions. See also William Madsen's (1967) rebuttal and statement on the origins of syncretism.

12. Note here Lafaye's (1976) account of the importance of the Virgin of Guadalupe in preconquest Spain and its transfer to Mexico. This contrasts somewhat with Arevas's (1974) argument for Chile, at least, that it was only in the eighteenth century that Mary replaced Christ in popular importance, though Lafaye also notes the gradual growth in the importance of Guadalupe in Mexican life.

13. Camargo (1961:125) does emphasize, however, that Umbanda is practiced

by a variety of class and racial groups, noting that 50 percent of Umbandists in São Paulo are Euro-Brazilian.

14. The importance of Protestantism as a source of identity has been analyzed for other areas as well. Schwartz (1972) looks at Protestant conversion in Guatemalan communities as it occurs along Indian-*ladino* lines, while Maynard (1981) discusses the hierarchical and internally diverse nature of "Protestant" identity in an Ecuadorian provincial capital with eighteen local churches of different denominations.

15. Certainly the involvement of both religion and politics in the history of rebellions among Indians and Latin American peasants generally is well documented (Cf. Bricker 1981; Campbell 1979; and Reed 1964).

16. For a general review of the church's role in politics, see the issue of the *Journal of Interamerican Studies and World Affairs* on "The Church and Politics in Latin America" (1979). Also see Brian Smith's (1975) essay on social change and the Latin American Catholic church.

17. Consider the recent issue of *Monthly Review* on "Religion and the Left." While examining the involvement of religion in popular consciousness and change more broadly, several articles focus especially on North America.

BIBLIOGRAPHY

Adams, Richard N. *A Community in the Andes*. American Ethnological Society Monograph Series, no. 31 (Seattle: University of Washington Press, 1959).

————, and Rubel, Arthur J. "Sickness and Social Relations." In *Handbook of Middle American Indians*, edited by M. Nash, 6:333–56 (Austin: University of Texas Press, 1967).

Aguirre Beltrán, Gonzalo. *Cuija, esbozo etnográfico de un pueblo negro* (México, D.F.: Fondo de Cultura Económica, 1958).

————. *Medicina y magia*. Colección de Antropología Social, vol. 1 (México, D.F.: Instituto Nacional Indigenista, 1963).

————. *Regiones de refugio: el desarrollo de la comunidad y el proceso dominical en mestizo América*. Instituto Nacional Indigenista, Serie de Antropología, núm. 17 (México, D.F.: Instituto Nacional Indigenista, 1967).

Antoine, Charles. *Church and Power in Brazil* (Maryknoll, N.Y.: Orbis Books, 1973).

Arevas, José M., S.J. "Religiosidad popular: en torno a un encuentro." *Mensaje* 23, no. 226 (1974): 47–49.

Arriaga, Pablo José. *The Extirpation of Idolatry in Peru* (Lexington: University of Kentucky Press, 1968).

Azevedo, Thales de. "Catholicism in Brazil: A Personal Evaluation." *Thought* 28, no. 109 (1953): 253–74.

————. "Problemas metodológicos da sociologia do Catolicismo no Brasil." *Revista do Museu Paulista* 14 (1963): 345–76.

————. *Cultura e situação racial no Brasil* (Rio de Janeiro: Editora Civilização Brasileira, 1966).

Azzi, Riolando. "Elementos para a história do catolicismo popular." *Revista Eclesiástica Brasileira* 36, no. 141 (1976): 95–131.

Bahamonde, W. O. "The Establishment of Evangelical Christianity in Peru, 1822–1900." Ph.D. dissertation, The Hartford Seminary Foundation, 1952.

Bastide, Roger. *Le Candomblé de Bahia (Rite Nagô)* (Paris: Mouton, 1958).

———. "The Present Status of Afro-American Research in Latin America." *Daedalus* 103, no. 2 (1974): 111–24.

———. *The African Religions of Brazil* (Baltimore: The Johns Hopkins University Press, 1978).

Bastien, Joseph W. *Mountain of the Condor: Metaphor and Ritual in an Andean Ayllu*. American Ethnological Society Monograph Series, no. 64 (New York: West Publishing Co., 1978).

Bedregal, Yolanda. "Literatura y artes aymaras dentro de la cultura boliviana." In *Los aymaras dentro de la sociedad boliviana*, 12:57–72. Cuadernos de Investigación CIPCA (La Paz: CIPCA, 1976).

Berger, Peter. *The Sacred Canopy* (Garden City, N.Y.: Anchor Books, 1967).

Berryman, Felipe. "Popular Catholicism in Latin America." *Cross Currents* 21, no. 3 (1971): 284–301.

Blaffer, Sarah. *The Black-man of Zinacantán: A Central American Legend* (Austin: University of Texas Press, 1972).

Bodley, John H. *Victims of Progress*. 2d ed. (Palo Alto, Calif.: Mayfield Publishing Co., 1982).

Bombart, Jean Pierre. "Les cultes Protestants dans une favela de Rio de Janeiro." *América Latina* 12, no. 3 (1969): 137–59.

Bonino, José M. "La Piedad popular en América Latina." *Cristianismo y Sociedad* 47 (1976): 31–38.

Braden, Charles. *Religious Aspects of the Conquest of Mexico* (Durham, N.C.: Duke University Press, 1930).

Brenner, Anita. *Idols Behind Altars* (New York: Payson and Clarke, 1929).

Bricker, Victoria Reifler. *Ritual Humor in Highland Chiapas* (Austin: University of Texas Press, 1973).

———. *The Indian Christ, the Indian King* (Austin: University of Texas Press, 1981).

Brintnall, Douglas E. *Revolt Against the Dead* (New York: Gordon and Breach, 1979).

Brown, Diana. "Umbanda and Class Relations in Brazil." In *Brazil, Anthropological Perspectives* edited by M. Margolis and W. Carter, 270–304 (New York: Columbia University Press, 1979).

Bruneau, Thomas. *The Church in Brazil, the Politics of Religion* (Austin: University of Texas Press, 1982).

Cabestrero, Teofilo. *Ministers of God, Ministers of the People* (Maryknoll, N.Y.: Orbis Books, 1982).

Camargo, Cándido Procopio Ferreira de. *Kardecismo e Umbanda: uma interpretação sociológica* (São Paulo: Livaria Pioneira, 1961).

Campbell, Leon G. "Recent Research on Andean Peasant Revolts, 1750–1820." *Latin American Research Review* 15, no. 1 (1979): 3–50.

Cancian, Frank. *Economics and Prestige in a Maya Community* (Stanford, Calif.: Stanford University Press, 1965).

———. "Political and Religious Organizations." In *Handbook of Middle American*

Indians, edited by M. Nash, 6:283–98 (Austin: University of Texas Press, 1967).

Carneiro, Edison. *Candomblés da Bahia* (Bahia: Publicação do Museu do Estado, 1948).

Carrasco, Pedro. *Tarascan Folk Religion: An Analysis of Economic, Social and Religious Interactions*. Middle American Research Institute, Tulane University, 17: 1–64 (New Orleans: Middle American Research Institute, Tulane University, 1952).

————. "The Civil-Religious Hierarchy in Mesoamerican Communities: Pre-Spanish Background and Colonial Development." *American Anthropologist* 63, no. 3 (1961): 483–97.

Carvalho-Neto, Paulo de. "Concepto y realidad del teatro folklórico latinoamericano." *Folklore Americano* 23 (1977): 101–15.

Casa de Rui Barbosa. *Literature Popular em Verso: Antologia* (Rio de Janeiro: Ministerio de Educação e Cultura, 1964).

Casagrande, Joseph B. "Religious Conversion and Social Change in an Indian Community of Highland Ecuador." In *Amerikanistische Studien: Festschrift für Hermann Trimborn*, 1, edited by R. Hartmann and U. Oberem (Augustin: Haus Völker und Kulturen, Anthropos Institut, 1978).

Cesar, Waldo A. *Para uma sociologia do Protestantismo Brasileiro* (Petrópolis: Editores Vozes, 1973).

————, ed. *Protestantismo e imperialismo na America Latina: questões abertas* (Petrópolis: Editor Vozes, 1968).

Chilcote, Ronald H. "The Politics of Conflict in the Popular Poetry of Northwest Brazil." *Journal of Latin American Lore* 5, no. 2 (1979): 205–31.

"The Church and Politics in Latin America." *Journal of Interamerican Studies and World Affairs* 21, no. 1 (February 1979).

Comblin, José. "Valoración cristiana de las religiones nativas o sincretismo religioso." In *Religiones nativas y religión cristiana*, edited by E. Rodríguez B. and A. Muriel A. (Oruru: n.p., 1972).

Correa, G.; Cannon, C.; Hunter, W.; and Bode, B. *The Native Theatre in Middle America*, Middle American Research Institute, Tulane University, vol. 27 (New Orleans: Middle American Research Institute, Tulane University, 1961).

Crumrine, N. Ross. *The Mayo Indians of Sonora: A People Who Refuse to Die* (Tucson: University of Arizona Press, 1977).

Currier, Richard L. "The Hot-Cold Syndrome and Symbolic Balance in Mexican and Spanish-American Folk Medicine." *Ethnology* 5, no. 3 (July 1966): 251–63.

Curry, Donald. "Lusíada: An Anthropological Study of the Growth of Protestantism in Brazil." Ph.D. dissertation, Columbia University, 1968.

Damboriena, Prudencio. *El Protestantismo en América Latina*, vol. 1. Estudios socio-religiosos latino-americanos, núm. 12. (Friburg: FERES), 1962.

Dávila, Mario. "Compadrazgo: Fictive Kinship in Latin America." In *Readings in Kinship and Social Structure*, edited by N. Graburn, 396–405 (New York: Harper and Row, 1971).

de Kadt, Emanuel. "Religion, the Church and Social Change in Brazil." In *The*

Politics of Conformity in Latin America, edited by C. Veliz, 192–220 (London: Oxford University Press, 1967).

————. *Catholic Radicals in Brazil* (London: Oxford University Press, 1970).

De Moura, Abdalazig. "O pentecostalismo como fenomeno religioso popular no Brasil." *Revista Eclesiástica Brasileira* 31 (1972): 78–94.

Demarest, Donald, and Taylor, Coley, eds. *The Dark Virgin: the Book of Our Lady of Guadalupe* (Fresno, Calif.: Academy Guild Press, 1957).

Denton, C. F. "Protestantism and the Latin American Middle Class." *Practical Anthropology* 18 (1971): 24–28.

Dow, James W. *Santos y sobrevivencia: funciones de la religión en una comunidad Otomí, México* (México, D.F.: Instituto Nacional Indigenista, Secretaría de Educación Pública, 1974).

Duviols, Pierre. *La lutte contre les religions autochtones dans le Pérou colonial* (Paris: Editions Ophrys, 1971).

Edmonson, Munro S. "Narrative Folklore." In *Handbook of Middle American Indians*, edited by M. Nash, 6:357–38 (Austin: University of Texas Press, 1967a).

————. "Play: Games, Gossip and Humor." In *Handbook of Middle American Indians*, edited by M. Nash, 6:191–206 (Austin: University of Texas Press, 1967b).

Edmonson, M.; Thompson, D.; Correa, G.; and Madsen, W. *Nativism and Syncretism*, Middle American Research Institute, Tulane University, vol. 19 (New Orleans: Middle American Research Institute, Tulane University, 1960).

Eduardo, Octavio da Costa. *The Negro in Northern Brazil: A Study in Acculturation*. American Ethnological Society Monograph Series, no. 15. (Seattle: University of Washington Press, 1966).

Ehms, Arno W. *Man, Milieu and Mission in Argentina* (Grand Rapids, Mich.: Eerdmans Publishing Co., 1971).

Fabrega, Horacio, Jr., and Silver, Daniel B. *Illness and Shamanistic Curing in Zinacantan* (Stanford, Calif.: Stanford University Press, 1973).

Facó, Rui. *Cangaceiros e Fanaticos* (Rio de Janeiro: Editora Civilização Brasileira, 1972).

Falla, Ricardo, S.J. "Juan el Gordo: visión indígena de su explotación." *Estudios Centro-Americanos* 268 (1970): 98–107.

Fals Borda, Orlando. *Peasant Society in the Colombian Andes* (Gainesville, Fla.: University of Florida Press, 1955).

Faron, Louis C. *Hawks of the Sun: Mapuches Morality and Its Ritual Attributes* (Pittsburgh: University of Pittsburgh Press, 1964).

Flora, Cornelia B. "Pentecostal Women in Colombia." *Journal of Interamerican Studies and World Affairs* 17, no. 4 (November 1975): 411–25.

————. *Pentecostalism in Colombia: Baptism by Fire and Spirit* (Cranbury, N.J.: Associated University Press, 1976).

Forman, Shepard. *The Brazilian Peasantry* (New York: Columbia University Press, 1975).

Foster, George. "Nagualism in Mexico and Guatemala." *Acta Americana* 2 (1944): 85–103.

——. "Cofradía and Compadrazgo." *Southwestern Journal of Anthropology* 9, no. 1 (1953a): 1–28.

——. "Relationships Between Spanish and Spanish-American Folk Medicine." *Journal of American Folklore* 66, no. 261 (1953b): 201–17.

——. *Culture and Conquest* (Chicago: Quadrangle Books, 1960).

Freyre, Gilberto. *The Masters and the Slaves* (New York: Knopf, 1966).

Friedlander, Judith. *Being Indian in Hueyapan* (New York: St. Martin's Press, 1975).

Galvão, Eduardo. *Santos e visagens* (São Paulo: Companhia Editora Nacional, 1955).

Gillin, John. *Moche, A Peruvian Coastal Community*. Smithsonian Institution of Social Anthropology, 3 (Washington, D.C.: Smithsonian Institution, 1945).

——. *The Culture of Security in San Carlos*, Middle American Research Institute, Tulane University, 16 (New Orleans: Middle American Research Institute, Tulane University, 1951).

González Sol, Rafael. *Fiestas cívicas, religiosas y exhibiciones populares de El Salvador* (San Salvador: Talleres Gráficos Cisneros, 1947).

Goodman, Felicitas D. *Speaking in Tongues, A Cross-Cultural Study of Glossolalia* (Chicago: University of Chicago, 1972).

——. "Disturbances in the Apostolic Church: A Trance-Based Upheaval in Yucatán." In *Trance, Healing and Hallucination*, edited by F. Goodman, J. Henney, and E. Pressel, 227–364 (New York: John Wiley and Sons, 1974).

Goslin, Thomas S. *Los evangélicos en la América Latina, siglo XIX: los comienzos* (Buenos Aires: La Aurora 1956).

Gossen, Gary. *Chamulas in the World of the Sun: Time and Space in a Maya Oral Tradition* (Cambridge: Harvard University Press, 1974).

Greenberg, James B. *Santiago's Sword* (Berkeley: University of California Press, 1981).

Gross, Daniel. "Ritual and Conformity: A Religious Pilgrimage to Northeast Brazil." *Ethnology* 10, no. 2 (April 1971): 129–48.

Gross, Sue Anderson. "Religious Sectarianism in the Sertão of Northeast Brazil 1815–1966." *Journal of Interamerican Studies* 10, no. 3 (July 1968): 369–83.

Gushiken, José. *Tuno: el curandero* (Lima: Universidad Nacional Mayor de San Marcos, Seminario de Historia Rural Andina, 1977).

Gutiérrez, Gustavo. *A Theology of Liberation* (Maryknoll, N.Y.: Orbis Books, 1973).

Harris, Marvin. *Town and Country in Brazil* (New York: W.W. Norton and Co., 1956).

Hartmann, Roswith. "Conmemoración de muertos en la sierra ecuatoriana." *Indiana* 1 (1973): 179–97.

Helms, James E. "Origins and Growth of Protestantism in Mexico to 1920." Ph.D. dissertation, University of Texas, 1955.

Herskovits, Melville J. "African Gods and Catholic Saints in New World Negro Belief." *American Anthropologist* 39, no. 4 (1937): 635–43.

——. "The Southernmost Outposts of New World Africanisms." *American Anthropologist* 45, no. 4 (1943): 495–510.

Hinds, Harold E., Jr. "Latin American Popular Culture A New Research Frontier:

Achievements, Problems and Promises." *Journal of Popular Culture* 14, no. 3 (1980): 405–12.

Holland, William. *Medicina Maya en Los Altos de Chiapas: un estudio del cambio sociocultural*. Colección de Antropología Social, vol. 2 (México, D.F.: Instituto Nacional Indigenista, 1963).

Homero Palma, Nestor. *Estudio antropológico de la medicina popular de la puna argentina* (Buenos Aires: Ediciones Cabargón, 1973).

Hoornaert, Eduardo. *Formação do catolicismo brasileiro, 1550–1800* (Petrópolis: Editora Vozes, 1974).

Hunt, Eva. *The Transformation of the Hummingbird: Cultural Roots of a Zinacantecan Mythical Poem* (Ithaca: Cornell University Press, 1977).

INDICEP. "El Jilakata: Apuntes sobre el sistema político de los aymaras." *Allapanchis Phuturinqa* 5 (1973): 33–44.

Instituto de Teologia do Recife. *A fé popular no Nordeste* (Salvador, Bahia: Editora Beneditima, 1974).

Iriarte, Gregorio. *Galerías de Muerte: vida de los mineros bolivianos* (Montevideo: Tierra Nueva, 1972).

Isbell, Billie Jean. *To Defend Ourselves: Ecology and Ritual in an Andean Village*. Latin American Monographs, no. 47 (Austin: University of Texas, Institute of Latin American Studies, 1978).

Iwánska, Alicja. *Purgatory and Utopia* (Cambridge: Schenkman Publishing Co., 1971).

Karasch, Mary. "Central African Religious Tradition in Rio de Janeiro." *Journal of Latin American Lore* 5, no. 2 (1979): 233–53.

Kardec, Alan. *Spiritualist Philosophy: The Spirit's Book* (Salem, N.Y.: Ayer and Co., 1976).

Kearney, Michael. *The Winds of Ixtepeji* (New York: Holt, Rinehart and Winston, 1972).

Kelly, Isabel. "Mexican Spiritualism." In *Alfred L. Kroeber: a Memorial. The Kroeber Anthropological Society Papers* 25 (1961): 191–206.

———. *Folk Practices in Northern Mexico* (Austin: University of Texas, Institute of Latin American Studies, 1965).

Kessler, J.B.A. *A Study of the Older Protestant Missions and Churches in Peru and Chile* (Goes, The Netherlands: Oosterbaan and le Cointre, 1967).

Kubler, George. "The Quechua in the Colonial World." In *Handbook of South American Indians,* edited by J. Steward, 2:331–410, Bureau of American Ethnology, Bul. 143 (Washington, D.C.: Smithsonian Institution, 1946).

Kurath, Gertrude Prokosch. "Drama, Dance and Music." In *Handbook of Middle American Indians*, edited by M. Nash, 6:158–90 (Austin: University of Texas Press, 1967).

Kusch, Rodolfo. "Interpretación de las religiones nativas." In *Religiones nativas y religión cristiana*, edited by E. Rodríguez B. and A. Muriel A. (Oruro, Bolivia: n.p., 1972).

La Farge, Oliver. *Santa Eulalia* (Chicago: University of Chicago Press, 1947).

Lafaye, Jacques. *Quetzalcóatl and Guadalupe: The Formation of Mexican National Consciousness, 1531–1813* (Chicago: University of Chicago Press, 1976).

Lalive d'Epinay, Christian. *El refugio de las masas: estudio sociológico del protestantismo chileno* (Santiago: Editorial El Pacífico, 1969).

La Maza, Francisco de. *El guadalupanismo mexicano* (México, D.F.: Porruay Obregón, 1953).

Laughlin, Robert M. *Of Wonders Wild and New: Dreams from Zinacantán,* Smithsonian Contributions to Anthropology, no. 22 (Washington, D.C.: Smithsonian Institution, 1976).

———. *Of Cabbages and Kings: Tales from Zinacantán,* Smithsonian Contributions to Anthropology, no. 23 (Washington, D.C.: Smithsonian Institution, 1977).

Lavenda, Robert H. "The Festival of Progress: The Globalizing World System and the Transformation of the Caracas Carnival." *Journal of Popular Culture* 14, no. 3 (1980): 465–75.

Leacock, Seth, and Leacock, Ruth. *Spirits of the Deep.* (New York: Natural History Press, 1972).

Leers, Frei Bernardo, O.F.M. *Religiosidade rural uma contribucao local* (Petrópolis: Editora Vozes Ltda., 1967).

Lekis, Lisa. *Folk Dances of Latin America* (New York: Scarecrow Press, 1958).

Lernoux, Penny. *Cry of the People* (Garden City, N.Y.: Doubleday, 1980).

Lewellen, Ted. *Peasants in Transition* (Boulder, Colo.: Westview Press, 1978).

Madsen, Claudia. *A Study of Change in Mexican Folk Medicine.* Middle American Research Institute, Tulane University, 25:89–201 (New Orleans: Middle American Research Institute, Tulane University, 1968).

Madsen, William. *Christo-Paganism: A Study of Mexican Religious Syncretism,* Middle American Research Institute, Tulane University, 19:105–80 (New Orleans: Middle American Research Institute, Tulane University, 1957).

———. *The Virgin's Children: Life in an Aztec Village* (Austin: University of Texas Press, 1960).

———. "Religious Syncretism." In *Handbook of Middle American Indians,* edited by M. Nash, 6:369–91 (Austin: University of Texas Press, 1967).

Marzal, Manuel María. *El mundo religioso de Urcos* (Cuzco: Instituto de Pastoral Andina, 1971).

———. "Es posible una iglesia indígena en el Perú?" *América Indígena* 33, no. 1 (1973): 107–24.

Maynard, Kent. "Christianity and Religion: Evangelical Identity and Sociocultural Organization in Urban Ecuador." Ph.D. dissertation, Indiana University, 1981.

Mecham, J. Lloyd. *Church and State in Latin America.* rev. ed. (Chapel Hill: University of North Carolina Press, 1966).

Medina, Carlos Alberto de. "Bom Jesus da Lapa, desenvolvimento e tradição." *América Latina* 15 (1972): 44–57.

Mendelson, E. Michael. "Ritual and Mythology." In *Handbook of Middle American Indians,* edited by M. Nash, 6:392–415 (Austin: University of Texas Press, 1967).

Millas, Jorge. *El desafío espiritual de la sociedad de masas* (Santiago: Ediciones de la Universidad de Chile, 1962).

Miller, Elmer S. "The Christian Missionary: Agent of Secularization." *Anthropological Quarterly* 43, no. 1 (January 1970): 14–22.

———. "The Argentine Toba Evangelical Religious Service." *Ethnology* 10, no. 2 (April 1971): 149–59.

————. "Shamans, power symbols and change in Argentine Toba culture." *American Ethnologist* 2, no. 3 (August 1975): 477–96.

Millones, Luís. "Los duendes de Casma. Religión popular en un valle de la Costa Norte." *Folklore Americano* 19 (1975): 81–92.

Mintz, Sidney, and Wolf, Eric. "An Analysis of Ritual Co-parenthood." *Southwestern Journal of Anthropology* 9, no. 4 (1950): 341–68.

Missionary Educational Movement. *Congress on Christian Work in Latin America.* 3 vols. (New York: Missionary Educational Movement, 1917).

Monteiro, Duglas T. Introduction to the Translation of *The African Religions of Brazil* by Roger Bastide, xv-xxviii (Baltimore: The Johns Hopkins University Press, 1978).

Monti, Daniel P. *Presencia del protestantisme en el Río de la Plata durante el siglo XIX* (Buenos Aires: Editorial La Aurora, 1969).

Movote Best, Efraín. "Dios, la virgen y los santos (en los relatos populares)." *Tradición* 5 (1953): 76–104.

Muratorio, Blanca. "Protestantism, Ethnicity, and Class in Chimborazo." In *Cultural Transformation and Ethnicity in Modern Ecuador*, edited by N. Whitten, Jr., 506–34 (Urbana: University of Illinois Press, 1981).

Nash, June. "Protestantism in an Indian Village in the Western Highlands of Guatemala." *Alpha Kappa Deltan* 30, no. 1 (1960): 41–58.

————. "The Passion Play in Maya Indian Communities." *Comparative Studies in Society and History* 10, no. 3 (April 1967/68): 318–27.

————. *In the Eyes of the Ancestors* (New Haven: Yale University Press, 1970).

————. *We Eat the Mines, and the Mines Eat Us* (New York: Columbia University Press, 1979).

Nash, Manning. "Political Relations in Guatemala." *Social and Economic Studies* 7 (1958): 65–75.

Nida, Eugene. "Mariology in Latin America." *Practical Anthropology* 4, no. 2 (1957): 69–82.

————. "The Relationship of Social Structure to the Problem of Evangelism in Latin America." *Practical Anthropology* 5, no. 3 (1958): 101–23.

Oliveira, Pedro Assis Ribeiro de. *Catolicismo popular no Brasil* (Rio de Janeiro: Ceris, 1970).

————. "Catolicismo popular e romaização do catolicismo brasileiro." *Revista Eclesiástica Brasileira* 36, no. 141 (1976a): 131–42.

————. "Catolicismo popular no Brasil—bibliografia." *Revista Eclesiástica Brasileira* 36, no. 141 (1976b): 272 80.

————. "Bibliografia sobre religiosidade popular." *Religião e Sociedad* 1 (1977): 181–94.

Ortiz, Renato. *A morte branca do feiticeiro negro* (Petrópolis: Editora Vozes, 1978).

Parsons, Elsie Clews. *Mitla, Town of Souls* (Chicago: University of Chicago Press, 1936).

Paz, Octavio. *The Labyrinth of Solitude* (New York: Grove Press, 1961).

Penton, Marvin J. "Mexico's Reformation: a History of Mexican Protestantism from its Inception to the Present." Ph.D. dissertation, Iowa State University, 1965.

Perreira de Queiroz, Maria Isaura. "O movimento messianico do Cotestado." *Revista Basileira de Estudios Políticos* 9 (1960): 118–39.

————. "Movements, messianique et dévelopement economique au Brésil." *Archive de Sociologie des Religions* 16 (1963): 109–21.

————. *O Messianismo no Brasil e no Mundo* (São Paulo: Universidade de São Paulo, 1965).

Pessar, Patricia R. "Unmasking the Politics of Religion: The Case of Brazilian Millenarianism." *Journal of Latin American Lore* 7, no. 2 (1981): 255–78.

Pierson, Donald. *Cruz Das Almas, A Brazilian Village.* Smithsonian Institution of Social Anthropology, 12 (Washington, D.C.: Smithsonian Institution, 1951).

Pike, Frederick B. "Religion, Collectivism and Intrahistory: the Peruvian Ideal of Dependence." *Journal of Latin American Studies* 10 pt. 2 (November 1978): 239–62.

Pollak, Angelina de. "El culto de María Leonza." *América Latina* 9, no. 1 (1966): 95–115.

————. *Cultos Afro-Americanos* (Caracas: Universidad Católica Andrés Bello, Instituto de Investigaciones Históricas, 1972).

Potter, Richard H. "Popular Religion of the 1930s as Reflected in the Best Sellers of Harry Emerson Fosdick." *Journal of Popular Culture* 3, no. 4 (1970): 712–28.

Pressel, Esther. "Umbanda Trance and Possession in São Paulo, Brazil." In *Trance, Healing and Hallucination* edited by F. Goodman, J. Henney, and E. Pressel (New York: John Wiley and Sons, 1974).

Quirk, Robert E. *The Mexican Revolution and the Catholic Church, 1910–1929* (Bloomington, Ind.: Indiana University Press, 1973).

Ravicz, Marilyn. *Early Colonial Religious Drama in Mexico; from Tzompantlí to Golgotha* (Washington, D.C.: Catholic University of America Press, 1970).

Ravicz, Robert. "Compadrazgo." In *Handbook of Middle American Indians*, edited by M. Nash, 6:238–52 (Austin: University of Texas Press, 1967).

Read, William, and Ineson, Frank A. *Brazil 1980: The Protestant Handbook* (Monrovia, Calif.: MARC, 1973).

Read, William; Monterroso, Victor, and Johnson, Harmon. *Latin American Church Growth* (Grand Rapids, Mich.: Eerdmans Publishing Co., 1969).

Redfield, Robert. *The Folk Culture of Yucatán* (Chicago: University of Chicago Press, 1941).

————,and Villas Rojas, Alfonso. *Chan Kom, A Maya Village* (Washington, D.C.: Carnegie Institution, 1934).

Reed, Nelson. *The Caste War of Yucatán* (Stanford, Calif.: Stanford University Press, 1964).

Reichel-Dolmatoff, Gerardo, and Reichel-Dolmatoff, Alicia. *The People of Aritama* (Chicago: University of Chicago Press, 1961).

Reina, Ruben E. "Annual Cycle and Fiesta Cycle." In *Handbook of Middle American Indians*, edited by M. Nash, 6:317–32 (Austin: University of Texas Press, 1967).

————and Schwartz, Norman. "The Structural Context of Religious Conversion in Petén, Guatemala: Status, Community and Multi-Community." *American Ethnologist* 1, no. 1 (February 1974): 157–91.

"Religion and the Left." *Monthly Review* 36, no. 3, (1984).

Ribeiro, René. *Cultos afrobrasileiros do Recife: um estudo de ajustamento social* (Recife: Instituto Joaquim Nabuco, 1952).

————. *Religião e relações raciais* (Rio de Janeiro: Ministério da Educação e Cultura, 1956).

————. "Brazilian Messianic Movements." In *Millennial Dreams in Action*, edited by S. Thrupp, 55–69 (New York: Schocken Books, 1970).

Ricard, Robert. *The Spiritual Conquest of Mexico* (Berkeley: University of California Press, 1966).

Richardson, Miles. *San Pedro, Colombia: Small Town in a Developing Society* (New York: Holt, Rinehart and Winston, 1970).

Richardson, Miles; Pardo, Marta Eugenia; and Bode, Barbara. "The Image of Christ in Spanish America as a Model for Suffering." *Journal of Interamerican Studies and World Affairs* 13, no. 2 (April 1971): 246–57.

Rivera, Julius. *Latin America*. Enlarged edition (New York: Irvington Press, 1978).

Roberts, Bryan. *El Protestantismo en dos barrios marginales de Guatemala*. Estudios Centroamericanos, núm. 2 (Guatemala: Seminario de Integración Social Guatemalteca e Instituto de Estudios Latinoamericanos, Universidad de Texas, 1967).

Rowe, John Howland. "Inca Culture at the Time of the Spanish Conquest." In *Handbook of South American Indians*, edited by J. Steward, 2:183–330, Bureau of American Ethnology, Bul. 143 (Washington, D.C.: Smithsonian Institution, 1946).

Rubel, Arthur J. "The Epidemiology of a Folk Illness: *Susto* in Hispanic America." *Ethnology* 3, no. 3 (July 1964): 268–83.

Salomon, Frank. "Andean Ethnology in the 1970s: A Retrospective." *Latin American Research Review* 17, no. 2 (1982): 75–128.

Sánchez-Arjona, Rodrigo. "La teología litúrgica y la pastoral de nuestras fiestas religiosas." *Allpanchis Phuturinqa* 7 (1974): 217–43.

Sánchez García, Julio, ed. *Calendario fólklorico de fiestas en la República Mexicana: fiesta de la fecha fija* (México, D.F.: Editora Porrua, 1956).

Saunders, J.V.D. "Organização social de uma congregação protestante no estado de guanabara, Brasil." *Sociologia* 22 (1960): 415–49.

Schwartz, Norman. "Protestantism, Community Organization and Social Status: Different Responses to Missions in a Guatemalan Town." *Cultures et Developpement* 4 (1972): 585–99.

Segundo, Juan Luís. *Liberation of Theology* (Maryknoll, N.Y.: Orbis Books, 1976).

Service, Elman R., and Service, Helen S. *Tobatí: Paraguayan Town* (Chicago: University of Chicago Press, 1954).

Sharon, Douglas. *Wizard of the Four Winds. A Shaman's Story* (New York: Free Press, 1978).

Sinclair, John H., ed. *Protestantism in Latin America: A Bibliographical Guide* (Pasadena, Calif.: William Carey Library, 1976).

Smith, Brian H. "Religion and Social Change: Classical Theories in the Context of Recent Developments in Latin America." *Latin American Research Review* 10, no. 2 (1975): 3–34.

————. *The Church and Politics in Chile* (Princeton: Princeton University Press, 1982).

Spicer, Edward H. *The Yaquis: A Cultural History* (Tucson: University of Arizona, 1980).

Stevens, Evelyn P. "Marianismo: The Other Face of Machismo in Latin America."

In *Female and Male in Latin America*, edited by A. Pescatello, 89–101 (Pittsburgh: University of Pittsburgh Press, 1973).

Taussig, Michael T. *The Devil and Commodity Fetishism in South America* (Chapel Hill: University of North Carolina Press, 1980).

Thompson, D. E. *Maya Paganism and Christianity: A History of the Fusion of Two Religions*, Middle American Research Institute, Tulane University, 19: 1–36 (New Orleans: Middle American Research Institute, Tulane University, 1954).

Torres Restrepo, Camilo. *Camilo Torres: biografía, plataforma, mensajes* (Medellín: Ediciones Carpel-Antorcha, 1966).

Turner, Victor, and Turner, Edith. *Image and Pilgrimage in Christian Culture* (New York: Columbia University Press, 1978).

Valdivia Ponce, Oscar. *Hampicamayoc: medicina folklórica y su substrato aborigen en el Perú* (Lima: Universidad Nacional Mayor de San Marcos, Dirección Universitaria de Biblioteca y Publicaciones, 1975).

Vallier, Ivan. "Religious Elites: Differentiation and Developments in Roman Catholicism." In *Elites in Latin America*, edited by A. Solari and S. M. Lipset, 190–232 (London: Oxford University Press, 1967).

Vergara, Ignacio. *El Protestantismo en Chile* (Santiago: Editorial del Pacífico, 1962).

Vessuri, Hebe M. C. "Aspectos del catolicismo popular de Santiago de Estero: ensayo en categorias sociales y morales." *América Latina* 14, nos. 1/2 (1971): 40–69.

Vogt, Evon Z. *Tortillas for the Gods* (Cambridge: Harvard University Press, 1976).

Wachtel, Nathan. *The Vision of the Vanquished: The Spanish Conquest of Peru Through Indian Eyes, 1530–70* (Hassocks, Sussex: The Harvester Press, 1977).

Wagley, Charles. *The Social and Religious Life of a Guatemalan Village*. Memoirs of the American Anthropological Association, 71 (Menasha, Wis.: American Anthropological Association, 1949).

———. *An Introduction to Brazil*. Rev. ed. (New York: Columbia University Press, 1971).

Warren, Donald, Jr. "Spiritism in Brazil." *Journal of Interamerican Studies* 10, no. 3 (July 1968): 193–405.

Warren, Kay B. *The Symbolism of Subordination, Indian Identity in a Guatemalan Town* (Austin: University of Texas Press, 1978).

Wasserstrom, Robert F. "The Exchange of Saints in Zinacantan: The Socioeconomic Bases of Religious Change in Southern Mexico." *Ethnology* 17, no. 2 (April 1978): 197–210.

Whitten, Norman E., Jr. *Black Frontiersmen; a South American Case* (Cambridge, Mass.: Shenkman Publishing Co., 1974).

Willems, Emilio. *Followers of the New Faith* (Nashville: Vanderbilt University Press, 1967).

———. *Latin American Culture: An Anthropological Synthesis* (New York: Harper and Row, 1975).

Williams, Edward J. *Latin American Christian Democratic Parties* (Knoxville: University of Tennessee, 1967).

Wolf, Eric R. "The Virgin of Guadalupe: A Mexican National Symbol." *Journal of American Folklore* 71, no. 279 (1958): 34–39.

Zalles, Jimmy. "La iglesia aymara dentro de la iglesia boliviana." In *Los aymaras dentro de la sociedad boliviana* 12:47–56. Cuadernos de Investigación CIPCA (La Paz: CIPCA, 1976).

Harold E. Hinds, Jr.

3 Comics

The comics (including both comic strips and books) are immensely popular throughout Latin America, especially in urban areas. Elite lawyers, staunch middle-class shopkeepers, and street kids all seem to read the comics in some form; if not daily, at least on occasion. Spanish and Portuguese translations of European and United States comics vie in the marketplace with Latin American varieties, themselves frequently imports from another Latin American nation, most notably Mexico or Argentina.

However, it is only recently that scholars have begun to study this phenomenon. Both the comics' popularity and the reluctance of "respectable" writers to take them seriously is captured by Paul Theroux in his 1979 travelogue, *The Old Patagonian Express*. In San Luis Potosí, Mexico, Theroux writes, "I went into the plaza and bought a Mexican newspaper. ...The rest of the [train] passengers bought comic books." And while traveling by train in northern Argentina, Theroux reports the following incident:

"With your permission," said Oswaldo, seating himself at my table. He carried a comic book. It was a Spanish one, about an inch thick, and its title was *D'Artagnan*—the name of the goonish swashbuckler in the cover story. It seemed fairly unambitious reading, even for a meat salesman.

"Want my book?"
I picked it up and glanced through it. *D'Artagnan* was a Spanish comic, luridly illustrated. "Super Album," it said. "Ten Complete Stories in Full Color." I looked at the stories: "Goodbye California," "We, the Legion," "OrGrund, Viking Killer." It was cowboys, detectives, cave men, soldiers, and ads for learning how to fix televisions in your spare time.
"I've got a book," I said.
"I'm offering it to you for nothing," said Oswaldo.
"I don't read comics."
"This one is beautiful."

Comics are for kids and illiterates, I wanted to say, but one was not supposed to criticize these people.

"Thank you," I said. "Do you ever read Argentine authors?"

"This," he said, tapping the comic book in my hand, "is an Argentine book. It is from Buenos Aires."

"I was thinking of the other kind of books. Without pictures."

"Stories?"

"Yes. Borges, for example."

"Which Borges?"

"Jorge Luis."

"I don't know him" (Theroux 1980: 68, 411, 415–16).

This dialogue illustrates beautifully why the comics remain understudied in spite of their popularity.

The historical sketch that follows must be treated as only the roughest outline and as possibly quite flawed; for the published sources are poor, fragmentary, and frequently contradictory. A surprising amount has been written, yet almost every aspect of the study of Latin American comics is in need of extensive research.

HISTORICAL OUTLINE

Virtually no information is available on the historical evolution of comics in Latin America prior to the last few years, except for Mexico, Argentina, and Brazil; so these comments will be largely devoted to these three nations. Many precursors to the comics in Latin America have been noted, ranging from the obvious, for example, the one-panel humor cartoon, to the seemingly farfetched, for example, pre-Columbian wall murals. The comics themselves did not appear in Latin America until after the turn of the century, several years after they had already gained considerable popularity in the United States.

Between about 1900 and 1929 the development of Latin America comic strips roughly followed United States trends, in large part because the first strips were translations of American ones. Early native strips were frequently modeled on United States genres and examples. Most predepression strips were devoted to humor or fantasy, although the family or domestic strip was not as popular as in the United States. As early as 1902 American strips appeared in Mexico, and within a year the first Mexican strip, the humorous *Don Lupito*, by Andrés Audiffred, was published. In the 1910s American strips became an essential part of Mexican newspapers. A dearth of Mexican strips lead *El Heraldo* [*The Herald*] in 1921 to commission the daily humor strip *Don Catarino* by Salvador Pruneda; and in 1925 *El Universal* [*The Universal*] sponsored a contest to discover new local talent. Perhaps the most famous of those discovered was Jesús Acosta Cabrera, whose humor strip about a disheveled tramp, *Chupamirto* [*Myrtle Sucker*], would continue until its creator's death in 1963.

About 1910 reprints of United States strips began to be published in Argentine magazines, such as *Tit-bits*, and in newspapers; and in 1912 the first Argentine strip, the humorous *Sarrasqueta* by Manuel Redondo, appeared. Noteworthy among the early humor strips was the vastly popular Amos-and-Andy-like strip, *El Negro Raúl* [*The Negro Raul*], created in 1916 by Arturo Lanteri, and Lanteri's long-lived, hilarious family strip, *Don Pancho Talero* (1922–1944). Most Argentine strips of the period followed United States models, but in Argentina central charcters were more likely to be adults than children. Although Brazil launched a major, long-lived publication devoted to the comics before either Argentina or Mexico did, it never developed a comics industry of major importance. *O Ticotico* [*The Brazilian Sparrow*], a comics newspaper, began publication in 1905. It mainly published foreign reprints, such as Richard Outcault's *Buster Brown*, or Brazilian imitations with minor alterations of foreign comics. However, it also published a number of Brazilian comics, for example, J. Carlos's *Lamparina* [*Slap*], a humor strip about the exploits of a black maid. In 1928 São Paulo's *A Gazeta* [*The Gazette*] began publishing a juvenile edition, a color tabloid that reprinted popular American strips, as well as publishing the Brazilian work of important comic creators such as Messias de Mello and Nino Borges.

The period of the late 1920s through the 1940s witnessed major changes. Adventure strips overwhelmed even the popular humor strip. And the comic book was born in the mid-1930s. Humor, funny animals, horror, war, science fiction, romance, adventure, and superheroes—all populated comic strips and books by the late 1930s. As in the earlier period, these United States trends influenced those in Latin America. The period from the late 1930s through the 1940s is referred to as Mexico's "Golden Age" of the comics. Indeed, two of Mexico's best and most influential comics first appeared only a year apart. In 1936 Germán Oliver Butze, who is widely regarded as *the* master among Mexico's comic creators, first published the humorous *Los Supersabios* [*The Superbrains*]; and in 1937 Gabriel Vargas gave us *La Familia Burrón* [*The Donkeyson Family*], a humorous saga about a lower-middle-class Mexico City family, whose hilarious doings still appear to this day. In 1934, the first Mexican comic book, *Paquín* [*Franky*], was published and was quickly followed by a host of imitators. By the late 1930s a few creators and artists began to make a livelihood from their work, but by and large profits and wages were low, and most continuing series had a steady turnover of talent.

The 1928–1949 period was one of tremendous creativity and growth for the comics in Argentina. Raúl Roux, in 1928, initiated the Argentine adventure strip with *El Tigre de los Llanos* [*The Tiger of the Plains*]; and in later decades he would become an outstanding specialist in gaucho comics.

Dante Quinterno's immensely popular humor comic *Patoruzú*, about a Pampas Indian who emulates Popeye and who discovers the urban foibles of Buenos Aires, appeared in 1931 and provided the monetary basis for the creation of a comics empire. The imprudent, mischievous, and childish star of the humor strip *Don Fulgencio*, created by Lino Palacio in 1935, delighted audiences in and out of Argentina for more than 40 years; it is probably Argentina's most popular strip. Guillermo Divito's gag strip, *El Doctor Merengue*, appeared in 1941, followed by Roberto Battaglia's delightful 1945 humor strip *Mangucho y Meneca*. While most of the period's memorable comics are humor strips, a profusion of adventure comics also appeared, the most outstanding being José-Luis Salinas's 1936–1946 *El Corsario Hernán* [*Hernán the Pirate*].

Numerous Argentine publications appeared that showcased the profusion of new comics. Only a few can be noted. In 1928 *El Tony*, the first Argentine magazine totally devoted to comics, began publication. About 1930 Argentine newspapers became seriously interested in the comics, both foreign and Argentine, as a means to increase circulation; and in 1931 the daily *Crítica* [*Criticism*], which already published numerous comics, became the first paper with a comics supplement in color. A major development was the 1935 appearance of the comics magazine *Patoruzú*, which, together with the strip of the same name, provided the financial basis for the creation of Latin America's only comics syndicate, Suraméricas, founded and headed by Quinterno. The influential comics magazine *Pif-Paf*, founded in 1937, introduced the characteristics of the English comics. The high demand for new creations probably accounts for a major innovation about 1945, the appearance of the script writer. Previously the creator both drew and wrote a comic.

The 1929–1949 period in Brazil was not particularly distinguished. A number of important new vehicles for the distribution of the comics, largely foreign reprints, did make their appearance. In 1934 the newspaper *A Nação* [*The Nation*] began an experiment that would be widely copied; it published a tabloid, color supplement, *Suplemento Juvenil* [*Juvenile Supplement*], devoted to the comics. And in one case, the supplement evolved into Brazil's first real comic book, *Gibi Mensal* [*Monthly Comicbook*]. Two Brazilian comics published in these supplements deserve, because of their great popularity, special note: Monteiro Filho's *Robert Sorocaba* and Francisco Armond and Renato Silva's *A Garra Cinzenta* [*The Gray Claw*], both adventure comics.

Nineteen fifty to the present has been a period of major setbacks and also of innovation in the comics. United States strips declined in quality and quantity, and for a time comic books were widely censored. Yet political satire, underground, and Marvel superhero comics flourished. The rest of the world no longer took its cues from United States comics. In Mexico during the contemporary period, while United States reprints did come to dominate newspaper comic strips, just the opposite prevailed in the comic book industry, where Mexican comics greatly outsell American titles. Perhaps the most important innovation during the period was Manuel de Landa's creation in the 1950s of "mini" comic books, pocket-size comics that sold at bargain-basement prices. By the early 1950s, individual artists began to found their own publishing houses. The most successful is undoubtedly Guillermo de la Parra and Yolanda Vargas's Editorial Argumentos, which publishes Mexico's best-selling romance comic, *Lágrimas, risas y amor* [*Tears, Laughter, and Love*]. Among the thousands of titles published since 1950, only a few can be singled out: the political satire comics, *Los Agachados* [*The Stooped Ones*] and *Los Supermachos* [*The Supermachos*], by Eduardo del Río (Rius); the Western *El Payo* [*The Hayseed*], by Guillermo Vigil; the slapstick humor-adventure comic *Chanoc*, by Pedro Zapiáin; the superhero *Kalimán*, Mexico's best-selling comic, by Modesto Vázquez González and Rafael Cutberto Navarro; *Memín Pingüín*, modeled on *Our Gang*, by Yolanda Vargas; Jorge Orlando Ortiz's adventure comic, *Torbellino* [*Whirlwind*]; and the multi-authored detective thriller, *La novela policiaca* [*The Mystery Novel*].

Argentina continues as a major center of comics creativity. The 1960s marked a low point, as several important comics magazines, such as Suraméricas' *Misterix*, folded. But the 1974 publication and great success of *Skorpio* led to the reissuing of defunct comics magazines, such as *Pif-Paf* and *Tit-bits*. In fact, the contemporary period in Argentina is marked by a wealth of outstanding talents and works. Perhaps best known throughout Latin America is *Mafalda* (1965–mid–1970s) by Joaquín Salvador Lavado [Quino]. The strip's main character, a precocious girl, comments upon the foibles and preoccupations of middle-class, bourgeois existence. Several outstanding Westerns also appeared, for example, Alberto Breccia's *Mort Cinder*; Hector Oesterheld and Hugo Pratt's *El sargento Kirk* [*Sergeant Kirk*]; and Roberto Fontanarrosa's *Las aventuras de Inodoro Pereira* [*The Adventures of Inodoro Pereira*], which demystifies Argentina's gaucho past. A fine science fiction strip is Oesterheld's mid-1950s *El Eternauta* [*The Eternalnaut*].

The contemporary period has been Brazil's most important. Before the 1959 publication of the very popular comic *Pererê*, by Alves Pinto [Ziraldo], which contains humorous, insightful reflections on contemporary Brazilian society and culture, it was difficult for writers and artists to earn a living from the comics. Even more successful than *Pererê* have been the comics by Maurício de Sousa. His humorous creations, which appear in the comic books *Mônica* and *Cebolinha* [*Onionette*] and in dozens of newspapers, are distributed all over Brazil by his own publishing firm. Aside from Ziraldo and Maurício de Sousa's creations, comics of note include Daniel Azulay's *Capitão Cipó* [*Captain Liana*], a critique of the superhero genre; Floriano Hermeto's strips, which are influenced by Guido Crepax's *Val-*

entina; Gedeone Malagola's strips, which are modeled on United States comics; and Henfil's black humor strips, with their right-on-the mark critiques of Brazilian customs.

Elsewhere in Latin America, even for the contemporary period, the historical record is mostly blank concerning comics, with the partial exceptions of Peru, Colombia, Cuba, and Chile. Juan Acevedo's Peruvian consciousness-raising comic *Cuy* [an indigenous rodent], is an incisive critique of Disney's Mickey Mouse comics. In Colombia, Ernesto Franco's humor strip, *Copetín* [*Half-pint*], chronicles the struggle for survival of a group of street waifs. In Cuba a paper shortage, especially of paper suitable for cheap, four-color printing, has prevented the development of a nationally distributed mass comics magazine. Comic strips, though, have appeared in various magazines, the best known of which is undoubtedly *Gugulandia*, by "Hernán H." It occupies the back page of *Dedeté* [*DDT*] and, like Johnny Hart's *B.C.*, it uses a prehistoric setting to critique contemporary civilization. During the Salvador Allende administration (1970–1973) in Chile, the government took over the Zig-Zag publishing corporation, which published most of Chile's pre-Allende comics, and which remains unstudied. Zig-Zag was renamed Quimantú and for two years published comics reflecting the administration's ideology, the best of which were the children's comic book *Cabro Chico* [*Little Kid*] and the adult comic *La Firme* [*Steadfast*].

GUIDE TO THE LITERATURE

Background Works

For the novice in the field of comics research, there are a number of English-language studies available. Inge's superb "Comic Art," which provides a brief history of the comics and bibliographic essays on reference works, research collections, historical and critical works, and anthologies and reprints, is the place to begin. The only work with a serious attempt at world-wide coverage is *The World Encyclopedia of Comics*, edited by Horn, which provides short entries on artists, writers, and individual strips or comic books or their central character(s). Although flawed, the best introduction to comics that attempts to relate them to their social context and to developments in other mass media is Reitberger and Fuchs's *Comics*. A short illustrated history of both strips and books is provided by Perry and Aldridge in *The Penguin Book of Comics*. Among useful works largely devoted to the study of comic strips are White and Abel, eds., *The Funnies*, which is particularly interested in the relationships between strips and culture; Couperie, et al., *A History of the Comic Strip*, which is especially good on the aesthetics, structure, and symbolism of strips; and Robinson, *The Comics*, which provides a well-illustrated capsule historical survey, together with essays by artists on their work. Useful studies primarily restricted to a study of comic books are Daniels, *Comix*, the best general introduction, although stronger on narrative content than art; Steranko, *The Steranko History of Comics*, largely devoted to superhero comics, and especially fine for its comments on art; Lupoff and Thompson, eds., *The Comic-Book Book* and *All in Color for a Dime*, collections of essays that assess comic book superheroes with a fan's enthusiasm and critical insight; Feiffer, *The Great Comic Book Heroes: The Origins and Early Adventures of the Classic Super-Heroes of the Comic Books—In Glorious Color*, which is a brief introduction; and Estren, *A History of Underground Comics*, the best introduction to those comics that rejected the stifling Comics Code Authority.

While Latin American scholars do on occasion cite English-language works, there exists a corpus of works published in Spain that are generally more available to Latin Americans. A broad overview of the history of comics and photonovels, combined with a sociological and formal analysis, is Gubern's *Literatura de la imagen* [*Pictorial Literature*]. Introductory coverage is also provided by Coma, *Los cómics* [*The Comics*], which surveys the means of distribution of comics, their art form, and their sociological and ideological content; and by Gasca's ambitious series of essays, *Tebeo y cultura de masas* [*Comics and Mass Culture*], devoted to the antecedents of comics, the influence of comics on literature, adult comics, pop art and comics, the use of comics to promote commercial products, the politicization of comics, similarities and influences between the cinema and comics, and the use of comics for didactic purposes. Several monographs offer excellent historical analyses. Coma's *Del gato Félix al gato Fritz* [*From Felix the Cat to Fritz the Cat*] is a superb general history of comics. Gasca, *Los cómics en España* [*The Comics in Spain*] is a profusely illustrated, scholarly history of Spain's comics. More specialized studies of comics in Spain include Martín's detailed, illustrated history of comics up to General Francisco Franco's dictatorship, *Historia del cómic español: 1875–1939* [*History of Spanish Comics: 1875–1939*]; Ramírez's study of post World War II humor comics, *La historieta cómic de postguerra* [*The Post-War Funnies*], with its extensive attention to the comics' creators and artists and brief examination of their sales and distribution; Ramírez's study of comics read by women between about 1940 and 1970, *El 'cómic' femenino en España* [*The Woman's Comic in Spain*], which especially focuses on developing a typology of comics based on narrative content and images, on types of plot development and resolution, on circulation, and on the relationship between the comics and socioeconomic and cultural trends; and Fernández and Vigil's *El cómix marginal español* [*Spain's Under-Ground Comix*], which combines interviews with artists of underground comics and examples of their works.

European general histories of a specific country's comics, genre studies, and period histories have found few Latin American imitators; but very general surveys—especially of United States and European comics—and more theoretical and analytical studies of form and ideological content have been imitated, and two books in particular have been immensely influential. Gubern's *El lenguaje de los cómics* [*The Language of Comics*] is a masterful general introduction—indeed, the best in Spanish—to the origins and development of comics, their production and distribution, and to sociological and semiological methods of analyzing them. Perhaps even more frequently cited by Latin American investigators is the eminent Italian scholar Eco, and, in particular, his collection of essays *Apocalípticos e integrados ante la cultura de masas* [*Attitudes of the Doomsayers and the Well-Adjusted toward Mass Culture*]. Eco's close reading of narrative and visual elements in individual frames and in sequences and especially his application of cinema techniques and semiology to the study of comics have been widely imitated and expanded upon by Latin Americans.

Besides these two seminal works, a number of other European studies available in Spanish and with a more theoretical bent are worth noting. Moix's *Los 'cómics'* [*The Comics*] probes the relationship between comics and other "pop" phenomena and the evolution of mythical archetypes in comics. Essays by Allegri, Calabrese, and Lutzemberger and Bernardi in *Cultura, comunicación de masas y lucha de clases* [*Culture, Mass Communication, and Class Conflict*] are noteworthy; respectively, they discuss narrative structures in comics, Italian "negro-crótica" adult] comics, and the construction of an alternative language for the comics. Baur's *La historieta como experiencia didáctica* [*The Comics as Educational Experience*] is an in-depth study of the Dutch-German comic *Bessy*, which stars a collie dog in a Wild West setting. *Bessy* is studied as a system of signs to convey various meanings (a modified use of the system of semiological analysis developed by Roland Barthes) and as a conveyor of ideological and economic messages. Baur then advances a method to teach secondary students how to analyze other comics in a similar manner. A more general theoretical approach to the semiological analysis of comics is Fresnault-Deruelle's essay "Lo verbal en las historietas" ["Language in the Comics"]. And finally, a study worth noting is Trabant's "Supermán," which is a detailed study of a sample of consumers of comics aged 10 and 11. It especially studies their reading habits; their attitudes toward comics; and their reaction, as measured by a "semantic differential" test, toward *Superman* comics' images and messages.

There exists no useful bibliographic guide, either general or more specialized, to published literature concerned with Latin American comics. Miller's annotated bibliography on popular Latin American "Graphics" includes comics, but barely scratches the surface. Kempkes's *International Bibliography of Comics Literature* has sections on forerunners, structure of comics, commercial aspects, readership and opinions, effects, use for educational purposes, use in related forms of expression, and judicial and other limiting measures against comics, but it contains few references to published studies on any aspect of Latin American comics. To date, the best guides remain the bibliographies appended to many of the monographs cited in this chapter.

A few biographical dictionaries have been compiled, but each has marked limitations. Horn's *The World Encyclopedia of Comics* includes multiple entries only for Mexico and Argentina, and even then coverage is spotty: for example, Mexico's leading superhero and romance comics, *Kalimán* and *Lágrimas, risas y amor* [*Tears, Laughter and Love*], are not included. The issue of *Artes de México* [*Mexican Arts*] devoted to "La historieta mexicana" ["The Mexican Comic"] is basically an illustrated biographical dictionary. Most of Mexico's creators and artists of comics are noted with brief biographies and a sample of their most famous work, but entries frequently fail to give pertinent information, such as dates and places of publication for works mentioned. Fossati's *Il fumetto argentino* [*The Argentine Cartoon*], a biographical dictionary of creators of Argentine cartoons, caricatures, comic strips, and comic books, also has serious limitations. No criteria for selection are provided, except that artists with Italian distribution received special priority. With few exceptions, pre-1940 artists and works are omitted. On the other hand, those artists and works noted are provided entries that frequently both evaluate artwork and narrative and trace patterns of influence. Further critical evaluation of Fossati's book is provided in Lindstrom's review essay "Latin American Cartooning." To these biographical dictionaries could be added Mexico's periodical *SNIF*, which lasted for only five numbers but provided a limited number of biographical sketches, together with extensive examples of creators' and artists' work: for example, creations of the Italian-Argentine Hugo Pratt and the Mexicans Víctor Uhthoff and Daniel Rossell.

Fanzines are also good sources of information about individual titles and their creators. Unfortunately, Mexico's only fanzine, *Motus Liber*, lasted for only one number, although the group that produced it continues to meet occasionally under the direction of Carlos Vigil, director of the publishing firm Editora Senda. In Argentina, informative columns by Carlos Trillo and Guillermo Saccomanno contain information on comic strips and comic books. Their columns are published by the Buenos Aires firm of Ediciones Record and appear under the headings of "La club de la historieta" ["The Comics Club"] in *Skorpio* and "Introducción a la historieta argentina" ["Introduction to the Argentine Comic"] in *Tit-bits*.

Conference proceedings and exposition catalogues may also provide basic source material on comics, but both types of literature have appeared very infrequently in Latin America. Examples of this type of literature's possibilities for the study of comics are provided by the 1968 catalogue of a Buenos Aires exposition, *La historieta mundial* [*The World's Comics*], and by Salomón's *El humor y las historietas que leyó el argentino* [*Humor and Comics Read by Argentines*], published biannually as a record of the Congreso Bianual de la Historieta de Córdoba [The Cordoba Biannual Congress of Comics].

Theoretical and General Approaches to the Study of Comics

The single most influential work on comics written in Latin America is without doubt Dorfman and Mattelart's *How to Read Donald Duck: Imperialist Ideology in the Disney Comic*. In a Marxist analysis, based on a close reading of the narrative text of a sample of comics sold in Chile, the authors conclude that Donald Duck is not just an innocent and socially harmless children's delight, but the embodiment of capitalist values and social oppression. Disney's messages (which are succinctly listed in Flora's "Roasting Donald Duck") and their penetration into dependent countries need to be carefully exposed, according to the authors. Their approach essentially ignores semiology or the idea that comics are composed of a system of signs to convey meanings and focuses instead on narrative more than visual elements.

This general approach is encountered in several other studies that also use either a Marxist/dependency mode of analysis or a more narrowly-focused class-based analysis. Montalvo's *Ensayos marxistas sobre los 'cómics'* [*Marxist Essays on the Comics*] is a rather pedestrian collection of essays, which predictably argues that United States comics reflect the commercial-bourgeois-industrial culture that produced them and that they represent a nefarious neocolonialism in their considerable penetration into the Third World. Two important exceptions to the generally ho-hum level of analysis in the collection are Jorge Vergara's essay, which contributes an important critical analysis of some twenty-one United States comics, most of which have been ignored by others influenced by Dorfman and Mattelart, and Montalvo's article, which analyzes the Colombian comic strip "Copetín" and concludes that the strip's philosophy parallels that of the bourgeois paper, *El Tiempo* [*The Times*], that prints it.

Dorfman further applied the *How to Read Donald Duck* approach in the book he co-authored with Jofré, *Supermán y sus amigos del alma* [*Superman and His Bosom Buddies*]. In addition to a reading of the Lone Ranger stories, he analyzed the Chilean comic strip *Mampato*, which he concluded was a mythic parable that paralleled the destruction of the Allende regime. His essay on *Mampato* also appears in *Reader's nuestro que estás en la tierra* [*Our Readers Who Art on Earth*], and in English translation in *The Empire's Old Clothes*. Vergara's "Comics y relaciones mercantiles" ["Comics and Commercial Relations"] and Bardini and Serafine's "La 'inocencia' de la historieta" ["The Comics' 'Innocence' "] are Marxist interpretations of United States comics and comics in general and are both clearly indebted to Dorfman-Mattelart, as is Herner's profusely illustrated *Mitos y monitos* [*Myths and the Funnies*]. Herner catalogues the basic narrative and visual structures of the comics, analyzes the capitalist-bour-geois-controlled production and distribution of Mexican comics, and in particular provides a Marxist reading of both United States and Mexican comics' contents. Curiously, Ludovico Silva's chapter on the comics in his 1971 *Teoría y práctica de la ideología* [*Theory and Practice of Ideology*] is a Marxist study of the ideological content of several United States comics, including Donald Duck; but in spite of the marked parallels between his analytic approach and that of Dorman and Mattelart, neither evidently knew of the work of the other.

There is also a group of studies that clearly applies Marxist-dependency analysis but is somewhat less strident and deterministic in doing so—al-though other reviewers might well group these works with those already discussed. The research group (originally under the direction of Jean C. Simard and now under Georges-A. Parent) at Laval University in Quebec has been particularly interested in the relationship between the structure of capitalist-bourgeois production of Mexican comics and their ideological content. The group's preliminary conclusions are found in Simard and Jarque's 1976 report to the Canadian Council of Arts and are also sum-marized more recently in Jarque's "La paraliteratura" ["Paraliterature"]. Both tend more toward theoretical discussion than toward analysis of em-pirical data.

Erreguerena, in a brief essay on the Mexican Western comic book *El Payo*, concludes that, despite first impressions, its apparently revolutionary content does not escape the influence of its bourgeois origin. Palacios Franco's thesis on the Mexican adventure comic book *Torbellino*, while using a Marxist framework of analysis, concludes that this comic is some-what progressive, from the point of view of the lower classes, despite its bourgeois origin. Gallo, in *Los cómics* [*The Comics*], also sees most comics as industrial-bourgeois-imperialist products but argues against a knee-jerk Marxist analysis and notes that there are important exceptions. Gallo's book is a hodgepodge of information, and more concerned with narrative content than iconographic elements, but it is worthy of consideration.

Largely because of the influence of Eco, semiological studies of the comics by Latin Americans have been nearly as popular as Marxist-de-pendency ones. Taken together, these studies do not appear to extend our understanding of semiological analysis, but they do either summarize this approach or routinely apply the theory to a particular body of popular literature. Studies that semiotically analyze a narrowly defined group of comics include Cornejo, on the political comic books of Rius (Eduardo del Río); Gauthier on *Peanuts'* Linus; Cirne on avant-garde comics, in-cluding Brazilian examples, in *Vanguarda* [*Vanguard*]; and Steimberg on the French comic strip *Lucky Luke*, and also on comics that are renditions of literary works in *Leyendo historietas* [*Reading Comics*]. More general applications of semiotics to the study of comics include a semiological study of the comics industry in Carlos Montalvo's *Ensayos marxistas*; a chapter on how comics teach us to think in Steimberg's book; Alfie's essay on the semiology of comics; and Cirne's frequent use of semiotics in *Para ler os quadrinhos* [*How to Read the Funnies*].

A variety of other theoretical and analytical approaches have been advanced for the study of comics. Vázquez González, in *La Historiética* [*The Comic Book Compendium*], argues that the semiotic and semantic analysis is unfathomable and then offers an illustrated catalogue of language specific to the comics that, while nearly encyclopedic in coverage, is difficult to follow because of his penchant for coining convoluted neologisms. Horn, in his review essay "Recent Mexican Scholarship on Comics," offers further comment on Vázquez González's efforts. Parent offers a "Focalization: A Narratological Approach to Mexican Illustrated Stories," which closely follows Gérard Genette's theories on narrative discourse. Prieto Castillo, in *Retórica y manipulación masiva* [*Rhetoric and Mass Manipulation*], applies the rules of rhetoric to the mass media, including Mexican comics. Pareja's *El nuevo lenguaje del cómic* [*The Comics' New Language*] observes that the narrative structure of comics is now decisively influenced by television and especially by television commercials. The use of the comics' more popular characters to advertise commercial products in children's magazines sold in Chile in 1971 is examined by Gastón in *La propaganda dirigida a los niños* [*Propaganda Directed at Children*]. The theories of D. McClelland on the achievement motive are applied to a group of comics sold in Panama in "Motivación al logro y motivación al poder en el contenido de historietas populares" ["Achievement Motivation and Power Motivation in the Content of Popular Comics"] by Escovar and Escovar. A feminist critique of the semipornographic Mexican comic, *El caballo del diablo:* Un estudio de caso [*"The Devil's Horse:* A Case Study"] is advanced by Guillermoprieto. Solórzano offers a broad-gauged psychological rendering of the comics; Katz uses Martin Heidegger's ideas to raise questions concerning the comics' relation to ideology, socioeconomic systems and aesthetics, and to critique theories of Cirne and Eco; and Massart, in "Literatura y paraliteratura" ["Literature and Paraliterature"], advances a method for the sociological study of young people's popular literature.

There are a number of rather general studies of comics that should be noted, but which do not fit easily into the categories given here. Ossa's *El mundo de la historieta* [*The World of Comics*] is a broadly sketched historical overview of the comics. Other basic introductions, either to comics in general or to an informed reading of their narrative and visual structures, include Alvarez Constantino's various editions of *La magia de los 'cómics'* [*The Magic of the Comics*], the later version of which is commented on in Foster's review essay, "Recent Works on Latin American Cartoon Art";

the chapter on "Los poderes de la historieta" ["The Comics' Powers"] in Steimberg's *Leyendo historietas*; the collection of essays, *Shazam!*, edited by de Moya; Cirne's *Para ler os quadrinhos* and *Bum!* [*Boom!*]; Cagnin's *Os quadrinhos*; and Baêta Neves's "Críticas às leituras formalistas da ideologia" ["Critiques on Formalist Readings of Ideology"]. Sweeping overviews of the Mexican comics scene are contained in essays by Sewell and Gutiérrez Vega and in "Los Supermachos" ["The Supermachos"]. Herner, in "El museo y la historieta" ["The Museum and the Comics"], offers a rationale for why comics are now regarded as works of art.

SOURCES ON THE HISTORY OF LATIN AMERICAN COMICS

There exists no general history of Latin American comics or of comics in any Latin American country except Argentina. A wide variety of sources offer very sketchy historical overviews of Mexican comics. In particular, see Aurrecoechea, "La historieta mexicana" ["The Mexican Comic"]; Monsiváis, "Impresiones sobre la cultura popular urbana en México" ["Impressions on Mexican Urban Culture"]; González, "Entrevista con Carlos Monsiváis" ["Interview with Carlos Monsiváis"]; de Valdés, "Crónica general de la historieta" ["General Chronicle of the Comics"]; del Río (Rius), *La vida de cuadritos* [*The Life of Small Frames*] and "Las historietas" ["The Comics"]; Siller, "Historia de la historieta" ["History of the Comics"]; Herner, *Mitos y monitos*; and Trejo, "La historieta mexicana." Coverage for Brazil is equally sketchy, but partial coverage is provided by material in Cirne's *A linguagem dos quadrinhos* [*The Comics' Language*], *Vanguarda*, and "Os novos quadrinhos brasileiros" ["New Brazilian Comics"]; de Moya, *Shazam!*; and Anselmo, *Histórias em quadrinhos* [*Stories in Comics*]. Coverage for Chile has been provided only for the period of the Salvador Allende government (1970–1973). Good to excellent critical surveys are found in Dorfman and Jofré, *Supermán y sus amigos del alma*; Nómez, "La historieta en el proceso de cambio social" ["Comics during the Process of Social Change"]; and Kunzle, "Art of the New Chile." Cuban comics have been studied only for the period of the Cuban Revolution and then only in Kunzle, "Public Graphics in Cuba." Brief notice of a number of comics, that is, a vague attempt at multicountry historical coverage, can be found in *SNIF*; Ossa, *El mundo de la historieta;* and Gallo, *Los cómics.*

The best two histories are both on Argentina. Bróccoli and Trillo's *Las Historietas* [*The Comics*] is a well-illustrated, coherent history of both comic strips and books from 1901 through the 1960s. (A useful companion to this volume is provided by the same authors' history of Argentine cartoon art in Trillo and Bróccoli, *El humor gráfico* [*Graphic Humor*].) The best history is undoubtedly Trillo and Saccomanno's illustrated *Historia de la historieta argentina* [*History of the Argentine Comic*], which offers coverage from the turn of the century on for all types of comics, as well as for cartoons, and includes interviews with artists and detailed reviews of major comics. Unfortunately, the encyclopedic coverage is more anecdotal than analytical, the volume contains numerous printing errors, and at times it is more like a fanzine than a professional history. See Foster's review essay for a more detailed review of this fundamental history. Further partial coverage of Argentine comics can be obtained from Fossati, *Il fumetto argentino*; Masotta, *La historieta en el mundo moderno* [*Comics in the Modern World*]; Steimberg, *Leyendo historietas*; Coma, *Del gato Félix al gato Fritz*; Bardini and Serafini, "La 'inocencia' de la historieta"; Ossa, *El mundo de la historieta*; and Roque, "Resurgimiento de la historieta argentina" ["Resurgence of the Argentine Comic"].

Creation, Production, Distribution, and Consumption of Latin American Comics

Several "how-to" manuals give insights into the artists' creation of comics. Llobera's *Dibujo del 'comic'* [*"Comic" illustration*] is a practical guide to the step-by-step drawing and scripting of a comic. Lipszyc and Vieytes's how-to manual, *Técnica de la historieta* [*Technique of the Comics*], is lavishly illustrated, including illustrations by many Argentine comics artists, and stresses the basics and how to develop one's own style. Del Río [Rius] offers humorous tips on how to make a comic in his *La vida de cuadritos*. An example of a completed narrative script, with instructions to the artist(s), is contained in Vigil, *El Payo*. Perhaps the best how-to manual is Acevedo's *Para hacer historietas* [*How to Make Comics*], which provides a detailed guide to the artistic creation of a comic. It is well illustrated, includes examples of Latin American comics artists' work, and is intended as a guide to the creation of alternative, populist comics. The most detailed breakdown of the processes involved in creating a comic and a profusely illustrated volume is Vázquez González, *La Historiética*. However, its usefulness is limited, since it relies entirely on examples from one company, Promotora K, which is headed by Vázquez González, and since it only describes the team approach to creating comics.

The conditions under which artists work and the editorial houses that produce or manufacture comics are little studied. Work conditions are described in Cardoso and Ortiz, "Autoentrevista" ["Self-interview"]; Herner, *Mitos y monitos*; and Vázquez González, *La Historiética*. Government censorship is detailed critically in Silva O., "Un asunto censurable, la censura" ["A Censurable Subject: Censorship"]; with enthusiastic approval in Vázquez González, *La Historiética*, which gives all the appropriate texts of laws regulating the industry; and caustically and with graphic examples in Vigil, *El Payo*. *SNIF*, show-cases outstanding strips in the hopes that Mexican comics will be upgraded. *SNIF* also includes critical commentary on the generally poor quality of art work in Reynoso, "Una mancha en un cómic" ["A Blot on a Comic"], and on the problem of plagiarism in "Del plagio como una de las bellas artes" ["Plagiarism as One of the Fine Arts"]. Data on Brazilian publishers of comics is found in Anselmo, *Histórias em quadrinhos*, and Enrique Lipszyc, "Publicaçaões brasileiras de histórias em quadrinhos" ["Brazilian Comics Publications"]; on Mexican publishers in Herner, *Mitos y monitos*; and on Argentine publishing firms in Trillo and Saccomanno, *Historia de la historieta argentina*.

Who produces comics, it is often argued, does make a difference. The argument that bourgeois control of the means of production means products that promote the interests of the bourgeoisie is advanced by many critics already mentioned, most notably, by Simard, Jarque, and Herner. Yet all of these fail to make careful distinctions between those who create the product, those who absorb the risks of production, and those who distribute the finished product. Indeed, the only sophisticated, careful consideration of these factors is in Flora's "Roasting Donald Duck."

Very little attention has been focused on how the finished product is distributed and the consequences of different means of distribution. Parlato et al., *Fotonovelas and Comic Books*, in a late 1970s survey, found essentially no data on distribution. Since then, Herner, in *Mitos y monitos*, has described the Mexican commercial distribution system and has provided sales data for most Mexican comic books; and Flora carefully considers different means of distribution in her model of developmental paths in alternative comics and photonovels in "Roasting Donald Duck."

The comics' audience has also been largely neglected. In fact, while nearly every study speculates about who reads comics, only a few have actually interviewed the medium's consumers. As part of a study of "Mexican Children's Use of the Mass Media," Rota interviewed forty-six children in fourth to sixth grades. He identified some forty needs in the children but found that they did not select comics as the preferred medium to gratify any of these needs. Mexican fourth to sixth grade students were also surveyed—some 3,300 of them—by Alvarez Constantino. Kids were asked why they liked comics, which comics they read most frequently, and how often they purchased comics; and preferences for United States comic-book heroes and Mexican historical figures were compared. Unfortunately, the presentation of this data in *La magia de los 'cómics'* is sufficiently unclear and unsystematic to make it difficult to use. In an appendix to *El cómic o la historieta en la enseñanza* [*The Comic Strip and Comic Book in Education*], Guerra summarizes a survey of Mexican secondary students. They were asked about their comic-book reading habits, and their answers form the basis of the author's plea that students be taught how to read comics critically. Alarcón also presents the findings of a survey of the reading habits of Mexican secondary students, including comics, in *El habla popular de los jóvenes en la ciudad de México* [*Popular Speech of Mexico City Youth*]. Undoubtedly the most thorough and sophisticated survey and study of adolescent consumption of comics and their opinion about them is presented in the second part of Anselmo's *Histórias em quadrinhos*. Also especially enlightening is Jacob's description of lower-class, Guatemala City childrens' comic-book trading groups and networks and the results of his media recognition questionnaire, which included both United States and Mexican comic-book personalities. Jacob's findings are most fully presented in his Ph.D. dissertation and summarized in "Urban Poverty, Children, and the Consumption of Popular Culture." The utility of the messages in educational comic books is evaluated in *Evaluation of the Effectiveness of Illustrated Print Media (Nonverbal) on Family Planning Attitudes among Colombians* and in Vigano, "Estudio sobre aceptación y efectividad de las fotonovelas e historietas en la comunicación de conocimientos en áreas rurales de Guatemala" ["Study of the Acceptance and Effectiveness of Photonovels and Comics in Communicating Knowledge in Rural Guatemala"].

Latin American Studies of United States Comics

The fact that Eco chose to provide an in-depth analysis of *Steve Canyon, Superman*, and Charlie Brown in *Apocalípticos*; that Dorfman and Mattelart studied Donald Duck; and that Dorfman analyzed the Lone Ranger in *Supermán* had an important impact on the study of comics by Latin Americans. Indeed, there are nearly as many, if not more, studies on United States comics, as on home-grown varieties. Del Río [Rius] in *La vida de cuadritos* and in "Las historietas" ["The Comics"], Masotta in *La historieta en el mundo moderno*, and Lipszyc in *Técnica de la historieta*— all provided historical surveys of United States comics. More than cursory examinations of individual titles or genres include a chapter in Montalvo's *Ensayos marxistas* on Disney comics; Gallo's essay on Marvel superheroes in *SNIF*; Steimberg's chapters on *Li'l Abner* and *The Little King* in *Leyendo historietas*; Masotta's chapter on *Dick Tracy* in *La historieta*; Luz's article on Tarzan and Serra's on *The Phantom*, both in *Revista de Cultura Vozes* [*Review of Cultural Voices*]; and a chapter on *The Phantom* in de Moya's *Shazam!* Many of these studies, while admiring the technical finesse of United States comics, are also quite critical of their ideological content. Given this fascination with United States comics, it is strange that few note that not all "United States" comics sold are in fact translations of stories written by Americans; but rather in some cases, they are stories written by Latin Americans that never appear in English-language editions. Concerning this, see especially Patten's discussion of *Blackhawk* comics in "Superman South. Part II."

Latin American Studies of Latin American Comics

Few studies have attempted to advance any sort of classification scheme for comics, and those that have been suggested are not particularly well developed. Semard and Jarque, in their preliminary report, classify Mexican comic books based on physical characteristics and sales. Herner, in *Mitos y monitos*, suggests a broad thematic division, as do Alvarez Constantino in *La magia* and Vázquez González in *La Historiética*, differentiating between adventure and romance comics based on art styles. And Acosta and Delhumeau divided comics into translations of United States comics, Latin versions of United States products, and largely original Latin American creations. Both Acosta and Delhumeau offer some surprising examples for the latter two categories that should be carefully considered.

There are a growing number of chapter- or article-length studies of individual titles, genres, or themes, the largest number being on Mexican products. For Mexico, Hinds has described and analyzed Guillermo Vigil's Western comic book *El Payo*, the multi-authored amateur detective thriller *La novela policiaca* [*The Mystery Novel*], Pedro Zapiáin's adventure comic book *Chanoc*, the multi-authored horror comic book *Tradiciones y leyendas de la colonia* [*Colonial Traditions and Legends*], Modesto Vázquez González and Rafael Cutberto Navarro's superhero comic book *Kalimán*, and the anonymous adventure comic *Arandú* (in the essay titled "Comics"). Hinds and Tatum have analyzed "Images of Women in Mexican Comic Books"; and Tatum has studied Yolanda Vargas Dulché and Guillermo de la Parra's romance comic book *Lágrimas, risas y amor*, as has Reséndiz in "El mito de Rarotonga" ["The Myth of Rarotonga"]. Other scholarly articles on Mexican comics include Guillermoprieto on the horror comic book *El caballo del diablo*, Vigil on Germán Butze's humor comic *Los Supersabios* [*The Wise Guys*], Mejía on Yolanda Vargas Dulché's humor comic book *Memín Pingüín*, Palacios Franco on Jorge Orlando Ortiz's adventure comic book *Torbellino*, Hunt and LaFrance on Palomo's political comic strip "El Cuarto Reich" ["The Fourth Reich"], Simard and Jarque on the multi-authored romance comic book *El libro semanal* [*The Weekly Novel*] (in their preliminary report), Steele on the adventure-romance comic book *Sangre india: Chamula* [*Indian Blood: Chamula*], and Patten on Mexican superhero comic books.

A chapter in Montalvo et al. *Ensayos marxistas* is devoted to Ernesto Franco's Colombian comic strip, *Copetín*, about a street waif and his gang. Dorman analyzes the futuristic Chilean adventure comic strip *Mampato* in chapters in *Reader's nuestro* and *The Empire's Old Clothes*. Steimberg has contributed a study of Dante Quinterno's Argentine humor strip and comic book about the good Indian confronted by civilization, *Patoruzú*, in a chapter in *Leyendo historietas*, which is reprinted in Masotta's *La historieta*. Other studies worthy of note on Argentine comics include discussions of

Héctor Oesterheld and Hugo Pratt's adventure strip *Ticonderoga* and of Alberto Breccia's adventure strip *Mort Cinder* in Masotta's *La historieta* and of Eduardo Ferro's humor comic strip *Langostino* [*Crawfish*], discussed in Steimberg's book. For Brazil there are excellent articles on *Pereré* by Alves Pinto [Ziraldo] and *Mônica* by Mauricio de Sousa; both are humor comic books and are extensively analyzed in Cirne, *A linguagem*.

While most comic strips and books have never attracted serious scholarly appraisal, a few, mostly political comics, have received disproportionate attention. The Argentine humor comic strip *Mafalda*, created by Joaquín Salvador Lavado [Quino], stars an acutely sensitive little girl who comments on national foibles and pretensions. Foster, in two articles, has analyzed *Mafalda* from a literary, sociological, and semiological point of view. Steimberg, in a chapter in *Leyendo historietas*, provides a broad overview of the strip; the essay by Escobar et al. in *El cómic es algo serio* [*The Comics Should Be Taken Seriously*] compares *Mafalda* and *Peanuts*; and Cirne's article in *Revista de Cultura Vozes* provides a semiological and ideological reading of the strip. The most important work on *Mafalda* is Hernández's controversial monograph *Para leer a Mafalda* [*How to Read Mafalda*]. Hernández reads *Mafalda* from a Peronist perspective and views it as a timid, bourgeois critique that suffers from a false liberalism and a pro-imperialist attitude.

Mexico's Eduardo del Río [Rius], creator of the political comic books *Los Supermachos* and *Los Agachados* [*The Stooped Ones*] and author of numerous illustrated books, has also attracted a great deal of attention. Interviews with Rius have been published by Herner in *Mitos y monitos*, by Tatum and Hinds in *Chasqui*, and by Proctor as an appendix to her Ph.D. dissertation. Tatum analytically describes Rius's comic-book work in articles in *Praxis* and *Iberoamericana*. Rius's use of satire is probed by Speck, and two semiological analyses of his comic books are offered by Cornejo. The most thorough study is Proctor's "Mexico's *Supermachos*: Satire and Social Revolution in Comics by Rius." Drawing on the first one hundred numbers of *Los Supermachos*, Proctor illustrates Rius's cartoon style and introduces his mythical town of San Garabato and its principal characters, then describes his satires on the Mexican Revolution, *machismo*, various types of institutional reform and traditional protest, and Mexican-Americans. Rius has had a host of imitators, all far less successful than he, and they are catalogued in Barta, "El fenómeno Rius" ["The Rius Phenomenon"].

Comics published during Salvador Allende's government (1970–1973) have also been a popular topic for commentators. When the Allende government took over the bankrupt publishing house of Zig-Zag and renamed it Quimantú, new comic books were created to reflect government philosophy, and in many cases old titles were altered to instill socialist values.

Nómez and Jofré have both described the varying fates and alterations of Zig-Zag's titles under Quimantú's stewardship. *La Firme*, a political comic book that revealed the political, social, and economic condition of Third World countries such as Chile, is generally introduced by Woll; and an intensive analysis of three different numbers of *La Firme* is contained in Kunzle's essays for *Praxis* and *Latin American Perspectives*. A close analysis of the firm's juvenile comic book, *Cabro Chico* [*Little Kid*] and brief descriptions of several adult adventure comic books are found in Kunzle, "Art of the New Chile."

Avant-garde comics—also referred to as comix or marginal, underground, or vanguard comics—are infrequently commented upon. *Garrapata* [*Cattle Tick*], a Mexican magazine that includes both political and avant-garde cartoons and comic strips, is briefly reviewed in Barata's "De monitos: Del cartón a la historieta" ["About Little Figures: From Cartoon Paper to Comics"]; and Rius in *La vida de cuadritos* provides samples of avant-garde work from *Garrapata*. Cirne, in *Vanguarda*, reviews a large number of avant-garde comic strips published in Brazil after 1960, with a special emphasis on those dated 1968 and after.

Comics, in large part because of the popularity of the genre, have been widely used in Latin America not only for commercial purposes, but also for education. For example, some church groups have adopted comics to better explain their messages, and one such attempt is described in Dineen, "Catechetics in Comics." Imitators of Rius, as catalogued by Barta, have attempted to use his comic-book style to advance government, commercial, and leftist causes. Jiménez Codinach, in "Historia e historieta" ["History and Comics"], describes the Mexican government's attempt to create a historically accurate educational comic book, *Episodios Mexicanos* [*Mexican Episodes*]. So that school children can read comics critically and then construct their own alternative comics, Fernández Paz, in *Cuadernos de Pedagogías* [*Pedagogical Notes*], offers a model to achieve these goals. As well as they could, the team of Parlato, Parlato, and Cain catalogued the use of comic books to promote educational and developmental goals around the world, and they discuss several Latin American examples in *Fotonovelas and Comic Books*. And Flora in "Roasting Donald Duck" describes a variety of alternative comics used to advance particular "alternative" messages. Her essay is particularly valuable for its close attention to risk factors involved in creation and distribution of these comics.

A variant on explicitly educational comics is the use of comics in the classroom to teach Spanish. Carrillo describes the use of Rius's political comics as teaching material in bilingual classes in the United States. Hall and Lafourcade, using Chilean examples, have authored "Teaching Aspects of Foreign Culture through Comic Strips," and Hall, who teaches in the Department of Spanish and Portuguese at Brigham Young University, has developed an impressive set of Spanish lessons using the Chilean humor comic strip and comic book *Condorito* [*Little Condor*], created by René Ríos (Pepo).

RESEARCH COLLECTIONS AND CENTERS

There are no research collections or centers for the study of the comics known to this reviewer. Trillo and Saccomanno note, in the prologue to their *Historia de la historieta argentina*, that for Argentine comics there simply are no archives or organized collections in libraries. For Mexico the situation is identical, although the national periodical library, the Hemeroteca Nacional, has a marvelous, well-catalogued newspaper collection. The Hemeroteca has collected comic books for many years, but the comic-book collection has only been catalogued for the last few years. Should it ever become catalogued and accessible, it will undoubtedly constitute the single most important comic-book research collection in Latin America.

Few comic-book or newspaper publishing houses maintain useful research collections, either because they have failed to retain back issues, because their archives are so disorganized as to prevent use by visiting scholars with limited time, or because they will not allow access to their archives. There do exist, however, a number of accessible, well-organized company archives, most of which remain untapped.

Private collections, assembled over the years by avid fans, do exist, but it is often difficult to locate them due to the lack of well-organized networks and organizations of fans and collectors. Generally, this approach would probably fare better in Argentina and Brazil than in Mexico.

The secondhand market for comic books can, with luck, provide a gold mine of material, often at very low prices. By their nature, secondhand shops are hard to find, since they are often tucked away on back streets of poor neighborhoods. The problem here, of course, is discovering these caches before the comics literally fall apart from multiple rereadings and resales.

For comic strips, the key resource is back files of newspapers. For a discussion of their general accessibility, see the chapter on newspapers in this collection. Without a doubt, newspaper collections remain the most accessible and untapped source for the study of comics.

POSSIBILITIES FOR FUTURE RESEARCH

There is a great need for catalogues of comic-book collections, especially of the collection in Mexico's Hemeroteca Nacional, as well as for detailed guides to newspaper collections. Any guide to comics that provided such basic information as title, dates published, publisher, and creators/artists would be very useful, as would a biographical dictionary for Latin America along the lines of Horn's *The World Encyclopedia of Comics*.

Very little is known about the comics' publishers, creators, and artists. Researchers would welcome interviews or studies that revealed the workings and economics of the industry; the processes by which material is selected and altered; the legal constraints, artistic trends, and opinions of consumer desires; writers' and artists' techniques, conditions of work, goals, class background, and world views; and the like. To these should be added studies of the industrial processes by which comic strips and books are manufactured and how they have changed over time.

Data on comic-book sales, newspaper circulation, and newspaper polls of reader preferences would allow us to better gauge comparative popularity; and data on secondhand sales and markets and rental arrangements are essential if accurate estimates are to be made of total readership. Very fuzzy guesses, often accompanied by ideological preconceptions about the nature of the comics' audience, must be replaced by an informed description of the real consumers of comics. Equally important, we must discover how consumers perceive individual products and, where possible, how the comics affect their lives. Also, the influence of fans on the continued creation of their favorite comics needs to be carefully considered. Certainly the assumption of passive consumption is not warranted in many cases.

There is a crying need for in-depth studies of individual titles, of genres, and of themes. While the study of comics that have a special attraction to the intelligentsia (mainly political comics) continues to be important, comics that appeal to a broad popular audience especially need to be studied— and studied not with smug condescension, but with critical insight and sympathy.

Histories of the comics of Mexico, Brazil, Chile, and Argentina would be most useful, although Argentina's present coverage is at least a decent beginning. Histories for other Latin American countries, which have probably not been exporters of the comics to any great degree (e.g., Cuba, Peru, Colombia, Nicaragua), should also be undertaken. Also needed are histories of genres—such as Westerns, romance, humor, and superheroes— and histories of themes—such as the image of the family, women, and politicians.

Although there would appear to be a surfeit of Marxist and semiological studies, at least in contrast to other unmet needs, there is still ample room for theoretical studies, based on hard data, on the socio-economic context within which comics are produced. Also, further careful studies of the ideological content of comics are needed. And certainly not everything has been said that could be about the nature of the comics' language.

To sum up, nearly everything remains to be done. We have only begun to explore this exciting new research frontier.

BIBLIOGRAPHY

Acevedo, Juan. *Para hacer historietas* (Madrid: Editorial Popular, 1981).

Acosta, Mariclaire. "La historieta cómica en México." *Revista de la Universidad de México* 28, no. 10 (June 1973): 14–19.

Alarcón, Alejandro. *El habla popular de los jóvenes en la ciudad de México* (México: B. Costa-Amic Editor, 1977).

Alfie, David. "Semiología del cómic." In *El cómic es algo serio*, 47–57 (México: Ediciones Eufesa, 1982).

Allegri, Luigi. "Historieta y estructuras narrativas." In *Cultura, comunicación de masas y lucha de clases*, translated by Aurora Chiaramonte, 57–80 (México: Editorial Nueva Imagen, 1978).

Alvarez Constantino, Higilio. "La magia de los cómics coloniza nuestra cultura." *Audiovisión* (México) 2, no. 7, 2, no. 8, 3, no. 9 (September–October 1975, November–December 1975, January–February 1976); 459–64, 573–83, 67–77.

———. *La magia de los 'cómics' coloniza nuestra cultura* (México: By the Author, Angel Urraza 272-2, 1978).

———. "La magia de los cómics coloniza nuestra cultura." *Respuesta: La opinión educativa en México* (México) 1, nos. 7–8 (March-April 1979): 23–26.

Anselmo, Zilda Augusta. *Histórias em quadrinhos* (Petrópolis: Editôra Vozes, 1975).

Artes de México (México) 158 (n.d.) Issue titled "La historieta mexicana." Entire issue devoted to the Mexican comic book.

Artes Visuales (México) 22 (June–August 1979). Special issue devoted to the comics.

Aurrecoechea, Juan Manuel. "La historieta mexicana: Fascículo desprendible y coleccionable." *SNIF: El Mitín del Nuevo Cómic* (México) 1, 2, 3, 4, 5 (August 1980, September 1980, n.d., n.d., n.d.,): 45–52, 9–16 (insert), 17–24 (insert), 25–32 (insert), 33–40.

Baêta Neves, Luiz Felipe. "Críticas às leituras formalistas da ideologia." *Revista de Cultura Vozes* (Petrópolis) 67, no. 7 (September 1973): 21–28.

Bardini, Roberto, and Serafini, Horacio. "La 'inocencia' de la historieta." *Cambio* (México) 5 (October/November/December 1976): 49–53.

B[arta], A[rmando]. "De monitos: Del cartón a la historieta." *SNIF: El Mitín del Nuevo Cómic* (México) 3 (n.d.): 82.

———. "De monitos: El fenómeno Rius." *SNIF: El Mitín del Nuevo Cómic* (México) 4 (n.d.): 11–14.

———. "De monitos: Gabriel Vargas e hijos sin sucesores." *SNIF: El Mitín del Nuevo Cómic* (México) 3 (n.d.): 40.

———. "De Monitos: Réquiem por *El Payo*." *SNIF: El Mitín del Nuevo Cómic* (México) 3 (n.d.): 25.

Baur, Elisabeth K. *La historieta como experiencia didáctica*. Translated by Pablo Kein (México: Editorial Nueva Imagen, 1978).

Bróccoli, Alberto, and Trillo, Carlos. *Las historietas* (Buenos Aires: Centro Editor de América Latina, 1971).

Cagnin, Antônio Luiz. *Os quadrinhos* (São Paulo: Editôra Atica, 1975).

Calabrese, Omar. " 'Fascio' e historieta . . . o bien la reacción de contrabando."

In *Cultura, comunicación de masas y lucha de clases*, translated by Aurora Chiaramonte, 81–92 (México: Editorial Nueva Imagen, 1978).

Cardoso, Antonio, and Ortiz, Orlando. "Autoentrevista: [Antonio] Cardoso y Orlando Ortiz se confiesan." *SNIF: El Mitín del Nuevo Comic* (México) 2 (September 1980): 45–46.

Carrillo, Bert B. "The Use of Mexican Comics as Teaching Material in Bilingual Classes." *Hispania* 59, no. 1 (March 1976): 126–28.

Cirne, Moacy. *Bum! A Explosão criativa dos quadrinhos*. 4th ed. (Petrópolis: Editôra Vozes, 1974. 1st ed., 1970).

———. *A linguagem dos quadrinhos: O universo estrutural de Ziraldo e Maurício de Sousa* (Petrópolis: Editôra Vozes, 1971).

———. "Mafalda: Prática semiológica e prática ideológica." *Revista de Cultura Vozes* (Petrópolis) 67, no. 7 (September 1973): 47–53.

———. "Os novos quadrinhos brasileiros." *Revista de Cultura Vozes* (Petrópolis) 67, no. 7 (September 1973): 65–68.

———. *Para ler os quadrinhos: Da narrativa cinematográfica à narrativa quadrinizada* (Petrópolis: Editôra Vozes, 1972).

———. *Vanguarda: Um projeto semiológico* (Petrópolis: Editôra Vozes, 1975).

Coma, Javier. *Del gato Félix al gato Fritz: Historia de los cómics* (Barcelona: Editorial Gustavo Gili, 1979).

———. *Los Cómics: Un arte del siglo XX* (Barcelona: Editorial Labor, [1978]).

El cómic es algo serio (México: Ediciones Eufesa, 1982).

Cómic Grupo de Estudio—México. *Motus Liber: Organo* (fanzine) (México) 1 (January 1973).

Cornejo, Leobardo. "Semiótica de Los Supermachos y Los Agachados de Rius." In *El cómic es algo serio*, 121–28 (México: Ediciones Eufesa, 1982).

———. "Elementos de retórica en Rius." *Cuadernos de Semiótica* (México) 2 (August 1982): 1–16.

Couperie, Pierre, et al. *A History of the Comic Strip*. Translated by Eileen B. Hennessy (New York: Crown Publishers, 1968).

Cultura, comunicación de masas y lucha de clases. Translated by Aurora Chiaramonte (México: Editorial Nueva Imagen, 1978).

Daniels, Les. *Comix: A History of Comic Books in America* (New York: Bonanza Books, 1971).

de Blas, Jean Paul. "El mundo mágico de Corto Maltés." *SNIF: El Mitín del Nuevo Cómic* (México) 2 (September 1980): 2–8.

Delhumeau, Antonio. "Historia cómica de la tragedia: Apuntes acerca de las virtudes del subdesarrollo en las historietas cómicas mexicanas." *Revista Mexicana de Ciencia Política* 19, no. 74 (October–December 1973): 19–23.

"Del plagio como una de las bellas artes." *SNIF: El Mitín del Nuevo Comic* (México) 3 (n.d.): 59.

del Río, Eduardo [Rius]. "Las historietas." *Los Agachados* (México) 66 (April 4, 1971).

———. *La vida de cuadritos: Guía incompleta de la historieta* (México: Grijalbo, 1983).

de Moya, Alvaro, ed. *Shazam!* (São Paulo: Editôra Perspectiva, 1970).

de Valdés, Rosalva. "Crónica general de la historieta." *Artes de México* (México) 158 (n.d.): 9–13, 84–86, 89–90.

Dineen, Louis. "Catechetics in Comics." *Columban Mission* 60, no. 2 (February 1977): 6–7.

Dorfman, Ariel. *The Empire's Old Clothes: What the Lone Ranger, Babar, and Other Innocent Heroes Do to Our Minds* (New York: Pantheon Books, 1983).

———. *Ensayos quemados en Chile: Inocencia y neocolonialismo* (Buenos Aires: Ediciones de la Flor, 1974). Contains "Entrevista exclusiva al Llanero Solitario."

———. *Reader's nuestro que estás en el tierra: Ensayos sobre el imperialismo cultural* (México: Editorial Nueva Imagen, 1980).

Dorfman, Ariel, and Jofré, Manuel. *Supermán y sus amigos del alma* (Buenos Aires: Editorial Galerna, 1974).

Dorfman, Ariel, and Mattelart, Armand. *How to Read Donald Duck: Imperialist Ideology in the Disney Comic*. Translation and introduction by David Kunzle (New York: International General, 1975).

———. *Para leer el Pato Donald: Comunicación de masa y colonialismo* (Valparaíso, Chile: Ediciones Universitarias de Valparaíso, 1971). Also republished by Siglo Veintiuno Editores in Buenos Aires, Argentina in 1972, and frequently thereafter.

Eco, Umberto. *Apocalípticos e integrados ante la cultura de masas*. Translated by Andrés Boglar (Barcelona: Editorial Lumen, 1968).

Ehmer, Hermann K., ed. *Miseria de la comunicación visual: Elementos para una crítica de la industria de la conciencia*. Translation and introduction by Eduard Subirats Rüggeberg (Barcelona: Editorial Gustavo Gili, 1977).

Erreguerena, María Josefa. "El Payo ¡Un hombre contra el mundo!" *Revista de la Universidad de México* (México) 33, nos. 2–3 (October–November 1978): 85–86.

Escobar, Marina; Orozco, Rebeca; and Watts, Marta. 'La proxémica en Mafalda y Peanuts." In *El cómic es algo serio*, 145–63 (México: Ediciones Eufesa, 1982).

Escovar, Luis A., and de Escovar, Peggy L. "Motivación al logro y motivación al poder en el contenido de historietas populares." *Revista Interamericana de Psicología* 7, nos. 3–4 (1973): 233–38.

Estren, Mark James. *A History of Underground Comics* (San Francisco: Straight Arrow Books, 1974).

Evaluation of the Effectiveness of Illustrated Print Media (Nonverbal) on Family Planning Attitudes Among Colombians. Program of Policy Studies in Science and Technology (Washington, D.C.: George Washington University, 1974).

Feiffer, Jules, comp. *The Great Comic Book Heroes: The Origins and Early Adventures of the Classic Superheroes of the Comic Books—In Glorious Color* (New York: Bonanza Books, 1965).

Fernández, Juan José, and Vigil, Luis, eds. *El comix marginal español* (Barcelona: Producciones Editoriales, 1976).

Fernández Paz, Agustín. "Práctica: Los cómics en la escuela." *Cuadernos de Pedagogías* (México) 74 (February 1981): 47–53.

Flora, Cornelia Butler. "Roasting Donald Duck: Alternative Comics and Photonovels in Latin America." *Journal of Popular Culture* (forthcoming).

Fossati, Franco. *Il fumetto argentino* (Genova: Pirella Editore, 1980).

Foster, David William. "Mafalda: An Argentine Comic Strip." *Journal of Popular Culture* 14, no. 2 (Winter 1980): 497–508.

———. "Mafalda . . . the Ironic Bemusement." *Latin American Digest* 8, no. 3 (June 1974): 16–18.

———. "Recent Works on Latin American Cartoon Art [Review Essay]." *Studies in Latin American Popular Culture* 3 (1984): 179–82.

Fresnault-Deruelle, Pierre. "Lo verbal en las historietas." In Metz, Christian, et al., *Análisis de las imágenes*, 182–204. Translated by Marie Thérèse Cevasco (Buenos Aires: Editorial Tiempo Contemporaneo, 1972).

Gallo, Miguel Angel. *Los cómics: Un enfoque sociológico* (México: Ediciones Quinto Sol, n.d.).

———. "Los superheroes de la Marvel." *SNIF: El Mitín del Nuevo Cómic* (México) 3 (October 1980): 76–81.

Gasca, Luis. *Los cómics in España* (Barcelona: Editorial Lumen, 1969).

———. *Tebeo y cultura de masas* (Madrid: Editorial Prensa Española, 1966).

Gastón, Enrique. *La propaganda dirigida a los niños* (Valparaíso, Chile: Ediciones Universitarias de Valparaíso, 1971).

Gauthier, Guy. "La mirada discreta de Linus." Translated by Jaime Goded Andrew. *Cuadernos de Semiótica* (México) 3 (September 1982): 1–16.

González, José Carlos. "Entrevista con Carlos Monsiváis [on Mexican comics]." *Artes Visuales* (México) 22 June–August 1979): 25–29, 44–46.

Gubern, Román. *El lenguaje de los cómics* (Barcelona: Ediciones Península, 1972).

———. *Literatura de la imagen* (Barcelona: Salvat Editores, 1973).

Guerra, Georgina. *El cómic o la historieta en la enseñanza* (México: Editorial Grijalbo, 1982).

Guillermoprieto, Alma. "*El caballo del diablo*: Un estudio de caso." Paper presented at Primer Simposio Mexicano Centroamericano de Investigación sobre La Mujer, México, November 7–9, 1977.

Gutiérrez Vega, Hugo. "Observaciones sobre el cine, la radio, la televisión y las historietas cómicas." *Revista Mexicana de Ciencia Política* 19, no. 74 (October–December 1973): 5 11.

Hall, Wendell, and Lafourcade, Enrique. "Teaching Aspects of the Foreign Culture through Comic Strips." In *Teaching Cultural Concepts in Spanish Classes*, edited by H. Ned Seelye, 86–92 (Springfield, Ill.: Office of the Superintendent of Public Instruction, 1972).

"Heraclio Bernal. El rayo de Sinaloa." *SNIF: El Mitín del Nuevo Comic* 5 (México): 2.

Hernández, Pablo José. *Para leer a Mafalda* (Buenos Aires: Editorial Precursora, 1976).

Herner, Irene. *Mitos y monitos: Historietas y fotonovelas en México* (México: Universidad Nacional Autónoma de México, Editorial Nueva Imagen, 1979).

———. "El museo y la historieta." *Revista Mexicana de Ciencia Política* (México) 76 (April–June 1974): 51–61.

Hinds, Harold E., Jr. "Algunas reflexiones sobre la historieta mexicana." *Artes Visuales* (México) 22 (June–August): 30–31, 46–47.

———. "Chanoc: Adventure and Slapstick on Mexico's Southeast Coast." *Journal of Popular Culture* 14, no. 2 (Winter 1980): 424–36.

———. "Comics: An Introduction to Mexico's Most Popular Literature." In *Pop-*

ular Culture in Mexico and in the American Southwest (tentative title). Edited by Linda B. Hall (San Antonio, Texas: Trinity University Press [forthcoming]).

―――. "If You've Been to Mexico Lately, Did You Notice What Most Mexicans Are Reading? Would You Believe It's Comics and Photonovels [Review Essay]." *Canadian and International Education* 11, no. 1 (1982): 73–79.

―――. "Kalimán: A Mexican Superhero." *Journal of Popular Culture* 13, no. 2 (Fall 1979): 229–38.

―――. "Literatura popular: 'No hay fuerza más poderosa que la mente humana'— Kalimán." *Hispamérica* (Buenos Aires) 18 (December 1977): 31–46.

―――. "*La novela policiaca:* Crime, Detectives, and Escapism." Paper presented at the VI Conference of Mexican and United States Historians, Chicago, September 8–12, 1981.

―――. "*Tradiciones y leyendas de la colonia:* Folklore and Colonial History for Popular Consumption." *Folklore Americano* 25 (June 1978): 101–9.

―――. "*El Payo: A Man Against the World:* A Mexican 'Western' Comic Book." *North Dakota Quarterly* 48, no. 2 (Spring 1980): 31–55.

―――. "*El Payo:* Una solución a la lucha mexicana entre los robatierras y los descamisados." *Hispamérica* (Buenos Aires) 31 (April 1982): 33–49.

Hinds, Harold E., Jr., and Tatum, Charles. "Images of Women in Mexican Comic Books." *Journal of Popular Culture* (forthcoming).

La historieta mundial: Catálogo de I Bienal Mundial de la Historieta (Buenos Aires, 1968).

Horn, Maurice. "Recent Mexican Scholarship on Comics [A Review Essay]." *Studies in Latin American Popular Culture* 2 (1983): 208–12.

―――, ed. *The World Encyclopedia of Comics* (New York: Chelsea House Publishers, 1976).

Hunt, Nancy L., and LaFrance, David G. " 'El Cuarto Reich': Economic Disaster, Torture and Other Laughs." *Studies in Latin American Popular Culture* 2 (1983): 36–43.

Inge, M. Thomas. "Comic Art." In *Handbook of American Popular Culture*, 3 vols, edited by M. Thomas Inge, 1:77–102 (Westport, Connecticut: Greenwood Press, 1978–1981).

J. F. T. "Malaguias Mora por teléfono." *SNIF: El Mitín del Nuevo Comic* (México) 1 (August 1980): 23.

Jacob, Jeffrey C. "The Children of Santa María: A Study of Culture and Poverty in Urban Latin America." Ph.D. dissertation, Cultural Foundations of Education, Syracuse University, 1974.

―――. "Urban Poverty, Children, and the Consumption of Popular Culture: A Perspective on Marginality Theses from a Latin American Squatter Settlement." *Human Organization* 39:3 (Fall 1980): 233–41.

Jarque Andrés, Francisco. "La paraliteratura: Producción y consumo." *Hispamérica* (Buenos Aires) 21 (December 1978): 37–52.

Jiménez Codinach, Estela Guadalupe. "Historia e historieta: *Episodios Mexicanos* (Estudio de caso)." Paper presented at the VI Conference of Mexican and United States Historians, Chicago, Illinois, September 10, 1981.

Katz, Chaim Samuel. "Ideologia e centro mas histórias em quadrinhos." *Revista de Cultura* (Petrópolis) 67, no. 7 (September 1973): 5–20.

Kempkes, Wolfgang. *International Bibliography of Comics Literature*. 2d rev. ed. (New York: R. R. Bowker/Verlag Dokumentation, 1974).

Kunzle, David. "Art of the New Chile: Mural, Poster, and Comic Book in a 'Revolutionary Process.' " In *Art and Architecture in the Service of Politics*, edited by Henry A. Millon, and Linda Nochlin, 356–81 (Cambridge, Massachusetts: The MIT Press, 1978).

————. "The Chilean Worker as Mythic Hero: 'The Shanks of Juan'." *Praxis* 1, no. 2 (Winter 1976): 199–219.

————. "Chile's *La Firme* Versus ITT." *Latin American Perspectives* 16 (Winter 1978): 119–33.

————. "Public Graphics in Cuba: A Very Cuban Form of Internationalist Art." *Latin American Perspectives* Issue 7, Supplement 1975, Vol. 2, No. 4 (1975): 89–110.

Lindstrom, Naomi. "Latin American Cartooning: Between Lovers and Critics [A Review Essay]." *Studies in Latin American Popular Culture* 1 (1982): 246–51.

Lipszyc, David, and Vieytes, Enrique J., eds. *Técnica de la historieta* (Buenos Aires: La Escuela Panamericana de Arte, 1966).

Lipszyc, Enrique. "Publicações brasileiras de histórias em quadrinhos." In *Catálogo da Exposição Internacional de História em Quadrinhos* (São Paulo, 1970).

Llobera, José. *Dibujo del 'cómic': Manuales prácticas AFHA* (Barcelona: Ediciones AFHA Internacional, 1973).

Lupoff, Dick, and Thompson, Don, eds. *All in Color for a Dime* (New Rochelle, New York: Arlington House, 1970).

Lutzemberger, María Grazia, and Bernardi, Sergio. "Introducción a una historieta alternativa." In *Cultura, comunicación de masas y lucha de clases*, translated by Aurora Chiaramonte, 93–102 (México: Editorial Nueva Imagen, 1978).

Luz, Marco Aurélio. "Tarzan, o Homen-Macaco." *Revista de Cultura Vozes* (Petrópolis) 67, no. 7 (September 1973): 29–46.

Martín, Antonio. *Historia del cómic espanol: 1875–1939* (Barcelona: Editorial Gustavo Gili, 1978).

Masotta, Oscar. *La historieta en el mundo moderno* (Buenos Aires: Editorial Paidos, 1970).

Massart, Pierre. "Literatura y paraliteratura: El estudio de la literatura infantil y juvenil." *Revista Internacional de Ciencias Sociales* 1 (1976): 193–213.

Mejía G., Francisco. "Edipín Pingüín." *Motus Liber: Organo* (Fanzine) (México) 1 (January 1973): 11

Metz, Christian; Eco, Umberto; Durand, Jacques; Péninou, Georges; et al. *Análisis de las imágenes*. Translated by Marie Thérèse Cevasco (Buenos Aires: Editorial Tiempo Contemporáneo, 1972).

Miller, Gary, comp. "Graphics." In "Latin American Popular Culture: An Introductory Bibliography," edited by Roger Cunniff. *Proceedings of the Pacific Coast Council on Latin American Studies* 5 (1976): 188–91.

Moix, Ramón-Terenci. *Los 'cómics': Arte para el consumo y formas 'pop'* (Barcelona: Llibres de Sinera, 1968).

Monsiváis, Carlos. "Impresiones sobre la cultura popular urbana en México: Segunda Parte." *Cuadernos Comunicación* (México) 22 (April 1977): 6–15.

Montalvo, Carlos; Vergara, Jorge; Pérez, Fernando; Rebetez, René; and Paramio,

Ludolfo. *Ensayos marxistas sobre los 'cómics'* ([Bogotá]: Ediciones Los Comuneros, 1976 [?]).

Nómez, Naín. "La historieta en el proceso de cambio social. Un ejemplo: De lo exótico a lo rural." *Comunicación y Cultura* (México) 2 (2d ed., 1978): 109–24.

Ossa, Felipe. *El mundo de la historieta* (Bogotá: Editores Colombia, 1978).

Palacios Franco, Julia Emilia. "Proposiciones para el análisis de un cómic mexicano: El caso de *Torbellino*." M.A. Thesis, Sociology, Iberoamerican University, 1978.

———. "*Los Supermachos* (98 números): Rius." *Motus Liber: Organo* (fanzine) (México) 1 (January 1973): 10.

Pareja, Reynaldo. *El nuevo lenguaje del cómic* (Bogotá: Ediciones Tercer Mundo, 1982).

Parent, Georges-A. "Focalization: A Narratological Approach to Mexican Illustrated Stories." *Studies in Latin American Popular Culture* 1 (1982): 201–15.

Parlato, Ronald; Parlato, Margaret Burns; and Cain, Bonnie J. *Fotonovelas and Comic Books: The Use of Popular Graphic Media in Development* (Washington, D.C.: Office of Education and Human Resources, Development Support Bureau, Agency for International Development, 1980).

Patten, Fred. "Superman South." *Alter Ego*, nos. 8 and 9 (August 1965; Winter 1965): 24–28; 4–12. Parts III and IV are available only in ms. form. They were to appear in nos. 10 and 11, but *Alter Ego* ceased publication for several years after the appearance of No. 9.

Perry, George, and Aldridge, Alan. *The Penguin Book of Comics: A Slight History* (New York: Penguin Books, 1967. Rev. ed. 1971).

Prieto Castillo, Daniel. *Retórica y manipulación masiva* (México: Editorial Edicol, 1979).

Proctor, Phyllis Ann Wiegand. "Mexico's *Supermachos*: Satire and Social Revolution in Comics by Rius." Ph.D. dissertation, University of Texas, 1972.

Ramírez, Juan Antonio. *El 'cómic' femenino en España: Arte sub y anulación* (Madrid: Editorial Cuadernos para el Diálogo, 1975).

———. *La historieta cómic de postguerra* (Madrid: Editorial Cuadernos para el Diálogo, 1975).

Reitberger, Reinhold, and Fuchs, Wolfgang. *Comics: Anatomy of a Mass Medium.* Translated by Nadia Fowler (Boston: Little, Brown, 1972).

Reséndiz, Rafael C. "El mito de Rarotonga." In *El comic es also serio* 129–243 (México: Ediciones Eufesa, 1982).

Revista de Cultura Vozes (Petrópolis) 67, no. 7 (September 1973). Entire issue devoted to "Quadrinhos e ideologia."

Reynoso, Ricardo. "Una mancha en un cómic." *Motus Liber: Organo* (fanzine) (México) 1 (January 1973): 16.

Robinson, Jerry. *The Comics: An Illustrated History of Comic Strip Art* (New York: G. P. Putnam's Sons, 1974).

Roque, Carlos. "Resurgimiento de la historieta argentina." *Análisis Latinoamericano* (New York) 1, no. 2 (1979): 47–49.

Rota, Josep. "Mexican Children's Use of the Mass Media as a Source of Need Gratification." *Studies in Latin American Popular Culture* 2 (1983): 44–58.

Serafini, Horacio, and Bardini, Roberto. "La inocencia de la historieta." *Cambio* (México) 5 (October-November-December 1976): 49–53.

Salomón, Antonio. *El humor y la historieta que leyó el argentino* (Córdoba, Argentina: Congreso Bianual de la Historieta de Córdoba. 1972, 1974, 1976, 1979 editions of conference proceedings).

Serra, Antônio. "O fantasma, ou atribulções dum édipo no 3° mundo." *Revista de Cultura Vozes* (Petrópolis) 67, no. 7 (September 1973): 55–65.

Sewell, Dorita. "The Comics in Mexico." Paper presented at the Seventh National Convention of the Popular Culture Association, Baltimore, Maryland, April 28, 1977.

Siller, David. "Historia de la historieta." *Revista Comunidad (CONACYT)* (México) (August 1977): 23–26.

Silva, Ludovico. *Teoría y práctica de la ideología* (México: Editorial Nuestro Tiempo, 1971).

Silva O., José L. "Un asunto censurable, la censura." *Motus Liber: Organo* (fanzine) (México) 1 (January 1973): 3–10.

Simard, Jean Claude, and Jarque Andrés, Francisco. "La paraliteratura mexicana," Rapport provisoire destiné au Conseil des Arts du Canada, Groupe de Recherche en Paraliterature Mexicane [*sic*], Département des Littératures, Université Laval, August 1976.

SNIF: El Mitín del Nuevo Comic. 4 Vols. (México: SEP/Editorial Penélope, August 1980).

Solórzano, Luz de Lourdes. "Psicología en la historieta." *Artes de México* (México) 158 (n.d.): 4–5, 83–84, 88.

Sotres Mora, Bertha Eugenia. "La cultura de los cómics." *Revista Mexicana de Ciencia Política* 19, no. 74 (October–December 1973): 13–17.

Speck, Paula K. "Rius for Beginners: A Study in Comicbook Satire." *Studies in Latin American Popular Culture* 1 (1982): 113–24.

Steele, Cynthia. "Ideology and Mexican Mass Culture: The Case of *Sangre India: Chamula.*" *Studies in Latin American Popular Culture* 2 (1983): 14–23.

Steimberg, Oscar. "La historieta argentina." *Todo es historia* (Buenos Aires) (April 1982): 83–94.

———. *Leyendo historietas: Estilos y sentidos en un 'arte menor'* (Buenos Aires: Ediciones Nueva Visión, 1977).

Steranko, James. *The Steranko History of Comics.* 2 Vols. (Reading, Pennsylvania: Supergraphics: 1970–1972).

"Los Supermachos." *México/This Month* 13, no. 5 (October 1967): 26–28.

Taibo, Paco Ignacio, II. "De la historia marginal a el desempleado [interview with Víctor Uhthoff]." *SNIF: El Mitín del Nuevo Cómic* (México) 2 (September 1980): 29.

———. "Muñoz, Sampayo y Alack." *SNIF: El Mitín del Nuevo Cómic* (México) 4 (n.d.): 50.

Tatum, Charles M. "Eduardo del Río: Comic Book Writer as Social Gadfly." Paper presented at the VI Conference of Mexican and United States Historians, Chicago, September 8–12, 1981.

———. "Eduardo del Río's *Los agachados* y *Los supermachos.*" *Praxis* (forthcoming).

————. "*Lágrimas, risas y amor*: La historieta más popular de México." *Hispamérica* (Buenos Aires) 36 (Fall 1983): 101–8.

————. "*Lágrimas, risas y amor*: Mexico's Most Popular Romance Comic Book." *Journal of Popular Culture* 14, no. 3 (Winter 1980): 413–23.

————. "Ruis [*sic*]: der Comics-Autor als Sozialkritiker und politischer Unruhestifter." *Iberoamericana* 13/14 (1982): 78–91.

Tatum, Chuck [Charles], and Hinds, Harold. "Eduardo del Río (Rius): An Interview and Introductory Essay." *Chasqui* 9, no. 1 (November 1979): 3–23.

Tenorio, Jesús Pavlo. "Fotonovelas y cómics son la lectura habitual del mexicano." *Señal* 54, no. 1829 (November 29, 1980): 24–25.

Theroux, Paul. *The Old Patagonian Express: By Train Through the Americas* (Boston: Cape Cod Scriveners Co., 1979; New York: Washington Square Press, 1980).

Trabant, Jürgen. "Supermán: La imagen de un héroe de cómic." In Ehmer, Hermann K. ed. *Miseria de la comunicación visual: Elementos para una crítica de la industria de la conciencia*, 273–99. Translation and introduction by Eduard Subiratus Rüggeberg (Barcelona: Editorial Gustavo Gili, 1977).

Thompson, Don, and Lupoff, Dick, eds. *The Comic-Book Book* (New Rochelle, New York: Arlington House, 1973).

Trejo, Patricia. "La historieta mexicana." *Hoy* (México) 1639 (October 23, 1971): 32–37.

Trillo, Carlos, and Bróccoli, Alberto. *El humor gráfico* (Buenos Aires: Centro Editor de América Latina, 1971).

————, and Saccomanno, Guillermo. *Historia de la historieta argentina* (Buenos Aires: Ediciones Record, 1980).

Vargas Dulché, Yolanda. "¿Qué es la historieta para mí?" *Artes de México* (México) 158 (n.d.): 14, 87, 90–91.

Vázquez González, Modesto. *La historiética: Todo lo relativo al lenguaje lexipictográfico* (México: Promotora K, S.A., 1981).

"Los verdaderos antecedentes de la fotonovela actual." *Artes de México* (México) 119 (1969): 18–27.

Vergara, Jorge. "Cómics y relaciones mercantiles." *Casa de las Américas* (Havana) 77 (March–April 1973): 126–42.

Vigano, Oscar. "Estudio sobre aceptación y efectividad de las fotonovelas e historietas en la comunicación de conocimientos en áreas rurales de Guatemala." Rural Education and Extra Scholastic Programs of Guatemala (Guatemala: Academy for Educational Development, 1976; mimeo).

Vigil, Guillermo Z. "Ensayo sobre la personalidad de los principales personajes del cómic 'Los Supersabios,' del dibujante y argumentista mexicano Germán Butze." *Motus Liber: Organo* (fanzine) (México) 1 (January 1973): 12–15.

————. *El Payo: O cómo escribo mi historieta* (México: Edamex, 1981).

White, David Manning, and Abel, Robert H., eds. *The Funnies: An American Idiom* (New York: The Free Press, 1963).

Wicke, Charles R. "The Burrón Family: Class Warfare and the Culture of Poverty." *Studies in Latin American Popular Culture* 2 (1983): 59–70.

Woll, Allen J. "The Comic Book in a Socialist Society: Allende's Chile, 1970–1973." *Journal of Popular Culture* 9, no. 4 (Spring 1976): 1039–1045.

Joseph Straubhaar

4 Television

Television is a form of popular culture present in all Latin American nations—even, as of 1981, in Belize. Television dominates other mass media and forms of popular culture in a number of the more urbanized and industrialized countries. Although restricted to urban areas in many countries, television is reaching far into rural areas in several countries, such as Brazil and Mexico.

In most Latin American countries, television broadcasting is predominantly a commercial enterprise, run by private companies and supported by advertising revenue. As a result, television programming is most often oriented toward entertainment rather than education, which accentuates its importance in popular culture. Although a good deal of television programming is imported from the United States, there is an increasing tendency to either produce programming locally or buy it from regional producers in Brazil, Mexico, or Venezuela. A number of distinctive programs and genres have been created by Latin American television producers. Nevertheless, programming policies have been intensely controversial in nearly all Latin American countries.

Despite varying government controls, television tends not to be an instrument of the state in Latin America to the degree that it is in many developing countries. Many researchers and critics have, in fact, urged greater government control and use of television in modernization and the formation of stronger national identities and cultures. Others fear abuse of government control over news and entertainment on television.

A BRIEF HISTORY

Television began early in Latin America compared with other developing countries. Mexico, Cuba, and Brazil inaugurated television broadcasting in 1950. Argentina followed soon after in 1951, Venezuela in 1952, Chile in 1954, Nicaragua in 1955, Uruguay in 1956, and Peru in 1958. Some smaller countries came later: Paraguay in 1965, Bolivia in 1969, and Belize in 1981.

In most Latin American countries, television started in one or two major cities, then gradually spread to smaller cities and even rural areas (Milanesi, 1978). Currently, 60 to 70 percent of Brazilians, Cubans, and Mexicans; 80 percent of Venezuelans; and 90 percent of Colombians have regular access to television, despite the long distances and rough terrain over which transmission must take place. In more urbanized countries, such as Argentina and Uruguay, television spread rapidly to the interior areas and today reaches over 90 percent of the population. In a few countries, such as El Salvador, Bolivia, and Paraguay, television in still limited to the major urban areas and remains a restricted urban "popular culture."

Television developed in most countries as a commercial system. Television industries developed and became profitable quickly in Argentina (Santos Hernando, 1977; Muraro, 1974, 1976; Ulanovsky, 1976), Brazil (Camargo, 1975; Mattos, 1982; McAnany, 1983; Moran, 1982; Prado, 1973; Sodré, 1977; Straubhaar, 1981, 1984), pre-Castro Cuba (Carty, 1978; Santana, 1976; Herd, 1979), Mexico (Emery, 1964; Noriega and Leach, 1979; Pedrero, 1969) and Venezuela (Alfonzo, 1983; Capriles, 1976; Izcaray, 1981; Pasquali, 1976). In most cases, these television stations and networks were developed by individual entrepreneurs who had other media empires, usually in radio. Goar Mestre created Latin America's first fully realized commercial network in Cuba, then, after it was nationalized, moved on to Argentina and Venezuela. Emilio Azcárraga created, with Rómulo O'Farrill and Miguel Alemán, the Mexican Televisa system. Genaro Delgado Parker shaped Peruvian television and the *telenovela* [soap opera] genre before his operation was taken over by the revolutionary government that came to power in 1968. Television in Brazil was started by Assis Chateaubriand and dominated after 1969 by Roberto Marinho. These examples influenced commercial broadcasters in other smaller countries in Central America (Alisky, 1955; Fonseca, 1977) and South America (Alisky, 1969; Dillner, 1979; Merino Utreras, 1973) to develop commercial television broadcasting.

However, some countries followed a noncommercial form of broadcasting. Colombia initiated television broadcasting under a government-controlled institute (INRAVISION), where commercial programming is used to finance educational programs (Fox, 1973, 1975; Caycedo, 1980). In Chile, universities operated television stations, first on a noncommercial, then a quasi-commercial basis (Fuenzalida, 1981; Caviedes, 1972; Fagen, 1974). In some countries, such as Peru (Alisky, 1959; Gargurevich, 1976, 1977; Atwood and Mattos, 1982; Ortega and Romero, 1977; Perrett, 1977; Rocca Torres, 1975) and Argentina, ownership of television has passed back and forth from industry to government, depending on the current regime's ideology concerning state control of media. In Cuba and Nicaragua, television stations were nationalized after the revolution and little prospect exists for a return to private, commercial operation (Alisky, 1960; Mahan and Schement, 1980; Nichols, 1982b; Werthein, 1977).

Commercial television broadcasting was often begun or developed in cooperation with U.S. television networks. From 1956 to 1962, several U.S. companies invested in or helped start local broadcasters: NBC in Mexico, Argentina, Peru, Uruguay, and Venezuela; ABC in Venezuela and Central America; Time-Life in Brazil; CBS in Uruguay. Time-Life and CBS also invested in production companies in Argentina, Peru, and Venezuela (Avila, 1982; Beltrán and Fox, 1979). Except for ABC's investments in Central America, all these ventures failed by the early 1970s (Fox, 1974, 1977). Latin American governments were not willing to countenance foreign investment in an area as sensitive as television broadcasting and production. Furthermore, most local broadcasters discovered that they did not need outside investments or technical assistance (Read, 1976; Straubhaar, 1984).

Dependence by Latin American broadcasters on imported equipment has not declined as much, although the sources of broadcasting and production equipment have diversified to include Western Europe and Japan as well as the United States (Caparelli, 1980; Marques de Melo, 1979). Television sets themselves are now manufactured locally in the larger Latin American countries, although often manufacturing is controlled by local branches of multinational corporations. Smaller countries still import sets from the United States, Japan, Western Europe, or the larger Latin American countries. In Cuba, both broadcasting equipment and sets are imported from the Soviet Union (Nichols, 1982b).

Most Latin American commercial television stations continue to depend to some degree on advertising revenues from foreign or multinational corporations. These advertisers, in turn, reinforce styles of programming that attract middle- and lower-middle-class consumers and tacitly discourage other kinds of programming, which would not appeal to their intended audiences (Arriaga, 1980; Fejes, 1980; Janus, 1981; Janus and Rocancaglio, 1981; Mattos, 1982, 1984).

Apart from actual foreign investment or ownership, a number of Latin American stations and networks affiliated with American networks in order to buy programming (Tunstall, 1977). In Mexico, the three commercial networks had programming ties for some time with ABC, CBS, and NBC, respectively. In 1968, ABC formed the Latin American Television International Network Organization (LATINO) to sell programs in Argentina, Chile, Colombia, Costa Rica, the Dominican Republic, Ecuador, El Salvador, Honduras, Guatemala, Mexico, Panama, Uruguay, Venezuela, Haiti, and the Antilles (Read, 1976). This ABC arrangement persists in some countries, but most broadcasters now tend to attend sales meetings in the United States themselves and select their own programming. When enough companies indicate interest in a given program, it is sent to Mexico City or Brazil for dubbing (Rogers and Antola, 1984).

Most Latin broadcasters also continue to rely on imported programs, usually from the United States, as a source of low-cost broadcast fare. In 1972, the Nordenstreng and Varis study of television program flows showed that many Latin American nations imported most of their programming and some imported almost all of it—primarily from the United States. The imported American programs have been feature films, series, cartoons, and other childrens' programs. Over time the imported American series have changed from situation comedies and Westerns to police and other action-type dramas (Straubhaar, 1983; Varis and Salinas, 1977).

By 1982, a study by Antola and Rogers in Argentina, Brazil, Chile, Mexico, Peru, and Venezuela showed that Latin American broadcasters in these countries now produce more of their own material and also buy relatively more from other Latin American countries and less from the United States than in the past. In smaller countries, programming is still purchased from abroad, but the sources are more diverse, including Mexico, Brazil, Venezuela, and Puerto Rico, as well as the United States.

The decline in imported American programs was predicted in 1972 by Cuban/Argentine producer Goar Mestre, who was involved with CBS and Time-Life for a while. "The Americans failed to realize that television here is a different animal from television in the United States. People in Argentina don't mind the occasional American program, but what they really like are shows with local flavor" (Green, 1972:66). Broadcasters interviewed by Rogers and Antola see a trend in viewer preferences "for locally produced programs, followed by another Latin American country's programs, and last, imported programs from the United States" (1984:6).

A number of North American program genres have been transplanted to Latin America. Commercial broadcasters have copied and adapted successful formats such as variety shows, soap operas, game shows, music reviews, magazine-type public affairs shows, and interview programs (Sodré, 1972; Wells, 1972). Some of these were also pushed by U.S. advertisers, anxious to sell products through familiar genres. Others, like *Sesame Street*, were imported for their perceived desirability as educational programs. *Sesame Street* was adapted very carefully, with joint Mexican-American and Brazilian-American teams translating the show's basic educational concept into locally produced versions of the show (Mayo, Araujo e Oliveira; Rogers, Guimarães; Pinto; Morett, 1984).

From these borrowed formats, from earlier radio genres, and from diverse other sources of inspiration, such as local circuses and theatre, several innovative popular culture television genres have been created in Latin America. Most notable are the *telenovelas*, which constitute most of the program sales between Latin American countries. Also noteworthy are variety, comedy, music, interview, and soccer programs.

Telenovelas originally emphasized romantic themes and family intrigues.

The classic of this form, which was originally produced in Mexico on radio and has been revived repeatedly as a television production, is *El derecho de nacer* [*The Birthright*], about a man's search for his parents. Another major theme has been upward mobility by the poor, as in the Peruvian *Simplemente María* [*Simply Maria*], where a peasant girl moves from the country to become first a maid then a seamstress. Partially based on the impact of *María*. a number of *telenovelas* have now been written that deliberately stress economic growth and developmental themes (Alisky, 1982; Orme, 1982). Historical themes and classics of literature have been used as material in some countries, such as adaptations of Jorge Amado novels in Brazil. In Brazil, *telenovelas* exemplifying various regions of the country—such as the Rio "good life" (*Beto Rockefeller*), São Paulo agricultural dynasties (*O Casarão*) [*The Big House*], Bahian culture (*O bem amado*) [*The Well Loved*], or northeast folklore (*Saramandaia*)—have been successful nationwide, but not always have they been exportable to other nations (Rohter, 1978; Straubhaar, 1982).

Variety programs are probably the next most important television genre that has developed in Latin America. Like *telenovelas*, variety shows developed from diverse sources: U.S. and European television musical variety shows, Latin American *teatro de revista* [revues], local circuses, and so on. The main elements of variety shows are charismatic show hosts, amateur performances, professional music, comedy, dance, games, interviews, political debates, lotteries or give-aways, fashion shows, circus-style oddities and stunts and weddings or match-making (Sodré, 1972). Few of these elements are exclusive to Latin America; most can be found in television in the United States and elsewhere. There are, however, some distinctive twists in the ways these elements are combined and emphasized in Latin America. For example, the personal style of variety-show hosts tends to be distinctive to the country or region where the program is produced. Given fairly equal production quality, local viewers, as reflected in ratings, seem to prefer familiar speech, body language, and jokes—although some hosts succeed with a "sophisticated" and "international" image.

Like all programming, variety shows started out live because of necessity. Unlike for *telenovelas*, however, the audience is often an important part of the program, so live broadcasting continued even after the advent of videotape technology in 1960. Audiences participate directly as amateur performers, interview subjects, game participants, or judges and as foils for the patter of show hosts and comedians. The marathon live variety show—often running for six to eight hours, usually on Saturdays and Sundays—is a major staple of Latin American television. Such "auditorium shows" [*shows de auditório*] have, due to general differences in group behavior and participatory styles, a different flavor in various parts of Latin America or in different regions, as is the case of Brazil, where shows are still produced locally.

Live variety shows have been particularly popular in Argentina, with programs such as *Sabados de* [*Saturday with . . .* the current leading show host] and *Feliz domingo* [*Happy Sunday*]. Mexico has shows such as *Siempre en domingo* [*Always on Sunday*] and Brazil has *Chacrinha* and the *Sílvio Santos Show*. Prerecorded variety programs are also very popular, offering slicker production and more special effects, as in Brazil's *Fantástico* [*Fantastic*] or Mexico's *Noche de gala* [*Gala Evening*].

Comedy is one of the most idiosyncratic forms of popular culture and one of the most likely to be produced locally. Comedy is a staple ingredient of variety shows. There are also a number of specific comedy shows now in virtually all of these Latin American countries, for example, in Brazil, Mexico, Peru, Chile, Argentina, and Venezuela that produce their own television programs.

Brazil has a variety of comedy programs: one-man shows like *Chico Anísio*, which has created characters for an entire small town; ensembles like *Os trapalhões* [*The Clodhoppers*]; and comedy-variety shows with staple characters or sketches and guest comics, such as *Planeta dos homens* [*Planet of Man*], which bears a loose resemblance to the U.S. program *Laugh-In*. Undoubtedly because of language barriers and cultural traditions, Brazil has not had much success in exporting its comedy programs to other Latin American nations, but Mexico creates some comedies that are popular in a number of other Spanish-speaking countries. In fact, comedy programs, such as *Chespirito* and *Hogar dulce hogar* [*Home Sweet Home*], are Televisa's second most popular export (after *telenovelas*).

The distinctiveness of Latin American nations' music programming on television depends in large part on the independent strength of the local musical traditions and industries—strongest in Brazil, Mexico, and Argentina. In these countries and some others, however, television also bolsters local music traditions and industries by offering showcases and sources of income to performers. In Brazil, for example, the music recording industry has been partially taken over by TV Globo, which promotes its own label's records with its television programs and vice versa (Straubhaar, 1981).

The interview program has been particularly adapted to the culture of poverty in Latin America. There are distinctive variations on scandal-mongering or muck-raking interviews that focus on poverty and its attendant physical and social ills (malnutrition, abandonment, crime, etc.). In another variation, show hosts interview those of the middle-class but, much like the majority of television advertisements, these interviews also offer a vicarious sense of participation to those in the lower-class (Straubhaar, 1983; Walger and Ulanovsky, 1974; Miceli, 1972).

Finally, some Latin American countries, most notably Brazil, have begun to produce or consider producing dramatic series like those successfully exported by the United States—self-contained hour or half-hour episodes within a continuing general plot and set of characters. Brazil has produced a police-action series (*Reporter*), a series about a truck driver (*Carga pesada*

[*Heavy Load*]), and others, including one about a recently divorced woman (*Malu mulher* [*Malu, a woman*]), which has been widely exported to Latin America, the SIN network in the United States, and several Scandinavian countries (Straubhaar, 1981).

The program genres discussed above dominate the production of most Latin American countries and the flow of programs between those nations. There are one or two exceptions, principally Cuba and possibly now Nicaragua. Like other Cuban media, television programming is used for education, political socialization, and mobilization. In 1976, programming was described by Santana as emphasizing education, women's issues, racial issues, children's development, support for popular liberation struggles abroad, history, class conflict, music, and sports. Cuban President Fidel Castro is particularly effective at linking together and politically mobilizing the whole country through speeches at televised rallies. In fact, his marathon speeches (often up to four hours in length) are a fascinating television genre in themselves (Szulc, 1982). Most programming is produced in Cuba, although some U.S. movies and series are shown, as are a number of Soviet and Eastern European programs. Cuban television is linked by satellite with the Soviet and Eastern European broadcasting consortium Intervision (Nichols, 1982).

REFERENCE WORKS

For each individual country, among the most consistent reference sources on television are the area handbooks or country studies produced by American University's Foreign Area Studies staff. Each volume covers one country and contains a section on mass media that gives basic data on television, sometimes including information on programming relevant to popular culture.

As a region-wide factbook, the UNESCO volume *World Communications: A 200 Country Survey of Press, Radio, Television and Film* (1975) is good but dated. On content, the UNESCO study, *The Cultural Value of Film and Television in Latin America*, by Estrada and Hopen (1968) is likewise useful but dated. Katz and Wedell's 1977 study of broadcasting in the Third World covers television content and structure in several Latin American countries (particularly Brazil and Peru). In terms of brief region-wide surveys, sections on television by Alisky (1974) and Rogoff (1981b) in handbooks on Latin America and the chapters on Latin America from Green's *The Universal Eye: World Television in the Seventies* (1972) and Tunstall's *The Media are American* (1977) are among the best. For historical perspective, Gutiérrez's 1961 essay "Television in Latin America" is also worthwhile.

The best single volume dedicated to a critical analysis of the various aspects of television across Latin America to date has been a 1976 issue of the Mexican journal *Nueva política* [*New Politics*]. The Mexican and Brazilian television systems, as well as program flows between a number of Latin American countries, are treated in the April 1984 issue of *Communication Research* edited by Jorge Schement and Everett Rogers. A volume on Latin America to be edited by Elizabeth Mahan, Joseph Straubhaar, and Sergio Mattos is planned in the Temple University series on regional broadcasting systems but will not be ready for at least one or two years.

There are several studies examining media-government relations throughout the area that cover many aspects of television. The most thorough and recent is *Latin American Media: Guidance and Censorship* (1981) by Marvin Alisky, who has also written on a number of individual Latin American broadcasting systems. Also worthy of note is *Keeping the Flame: Media and Government in Latin America* by Robert Pierce, with John Spicer Nichols (1979). There are collections on Third World media systems by George Gerbner (1977) and Emile McAnany (1980) that include papers on various Latin American television systems, television flows, and developed country influence on Latin television.

There are several comprehensive but somewhat dated bibliographies on broadcasting in Latin America. Lichty (1971), Sparks (1971), and Harwood (1972) covered periodicals, dissertations, and monographs on world broadcasting, including Latin America. In a remarkable effort, CIESPAL (Centro Internacional de Estudios Superiores de Periodismo para América Latina [International Center of Graduate Journalism Studies for Latin America]) compiled a two-volume study of Latin American communication research, *Comunicación social y desarrollo: compendios de investigación de y sobre América Latina* [*Social Communication and Development: Research Compendium of and about Latin America*] covering most work up to 1976. In 1978, *Journal of Broadcasting* had bibliographies by Daniel Appelman and Mary A. Gardner.

There are several comprehensive and up-to-date country-specific and regional bibliographies. INTERCOM (Associação Brasileira de Estudos Interdisciplinares de Comunicação [Brazilian Association for Interdisciplinary Studies of Communication]) publishes very thorough annual bibliographies of communication monographs in Brazil (the *Bibliografia brasileira de comunicação* [*Brazilian Communication Bibliography*]), as well as a bimonthly newsletter with a bibliographic update (*Bibliografia Correinte de Comunicação* [*Current Bibliography of Communication*]) on monographs and selected serials from Brazil, other Latin American countries, and Lusophone Africa. The bibliographies' editor, José Marques de Melo, also wrote a valuable inventory of American research on diffusion of innovations and communication in Brazil (1974). John Lent has compiled a very thorough volume, *Caribbean Mass Communications: A Comprehensive Bibliography* (1981).

HISTORICAL AND CRITICAL WORKS

Criticism and analytic research on television in Latin America have centered on a few major themes: the role of entertainment versus education; private versus governmental ownership or control; the effect of televised messages on the habits and ideologies of viewers; the importation of programs versus nationalization of production; and centralization of production and its effects on national or regional cultures.

Many of the studies in Latin America criticized television for devoting too much time to pure entertainment and not enough to information, education, and culture. A 1969 Universidad de Lima [University of Lima] survey of viewing behavior showed that entertainment did indeed dominate programming and that most viewers preferred it. Sports, popular music, and imported films were most widely watched, followed by theatre, *telenovelas*, classical music, ballet, and documentaries. Current studies in various Latin American countries reach similar conclusions, except that most find the *telenovela* genre increasingly dominant. In Brazil, for instance, as of 1977, *telenovelas* were most widely watched, followed by American series and feature films, news, cartoons and other children's programs, variety programs, interview programs, music, sports, and comedy (Straubhaar, 1982).

More interpretive studies link the emphasis on entertainment over education to a second major research theme, the commercial nature of television in most of Latin America. Structural studies comparing and criticizing the commercial development of television across Latin America have been made by Schenkel (1973), Wells (1972), Faraone (1973), and Beltrán and Fox de Cardona (1980). This has focused debate on private versus public ownership/control of television production and broadcasting. A few researchers, such as Maldonado Quijano (1966) and Camargo and Pinto (1975), have focused on problems of censorship and state intervention and favor private ownership to limit state control. One of the most thorough studies, the Venezuelan government-sponsored Proyecto Rattelve [Rattelve Project] in 1975, recommended a truly mixed broadcasting system, with a stronger state component (Pasquali, 1976; Capriles, 1976).

Analyses of program content have led to specific critiques of commercially motivated programming and its effects. Nelida Baigorria (1966) writes on such programs' deleterious effect on language and culture, Luis Beltrán (1978) on the "conservatism, materialism and conformism" inspired by commercial programs, and Dias (1968) on consumerism, which is a prime focus of criticism. Wells defines consumerism as "the increase in consumption of the material culture of the developed countries" (1972:43). This includes absorption of foreign, nonindigenous values, such as materialism, as well as use of artifacts produced in or inspired by developed country industries (Ordóñez Andrade and Reyes, 1976; Arenas, 1975).

There are, beyond this basic critique, two lines of thought on consumerism and television in Latin America.

Dias (1975) and Fadul (1974) see evidence of television serving only the consumption habits of a relatively restricted upper and middle class. Faraone (1973) cites as an example the introduction of color television in many Latin American countries when economic indicators would have made other investments more advisable. Gordon (1970) and Miceli (1972) see television as middle-class oriented but expansive, even missionary, instead of restrictive. They perceive commercial television, both in advertising and programming, as seeking to change the dress, values, and consumption habits of lower-class viewers to bring them into the consumption economy and to cause them to emulate the middle-class as much as possible.

The concept of "leisure" or "free time" in its relationship to television as an entertainment medium is criticized by authors such as Armand Mattelart (1976). This view tends to see such time, particularly for working-class viewers, as pre-empted by the mass media, particularly commercial television, and filled with programming that ideologically supports existing regimes and the capitalist economic system (Michèle Mattelart and Piccini, 1973; Marques de Melo, 1981; Thiollent, 1982). Similarly, many see Latin American television as leveling differences between socioeconomic groups, "demobilizing workers," and reducing class consciousness (Caparelli, 1982; da Via, 1977; Gadotti, 1982).

Content analyses in Brazil by Marques de Melo (1971) and Venezuela by Rincón (1968) and Eduardo Santoro (1976) found that *telenovelas* tended to encourage a sense of fatalism and resignation to one's lot in life. These analyses also emphasized that villains were typically working class and often black or Indian, that good inevitably triumphed over evil, and that problems were best solved by love, not action (Beltrán, 1978). Some surveys of viewers show that such messages are getting through. Colomina de Rivera (1968) found in Venezuela that *telenovelas* were, in fact, watched more often by poor women who seemed to use them for escape and wish fulfillment to cope with difficult life situations. In São Paulo, Marques de Melo (1971) also found *telenovelas* used for "substitute gratification" by housewives.

Wish fulfillment and fatalism are also major themes of another staple television genre in Latin America, the interview program. In some São Paulo programs, Miceli (1972) observes that interviewees are typically successful and middle class, offering wish fulfillment to poorer viewers. However, Walger and Ulanovsky (1974) note programs in Buenos Aires in which interviewees are usually poor or distressed, reinforcing fatalism about life and offering many a sense that others are worse off than they are.

Somewhat conflicting messages tend to come from imported U.S. television series, which form an important part of popular culture in Latin

America. Eduardo Santoro in Venezuela and Tapia Delgado in Peru found that these series stressed individualism, even ruthlessness, and the acquisition of material possessions, although they also reinforce resignation to poverty by those who lose out in this game (Fleischman and Fuenzalida, 1982; Santoro 1976:279–93; Tapia Delgado, 1973).

There is a specific problem with the level of violence encountered in many imported U.S. television series. Studies by Straubhaar (1980) in Brazil, Eduardo Santoro (1976) in Venezuela, and Merino Utreras (1976) in Ecuador found a significant number of imports with a disturbing amount of violence. Most studies in Latin America of television's effects on children have focused on violence, although consumerism and individualism have also been critical concerns (Grupo de Mídia, 1978; Pfromm Neto, 1978; Quiroga, 1967).

Imported U.S. television programs have been a major focus of critical attention in Latin America. This is due in part to preoccupation with U.S. television content themes, such as violence, materialism, consumerism, and individualism, which many Latin American critics see as undesirable cultural imports. Critics are also concerned that even more ostensibly benign content may be alienating, in that it comes from another culture with different norms, values, and ideals. Many fear that what is distinctive about national and regional cultures in Latin America may be lost as people watch U.S. television programs or local programs that closely imitate them, instead of participating in traditional activities and family or neighborhood discussions, where national or indigenous culture has usually been transmitted. Some assume that foreign influences via television will be assimilated by Latin American cultures as have earlier waves of foreign influence through other media (Beltrán, 1978; Bibliowicz, 1980; Pasquali, 1976; Marques de Melo, 1971; Eduardo Santoro, 1976; Straubhaar, 1981).

A major focus of critical studies has been the "nationalization" of television programming in Latin America. A number of issues have been discussed. On a practical level, problems include the cost and production quality of local programs versus imports. On the societal level, researchers try to establish what the cultural impact of imported programs and various types of nationally produced programs may actually be. Studies have been done by Caviedes (1972) on Chile; Bibliowicz (1980) on Colombia; Straubhaar (1981) and Marques de Melo (1971) on Brazil; Rota (1985), Rebeil (1985), and Montoya and Corella (1982) on Mexico; Rogoff (1981a) on Argentina; Pasquali (1976), Colomina de Rivera (1968), and Rincón (1968) on Venezuela; and Beltrán (1978) on general developments in Latin America. Tunstall (1977) and Katz and Wedell (1977) have also written general surveys of television in which problems with the content of imports and possibilities for local production in at least some Latin America countries are viewed favorably.

As the number of television programs imported from the United States has been reduced in many Latin American countries, the focus of research has shifted increasingly to the nature of what will replace them. Studies, such as that by Rogers and Antola, are being done to chart program flows within Latin America. Little has been done yet to examine the cultural impact of Brazilian or Mexican programs in the smaller countries that import them. More work has been done in various countries concerning foreign influences on the programs produced locally to replace imports. Straubhaar (1982), Sodré (1972, 1976), and Beltrán (1978) have discussed American influence on the content and impact of *telenovelas* and variety shows.

Particularly intense critical scrutiny was given to the local adaptations of the U.S. educational television program *Sesame Street* in Mexico and Brazil. These adaptations had educational ambitions well beyond the usual imported entertainment programs, and more than the usual care was given to make *Plaza Sesamo* fit into national cultural patterns (Mayo, Araujo y Oliveira; Rogers; Guimarães; and Morett). Nevertheless, results were generally judged as mixed. Critics charged these productions with carrying many of the same messages that other "alienating" cultural imports carried: consumerism, submission to authority, resolution of problems by outside intervention rather than individual initiative, and other "middle-class" values. The Mexican adaptation was not allowed to be aired in Peru because of government opposition. Both Brazilian and Mexican productions were eventually stopped because of criticism from educators (Armand Mattelart, 1973; Díaz-Guerrero, 1976; Goldsen and Bibliowicz, 1976; Pérez Barreto, 1973).

Studies criticizing concentration of television in the hands of a few broadcasters, often parallel to critiques of commercial development of television, have been made by Dias (1968), Schenkel (1973), Muraro (1974, 1980), Portales (1981), and Sodré (1977). Concentration of programming decisions into a few hands has been seen as dangerous, since certain ideologies, commercial interests, class interests, social aims, and regional identities may be propounded at the expense of competitors.

Among culturally focused studies on this issue, television has been seen as homogenizing regional groups in terms of cultural preferences and tastes, leading to what Anamaria Fadul (1976) called "the decadence of regional culture." In fact, at least in Brazil, Mexico, and Argentina, an increasing concern is that television programs produced in one or two major cities are eroding regional cultures, even regional accents.

However, the study of Televisa in Mexico by Noriega and Leach (1979) defends the idea that the concentration of production and program control of all three Mexican commercial networks under Televisa meets the public good better than "no holds barred competition" for viewers, which leads to programming for the lowest common denominator of taste. In contrast, Noriega and Leach (1979) find that the five Mexican channels segment the audience and differentiate their programs: Channel 2 emphasizes the middle class, with *telenovelas*, children's programs, sports, comedy, and news; Channel 4 emphasizes the urban lower-middle class, with Mexican feature films and a four-hour magazine show on Mexico City neighborhoods; Channel 5 targets middle-class youth with imported series and *telesecundaria* [televised secondary school education]; and Channels 8 and 13 emphasize culture and education.

RESEARCH AND RESOURCE CENTERS

Materials for serious study of Latin American television as popular culture can be found in several academic, government, and industry organizations in Latin America and the United States. None of these sources is complete—most emphasize one or two countries, certain aspects of television research, and/or collections of programs. Following is a brief overview of what is available in several locations.

The most accessible and broad-ranging source for American scholars is in Washington, D.C. at the Library of Congress. Its collection has monographs and journals from all over Latin America, selected by Library of Congress regional offices in several countries, and may be expanded to include some videotapes of Latin American television programs.

Los Angeles is both a commercial and academic center for Latin American television. Televisa (Mexico), TV Globo (Brazil), and other broadcasters have commercial offices there. California State University at Northridge has sponsored a conference/festival on Brazilian film and television and is setting up an archival collection of materials. The Annenberg School of Communication at the University of Southern California has several researchers (Jorge Schement, Félix Gutiérrez) working on Mexican television and Spanish-language broadcasting in the United States. The Graduate Library at the University of California, Los Angeles, has a large collection of Spanish and Portuguese monographs and serials, including some on television.

Stanford University has researchers in several departments working on Latin American television: in the Communications Department (Everett Rogers, Steven Chaffee, Nicholas Valenzuela), Latin American Studies Center (Jorge Schnitman), and the School of Education's Stanford International Development Education Committee (Edmundo Fuenzalida). The University of Texas at Austin has a strong program in Latin American communications—an overlap between the Communications and Latin American Studies programs (Rita Atwood, Emile McAnany)—as well as a good Latin American library collection.

There are other active current researchers on Latin American television at Michigan State University (Joseph Straubhaar, Felipe Korzenny—Telecommunications Department), Arizona State University (Marvin Alisky), University of Wisconsin-Madison (John McNelly—Journalism), Pennsylvania State University (John Nichols—Journalism), and Yale University (Elizabeth Mahan—Latin American Studies).

At several points in time, the best Latin American center for communication studies has been the Centro Internacional de Estudios Superiores de Periodismo para América Latina [The International Center of Graduate Journalism Studies for Latin America, CIESPAL], in Quito, Ecuador. The center was strong in the late 1960s to mid-1970s and produced valuable conferences, reports, bibliographies, and research summaries, and a research journal, *Chasqui* (1973–1976). After a hiatus, CIESPAL has picked up again in activity and renewed publication of *Chasqui* in 1981.

The other major locus for multicountry studies in Latin America has been the Instituto Latinamericano de Estudios Transnacionales [Latin American Institute for Transnational Studies, ILET], with centers in Mexico City and Santiago, Chile. The Mexico City center produced a number of critical studies on commercial media, including television, advertising, and Latin American dependency on the developed countries. Some of the Mexico City staff have moved to Chile (Rafael Roncaglio) or the United States (Noreene Janus), but both centers remain active in research.

In Mexico, there are a number of researchers and a variety of reference sources at a number of institutions besides ILET. Beatriz Soliz and Javier Esteinou are at the Universidad Autónoma Metropolitana [Autonomous Metropolitan University]. Tatiana Galván is at the Universidad Nacional [National University] and Patrícia Arriaga is at CEESTEM—Centro de Estudios Económicos y Sociales del Tercer Mundo [Center for Third World Economic and Political Studies]. Televisa itself employs or has employed several researchers (John Page, Fernando Morett) and Televisa has program archives which may become accessible to researchers.

Brazil has also become a major center for television studies in Latin America. Although most work is focused on Brazil itself, a number of researchers are beginning to take a more comparative focus. The coordinating body for academic research is INTERCOM. Beside its bibliographies, INTERCOM has annual conferences that draw researchers from all of Latin America and usually produce thematic collections of essays.[1] There are active researchers at a number of Brazilian universities. José Marques de Melo and Carlos Eduardo Lins da Silva are at the Universidade de São Paulo [University of São Paulo] and the Instituto Metodista de Ensino Superior [Methodist Institute of Advanced Studies]. Regina Festa, Fernando Santoro, and José Moran are also at the latter institute, and Nely de Camargo is at the former. Muniz Sodré is at the Universidade Federal do Rio de Janeiro [Federal University of Rio de Janeiro], Sergio Mattos is at the Universidade Federal da Bahia [Federal University of Bahia], and Sergio Caparelli is at the Universidade Federal do Rio Grande do Sul [Federal University of Rio Grande do Sul].

The state government of São Paulo maintains the Fundação Padre Anchieta [Father Anchieta Foundation], which produces programs for the state-owned educational channel and conducts or sponsors some research. Of particular note are two television series produced by the foundation on the history of Brazilian television and the history of the Brazilian *telenovela*. Some São Paulo advertising and commercial researchers also conduct independent studies under the auspices of an informal body called the Grupo de Mídia [Media Group]. TV Globo also conducts extensive research and has worked with some outside researchers.

There are several major researchers on television in Venezuela, principally Antonio Pasquali and Carlos Muñoz at the Universidad Central de Venezuela [Central University of Venezuela]. There are also a number of influential researchers in other countries: Heriberto Muraro and Elizabeth Fox in Argentina, Juan Gargurevich in Peru, and Luis Ramiro Beltrán and Azriel Bibliowicz in Colombia, among others.

FUTURE DIRECTIONS

Research on television in Latin America has been concentrated in historical and structural studies of the medium itself and how it relates to society. Some content analyses have been done of various types of programs, usually with an eye to their effect on society, and some viewer surveys have been conducted to examine programs' social impact. There is a need for more analysis of program content and for serious criticism of various television genres as popular art or popular culture. More impact studies need to be done, particularly interview studies that are based on the viewers' own thoughts and reactions.

Substantively, the trend to look at the internal dynamics of Latin American television programs as popular culture should continue, even expand. Too many studies have been focused solely on television industry structures, relations with government, political history, and foreign influence. It is at least arguable that now there are identifiable Latin American television genres, and they need much more serious study and criticism.

NOTES

1. Examples of INTERCOM conference proceedings include the following volumes edited by José Marques de Melo: *Comunicação e incomunicação no Brasil* (São Paulo: Loyola, 1976), *Comunicação e classes subalternas* (São Paulo: Cortez Editora, 1980), *Populismo e comunicação* (São Paulo: Cortez Editora, 1981). Cf. Joseph Straubhaar, "The Brazilian Society for Interdisciplinary Study of Communication and Its Bibliography of Communication," *Studies in Latin American Popular Culture* 2 (1983): 262–267.

BIBLIOGRAPHY

Comparative Bibliographies

Appleman, Daniel. "The Mass Media of Latin America: Selected Information Sources." *Journal of Broadcasting* 22, no. 2 (Spring 1978): 217–40.

Comunicación social y desarrollo: compendios de investigación de y sobre América Latina. Vols. 1, 2 (Quito: CIESPAL, 1977).

Gardner, Mary A. "Central and South American Mass Communication: Selected Information Sources." *Journal of Broadcasting* 22, no. 2 (Spring 1978): 196–216.

Harwood, Kenneth. "A World Bibliography of Selected Periodicals on Broadcasting." *Journal of Broadcasting* 16 (Spring 1972).

Lent, John A. *Caribbean Mass Communications: a Comprehensive Bibliography* (Los Angeles: Crossroads Press, 1981).

Lichty, Lawrence W. "World and International Broadcasting: a Bibliography." (Washington, D.C.: Association for Professional Broadcasting Education, 1971). (Mimeographed).

Marques de Melo, José. "American Studies Related to Communication, Modernization and Diffusion of Innovations in Brazil: A Bibliographical Approach." (Madison: University of Wisconsin, Department of Agricultural Journalism, 1974).

————,ed. *Bibliografia brasileira de comunicação* (São Paulo: Cortez Editoria INTERCOM. Volumes for 1977, 1978, 1979–80, 1981, 1982 to date).

Sparks, Kenneth R. "A Bibliography of Doctoral Dissertations in Television and Radio." (Syracuse: Syracuse University School of Journalism, 1971 mimeo).

Straubhaar, Joseph D. "The Brazilian Society for Interdisciplinary Study of Communication and Its Bibliography of Communication." *Studies in Latin American Popular Culture* 2 (1983): 262–67.

Books and Articles

Alfonzo, Alejandro. "El caso venezolano." *Chasqui* 3 (1983).

Alisky, Marvin. "The Mass Media in Central America." *Journalism Quarterly* 32 (1955): 479–86.

————. "Broadcasting in Peru." *Journal of Broadcasting* 3 (1959): 120–27.

————. "Confused Cuba: Printers Who Edit—Government by Television." *Nieman Reports* 14 (April 1960): 12–14.

————. "Uruguay's Utopian Broadcasting." *Journal of Broadcasting* 13 (1969): 277–83.

————. "Radio and Television." In *Encyclopedia of Latin America.* Edited by Helen Delpar (New York: McGraw-Hill, 1974).

————. *Latin American Media: Guidance and Censorship* (Ames: Iowa State University Press, 1981).

————. "The Mexican Government's Use of Media to Bolster Family Planning." (Washington, D.C.: Latin American Studies Association, March 6, 1982).

Antola, Livia and Rogers, Everett. "Television Flows in Latin America." *Communication Research* 11, no. 2 (1984).

Arenas, Pedro José. *La televisión y nuestra conducta cotidiana* (Buenos Aires: Editorial Curato Mundo, 1975).

Arriaga, Patricia. *Publicidad, economía y comunicación masiva: Estados Unidos y México* (México, D.F.: Nueva Imagen, 1980).

Atwood, Rita, and Mattos, Sergio. "Mass Media Reform and Social Change: The Peruvian Experience." *Journal of Communication* 32, no. 2 (Spring 1982): 33–45.

Avila, Carlos Rodolfo Amendola. *A televisão* (São Paulo: Cortez, 1982).

Baigorria, Nelida, "Idioma y estética en los programas de la radiofusión y la televisión." In *La radiodifusión y la televisión frente a la necesidad cultural de América Latina* (Quito: CIESPAL, 1966).

Beltrán, Luis Ramiro. "TV Etchings in the Minds of Latin Americans: Conservatism, Materialism and Conformism." *Gazette* 24, no. 1 (1978) pp. 61–65.

Beltrán, Luis Ramiro, and Fox de Cardona, Elizabeth. "Latin America and the United States: Flaws in the Free flow of Information." In *National Sovereignty and International Communication*, edited by Kaarle Nordenstreng and Herbert I. Schiller, 33–64 (Norwood, N.J.: Ablex, 1979).

———. *La comunicación dominada: los Estados Unidos en los medios de comunicación de América Latina* (México, D.F.: ILET/Nueva Imagen, 1980).

Bibliowicz, Azriel. "Be Happy Because Your Father Isn't Your Father. An Analysis of Columbian *Telenovelas*." *Journal of Popular Culture* (Winter 1980): 476–85.

"30 años de TV." *Briefing* (São Paulo) September 1980.

Camargo, Nely de. "Política de comunicacao: technologia e as perplexidades do desenvolvimento." In *Comunicação de Massa, impasse brasileiro*, edited by R. A. Amaral Vieira (Rio de Janeiro: Forense, 1978).

Camargo, Nely de, and Pinto, Virgilia Noya. *Communication Policies in Brazil* (Paris: UNESCO Press, 1975).

Caparelli, Sérgio. *Comunicação de massa sem massa* (São Paulo: Cortez, 1980).

———. "Televisão e mobilização popular." *Cadernos INTERCOM* 1, no. 2 (São Paulo, 1982).

Capriles, Oswaldo. "Venezuela." *Nueva Política* 3 (1976): 143–78.

Carty, James W. *Cuban Communications* (Bethany, West Va.: Bethany College, 1978).

Caviedes, José L. "La televisión entusiasta." *Revista EAC Artes de la Comunicación* 2 (Chile, 1972): 110–13.

Caycedo, Gustavo Castro. *La televisión en negro* (Bogotá: Hispana, 1980).

Christol, Susan. "Television as an Acculturation Resource in the Third World: Mexico, a Case Study." Conference on Culture and Communication, Temple University, April 9–11, 1981.

Colomina de Rivera, Marta. *El huesped alienante: un estudio de audiencia y efectos de las radio-telenovelas en Venezuela* (Maracaibo: Universidad del Zulia, 1968).

Contreras, Eduardo; Larsen, James; Mayo, John K.; and Spain, Peter. "Cross-cultural Broadcasting." *UNESCO Reports and Papers on Mass Communication* 77 (1976).

da Via, Sara Chucid. *Televisão e consciência de classe* (Petrópolis, Brazil: Editora Vozes, 1977).

Dias, Marco Antonio. "Concentração e seus efeitos no televisão." Universidade Nacional de Brasília, 1968 (mimeographed).

———. "Responsibilidade cultural da radiodifusão." Proceedings of the Simpôsio sobre radiodifusão, Associação Brasileira de Teleducação, Brasilia, August 1975.

Díaz-Guerrero, Rogelio; Reyes-Lagunes, Isabel; Witzke, Donald; and Holtzman, Wayne. "Plaza Sésamo in México: an Evaluation." *Journal of Communication* 26, no. 2 (Spring 1976): 145–54.

Dillner, Gisela. *Massenkommunikation in Ecuador* (Frankfurt: Vervuert, 1979).

Dizard, Wilson. *Television: a World View* (Syracuse, N.Y.: Syracuse University Press, 1966).

Emery, Walter B. "Broadcasting in Mexico." *Journal of Broadcasting* 8 (Spring 1964): 185–202.

Espinoza, U. H. *El poder económico en el sector de los medios de communicación de masas* (Lima: Universidad Nacional Frederico Villareal, 1971).

Estrada, Luis P., and Hopen, D. *The Cultural Value of Film and Television in Latin America* (Paris: UNESCO, 1968).

Fadul, Anamaria. "The Function of Mass Media in Capitalism: the Latin American Experience." M.A.thesis, University of Tampere, Finland, 1974.

———. "Decadéncia da cultura regional: a influéncia do radio e da TV." In *Comunicação/incomunicação no Brasil*, edited by José Marques de Melo (São Paulo: Loyola, 1976).

Fagen, Patricia. "The Media in Allende's Chile." *Journal of Communication* 24, no. 1 (Winter 1974): 59–70.

Faraone, Rogue. "Medios de comunicación de masas en América Latina." *ISAL* 4, no. 45 (Montevideo, 1973).

Fejes, Fred. "The Growth of Multinational Advertising Agencies in Latin America." *Journal of Communication* 30, no. 4 (Autumn 1980): 36–49.

Figueroa Herbas, Jorge Roberto. "Influencia de la televisión como medio de comunicación en los niños." Ph.D. dissertation, Universidad Católica del Perú, 1970.

Fleischman, Roberta, and Fuenzalida, Edmundo. "The Contribution of U.S. Film Series in Television on Venezuelan Women's Socialization." Conference on Flow of Media in the Americas, Stanford University, December 1982.

Fonseca, Jaime. *Communication Policies in Costa Rica* (Paris: UNESCO Press, 1977).

Fox de Cardona, Elizabeth. "The U.S. Television Industry and the Development of TV in Latin America: The Colombian Case." M.A. thesis, University of Pennsylvania, 1973.

———. "La televisión norteamericana en Américan Latina." *CHASQUI* 6 (1974): 53–72.

———. "Multinational Television." *Journal of Communication* 25, no. 2 (Spring 1975): 122–27.

———. "American Television in Latin America." In *Mass Media Policies in Changing Cultures*, edited by George Gerbner (New York: Wiley & Sons, 1977).

Fuenzalido, Valeri. *Estudios sobre la televisión chilena* (Santiago: Corporación de Promoción Universitaria, 1981).

Gadotti, Moacir. "Televisão como educador permanente das classes trabalhadoras." *Cadernos INTERCOM* 1, no. 2 (São Paulo, 1982).

Gargurevich, Juan. "El estado y la televisión—Perú." *Nueva política* 1, no. 3 (July 1976): 127–42.

———. *Introducción a la historia de los medios de comunicaciones en el Perú* (Lima: Horizontes, 1977).

Gerbner, George, ed. *Mass Media Policies in Changing Cultures* (New York: Wiley Interscience, 1977).

Goldsen, Rose, K., and Bibliowicz, Azriel. "Plaza Sésamo: 'Neutral' Language or 'Cultural Assault'?" *Journal of Communication* 26, no. 2 (Spring 1976): 124–26.

Gordon, Alicia. "La televisión en Concepción, sus efectos y las apiraciones de los usuarios." M.A. thesis, Universidad de Concepción, Chile, 1970.

Graziano, Margarita. "Los dueños de la televisión argentina." *Comunicación y Cultura* 3 (Buenos Aires, 1974).

Green, Timouthy. *The Universal Eye: World Television in the Seventies* (London: The Bodley Head, 1972).

Grupo de Mídia. "Alguns aspectos de audiéncia infantil aos meios de comunicação." *Cadernos de Comunicação PROAL* 4 (São Paulo, 1978): 52–66.

Gutiérrez, Lazardo B. "Television in Latin America." *Journal of Telecommunications* 28 (November 1961).

Herd, Jan, ed. *Mass Media in/on Cuba and the Caribbean area: The role of the television, radio and the free press* (Erie, Pa.: Mercyhurst College, 1979).

Izcaray, Fausto. *Estudio sobre medios de comunicación social y consciencia del desarrollo: informe cuantitativo 1974* (Barquisimeto, Venezuela: Fundación para el Desarrollo de la Región Centro Occidental de Venezuela, 1975).

———. "Mass Media Saturation Conditions and Information Gaps in Venezuela." Ph.D. dissertation, University of Wisconsin, Madison, 1981.

Janus, Noreene. "Advertising and the Mass Media in the Era of the Global Corporations." In *Communication and Social Structure: Critical Studies in Mass Media Research*, edited by Emile McAnany, Jorge Schnitman, and Noreene Janus (New York: Praeger, 1981).

Janus, Noreene, and Rocancaglio, Rafael. *Publicidad, comunicación y dependencia* (México, D.F.: Nueva Imagen, 1981).

Katz, Elihu, and Wedell, George. *Broadcasting in the Third World* (Cambridge, Mass.: Harvard University Press, 1977).

Mahan, Elizabeth. "Commercial Broadcast Regulation: Structures and Processes in Mexico and the U.S." Ph.D. dissertation, University of Texas. 1982.

Mahan, Elizabeth, and Schement, Jorge. "Broadcasting in Cuba and the United States: Systems, Structures, and Practices." Proceedings of the International Communication Association, 1980.

Maldonado Quijano, Gonzalo. "Libertad de expresión y ética en la radiodifusión y la televisión." In *La radiodifusión y la televisión frente a la necesidad cultural de América Latina* (Quito: CIESPAL, 1966).

Marques de Melo, José. "As telenovelas em São Paulo: estudio de Publico receptor." In *Comunicação social: teoria e pesquisa* (Petrópolis, Brazil: Editora Vozes, 1971).

———, ed. *Comunicação e incomunicação no Brasil* (São Paulo: Loyola, 1976).

————. "A televisão como instrumento do neocolonialismo: evidencias do caso brasileiro." *Comunicação e Sociedade* 1 (São Paulo 1979): 167–82.

————, ed. *Comunicação e classes subalternas* (São Paulo: Cortez Editora, 1980).

————, ed. *Populismo e comunicação* (São Paulo: Cortez Editoro, 1981).

————, ed. *Telemania, anestético social* (São Paulo: Loyola, 1981).

————. "Escapismo e dependéncia no programação da TV brasileira." *Comunicação e Sociedade* 5 (São Paulo, 1981): 147–60.

———— ed. *Comunicação, hegemonia e contra informação* (São Paulo: Cortez Editora, 1982).

————, ed. *Pesquisa em comunicação no Brasil* (São Paulo: Cortez Editora, 1983).

Mattelart, Armand. "La industria Sésamo." *Revista Mexicana de Ciencia Política* (México, D.F.) (October 1973).

————. *La cultura como empresa transnacional* (México, D.F.: Era, 1976).

————. *Multinational Corporations and the Control of Culture: The Ideological Apparatus of Imperialism* (Atlantic Highlands, N.J.: Humanities Press, 1979).

Mattelart, Michèle, and Piccini, Mabel. "La televisión y los sectores populares." *Comunicación y Cultura* 3, no. 11 (Buenos Aires, 1973).

Mattos, Sérgio. *The Development of Communication Policies under the Peruvian Military Government 1968–1980* (San Antonio: V. Klingensmith Independent Publisher, 1981).

————. "Domestic and Foreign Advertising in Television and Mass Media Growth: A Case Study of Brazil." Ph.D. dissertation, University of Texas, Austin, 1982.

————. *The Impact of Brazilian Military Government on the Development of TV in Brazil* (San Antonio: V. Klingensmith Independent Publisher, 1982).

————. "Advertising and Government Influence on Brazilian Television." *Communication Research* 11, no. 2 (1984): 203–20.

Mayo, John K.; Araujo y Oliveira, João Batista; Rogers, Everett M.; and Guimarães, Sonia Dantus Pinto. "The Transfer of *Sesame Street* to Latin America." *Communication Research* 11, no. 2 (1984) 259–80.

McAnany, Emile. "The Logic of Cultural Industries in Latin America: The Television Industry in Brazil." In *Changing Patterns of Communications Control*, edited by Vincent Mosco and Janet Wasko (Norwood, N.J.: Ablex, 1983).

————, ed. *Communication in the Rural Third World: The Role of Information in Development* (New York: Praeger, 1980).

Menasse, Ricardo, and Selene, Susana. "Un estudio sobre la publicidad en la televisión comercial mexicana." *Revista Mexicana de Ciencias Políticas y Sociales* 86/87.

Merino Utreras, Jorge. "La televisión en el Ecuador.' *CHASQUI* 3 (1973): 11–32.

————. "La violencia en los programas de televisión.' *CHASQUI* 14 (July 1976): 33–42.

Miceli, Sérgio. *A noite da madrinha* (São Paulo: Perspectiva, 1972).

Milanesi, Luis Augusto. *O paraíso via EMBRATEL* (Rio de Janeiro: Paz e Terra, 1978).

Montoya, Alberto, and Rebeil Corello, María Antonieta. "Commercial Television as an Educational and Political Institution: A Case Study of its Impact on the Students of Telesecundaria." Western Regional Conference of the Comparative and International Education Society, October 22–24, 1982.

Moraes, Renato de. "O poder da Globo, mamãe de todos das noites." *Senor* (São Paulo, May 1980): 32–43.

Morán, José Manuel. "Contradições e perspectivas da televisão brasileira." *Cadernos INTERCOM* 1, no. 2 (São Paulo, 1982).

Moschner, Meinhard. *Fernsehen in latinamerika* (Frankfurt am Main: P. Lang, 1982).

Muñoz, Carlos C. *Televisión, violencia y agresión* (Caracas: Universidad Central de Venezuela, 1974).

Muraro, Heriberto. *Neocapitalismo y comunicación de masa* (Buenos Aires: Universitaria, 1974).

———. "La TV en la Argentina." *Nueva política* 1, no. 3 (México, D.F., July 1976): 95–145.

———. "Television and Film in Argentina." In *Transnational Communication and Cultural Industries*, by Thomas Gubach and Tapio Varis. *UNESCO Reports and Papers on Mass Communications*, No. 92 (Paris: UNESCO, 1980).

Nichols, John. "Republic of Cuba." In *World Press Encyclopedia*, edited by George Thomas Kurain (New York: Facts on File, 1982a).

———. "The Mass Media: Their Functions in Social Conflict." In *Cuba—Internal and International Affairs*, edited by Jorge Domínguez (Beverly Hills: Sage, 1982b).

Noriega, Luis Antonio de, and Leach, Frances. *Broadcasting in Mexico* (Boston: Routledge & Kegan Paul, 1979).

Nordenstreng, Kaarie, and Varis, Tapio. "Television Traffic—a One Way Street?" *UNESCO Reports and Papers on Mass Communication* No. 70 (Paris: UNESCO, 1974).

———. "La homogeneidad del estado nacional y la corriente internacional de la televisión." *CHASQUI* 7 (December 1974): 55–86.

Nueva Política 1, no. 3 (July 1976): special issue on mass media in Mexico.

Ordoñez Andrade, Marco, and Encalda Reyes, Marco. "Comunicación internacional y contaminación ideológica." *CHASQUI* 13 (April 1976).

Orme, William A., Jr. "Using TV to Send a Social Message." *R & D Mexico* (June 1982): 15–17.

Ortega, Carlos, and Romero, Carlos. *Communication Policies in Peru* (Paris: UNESCO Press, 1977).

Pasquali, Antonio. *Comunicación y culture de masas* (Caracas: Monte Avila, 1976).

Paula Oliva, Francisco de. "Realidad de los medios de comunicación de masas en América Latina." *CHASQUI* 11 (1975): 81–90.

Pedrero, Enrique González. *Los medios de comunicación de masas en México* (México, D.F.: Universidad Nacional Autónoma, 1969).

Pérez Barreto, Samuel. "El caso 'Plaza Sésamo' en el Peru." In *Imperialismo y medios masivos de comunicación* (Lima: Causachun, 1973).

Perreira da Luz, Inez. "TV: Mulher e a comunicação comunitaria." In *Ideologia, cultura e comunicação no Brasil*, edited by José Marques de Melo (São Paulo: Cortez Editora, 1982).

Perrett, Heli E. de Sagasti. "Mass Media Revolution in Peru." In *Mass Media*

Policies in Changing Cultures, edited by George Gerbner (New York: Wiley & Sons, 1977).

Pfromm Neto, Samuel. "Efeitos da violéncia televisada sobre criancas." *Cadernos de Comunicação PROAL* 4 (1978): 26–39.

Pierce, Robert N. "Costa Rica's Contemporary Media Show High Popular Participation." *Journalism Quarterly* 47 (Fall 1970): 544–52.

Pierce, Robert, with Nichols, John Spicer. *Keeping the Flame: Media and Government in Latin America* (New York: Hastings House, 1979).

Portales, Diego. *Poder económico y libertad de expresión* (México, D.F.: Nueva Imagen, 1981).

Prado, João Rudolfo do. *TV: quem vê quem?* (Rio de Janeiro: Eldorado, 1973).

Proyecto Rattelve—Diseño para una nueva política de radiodifusión del estado venezolano. Informe del Comité de Radio y Televisión de la Comisión Preparatoria del Consejo Nacional de la Cultura (Caracas, Venezuela: Government of Venezuela, 1975).

Quiroga, Héctor Solís. "Influence of TV on Child and Adolescent Behavior." *Revista interamericana de sociología* 71, no. 4 (1967).

Read, William H. *America's Mass Media Merchants* (Baltimore: Johns Hopkins University Press, 1976).

———. "Global TV Flow: Another Look." *Journal of Communication* 26, no. 3 (Summer 1976): 69–73.

Rebeil Corella. "What Mexican Youth Learn from Commercial Television." *Studies in Latin American Popular Culture* 4 (1985): 188–99.

Rincón, César David. "Notas sobre el contenido de las tele/radio-novelas." In *El huesped alienante: un estudio de audiencia y efectos de las radio-telenovelas en Venezuela*, edited by Marta Colomina de Rivera (Maracaibo: Universidad del Zulia, 1968).

Rogers, Everett, and Schament, Jorge. "Media Flows in Latin America." Special issue of *Communication Research* 11, no. 2 (1984): 305–319.

Rocca Torres, L. *El gobierno militar y las comunicaciones en el Perú* (Lima: Ediciones Populares los Andes, 1975).

Rogoff, Edmond. "His Master's Voice: Television in Argentina." Conference on Latin American Popular Culture, Las Cruces, New Mexico, 1981a.

———. "Latin American Television: An Overview of Past Experiences and Future Perspectives." In *Latin American Prospects for the 1980's: What Kinds of Development*, Vol. 3 (Ottawa: Norman Paterson School of International Affairs, 1981b).

Rohter, Larry. "The Noble Hours of Brazilian Television." *American Film* 3, no. 4 (February 1978): 56–59.

Rota, Josep. "The Content of Mexican Commercial Television, 1953–1976." *Studies in Latin American Popular Culture* 4 (1985).

Rubio Barthell, Rodrigo, *TV en close-up* (Mérida, México: Fondo Editorial de Yucatán, 1970).

Santana, Joaquín. "Cuba." *Nueva política* 1, no. 3 (July 1976): 109–12.

Santoro, Eduardo. *La televisión venezolana y la formación de estereotipos en el niño* (Caracas: Universidad Central de Venezuela, Ediciones de Biblioteca, 1976).

Santoro, Luis Fernando. "Tendencias populistas no TV brasileira ou as escassas possibilidades de acesso as antenas." In *Populismo e comunicação*, edited by José Marques de Melo (São Paulo: Cortez Editora, 1981).

Santos Hernando, Gregorio. *Viente y cinco años de TV Argentina* (Buenos Aires: Herpa, 1977).

Schenkel, Peter. "La estructura del poder de los medios de comunicación en cinco países latinoamericanos." *ILDIS, Estudios y documentos* 21 (1973).

Schiller, Herbert I. *Mass Communications and American Empire* (Boston: Beacon Press, 1971).

———. *Communication and Cultural Domination* (White Plains, N.Y.: International Arts and Sciences Press, 1976).

Sodré, Muniz. *A comunicação do grotesco: um ensaio sobre cultura de massa no Brasil* (Petrópolis, Brazil: Editora Vozes, 1972).

———. *O monopolio da fala* (Petrópolis, Brazil: Editora Vozes, 1977).

Straubhaar, Joseph. "Television and Violence in Brazil: the Impact of Imported American Programs, Brazilian Industry and the Brazilian Government on Society." Proceedings of the Northeast Conference on Latin American Studies, Dartmouth, New Hampshire, October 4, 1980.

———. "The Transformation of Cultural Dependence: the Decline of American Influence on the Brazilian Television Industry." Ph.D. dissertation, The Fletcher School of Law and Diplomacy, Tufts University, 1981.

———. "The Development of the *Telenovela* as the Paramount Form of Popular Culture in Brazil." *Studies in Latin American Popular Culture 1* (1982): 138–50.

———. "Brazilian Variety Television Programs: Popular Culture, Industry and Censorship." *Studies in Latin American Popular Culture* 2 (1983): 71–78.

———. "Estimating the Impact of Imported versus National Television Programming in Brazil." In *Studies in Communication*, Vol. 1, edited by Sari Thomas (Norwood, N.J.: Ablex, 1985).

———. "The Decline of American Influence on Brazilian Television." *Communication Research* 11, no. 2 (1984): 221–240.

Szulc, Tad. "Cuban Television's One-Man Show." In *The Eighth Art*, edited by R. L. Shayon (New York: Holt, Rinehart & Winston, 1982).

Tapia Delgado, Gorki. " 'Los Picapiedra: aliados del imperialismo ideología y medios de comunicación de masas.' " *Textual Revista del Instituto Nacional de Cultura* 8 (Lima, 1973).

Televisión argentina: un enfoque nacional (Buenos Aires: Proartel, 1969).

Thiollent, Michel. "Televisão, trabalho e vida cotidiana." *Cadernos INTERCOM* 1, no. 2 (São Paulo, 1982): 44–55.

Thomas, Gerald. "Closely Watched TV." *Index on Censorship: Brazil* 8, no. 4 (July 1974): 43–46.

Tunstall, Jeremy. *The Media are American* (New York: Columbia University Press, 1977).

Ulanovsky, Carlos. *1951–1976, televisión argentina 25 años después* (Buenos Aires: Hachette, 1976).

Universidad de Lima, Instituto de Investigaciones Económicas y de Mercado. *Análisis del público televidente limeño, gustos, hábitos, preferencias* (Lima: Editorial Stylo, 1969).

Valenzuela, Nicholas. "*Televisa* and Television in Mexico." Ph.D. dissertation in progress, Stanford University, Communication Department.

Varis, Tapio, and Salinas Bascur, Raquel. "Communicaciones transnacionales: cine y televisión." *CHASQUI* 16 (1977): 9–22.

Vela Jones, Javier. "Los informativos radiovisuales: plagio y empirismo en el periodismo radial y de televisíon." *CHASQUI* 5 (April 1974): 104–31.

Velsaco, Miguel Aleman. "El estado y la televisión." *Nueva política* 1, no. 3 (México, D.F., 1976): 193–200.

Walger, Sylvina, and Ulanovsky, Carlos. *TV, guía negra* (Buenos Aires: La Flor, 1974).

Wells, Alan. *Picture Tube Imperialism* (MaryKnoll, N.Y.: Orbis Books, 1972).

Werthein, Jorge. "Educational Television in Cuba." In *Mass Media Policies in Changing Cultures*, edited by George Gerbner (New York: Wiley & Sons, 1977).

World Communications: A 200-Country Survey of Press, Radio, Television and Film (Paris: UNESCO Press, 1975).

Eric A. Wagner

5 Sport

Sport, as a social institution, has only recently been studied. Emerging primarily in Europe, interest spread through North America in the 1960s and 1970s. In Latin America, there are only the barest beginnings of the academic study of sport, and these first efforts are mainly the work of North Americans.

Nicholas Mullins, in *Theories and Theory Groups in Contemporary American Sociology* argues that as academic specialities emerge, they progress through four stages of development: the normal, network, cluster, and specialty stages. In North America, the normal stage of the study of sport probably lasted until about the mid-1960s and was characterized by "isolated studies by isolated scholars" (Loy, McPherson, and Kenyon 1979:10). The network stage, lasting at least until the early 1970s, centered around the building of known networks of sport scholars; active research communication was a key element of this stage. The cluster stage in North America emerged by the mid-1970s, when groups of professionals in one university began to focus their work primarily on sport. The University of Waterloo in Canada and the University of Massachusetts in the United States are good examples. In the specialty stage, into which North America has probably entered, sport has become a research area with specialists and a distinctive subject matter and is defined by other disciplines as legitimate and integrated into them.

In Latin America, there is little doubt that the academic study of sport is still in the normal stage. It has not passed beyond the point of isolated scholars engaged in individual studies. Despite early and recent attempts, there is not yet a network of Latin American-oriented sports specialists. The discipline of sociology is an example of this stage of development. In 1966, Ruíz Aguilera of Cuba produced a paper titled the "Situation of the Sociology of Sport in the Latin American Countries." In 1982, one of the sessions of the International Committee for Sociology of Sport at the World Congress of Sociology in Mexico City was devoted to sport in the Latin

American world. Nonetheless, a Latin American sports sociologist network is far from reality.

Perhaps this lack of a network is not surprising. Modern sociology is very recent in most of Latin America, and almost everywhere else, it is a post-World-War-II phenomenon. Much of this early sociology was started by North Americans working in Latin America during and just after the Second World War, with Lowry Nelson in Cuba, T. Lynn Smith in Brazil and Colombia, Carl C. Taylor in Argentina, and Elman and Helen Service in Paraguay. It took a long time after that for university sociology departments to be organized. For example, in Colombia, as late as the end of the 1960s, there were only a handful of doctoral-level sociologists, and university departments were still being organized, such as at the Universidad del Valle in Cali. It is little wonder that such specialized areas as the sociology of sport have yet to be developed; only in 1981 did the author discover a Colombian sociologist who might be interested in the area of sport.

Given that the academic study of sport is still in its incipient stage in Latin America, this chapter will review those isolated studies that have appeared and suggest some directions in which the academic study of sport might develop.

HISTORIC AND BIBLIOGRAPHIC REVIEW

Surprisingly, there are nearly as many studies of pre-Columbian sport as there are of contemporary sport. Most of these studies are anthropological and descriptive, though they sometimes analyze the relationship between social structure and sport. That so many studies of early sport have appeared is testimony to the important place of sport in these societies; "the playing of games by native Americans was an integral part of their cultures" (Cheska 1981:51). Perhaps the most important of these were the rubber ball games played in courts throughout Mesoamerica.

The Rubber Ball Game was popular in Mesoamerica, the Caribbean Islands, and in Arizona territory from approximately 100 to 1500 A.D. . . . An inventory taken in 1969 of known ball courts identified in Mesoamerica totaled 269, in the Caribbean Islands 24, and in Arizona 87. . . . The unique ball used was of solid rubber made from the latex of the rubber tree. It should be noted that this was the first known use of a rubber ball in the world [Cheska 1981:66].

In a few of these studies of early sport, such as Frans Blom's *The Maya Ball Game Pok-Ta-Pok (Called Tlachtli by the Aztec)*, Celso Enríquez's *Sports in Pre-Hispanic America*, William A. Goellner's "The Court Ball Game of the Aboriginal Mayas," Gerdt Kutscher's "Ceremonial Badminton in the Ancient Culture of Moche (North Peru)," and S. Jeffrey K.

Wilkerson's "Man's Eighty Centuries in Veracruz," emphasis is placed on the central role that religious, political, and social ceremonies played in sports events. A recent paper by Kathleen A. Cordes, "Sports and Games of the Aztec and Maya Indians," argued that the ceremonial ball game probably occurred quite early in the culture of the central American Indians and served to integrate religious, social, and political institutions. Some of the studies attempt to survey games and sport in the Americas by looking at more than one sport and/or area. In addition to the Cheska, Cordes, and Enríquez studies, these include Alberto F. Cajas's "Physical Activities in Ancient Peru," S. F. deBorhegyi's "America's Ballgame," John M. Cooper's "Games and Gambling," M. F. Kemrer, Jr.'s, "A Re-Examination of the Ball-Game in Pre-Columbian Meso-America," J. Smith's "The Native American Ball Games," T. Stern's *The Rubber-Ball Games of the Americas*, and Brian Sutton-Smith's *The Games of the Americas*. The latter is an especially useful source.

The majority of the anthropological studies are more limited in scope, confining themselves to discussions of one sport or one group of people; these generally tend to be more descriptive, with limited analysis, and therefore are of only minor use to the study of Latin American sport. Among these descriptive studies are Arthur J. O. Anderson's "Home Diversions of the Aztec Chief," S. F. deBorhegyi's "Ball-Game Handstones and Ball-Game Gloves," C. F. Ekholm's "The Probable Use of Mexican Stone Yokes," M. R. Gilmore's "The Meso-American Rubber Ball Games," Isabel Kelly's "Notes on a West Coast Survival of the Ancient Mexican Ball Game," C. Lumhotz's "Tarahumari Life and Customs," J. Norman's "The Tarahumaras: Mexico's Long Distance Runners," E. Pasztory's "The Historical and Religious Significance of the Middle Classic Ball Game," A. Ledyard Smith's "Types of Ball Courts in the Highlands of Guatemala," W. R. Swezey's "The Ballgame La Pelota Mixteca," and two studies by E. B. Tylor, "On the Game of Patolli in Ancient Mexico and Its Probable Asiatic Origin," and "Backgammon Among the Aztecs." All of these studies do, of course, provide some useful historical background.

There is a gaping hole in the literature about Latin American sport and games from the pre-Columbian period to the advent of modern sports in the late 1800s and early 1900s. Writers simply neglected this aspect of social life during the long colonial period. There are some brief accounts of this topic, but most are buried, generally as descriptive asides, in studies of other aspects of Latin American society. It is virtually impossible to review all the colonial materials about Latin America to the end of ferreting out bits and pieces about sport. Happily, a few colonial studies of game and sport do exist, and persistent searching will yield others. One of these studies is Eugenio Pereira Salas's *Juegos y alegrías coloniales en Chile* [*Colonial Games and Pastimes in Chile*], which is quite interesting. Horse racing, bull fights, cock fighting, *bolos* (which appear to be something like billiards), pelota, fencing, and gambling games are among those discussed. While there is little in the way of social analysis in this work, some of the description is fascinating. For example, the social class composition of various sport activities is sometimes mentioned. A shorter but useful study of games and diversions of the Chileans is Oreste Plath's *Juegos y diversiones de los chilenos* [*Games and Diversions of the Chileans*]. One work that is only marginally in the realm of sport is an examination of the *boleadora* by Alberto Rex González, *La Boleadora: sus áreas de dispersión y tipos* [*The Boleadora: Types and Areas of Dispersion*]. The *boleadora*, or *bolas*, is a missile consisting of two or more balls or stones tied by a rope or leather cord and swung so it will wind around and become entangled in the legs of cattle and occasionally wild game. Rex González's study examines the function, types, and distribution of the *bolas*, showing that it is widely distributed in Latin America. One short discourse, *Port Royal and Its Harbour: With Short Notes On Its History, Legends, Sports, Pastimes and Avocations*, has sports in its subtitle, but like many works of the 1800s and early 1900s, sports means hunting and fishing. The same is true of F. G. Aflalo's *Sunshine and Sport in Florida and the West Indies*. While he mentions jai-alai in Cuba, and polo, lawn tennis, and racing in Jamaica, the bulk of the text is about fishing.

The coming of modern sport to Latin America, which occurred in most places during the second half of the nineteenth century, is not well documented. Piecing together the few references that exist, makes it clear that modern sports, such as soccer, baseball, and basketball, were brought from Europe or North America, generally by merchant seamen. Unquestionably, these sports were in many cases similar to ancient Latin American sports, and they were modified in various ways by the new cultural context. Nonetheless, these modern sports were primarily of British origin, and they spread rapidly to most of the world through British commerce and colonialism. Soccer, for example, as Eric Dunning so vividly portrays in "The Development of Modern Football," evolved through a series of stages from a wild folk game, to acceptance and the development of rules for the game in British public schools, and subsequent dissemination to the larger society. Dissemination to the outside world started about 1860. Shortly afterward, British seamen introduced soccer to various parts of Latin America. Janet Lever reports that "British sailors visiting the port city of Rio de Janeiro first introduced the sport in 1864" (Lever 1972:140), while Robert Levine reports that soccer has been "Brazil's national sport since it was introduced in the 1890s by elite youths schooled in Europe" (Levine 1980:453). March Krotee states that "soccer was reportedly being played in Buenos Aires in 1864" and "permeated the 60–mile liquid barrier of the River Plata to Uruguay where the populace of Montevideo quickly took to the game with enthusiasm" (Krotee 1979:143). In "Mexicans at Play—

A Revolution," Norman Hayner notes that "soccer football" was introduced "long before" 1900.

At almost the same time that soccer was being introduced to Mexico
and South America, baseball was being disseminated from the United
States to the Caribbean, Central America, and northern South America.
Luis Hernández, in "Un siglo de béisbol en Cuba" ["A Century of Baseball
in Cuba"], reports that in 1864, a bat and baseball were brought to Cuba
by Nemesio Guillot, a Cuban who had studied in the United States. Both
Luis Hernández and Enrique Capetillo, in "103 años de lucha, 105 años
de béisbol" ["103 Years of Struggle, 105 Years of Baseball"], report that
in 1866, a ship from the United States docked in Matanzas, Cuba, and the
ship's men invited the Cuban cargo handlers to join them in an exhibition
game of baseball. By 1878 the game of baseball was firmly rooted in Cuban
soil. Norman Hayner, in "Mexicans at Play—A Revolution," noted that
in Mexico baseball was introduced "at least by 1900." Nicaraguans were
playing in organized baseball leagues in the 1890s (Stansifer 1981), but the
exact date of the introduction of baseball is not known. It did disseminate
rapidly and widely; by the early 1960s Mary Helms, in *Asang: Adaptations
to Culture Contact in a Miskito Community*, noted that even the isolated
Miskito Indians of Nicaragua's Atlantic coast region were regularly playing
baseball and had made it an integral part of their social life. Colombians
took up the sport of baseball shortly afterward. In 1903, two months before
Panama was separated from Colombia, Edel Casas and Severo Nieto in
"El béisbol en Colombia" ["Baseball in Colombia"] report that two brothers returned to Cartagena from studies in the United States with "various
modern implements of the game" and began playing baseball; in 1916 the
first baseball league began in Cartagena. Even today, the diffusion of
baseball through Latin America continues. Baseball came to Chile at least
by 1965, and has been brought to the northern Chile mines by a large
group of Japanese mining engineers.

Basketball, about which little has been written, but which is one of the
more popular Latin American sports, came into Latin America at least by
the early 1900s. Norman Hayner in "Mexicans at Play—A Revolution"
reported that the first basketball was brought to Mexico from the United
States "in the trunk of a YMCA physical director about 1907."

While the reasons why specific sports became more popular in some
areas of Latin America than in others have not been explored, it is generally
presumed that in sports Latin American countries reflect dominant colonial
or quasi-colonial influences in the late nineteenth and early twentieth centuries. Great Britain, with its substantial railroad and trading interests in
southern and Andean South America in the late 1800s, brought soccer.
The United States, with its commercial and military interest, brought baseball. It is no accident that those Latin American countries which today

have the strongest interest in baseball (Cuba, Nicaragua, the Dominican Republic, Panama, Venezuela, and Colombia) were the countries where the United States influence was the strongest. Where soccer is dominant (for example Brazil, Argentina, Chile, Uruguay, and Peru), the European presence was strongest. Fuller examination of the dissemination and acceptance of sport remains for future scholars.

Contemporary social science works about sport are few. In broad terms, they can be divided into two types. First are those works that, while undertaken from a social science perspective, are essentially descriptive. Second are studies that attempt some analysis of the society, or groups of societies, through an examination of the institution of sport. Unfortunately, with the exception of Janet Lever's brilliant *Soccer Madness*, theoretically oriented studies of the sociology of Latin American sport do not yet exist.

Among the descriptive studies, by far the largest number are concerned with Cuba. R. J. Pickering, in what is probably the best overall description of sport in Cuba, summarizes the development, organization, physical education, competition, and goals of sport in post-1959 Cuba in his chapter in James Riordan's *Sport under Communism: The U.S.S.R., Czechoslovakia, the G.D.R., China, Cuba*. Leonard Hampson, in "Socialism and the Aims of Physical Education in Cuba," examines physical education and socialist ideology. Manfred Komorowski, in "Cuba's Way to a Country with Strong Influence in Sport Politics: The Development of Sport in Cuba since 1959," shows that involving masses of people in sport, improving teacher training, better physical education programs in schools, and research on sport have all helped Cuba develop into a major sporting power in the last several decades. Eric Wagner, in "Baseball in Cuba," has studied the development, international competition, and contemporary status of baseball in Cuba and in "Sport after Revolution: A Comparative Study of Cuba and Nicaragua," examined the organization of and participation in sport in those countries.

Other descriptive studies are more scattered. Renato Requixa, in "Forms contemporaines d'emploi du temps libre au Brésil" ["Contemporary Forms of the Employment of Free Time in Brazil"], concluded that while sport is extensively discussed and debated, physical participation is low. In "The *Pelea de Gallo* (Cockfight) Along the Río Bravo/Río Grande: Mexican Popular Culture and Mexican American Folk Culture," Gary Joe Mounce looks at the social functions of the cockfight in northern Mexico, concluding that it is a widespread aspect of popular culture and a thriving business. Perhaps the most massive descriptive study of sport in Latin America is *El deporte en Venezuela* [*Sport in Venezuela*], by Luis Felipe Rodríguez and others. The result of an extensive symposium, this volume looks at the evolution of sport in Venezuela, its organization, its technical level, school and military sport, mass and elite sport, the international relations of sport, sport information, and a number of other topics. Norman Hayner, in his brief account of Mexicans at play, gives a vivid description of sport in Mexico about 1950 and provides some limited facts about the development of sport and its level of participation in that year. Eric Wagner, in "Sport and Revolution in Nicaragua," "Sport after Revolution: A Comparative Study of Cuba and Nicaragua," and "Sport Participation in Latin America" provides an account of the evolution of sport in Nicaragua, the philosophy and goals of sport under the Sandinista government, the organization of sport, and a discussion of the levels of participation in sport. The same author also examines the organization of sport and the level of participation in Belize in "Sport Participation in Latin America." Jeffrey Jacob, as part of a study of urban poverty and marginality in Guatemala ("Urban Poverty, Children and the Consumption of Popular Culture: A Perspective on Marginality Theses from a Latin American Squatter Settlement"), gives an enjoyable account of the passion for soccer of boys in a poor barrio. Lastly, Hilmi Ibrahim and Jay Shivers in *Leisure: Emergence and Expansion* examine the development of leisure in a number of countries; Mexico is the one Latin American country included.

Among the more analytical studies, most look at the relation between sport and politics; some of these studies focus on internal politics, while others examine the international level. In his recent paper, "Sport as Civil Society: The Argentinian Junta Plays Championship Soccer," Neil Larsen shows how Argentina's hosting of the 1978 World Cup soccer championships might affect the legitimacy and support for the military government—and might help unleash a resurgent nationalism of the popular classes that could be difficult for the military to control. Steve Ropp's study, "Boxing and the Torrijos Regime: Sports and Politics in Panama," shows that "sports heroes have played an important role in linking the Black urban masses politically to the White urban elite" and that boxing has been "used by the military government as a means of identifying the National Guard with the urban masses" and "serves as a vehicle for unifying Panamanians as a nation in the world context" (Ropp 1981:6–7). Robert Levine, in "The Burden of Success: Futebol and Brazilian Society through the 1970s," shows how soccer has been used to foster national integration and gain support for unpopular military regimes; sport, in other words, is seen as a political weapon. In "Cricket, Literature and the Politics of Decolonization—The Case of C.L.R. James," Helen Tiffin examined cricket as a means of bringing British political and moral values into West Indian culture. A broad analysis of the place of sport in society, including materials on the relationship between sport and politics, is found in Richard Cashman and Michael McKernan's *Sport in History: The Making of Modern Sporting History*. In a thesis, *Sport and Political Systems*, Robert Alan Mechikoff looks at the role of sport in various modern political systems. Also in the international political context, a useful study by Ebenezer Chu, "The Nature and Scope of International Amateur Sports Participation by Selected

Countries and the Implications for International Relations," shows the relationship between international relations and international amateur sports participation and presents interesting material on Brazil and Cuba.

Undoubtedly the most important book so far in the analysis of Latin American sport is Janet Lever's *Soccer Madness*. In this seminal work on Brazilian soccer, Lever argues that sport serves as a major mechanism for social integration at all levels of Brazilian society. It helps individuals to find meaning in their lives and to break the ice in conversations with strangers, it bridges gaps among various social groups, it gives direction and meaning to community cohesiveness and involvement, and the national teams instill pride in many Brazilians. Soccer, she argues, helps bring the whole society together; the institution of sport "helps complex modern societies cohere."

In addition to analyzing the integrative functions of the institution of sport, Lever provides data about the role of soccer in the lives of working-class Brazilians. She describes the organization of sport in Brazil, the problems faced by coaches and referees, and a little of the development of some of the more famous Brazilian soccer clubs. Pervading the book is the passion and joy that Brazilians express for their soccer.

Of the remaining analytical studies, two focus at least partly on the relationship between sport and the socioeconomic situation in a country. In an analysis of the close relationship between sport and the sociocultural process in Uruguay, March Krotee, in "The Rise and Demise of Sport: A Reflection of Uruguayan Society," showed that socioeconomic stability and success in sport seemed to be related. "If history is any indication," he argued, "the outcome of Uruguay's performance on the playing field will serve to mirror its sociocultural progress" (Krotee 1979:154). Janet Lever, in "Soccer as a Brazilian Way of Life," notes the fanaticism for soccer of the Brazilian people. In São Paulo, production rises when the most popular team wins. However, "professionalism has greatly reduced soccer as a stepping stone to a more permanent career," and mobility via soccer is not easy (Lever 1972: 149, 152). Finally, two studies examine the "Soccer War" between Honduras and El Salvador. Mary Jeanne Reid Martz's *The Central American Soccer War: Historical Patterns and Internal Dynamics of OAS Settlement Procedures* deals almost totally with the legal and political mechanisms used by the Organization of American States in solving disputes and has almost nothing that would be of interest to the student of sport. William H. Durham's *Scarcity and Survival in Central America: Ecological Origins of the Soccer War* has a little more material that might be useful to a student of sport but concentrates on analyzing the lack of adequate land for the poor people of El Salvador and their struggles for land with large landowners as the basic underlying cause of the war.

RESEARCH AND INFORMATION SOURCES

As a field characterized by isolated studies by isolated scholars, information sources for the study of Latin American sport are few. Most information still has to be gleaned from studies that focus on topics other than sport or from isolated descriptive studies. Certainly, there is a great deal of sport description in newspapers throughout Latin America. While these materials may be quite useful as primary data and to piece together the historical development of sport, they would require much research effort before they could be of use in the social analysis of sport. One regional newspaper, the Central American edition of *La Nación Internacional* [*The Nation International*], published in San José, Costa Rica, covers Central American sport on a weekly basis. Occasionally, *The Times of the Americas*, published in Washington, D.C., will have an article on sport. Newspapers in all large Latin American cities have daily coverage of sport. In addition, many countries have daily newspapers devoted exclusively to sport, such as *Jornal dos sports* [*Sports Journal*] in Rio de Janeiro, Brazil. There are also two sports dailies in São Paulo, Brazil. Most countries also have sport magazines. In Cuba, the two primary magazines devoted to sport are *El Deporte: Derecho del Pueblo* [*Sport: Right of the People*] and *Semanario Deportivo LPV* [*Sport Weekly*]. (The LPV stands for "Listos para vencer" ["ready for winning"], which indicates something of the propaganda use of sport in Cuba.) Both of these magazines carry articles analyzing sport and articles on the history of sport in Cuba and occasionally in other Latin American countries. They also report results and records and are quite useful to the student of sport.

Most academic journals devoted to the study of sport carry materials relating to Latin America only rarely. Nonetheless, they must be examined, because there are no academic journals that deal exclusively with the study of Latin American sport. Among these general sport journals are the *International Review of Sport Sociology, Journal of Popular Culture, Studies in Latin American Popular Culture, Journal of Leisure Research, Canadian Journal of the History of Sport and Physical Education, International Journal of Sport Psychology, Sport Sociology Bulletin, Journal of Sport Behavior, Review of Sport & Leisure, Exercise and Sport Sciences Review, Journal of Sport History, Journal of the Philosophy of Sport, Stadion, Leisure Sciences, Journal of Sport and Social Issues, Arena Review, Canadian Journal of Applied Sport Sciences, Research Quarterly,* and the *Sociology of Sport Journal.* In a class by itself is the *Sociology of Leisure and Sport Abstracts,* published in the Netherlands. This review of social science literature consists of abstracts prepared by the information retrieval system for the sociology of leisure and sports (SIRLS) at the University of Waterloo, Canada. Started in 1980, the journal has appeared three times a year and generally has around three hundred items abstracted. There are usually several references pertaining to Latin America in each issue.

The most useful general bibliographic reference is Günther R. F. Lüschen and George H. Sage's *Handbook of Social Science of Sport*. This contains an international classified bibliography on the sociology of sport with more than five thousand entries. Also of use is Brian Sutton-Smith's *The Games of the Americas*, which is a reprinting of a number of anthropological studies of play and games.

FUTURE RESEARCH

The study of Latin American sport might well proceed along two fairly distinct but simultaneous lines. In the first, attempts might be made to trace the parallel development of sport and society. Reflecting one of the dominant themes of the literature on sport, this macro-level approach could center on the symbiotic interplay of sport and society, showing how the values of sport and society are interrelated, how organization and structural characteristics of sport and society are similar, and how trends in one are reflected in trends in the other.

Such an approach is pregnant with possibilities for research. For example, sport could be studied as a means of unifying the country and of implementing some measure of understanding between rich and poor, educated and uneducated, young and old, male and female. A common interest in a sport is a great amalgamizer. Through sport can come a beginning of understanding among widely diverse peoples. No wonder many developing countries stress sport so greatly. Such an approach has possibilities not only within countries but among them. The German Democratic Republic is perhaps the best example, with that country turning "to sports as a medium of cultural diplomacy to obtain its foreign policy goals" (Strenk 1978: 348–49). In Latin America, Cuba is clearly pursuing such a policy, and it is certainly possible that Nicaragua will attempt to use sport as one of a number of means to international recognition. And certainly no one can deny that Brazilian success in World Cup soccer competition was an important element in evolving national pride and a sense of worth as a nation.

The second line along which the study of Latin American sport might proceed is a micro-level description of various aspects of sport in various societies. A number of these studies are needed in conjunction with macro-level studies of Latin American sport. A number of these descriptive studies already exist, as indicated earlier in this chapter, but more are needed, and it is these isolated studies by isolated scholars that will eventually lead to the network stage in the study of Latin American sport.

BIBLIOGRAPHY

Aflalo, F. G. *Sunshine and Sport in Florida and the West Indies* (Philadelphia: George W. Jacobs & Co., Publishers, 1907?).

Allardt, E. "Basic Approaches in Comparative Sociological Research and the Study of Sport." In *The Cross-Cultural Analysis of Sport and Games*, edited by G. Lüschen, 14–30 (Champaign, Ill.: Stipes Publishing Co., 1970).

Allison, Lincoln. "Association Football and the Urban Ethos." In *Manchester and São Paulo: Problems of Rapid Urban Growth*, edited by John D. Wirth and Robert L. Jones, 203–28 (Stanford, Calif.: Stanford University Press, 1978).

Allsop, K. "Birds of a Feather." *Spectator* (July 1960): 205–10.

Anderson, Arthur J. O. "Home Diversions of the Aztec Chief." *El Palacio* 55 (1948): 125–27.

Appleton, L. E. *A Comparative Study of the Play Activities of Adult Savages and Civilized Children* (Chicago: University of Chicago Press, 1910).

Blanchflower, D. "Brazilians." *New Statesman* 66 (November 1963): 628.

Blasig, R. "The Practice of Sports Among the Indians of America." *Mind and Body* 24 (1933): 216–19.

Blom, Frans. *The Maya Ball Game Pok-Ta-Pok (Called Tlachtli by the Aztec).* Tulane University of Louisiana Middle American Research Series, Publication No. 4, "Middle American Papers." New Orleans, Louisiana, 1932.

Cajas U., Alberto F. "Physical Activities in Ancient Peru." *Olympic Review*, 150, 151, 152/153 (1980): 176–78, 235–39, 342–49.

Capetillo, Enrique. "103 Años de Lucha, 105 Años de Béisbol." *Semanario Deportivo LPV* (November 30, 1971): 14–17.

Casas, Edel, and Nieto, Severo, "El Béisbol en Colombia." *Semanario Deportivo LPV* (December 8, 1970): 9.

Cashman, Richard, and McKernan, Michael. *Sport in History: The Making of Modern Sporting History* (St. Lucia, Queensland, Australia: University of Queensland Press, 1979).

Catabrano, D. A. "La Cultura, el Deporte, y la Juventud Chilena." *Cuadernos Americanos* 200, no. 3 (1975): 55–68.

Cheska, Alyce Taylor. "Games of the Native North Americans." In *Handbook of Social Science of Sport*, edited by Günther R. F. Lüschen and George H. Sage, 49–77 (Champaign, Ill.: Stipes Publishing Company, 1981).

———. "Sports Spectacular: A Ritual Model of Power." *International Review of Sport Sociology* 14 (1979). 51–72.

Chu, Ebenezer J. "The Nature and Scope of International Amateur Sports Participation by Selected Countries and the Implications for International Relations." Ph.D. dissertation, New York University, 1976.

Cooper, John M. "Games and Gambling." *Bureau of American Ethnology Bulletin* 143 (1949): 503–24.

Cordes, Kathleen A. "Sports and Games of the Aztec and Maya Indians." Paper presented at the Association for the Anthropological Study of Play, Fort Worth, Texas, April 1981.

deBorhegyi, S. F. "Ball-Game Handstones and Ball-Game Gloves." In *Essays in Pre-Columbian Art and Archaeology*, edited by Samuel K. Lothrop et al. (Cambridge, Mass.: Harvard University Press, 1961).

————. "America's Ballgame." *National History* 69 (1969): 48–59.

Dodder, Richard A.; Fromme, Marie Lim; and Holland, Lorell. "Psychosocial Functions of Sport." *Journal of Social Psychology* 116 (1982): 143–44.

Dunning, Eric. "The Development of Modern Football." In *Sport: Readings from a Sociological Perspective*, edited by Eric Dunning, 133–51 (Toronto: University of Toronto Press, 1971).

Durham, William H. *Scarcity and Survival in Central America: Ecological Origins of the Soccer War* (Stanford, Calif.: Stanford University Press, 1979).

Ekholm, C. F. "The Probable Use of Mexican Stone Yokes." *American Anthropologist* 48 (1946): 593–606.

Enríquez, Celso. *Sports in Pre-Hispanic America* (Mexico City: Litográfica Machado, 1968).

Escobar, G. "The Role of Sports in the Penetration of Urban Culture to the Rural Areas of Peru." *Kroeber Anthropological Society Papers* 40 (1969): 72–81.

Flynn, P. "Sambas, Soccer, and Nationalism." *New Society* 18, no. 464 (1971): 327–30.

Gilmore, M. R. "The Meso-American Rubber Ball Games." *Indian Notes* 3 (1926): 293–95.

Glanville, B. "Playing Away." *New Statesman* 95 (April 1978): 577–78.

Glassford, R. G. "The Meso-American Rubber Ball Games." In *Proceedings of the First International Seminar on the History of Physical Education and Sport* (Netanya, Israel: Wingate Institute, 1969).

Goellner, William A. "The Court Ball Game of the Aboriginal Mayas." *The Research Quarterly* 24 (1953): 147–68.

Gomes de Freitas, L. G. "Antigos Jogos Desportivos da Campanha." *Revista do Museo Julio de castillos* 6, no. 7 (1957): 12–19.

Guttmann, Allen. *From Ritual to Record: The Nature of Modern Sports* (New York: Columbia University Press, 1978).

Hampson, Leonard. "Socialism and the Aims of Physical Education in Cuba." *Physical Education Review* 3 (1980): 64–82.

Hayner, Norman S. "Mexicans at Play—A Revolution." *Sociology and Social Research* 38 (1953): 80–83.

Helms, Mary W. *Asang: Adaptations to Culture Contact in a Miskito Community* (Gainesville, Fla.: University of Florida Press, 1971).

Hernández, Luis. "Un Siglo de Béisbol en Cuba." *Semanario deportivo LPV* (December 2, 1969): 8–9.

Hull, Adrian Louis. "The Linguistic Accommodation of a Cultural Innovation as Illustrated by the Game of Baseball in the Spanish Language of Puerto Rico." Ph.D. dissertation, Columbia University, 1963.

Ibrahim, Hilmi, and Shivers, Jay S. *Leisure: Emergence and Expansion* (Los Alamitos, Calif.: Hwong, 1979).

Instituto Nacional de Deporte, Educación Física y Recreación (INDER). *Guía de Béisbol '79* (Ciudad de la Habana, Cuba: Editorial ORBL, 1980).

Jacob, Jeffrey C. "Urban Poverty, Children and the Consumption of Popular Culture: A Perspective on Marginality Theses from a Latin American Squatter Settlement." *Human Organization* 39 (1980): 233–41.

James, C. L. R. "Cricket in West Indian Culture." *New Society* 36 (1963): 8–9.

Kelly, Isabel. "Notes on a West Coast Survival of the Ancient Mexican Ball Game." *Notes on Middle American Archaeology and Ethnology* 1 (1943): 163–74.

Kemrer, M. F., Jr. "A Re-Examination of the Ball-Game in Pre-Columbian Meso-America." In *Crámica de cultura maya*, 1–25 (Philadelphia: Temple University, 1968).

Komorowski, Manfred. "Cuba's Way to a Country with Strong Influence in Sport Politics: The Development of Sport in Cuba since 1959." *International Journal of Physical Education* 14 (1977): 26–32.

Krotee, March L. "The Rise and Demise of Sport: A Reflection of Uruguayan Society." *The Annals of the American Academy of Political and Social Science* 445 (1979): 141–54.

Kutscher, Gerdt. "Ceremonial Badminton in the Ancient Culture of Moche (North Peru)." In *Proceedings of the Thirty-Second International Congress of Americanists*, 422–32. Copenhagen, Denmark, 1958.

Larsen, Neil. "Sport as Civil Society: The Argentinian Junta Plays Championship Soccer." Paper presented at the Latin American Studies Association, Washington, D.C., March 1982.

Lever, Janet. "Soccer as a Brazilian Way of Life." In *Games, Sport and Power*, edited by Gregory P. Stone 138–59 (New Brunswick, N.J.: Transaction Books, 1972).

———. "Soccer in Brazil: Integration Through Conflict." Paper presented at the World Congress of Sociology, Mexico City, August, 1982.

———. *Soccer Madness* (Chicago, The University of Chicago Press, 1983).

Levine, Robert M. "The Burden of Success: Futebol and Brazilian Society through the 1970s." *Journal of Popular Culture* 14 (1980): 453–64.

Loy, John W.; McPherson, Barry D.; and Kenyon, Gerald S. *The Sociology of Sport as an Academic Specialty: An Episodic Essay on the development and Emergence of an Hybrid Subfield in North America* (Calgary, Canada: Canadian Association for Health, Physical Education and Recreation [CAHPER], 1979).

Lumholtz, C. "Tarahumari Life and Customs." *Scribner's Magazine* 3 (1894): 296–311.

Lüschen, Günther R. F., and Sage, George H., eds. *Handbook of Social Science of Sport* (Champaign, Ill.: Stipes Publishing Company, 1981).

Mafud, J. *Sociología del fútbol* (Buenos Aires, 1967).

Manning, Frank E. "Celebrating Cricket: The Symbolic Construction of Caribbean Politics." *American Ethnologist* 8 (1981): 616–32.

Martindale, Colin Arthur. "The Role of Sport in Nation Building: A Comparative Analysis of Four Newly Developing Nations in the Commonwealth Caribbean." Ph.D. dissertation, City University of New York, 1980.

Martz, Mary Jeanne Reid. *The Central American Soccer War: Historical Patterns and Internal Dynamics of OAS Settlement Procedures* (Athens, Ohio: Ohio University Center for International Studies, 1978).

Mechikoff, Robert Alan. "Sport and Political Systems." M.A. thesis. Calfornia State University, 1975.

Medalha, José. "Duties of Sport Administrators in Selected Brazilian Sport Associations with Implications for Professional Preparation." P.E.D. dissertation, Indiana University, 1982.

Mounce, Gary Joe. "The *Pelea de Gallo* (Cockfight) Along the Río Bravo/Río Grande: Mexican Popular Culture and Mexican American Folk Culture." Paper presented at the Conference on Popular Culture in Latin America, Las Cruces, New Mexico: Juárez, Mexico—El Paso, Texas, March 1981.

Mullins, N. C. *Theories and Theory Groups in Contemporary American Sociology* (New York: Harper and Row, 1973).

Norman, J. "The Tarahumaras. Mexico's Long Distance Runners." *National Geographic* 149 (1976): 702–18.

Nufio, O. "Radiografía de la guerra del fútbol o de las Cien Horas." *Revista Mexicana de Sociología* 32, no. 3 (1970): 659–90.

Pasztory, E. "The Historical and Religious Significance of the Middle Classic Ball Game." In *Religión en Meso-América,* edited by J. L. Minh and N. C. Terjero, 441–45 (Mesa Redonda, México: Sociedad Mexicana de Antropología, 1972).

Patterson, O. "The Cricket Ritual in the West Indies." *New Society* 352 (1969): 988–89.

Pereira Salas, Eugenio. *Juegos y Alegrías Coloniales en Chile* (Santiago de Chile: Empresa Editora Zig-Zag, S.A., 1947).

Pickering, R. J. "Cuba." In *Sport Under Communism: The U.S.S.R., Czechoslovakia, The G.D.R., China, Cuba,* edited by James Riordan, 141–74 (London: C. Hurst & Company, 1978).

Pierce, Chester M.; Stillner, Verner; and Popkin, Michael K. "On the Meaning of Sports: Cross Cultural Observations of Super Stress." *Culture, Medicine and Psychiatry* 6 (1982): 11–28.

Plath, Oreste. *Juegos y Diversiones de los Chilenos* (Santiago de Chile: Imp. Cultura, 1946).

Pointu, R., and Fidani, R. *Cuba: Sport en Révolution* (Paris: Editeurs Français Réunis, 1975).

Port Royal and Its Harbour: With Short Notes on Its History, Legends, Sports, Pastimes and Avocations (Jamaica: Aston W. Gardner & Co., 1893).

Requixa, Renato. "Forms contemporaines d'emploi du temps libre au Brésil." *Loisir-Information/Leisure-Newsletter* 7 (1979): 7–10.

Rex González, Alberto. *La Boleadora: Sus Áreas de Dispersión y Tipos* (Argentina: Universidad Nacional de Eva Perón, 1953).

Riess, S. A. "Baseball Myths, Baseball Reality, and the Social Functions of Baseball in Progressive America." *Journal of the History of Sport and Physical Education* 3 (1977): 273–311.

Riordan, James, ed. *Sport under Communism: The U.S.S.R., Czechoslovakia, the G.D.R., China, Cuba* (London: C. Hurst & Company, 1978).

Robinson, John P. "Time Expenditure on Sports Across Ten Countries." *International Review of Sport Sociology* 2 (1967): 67–87.

Rodríguez, Luis Felipe. *El Deporte en Venezuela* (Caracas, Venezuela: Dirección de Cultura, Universidad Central de Venezuela, 1968).

Ropp, Steve C. "Boxing and the Torrijos Regime: Sports and Politics in Panama." Paper presented at the Conference on Popular Culture in Latin America, Las Cruces, New Mexico—Juárez, Mexico—El Paso, Texas, March 1981.

Ruíz Aguilera, R. "Situation of the Sociology of Sport in the Latin American Countries." Havana, Cuba, 1966. (Mimeographed.)

Russell, David. "Baseball, Hollywood, and Nicaragua." *Monthly Reivew* 34 (March, 1983): 22–29.

Sackmary, B. D. "The Sociology of Science: The Emergence and Development of a Sociological Specialty." Ph.D. dissertation, University of Massachusetts (Amherst), 1974.

Seppänen, Paavo. "Olympic Success: A Cross-National Perspective." In *Handbook of Social Science of Sport*, edited by Günther R. F. Lüschen and George H. Sage, 93–116 (Champaign, Ill.: Stipes Publishing Company, 1981).

Silver, B. B. "Social Structure and Games: A Cross-cultural Analysis of the Structural Correlates of Game Complexity." *Pacific Sociological Review* 21 (1978): 85–102.

Slack, Trevor. "Cuba's Political Involvement in Sport Since the Socialist Revolution." *Journal of Sport and Social Issues* 6 (1982): 35–45.

Smith, A. Ledyard. "Types of Ball Courts in the Highlands of Guatemala." In *Essays in Pre-Columbian Art and Archaeology*. Edited by Samuel K. Lothrop et al, 100–125 (Cambridge, Mass.: Harvard University Press, 1961).

Smith, David Horton. "Participation in Outdoor Recreation and Sports." In *Participation in Social and Political Activities*, edited by David Horton Smith, Jacqueline Macaulay and Associates, 177–201 (San Francisco, Calif.: Jossey-Bass Publishers, 1980).

Smith, J. "The Native American Ball Games." In *Sport in the Sociocultural Process*, edited by Marie M. Hart (Dubuque, Iowa: Wm. C. Brown, Co., 1972).

Stansifer, Charles L. Personal communication, 1981.

Stern, T. *The Rubber-Ball Games of the Americas* (Seattle: Wash.: University of Washington Press, 1949).

Strenk, Andrew. "Diplomats in Track Suits: Linkages Between Sports and Foreign Policy In The German Democratic Republic." In *Sport and International Relations*, edited by Benjamin Lowe, David B. Kanin, and Andrew Strenk, 347–68 (Champaign, Ill.: Stipes Publishing Company, 1978).

Sutton-Smith, Brian, ed. *The Games of the Americas* (New York: Arno Press, 1976).

Swezey, W. R. "The Ballgame La Pelota Mixteca." *Revista* 1 (1973): 21–24.

Szalai, Alexander. *The Use of Time: Daily Activities of Urban and Suburban Populations in Twelve Countries* (The Hague, Netherlands: Mouton, 1972).

Tiffin, Helen. "Cricket, Literature and the Politics of Decolonization—The Case of C.L.R. James." Paper presented at The Making of Sporting Traditions II, Kensington, New South Wales, Australia, June 1979.

Tylor, E. B. "On the Game of Patolli in Ancient Mexico and Its Probably Asiatic Origin." *Journal of the Anthropological Institute of Great Britain* 8 (1878): 116–31.

———. "Backgammon Among the Aztecs." *Macmillan's Magazine* 39 (1878): 142–50.

Wagner, Eric A. "Baseball in Cuba." *Journal of Popular Culture* 18 (Summer 1984): 113–120.

———. "Sport after Revolution: A Comparative Study of Cuba and Nicaragua." *Studies in Latin American Popular Culture* 1 (1982): 65–73.

———. "Sport and Revolution in Nicaragua." In *Nicaragua In Revolution*, edited by Thomas W. Walker, 291–302 (New York: Praeger Publishers, 1982).

———. "Sport Participation in Latin America." *International Review of Sport Sociology* 17 (1982): 29–39.

———. "Sport Participation in Latin America." In *Körperkultur und Sport in der Lebensweise sozialer Gruppen* (Volume 2), pp. 65–80. Proceedings of the VIIth International Symposium of the International Committee for Sociology of Sport (Leipzig, German Democratic Republic: German College for Physical Education, 1982).

Wilhelm, Daniel J. "Tropical Baseball: Staying Well in Nicaragua." *The Physician and Sportsmedicine* 7 (June 1979): 141–45.

Wilkerson, S. Jeffrey K. "Man's Eighty Centuries in Veracruz." *National Geographic* 158 (August 1980): 203–31.

Wood, E. R., and Carrington, L. B. "School, Sport and the Black Athlete." *Physical Education Review* 5 (1982): 131–37.

Yuriev, Grigory V. "The Muscled Missionaries of Marxism: Sports as a Soviet Political Weapon." *Analysis of Current Developments* 9 (1962–1963): 1–5.

Zurcher, L. A., and Meadow, A. "On Bullfights and Baseball: An Example of Interaction of Social Institutions." *International Journal of Comparative Sociology* 8 (1967): 99–117.

Cornelia Butler Flora

6 Photonovels

A HISTORICAL-SOCIOLOGICAL OVERVIEW

Fotonovelas [Photonovels]—romantic stories presented as balloon-captioned photographs—are, next to comic books, the most widely distributed printed material in Latin America. That phenomenal popularity—and profitability—is due to a combination of technological development, printing capacity, and cultural patterns.[1] Yet *fotonovelas* are almost orphans of Latin American mass media. Few claim to aspire to produce them, few admit to reading them, and no institution maintains systematic collections of even single titles, much less the thousands of titles that have been offered on newsstands and through neighborhood rental markets throughout Latin America.

Europe was the initial source of *fotonovelas* for Latin America. Saint-Michel links the birth of the first *roman-photo* [Photonovel], as he terms it, to the introduction of photography and the production, in 1834, of "Les Mésaventures de Jean-Paul Choppart" ["The Misadventures of Jean-Paul Choppart"], which used the form of captioned photographs to tell a romantic story (Saint-Michel 1979). Such publications reoccurred periodically in France with little lasting impact. For example, in 1900 a series of short fables was published using the same format and the romantic theme.

With the growth of the movie industry in Europe, it was logical to take still photographs from movies and caption them, and this has occasionally been done with popular movies since 1915 (Curiel 1978: 25). Movies as a medium accustomed people to accepting photographs as part of fiction, but it was not until after the Second World War that the movie industry was established to the degree that the *Roman-photos* became a systematic by-product. However, only the photographic image is the same. The *fotonovela* converted the continuous, moving and speaking image of the movie into a discontinuous, static and mute image. More imagination was required on the part of the reader to decode the story presented. Nevertheless, the sellers of *fotonovelas* like to term them *cine de bolsillo* [pocket movies].

The first commercial *fotonovela* publication's title was borrowed from the 1932 Hollywood movie *Grand Hotel*. The del Duca brothers, who owned the Cine del Duca movie company, launched *Grand Hotel* in Italy in 1945.[2] The first number sold fifty thousand copies the first week; the one million copies of the second number published the next week were also sold out. The idea to produce stories for *fotonovela* production, independent of any movie, but using the technical innovations, the aspiring actors, and the creative talent of a strong movie industry, was a success in Italy. They were known as *fumettis* after the "cloud of smoke" above the characters' heads where speech was printed. A new publishing empire was born. Using the same photographs, it proved easy enough to translate the captions to French, and, a bit later, to Spanish. Circulation was very high among the working classes in all three languages. Distribution then moved to the ex-colonies. Del Duca soon launched a coproduction company in France. The first title there was introduced through the women's magazine *Confidences [Confidings]*. Special *roman-photos* were made in France aimed specifically at Africa.

The *roman-photos* were aimed at women and appeared both as separate magazines and as parts of women's magazines. Often the second form served as a way to introduce potential readers to the first form. As the number of titles proliferated, the monopoly of the del Ducas was broken, although they continue to dominate the market in Italy. Other publishers, including Rizzoli and Mondadori, produced a second tier of *Roman-photo* publications. As off-set printing became more widely available, the potential for quick publication, with quick translation, grew. Yet *fotonovela* circulation met cultural barriers, as their popularity was largely restricted to Catholic and Latin populations with their "lower cultural level and degree of literacy than populations from northern European Protestant roots" (Gubern 1974:19–20).

The first *fotonovelas* sold in Latin America came to the northern part of the continent from Spain and to the southern cone from Italy. The Spanish production of *fotonovelas* built not only on the film industry, but on a tradition of romantic tales for women, which included the cheap romantic novel and the *tebeo feminino* [feminine comic], the romantic comic book that emerged in fascist Spain. For the Spanish-language *fotonovela*, one author's name is synonymous with the development of the genre, Corín Tellado. Corín Tellado first published only printed stories sold in cheap paperback editions of around 128 pages each. This limited the audience in Latin America to literate, middle-class women. The photographic format changed the prerequisites for readership, and a massive following, particularly in urban areas, resulted. The *fotonovela Corín Tel-*

lado, like the novel, at first was published in Spain and exported. As transportation costs became higher, the locus of production shifted. Miami became the site for publication of the *fotonovela* for the northern part of Latin American and Santiago de Chile for the southern part.

Initial production of *fotonovelas* in Latin America took advantage of several factors: close ties with Italian production companies; the introduction of modern magazines to the continent in the 1950s; the strong printing industry that had developed in southern-cone countries and particularly in Argentina, in part due to government subsidy for the production of school books; the establishment of film and television industries in the southern cone; and the capital and creative linkages among Italy, Brazil, and Argentina, which were a by-product of the stream of Italian immigrants. Later, production moved to Chile, Mexico, and Miami (via the Cuban exile connection). International linkages in *fotonovela* publishing remain strong, particularly as the economic swings in the southern-cone countries make it more or less profitable to produce domestically or import material.

During the relative economic prosperity of the 1950s and early 1960s, *fotonovela* production boomed in Argentina. A large domestic market was eager to buy, particularly in the working class areas of Buenos Aires and in the provinces. Editorial Abril, which had linkages to Italy and Brazil, began publishing *fotonovelas* in early 1950, putting out a number of titles. Both singers and other performers found it advantageous to work as "models" in *fotonovelas*, for, although the pay was minimal, the exposure they got increased sales of records and concert tickets. As television grew in importance, dual productions of *fotonovelas* and *telenovelas* [television soap operas] emerged. In Peru in the late 1960s and early 1970s, a favorite *telenovela*, *Simplemente María* [*Simply Mary*] spun off a highly popular *fotonovela* to accompany it. In that era in the southern cone, *fotonovelas* probably reached their peak of respectability and creativity.

In Brazil, the Italian connection had a great influence on the type of *fotonovelas* that emerged beginning in late 1951, as did the relatively repressive political climate after the 1964 military take-over. Brazilian publishing houses, especially Editora Abril, drew techniques and staff from its Argentina counterpart, Editorial Abril. The *fotonovelas* produced domestically in Brazil showed little difference from those produced in Italy and translated for publication. (Halbert 1974: 30). An important exception was the Brazilian *fotonovela* *Sétimo céu* [*Seventh Heaven*], which began publication in the late 1950s and which continued publication of Brazilian-produced materials—despite its disadvantageous economic position vis-à-vis imported materials—until the end of the 1970s.

For nearly twenty years the *fotonovela rosa* [pink photonovel] dominated the Latin American popular culture landscape. The *fotonovela rosa* was populated by poor, pure women confronting rich, evil women to win the love of rich, cynical men who were forever torn between their base instincts (sex, represented by the wiles of the evil, rich female) and their nobility (marriage, represented by the virtue of the poor heroine). Nobility and virtue came together at the end as fortune's reward for her groveling passivity and his astonishing wealth, unless prevented by a tragic death, in which case the spirits of the protagonists were eventually united.

These *fotonovelas* of mystification and escape generally were purchased from a European publishing house but then selected, censored, and translated to fit the political and economic realities of the national publishing industry. The publishing companies in Latin America were responding to potential censorship and easy profit in the first stage of *fotonovela* penetration into mass consumption. The medium, as represented by the *fotonovela rosa*, was in no way congruent with national reality. The *fotonovela rosa* systematically avoided any reflection of a non-European, non-upper-class milieu. (That the heroine was poor confounded that contradiction, for, despite the text that stressed her poverty, our poor, pure heroine always had an upper-middle-class home, wardrobe, hair style, and manicure which, apparently, made her temporary poverty less repellent to the fastidious hero.)

Production of *fotonovelas* was separated from consumption along four dimensions in Latin America: social class (produced by the upper class for the working class), gender (produced by men for women), continent (produced in Europe for Latin America), and race (produced by whites for blacks, Indians, and mestizos). This separation led to an antiseptic setting that became less and less appealing during the 1970s. The traditional *fotonovela rosa* lost its ability to mystify and thus its appeal, which before had sold millions of magazines a week throughout the continent. The occasional *fotonovelas* during the mid-seventies that touched more realistic life situations proved more popular and suggested the potential of a more *criolla* [creole] type of *fotonovela* that broke down at least some of the dimensions separating the reader from content. *Simplemente María* is the archtypical *fotonovela* that heralded the shift from the *fotonovela rosa*— the *fotonovela* of total escape—to the *fotonovela* of disintegration-integration via the mechanism of consumption as salvation.

María, of *Simplemente María*, is a young, illiterate girl of decided Indian heritage from a small town. Believing he loves her, she is deceived by a young upper-middle-class student. Pregnant and humiliated, she must make a new life for herself and her child—which she does as a seamstress/dress designer. She accepts her destiny to suffer because she has sinned—but her perseverance in the face of oppression yields economic as well as spiritual rewards.

Beginning in the late-1960s, but only becoming the norm by the mid-1970s, the protagonists in *fotonovelas* sold in Latin America became more middle class. In part, this reflected a shift in European tastes, as Italian publishers found that a politically mobilized working class no longer sought out stories of nice girls marrying millionaires. The problems addressed included those of making a living as well as finding true love. The solutions to the two problems generally were portrayed as ultimately compatible, although momentarily in conflict. This new genre of *fotonovela*, which has been termed the *fotonovela suave* [soft photonovel] (Flora [*JPC*] 1980:525), entered the market as new editorial companies formed to penetrate growing markets.

The *fotonovela suave* emerged as the number of publishers of *fotonovelas* grew. The market seemed insatiable, although risky. While some titles sold millions weekly or biweekly, other titles died after two or three issues. There was little systematic surveying of audience, and a lot of trial and error was involved in introducing a title that would bring in the profits possible in *fotonovela* publishing. *Fotonovelas* in the southern-cone countries carried more advertising, which tended to be the major source of profit. In Mexico and the Andean countries, there was little advertising. Profits came from sales only—the higher the volume, the lower the unit costs and the higher the profit.

But publishing was not the only place in *fotonovela* production and distribution where profits were made. Indeed, distributing *fotonovelas*—generally as one more title or genre in an already large repertoire of magazine titles—was more profitable and more tightly controlled than production. Only in Peru in the 1980s was there a large number of distributors of magazines, including *fotonovelas*. Elsewhere in Latin America, one, two, or at the most, three distributing companies, often multinationally linked or owned, distribute the magazines. Often these distributors are vertically linked to publishing houses, but not always. Such control of distribution can ultimately limit who has the opportunity to publish.

Distribution of *fotonovelas* is profitable whether the magazine is printed in the country where it is distributed or elsewhere. Del Duca, beginning in France in the 1930s, devised a method of distribution of romance magazines that is still profitable today. The magazines bear no date nor any seasonal theme. They are identified only by number. The runs are first sent to the larger cities in a country, where they remain on the newsstands until the next number in the series title appears—usually one or two weeks. The dealer then returns them to the distributor who ships them off to the second tier of towns, and so on, down to provincial sellers who simply handle whatever may be left.

In Latin America, that tier system works not only within countries, but across countries. For example, Mexican-made *fotonovelas* are printed in Colombia, after having been first produced, printed, and distributed in Mexico and then shipped to Central America and the Caribbean. The issues go first to major cities, then minor ones, then rural areas in Mexico, then on to work their way down the Central American isthmus. At the same time the magazines are sent to secondary Mexican markets, they are shipped to Spanish-speaking markets in the United States through closely held distribution networks. The Colombian publishing house arranges with a printer to print the magazines from the camera-ready mounted photographs and captions. Then the publisher sends them to one or two distributors who distribute them throughout the country. One of the distributors is tied to the Venezuelan publishing house, Bloque de Armas, and the other to the Carvajal paper empire, with linkages to Chile (an important source of timber for paper). Those that are not sold in Colombia go to Venezuela, then Ecuador, and finally Peru and Bolivia. Because of currency difficulties, Peru and Bolivia seldom remit much foreign exchange. Thus there is more competition among distributors in those countries, who distribute *foto-novelas* produced as long as two years earlier in another country. The same tiered distribution system works even within these countries. For example, in Ayacucho, Peru, in 1980, "new" *fotonovelas* were for sale that had been printed in Mexico in 1975. One reason cross-national sales are so profitable is that magazines, including *fotonovelas*—unlike books—are exempt from tariff restrictions because they are classified as news media and thus part of a population's basic right to information.

The one place that little profit is to be made is in the creative content of *fotonovelas*. Very few in-house *fotonovela* units are now functioning in Latin America. Production is generally farmed out on contract. Free lancers produce *fotonovelas* and then try to peddle them to publishing houses under established titles. In Mexico, a number of successful production companies have been established. Even there, however, writers, models, and photographers make relatively little. In the most successful enterprises, speed is valued over creativity, and no more than four days can be allotted to one *fotonovela* from conception to camera-ready copy.

Production of camera-ready copy requires the preparation of a story line, with characters and settings designated, scripting by scene and setting to facilitate costuming and sets, hiring models (who generally provide their own makeup and costumes, according to the instructions of the director), and arranging for sets (only the largest Mexican producers have an established site where they can shoot; other producers must borrow all settings, from restaurants, to offices, to bedrooms). Photographers must be contracted, and film bought. The scenes are then shot, and the proofs developed as quickly as possible. The director then attempts to link the script to the photographs, writing out the captions in the process. Some directors work from a set script; others use a vague outline worked out by scene and put in the captions once they see the photographs. Special machines are then needed to put the captions into proper form so that they fit the photographs. The desired photographs are then quickly printed in the proper size and mounted on cardboard, with the captions mounted appropriately over the photographs. The *fotonovela*, if approved by the publisher, is now ready to be printed.

The complicated process of original production—which can be even more involved if special makeup, settings, or costuming is desired—must be contrasted to the use of "canned" *fotonovelas* produced elsewhere and "recycled." In Argentina, large Italian publishing houses, which operate at a large enough scale to maintain constantly busy *fotonovela* production crews, supply the originals. The desired *fotonovelas* are selected by an Argentine reader in Buenos Aires who chooses from already published Italian *fotonovelas* shipped to her by the Italian mother house. This selection was necessary because of the censorship laws prevalent under the military regime of Argentina. Under the current civilian administration, selection anticipates readers' taste. Selection under the military government involved not only artistic criteria (basically, did the reader like it or not), but criteria of censorship—too much nudity (which can often be avoided by simply taking out a picture and inserting a short text euphemistically describing the "action"), criticism of the military, strikes, labor organizations, or anything that might be deemed "subversive" in the Argentine context. The Italian supplier is then informed of the choice, and the proper set of mounted photographs—with the captions removed—is duly sent, generally in batch lots. The text is then translated (and often simplified), the captions prepared and mounted, and the *fotonovela* sent to the printer. That long and elaborate process costs less than original production. But the process keeps any *fotonovela* from dealing with *timely* subjects.

In the case of Colombian *fotonovela* publication, the alternative to locally produced *fotonovelas* is even easier. No selection takes place, although often the *fotonovela* to be used has been published earlier in Mexico. Some publishing houses in Colombia simply buy a title that has been popular in Mexico and hope that Colombian tastes are similar. Other publishing houses, particularly Editorial Cinco, puts out Mexican produced *fotonovelas* under their own titles. As with the Argentine case, the photographs—this time with the captions still mounted—are shipped to the publisher, usually in a traveler's briefcase to avoid customs duties. Sometimes attempts are made to change the most offensive Mexican slang. Most often, no changes in the text are made, thus avoiding any national input—or local wages to be paid.

The key element in the production of *fotonovelas* is low cost of production. This is done by contracting out a large portion of the labor in order to pay the maintenance costs of as few staff as possible. Of the small permanent staff, the same three or four persons will work on all the titles a publishing house puts out. Although the publishing houses attempt to create a separate indentity for each *fotonovela* title published, upon examining them, it is often hard to distinguish between titles. As a result, most *fotonovelas* are bought because of their cover rather than their content. Only the most popular *fotonovelas* are bought for their titles. In response to this, one Colombian publishing house ran European covers (with blonds playing tennis, for example) on Mexican *fotonovelas* (with dark-skinned brunettes in Mexico City offices), because they considered them more attractive.

Publishing companies fall along a continuum of degree of division of labor, rationalization of the method of production, and professionalization of the staff. Degree of division of labor corresponds with the expansion of the publishing enterprise and the sales. As press runs expand, additional staff is hired to deal with the complexities of marketing and distribution. The most highly differentiated publishing houses are also distributors, often in several countries.

Despite the economic disincentives for original production, the number of *fotonovela* titles whose content is produced in Latin American has grown enormously in the last few years. This is an indirect rather than a direct result of the profits gained from publishing. If a producer of content can present a completed, camera-ready, mounted *fotonovela* for the same price as the imported version, it may be printed. The hope is that volume can make up for low return on the initial investment.

As many new people began producing *fotonovelas*, in response in part to expanded printing capacity as modern graphic techniques were introduced throughout Latin America, the variety in content grew as well. The introduction of new genres proved to publishers that something slightly different from maid-marries-millionaire might also be profitable. That was particularly the case in Mexico, where production capacity was high, the state subsidized paper, and official censorship was much less than in other nations with potentially large internal markets.

At first the *rosa* theme predominated in the Mexican-produced *fotonovelas*. However, as the number of *fotonovela* producers increased—and the resources supporting production proportionally decreased—both the costs of production and the social class of the protagonists, as well as the differences in age and social class of hero and heroine, declined. More varied plot devices were introduced to allow star-crossed lovers eventually to be united. For example, evil wives of rich heroes conveniently expired of exotic illnesses or bizarre accidents in the Spanish *fotonovela rosa*. Once fate had thus acted to remove that otherwise unassailable barrier, the long-suffering but noble hero was free to marry the passive heroine, who had silently loved him from afar. In the Mexican *fotonovela rosa*, the heroine maintained her classical subservient position and passive demeanor. But now the marital bonds could be severed by divorce, and the first wife need not be struck dead to remove the obstacle separating the clearly preferable romantic attachment. This change came not from a Mexican queasiness in facing death, but seemed to arise from a desire on the part of authors to be more realistic in the light of changing laws and norms.

As the *fotonovela rosa*'s popularity declined, *suaves* began to capture more of the market. Males were part of the readership to a greater degree than was assumed in the *fotonovela rosa*, as indicated by the proportion of letters they wrote to the *fotonovelas* (Flora [*JPC*] 1980:530).

Social class, as in the case of *Simplemente María*, became more explicit in *suaves*. Class differences were represented as artificial, something that could be overcome by true love and a determination to follow one's fate. While the hero was always portrayed as having a lower-class background than his competitor for the heroine (a "rule" of *fotonovela* writing), class differences were used to demonstrate that even these obstacles could not interfere with the cosmic flow of ultimate justice, of which true love was final vindication.

The *fotonovela suave* focused on a "salvation through consumption" theme. (Flora and Flora 1978: 146–149). Problems of social class differences could be resolved by buying more products. The *fotonovela suave* is the genre of *fotonovelas* with the largest number of advertisements per issue. Generally items aimed at the socially aspiring urban poor (correspondence courses, bust-building apparatuses) are featured. Social class then becomes defined by the number of items one owns rather than by one's relation to the means of production.

While in the Brazilian and Argentine *fotonovelas* consumer items, particularly clothes, makeup, and hair styles, are stressed in the story as the key to "salvation" (capturing the proper man), in the Colombian-produced *fotonovela suave*, the key consumption item is education. Much stress is laid on the necessity of the hero continuing his studies, despite his impulse to marry and get a job right away to support his wife and children. The message is "wait, study, and have a better life." With the waiting, sex before marriage for women is acceptable (it always was for men), although it must be confined to the intended or attributed to briefly losing one's self-control, usually as a result of grief or alcohol.

In the *fotonovelas suaves* that portray married couples, the consumption as salvation theme is more explicit. Usually the marriage is suffering because the husband is stingy with both his money and his attentions. Through the intervention of an attentive rival, usually a creation of the husband to see if his wife is really faithful and loves him, the husband learns by her warm and passionate response to the generous man of fiction that he has erred in his ways by not spending more on her; the monetary and emotional expenditures thus become equated.

The *fotonovela suave* combines the ideal of bettering one's self through consumption with the lesson that one should not desire to totally leave one's station in life. Not accepting the limits of the economic system by seeking "easy" ways around it is properly punished. In the Colombian *fotonovela suave*, drug trafficking is the "quick fix" leading to higher levels of consumption. Naturally, the drug trafficker is punished, at least in the *fotonovela*. In Mexico, the easy life is symbolized by the wicked world of the nightclub where prostitution abounds. Innocent girls get lured to such dens of iniquity thinking they will only be dancing for a living. The *foto-novela suave* teaches that purity should not be sacrificed even for the possibility of radically changing one's potential for consumption. Those who attempt to stray from the straight and narrow path of middle-class romance are severely punished.

The *fotonovela suave* from Europe published in the southern cone tend to have more complex plots and longer, more expensive presentation, aided by higher quality, larger-sized paper. Their high cost and complexity fit the higher literacy and standard of living of the readers in the southern-cone countries. In the *fotonovela suave* produced in Colombia and Mexico, the format of the magazine imposes certain conventions. Because of costs of production, each *fotonovela* is 30 pages, contains from 110 to 130 different vignettes, or pictures, has a size of 20 by 13 1/2 centimeters, and is printed on newsprint, which gives pictures lower contrast. The number of characters is reduced, and the few that are presented tend to be unidimensional. The amount of dialogue is reduced, in part because of smaller page and vignette size.

In the Mexican *fotonovela suave*, the average number of words per vignette is fourteen. In the Argentine, it is thirty two. Thus, the systematic shortening of the format in the northern countries of Latin America, done in part to keep costs or production down and sales up, leads to a greater dependency on pictures and the skill of the models in showing emotions. Often, as a result, onomatopoeia is used across the face of photographs to make the action/emotion clearer. The number of characters is limited to three or four at most. Size imposes strict limits on plot development and keeps costs down. Given such limitations, it is much easier to write about an on-going relationship rather than to establish one. If one is established, the bond must be rapidly formed, through meaningful glances that result in love at first sight. That instantaneous formation of true love generally occurs in the first vignette, or frame, of the *fotonovela suave*, without development of either character.

Whereas the *fotonovela suave* admitted to sex, with an underlying threat of violence if sexual norms were openly defied, it had to compete with other media that were getting more and more sexually explicit, particularly in the northern parts of Latin America, where state censorship was less extreme. *Radionovelas* [radio soap operas] and *telenovelas* filled the airways, bringing the same story with a more fluid presentation. Movies, following a western world trend, were becoming more sexually explicit. To compete, particularly with the electronic media, the printed form used its major advantage—the option of being more explicit sexually. Explicit sex and sexuality, as well as constant physical violence, particularly that of men against women, are the hallmark of the third genre of *fotonovelas* in Latin America, the *fotonovela roja* [red photonovel].

The *fotonovela rosa* generally was titled according to the name of the author (or reputed author): Corín Tellado, Seline, or, in the case of the southern-cone *fotonovelas*, with names that implied fate, such as *Destino* [*Destiny*]. The *fotonovela suave* took on names that spoke frankly of love, such as *Fotoromances* [*Photo Romances*], *Novelas de amor* [*Novels of Love*], *Secretos de corazón* [*Secrets of the Heart*]. In contrast, the *fotonovela roja* had titles that spoke of life as it is, with all its tragedy and pitfalls: *Casos de la vida* [*Cases of Life*], *Pecado mortal* [*Mortal Sin*]. Not only did titles imply greater realism, but the main characters became more earthy as well. Social class declined. Middle-class characters are practically absent, and even the stable working class is a rarity. The majority of characters are now lumpen proletariat. The models have darker hair and darker skins. Their wardrobes are less elaborate, and the setting shifts to the poorer part of town.

The covers on both the *fotonovela rosa* and the *fotonovela suave* strike a romantic and tender note, using head shots, or, in a few cases, shots from the waist up of male and female characters in close and loving proximity. In contrast, the *fotonovela roja* always has full body shots, with the women either in the scantiest of bikinis or underwear or with strategically torn clothing. Over half of the covers feature explicit violence or threat of violence. On these covers, female sexuality is portrayed as an irresistible temptation to men, leading toward sin and away from reasoned interaction and solidarity between the sexes. The violence portrayed reinforces the individualistic mode of problem solution. Woman's released sexuality inevitably leads to tragedy.

The *roja* genre combines the morality tale of the importance of keeping to the straight and narrow path with photographs that approach soft-core pornography in their explicitness. A favorite shot is up the heroine's miniskirt, focusing on her upper thigh. The woman thus photographed usually has one leg raised to emphasize this particular anatomical part. Such poses are excusable because of the moral message of the story. Whether or not readers are impressed by the pictures or the text has not been resolved, although preliminary research suggests that the "morals" serve as a justification for reading the *fotonovela roja*.

Readers of the *roja* genre explain their choice of reading matter in terms of the stories being "real" and giving them instruction on how one should meet actual problems. This rationale is believable because the characters are poor and their problems involve money as well as love and that the money problems are not solved by coming into an unexpected inheritance or marrying a millionaire. The *fotonovela roja*, for a majority of working-class and lumpen-proletariat Latin Americans, presents real life. Such codification of plots gives order, meaning, and commonality to life's inexplicable twists and turns. The reader is reassured that her own life is also meaningful and ordered, despite outward appearances.

The *roja* genre teaches lessons of antisolidarity. Not only best friend, but even brother, sister, father, and mother betray the heroes and heroines of the *fotonovela roja*. Most telling is that now the mother, closely linked to saintliness in most Latin American cultures, betrays the fruit of her womb to obtain her own narrow and selfish ends. The working class indeed has been separated into the easily manageable "potatoes in the sack" alluded to by Marx.

The *rojas'* tales of violence, family disintegration, and the destructive powers of sexuality awakened ring true in many of the *barriadas* [lower-class neighborhoods] of Mexico City, Bogotá, and Lima, where the *fotonovela roja* is very popular and outsells both the *rosa* and *suave* type of *fotonovela*. Incest and rape are a common occurrence in the *fotonovela roja* and a common occurrence in the population. No other medium talks about it so directly. Indeed, in a series of conversations with poor women in marginal neighborhoods of Bogotá, they pointed out that rape of young girls is a major problem, made even more difficult because the "shame" involved discourages parents from reporting the rapes.[3]

Although the stock versions of *rosa* (the Cinderella romance), *suave* (more realistic middle-class plots), and *roja* evolved and dominated the markets at the height of their respective eras (1950–1970 for the *rosas*, 1970–1978 for the *suaves*, and 1979–present for the *rojas* in the Andean countries and Mexico), other subgenres also have emerged. Perhaps the most blatantly commercial and exploitative, even more so than the *fotonovela roja*, is the *fotonovela picaresca* [picaresque photonovel]. Whereas in other genres, true love and its vicissitudes are the major focus around which plot and pictures revolve, in the *picaresca* subgenre the focus is solely on overt sexuality. The *picaresca* takes prurient photographs, uses lower-class models and settings, and totally separates sex from love. Seemingly aimed at a 13–year-old male's imagination, the stories center around young men whose recently uncovered sexual powers drive women mad, causing generously endowed and scantily clad women, usually unnaturally blond and married to older, obviously impotent males, to fight each other for the chance to get into bed with the "hero." Such titles as *Sexy risas* [*Sexy Laughs*] and *Fiebre de pasiones* [*Fever of Passions*] typify the *picarescas*. Readership of the *fotonovela rosa* can be presumed to be predominantly female, but the *fotonovela picaresca* clearly is aimed at a male audience.

Indeed, the *picaresca* type is downright insulting to women, although those who produce it mistake unbridled female lust for liberation. Women in these tales have only one interest—sexuality. The hero may either trick the woman (there are never heroines) into the initial sexual encounter, or simply be available at the right time and the right place. The cuckolded husband completes the "humorous" triangle in many of the plots. Anti-solidarity reaches a new high, with no emotional attachment or long-term commitment by any of the characters. Needless to say, neither moral nor class consciousness is presented.

None of the commercial *fotonovela* genres offers collective solutions to problems. In the southern cone, rejection of collective solutions has become part of self-censorship. The *fotonovela* producers in the rest of Latin America do not explicitly reject collective action and solidarity, but individualization of problems and their solutions is the overwhelming message presented. Only when examining the noncommercial *fotonovelas*, undertaken as political and educational projects, does one find the individualistic and antisolidarity message countered by awareness of class and ethnic identity.

During the 1970s, activists working with peasants and workers in Latin America began to realize the great popularity of the *fotonovela* among these groups. At that time, many studies were being published attacking both *fotonovelas* and comics for their reactionary content. (See, for example, Erhart 1973:93–101; Colomina 1976; and Mattelart 1970:221–80). As a result, a number of disparate and isolated publications with similar format but with the changed message emerged.

Perhaps one of the most interesting of the resulting *fotonovelas* came out of Educador through an AID (Agency for International Development) grant to the Massachusetts Institute of Technology, working through CEMA (Centro de Motivación y Asesoría [Center for Motivation and Advising]), a local population education group. The project was aimed at using a variety of popular cultural manifestations for organizing indigenous communities. The peasant groups were involved in the creation, production, *and* consumption of that type of *fotonovela* (Parlato, Parlato, and Cain 1980), although it could only survive with its foreign subsidy.

Two other alternative *fotonovelas* are worth noting. In Peru, during the declining days of the right-wing military government, a radical political group changed the scene of Maxim Gorki's play *The Mother* and made it into a *fotonovela*. The drama was high, and the class solidarity was strong, as was the political message. The direct "preaching" presented every few pages, however, tended to alienate those not already convinced.

In Southern California, *fotonovelas* for the Mexican-American community were produced by a collective based at California State University, Los Angeles. The photography and use of graphics were particularly innovative. A member of the collective, Kay Torres, has been working with community groups, such as women's centers and unions, to produce "message" *fotonovelas* aimed at Hispanic audiences. (Torres 1983: 18–23).

REVIEW OF THE LITERATURE

There is no one standard work on *fotonovelas* in Latin America. Habert's work on the Brazilian *fotonovela* to 1972 is the closest thing to a complete treatment of the development of the medium within a single country. Almost all the work (Flora, Curiel, and Hill and Browner are exceptions) focus exclusively upon the *fotonovela rosa*.

The studies and analyses presented have emphasized content. Most studies that have been published have come from the critical Adorno (1967) and Barthes (1973) schools of mass-media analysis, as modified for Latin America in the seminal work of Dorfman and Mattelart (1975). They focus on the mystification present in the *fotonovelas* and link the content with the maintenance of a conservative and repressive status quo. Three of the best studies, those by Michèle Mattelart and that by Marta Colomina, approach the problem from a feminist persective, critiquing *fotonovelas* because of their cultural oppression of women. The work of Mattelart, as well as that of Flora and Flora, specifically links the oppressive content of *fotonovelas* with an emphasis on individual solutions to collective problems, to the underdevelopment and economic dependency of Latin America.

Michèle Mattelart undertook the first analysis of Latin American *fotonovelas* in the critical atmosphere of the Eduardo Frei regime in Chile in the late 1960s, which was a prelude to Salvador Allende's popular united election victory in 1970. Using sociological semiotics colored by a Marxist understanding of class structure in a dependent capitalist setting, she focused on *fotonovelas* as a purveyor of the culture of feminine oppression.

Like all authors who undertake studies of *fotonovelas*, she had difficulty obtaining a complete sample, even of recent issues. Her analysis is based on forty-seven issues published between 1966 and 1969. In her groundbreaking essay, she concludes that the *fotonovela* genre is a commercial adaptation to the new exigencies of a consumption society. Emotionalism imparts realism to the medium, through such mechanisms as abnormal families (orphans, bastards), abnormal love relationships (great differences in age or social status) and crisis situations. Suspense is sexual suspense, implied but not explicit in the *fotonovelas rosa* that predominated in that era. Sexuality is pathological in its consequences.

Mattelart found social duality an important element used by *fotonovelas* to invoke "realism" concerning social class differentials, yet at the same time used to deny their importance. Love was able to overcome any antagonism of polar social origins. Social status is thus related to property of consumption—home, furniture, vacation house—not ownership of means of production and control over the labor power of others. Wickedness is presented as an individual characteristic. Any exploitation that takes place is therefore due to a personality defect, not class relations: the order of the heart is more important than the social order.

Mattelart, in her deep analysis of *fotonovelas*, perceived distinct norms of conduct for men compared to women. Virginity in the *fotonovela rosa* was held as the ultimate feminine attribute to be exchanged for the ultimate feminine desire, marriage to a man who respects her and supports her.

She is highly distrustful of the feminine culture the *fotonovela* reinforces and questions the potential of creating alternative content in the same medium.

Mattelart's original article, first printed in Chile in a special issue of *Cuadernos de la realidad nacional* [*Journal of the National Reality*] in March 1970, was reprinted in Mexico in 1977 in a collection of her work entitled *La cultura de la opresión feminina* [*The Culture of Feminine Oppression*]. The primary intervening event was the bloody military coup in 1973 that eliminated Salvador Allende and signaled the beginning of both economic and political repression. In the introduction to this volume, Mattelart predicts the reactivation of the pseudoamorous culture of the *fotonovela* under the military dictatorships that were the grim reality of Latin America at that time. That feminine culture, epitomized by the *fotonovela rosa*, was necessary to fill the abyss between the structure of motivations created by a society of consumption and the economic reality that each day reduced the purchasing power of the working class and made its existence more precarious. (Mattelart 1977: 14). She saw the strong demarcation between male and female roles, lauded in the *fotonovela rosa*, as a mainstay of oppressive right wing totalitarianism. (Mattelart 1977: 24).

My initial studies of *fotonovelas* began in 1971 (Flora 1971 and Flora 1973). They took from Mattelart's work the theme of stereotypical female role behavior, particularly passive behavior, and its implications for change. In that early work based on the *fotonovela rosa*, various genres of women's magazine fiction, determined by class and culture, were compared quantitatively and qualitatively. The passive female ideal was prevalent in Latin American women's magazines, with no significant differences present between middle-class women's magazines and the *fotonovelas*. Authors of the Corín Tellado type dominated both media. Differences between the printed word and its photographic representation did not affect portrayal of a feminine ideal.

In a 1977 study conducted with a nonrepresentative sample of *fotonovelas* throughout Latin America, Jan Flora and I attempted a structural analysis that more closely linked economic and political structures to symbols and themes. Fewer male-female differences in ideal behavior were encountered, as the *fotonovela suave* began shifting the form and formula.

In the mid-1970s, Marta Colomina and her students in the school of social communication in the University of Zulia in Venezuela undertook a comprehensive study of women's mass culture from the perspective of the cultural industry. She looked at both the *fotonovela rosa* and the *fotonovela suave*, although she did not identify them that way. The content of a diverse, nonrepresentative sample of ten *fotonovelas* was analyzed and found to support the same stereotypes presented in the rest of the cultural industry oriented toward women.

Colomina concludes that the readers of *fotonovelas* are the "new illiterates," who mechanically internalize the ideology that oppresses them and thus reproduce the social structure that enriches their oppressors.

Fernando Curiel's examinationn of the photonovelistic text of *fotonovelas* relates them not to women's magazines but to films and comics. Curiel thus challenges the assumption that the *fotonovela* is a female-oriented genre. Instead, he links its development in Mexico to particularly Mexican cultural roots. He challenges the contention that the *fotonovela* form is unique to the Latin and Catholic world, citing particularly U.S. soap operas. While Hill (1982) points out that both deal with controversial issues, Aufedeheide (1984) has shown that U.S. soap operas are quite different from *telenovelas*—and *fotonovelas*—in that they go on forever, while the Latin variety has a distinct beginning and end.

Curiel uses a structuralist semiotic framework for analysis, stressing the limited range of photographic conventions in *fotonovelas*. He points particularly to the use of onomatopoeia but fails to note that it is a relatively new *fotonovela* convention introduced by Mexican *fotonovela* producers, particularly of the *fotonovela roja*. This links the Mexican *fotonovela* more to comics than those produced in other regions.

Curiel's typology of *fotonovelas*, Hill (1982) contends, is less than exact, and his criteria for classification are not clearly stated. He clearly prefers the *suave* type, a hybrid between the *rosa* and the *roja*, but he does not explicitly acknowledge this preference.

Curiel also differs from some of the earlier students of *fotonovela* in that he is himself a reader of *fotonovelas*. He refuses to label them as "garbage" but instead accepts them as a valid mass medium.

Hill and Browner analyzed *fotonovelas* published in Mexico in the late 1970s, the era of the *fotonovela suave* and the beginning of the *roja*. Not surprisingly, they found a more complex picture of gender roles than those presented in studies carried out in the late 1960s (Mattelart) and early 1970s (Flora and Colomina); furthermore, they more systematically looked at male and female roles than did the earlier studies. They found messages concerning gender were ambivalent but those related to social class were strong.

Hill and Browner carried out both quantitative and deep structural analyses of a sample of 75 Mexican *fotonovelas* purchased in Puebla in 1977 and 1978. They found male and female characters to be equally passive and both much more likely to be evaluated positively for being passive than for being active. For women, active females were associated with unhappy endings and passive females with happy endings. Extreme *machismo* [males characterized by arrogance, sexual aggressiveness, and domination of women by violence] was consistently portrayed negatively. For men, passivity or activity was not related to type of ending. Their findings reinforce the destructive potential of both female and male sexuality. They also stress the complementarity/polarity of positively sanctioned couples but demonstrate that neither males nor females are necessarily always active or passive. Indeed, they found an *interchangeability* of gender role performance also found by Flora regarding servant/master relationships. Hill and Browner see the growth of gender interchangeability as a structural outcome of the proliferation of *fotonovela* production.

Hill and Browner link *fotonovelas* to other romantic literature in terms of metaphoric presentation of social hierarchy. Their analysis of recent *fotonovelas* leads them to suggest that the major hierarchy is not gender but instead social class and, to a lesser degree, rural and urban differences. In contrast to gender, polarization by class and degree of urbanization is stark. They found "a consistently strong and stereotyped association between lower-class goodness and upper-class evil in affairs across class boundaries" (Hill and Browner 1982: 57).

Hill and Browner, through the use of deep structure analysis, conclude that the *fotonovela* has taken on some aspects related to religious ritual in other cultural settings, as the biological pole of the *fotonovelas* becomes more sexual and more violent and their ethical commentary more explicit.

RESEARCH COLLECTIONS AND RELATED PROBLEMS

There are no systematic collections of *fotonovelas*, not even those that have proven most popular. Editorial Abril in Argentina apparently has archives containing some of the titles it has published, but access is difficult, if not impossible. Most publishers do not keep a complete set of the *fotonovelas* that have gone out under their imprint. The printers likewise keep no copies. The distributors have only the unsold copies they are about to ship down the distribution chain. Even authors of scripts have not retained copies of most of the productions of their published work. It is indeed an ephemeral set of publications.

Analyses have often been based on people's private collections or on samples rented from neighborhood "lending libraries." Sampling is often done through buying collections from stalls in a particular village or part of a city. Quantitative analyses have often been based on items available, rather than on a strict adherence to rules of random sampling.

The lack of availability of back issues stems from the social status of the medium. *Fotonovelas* are depreciated by the very people who produce them. At worst, they are defined as weapons capable of potential damage, whose marketing, like alcohol or firearms, must be done in light of profits rather than use. Others involved in their publication are less cynical but still depreciate the medium. *Fotonovelas*, according to the second group, are, in general, very bad. They participate in order to raise their level, however slightly, through particular innovations in plots or characters.

The large turnover of titles, as well as the economic insecurity of the publishers, contributes to the difficulties in pulling together complete collections of a particular title or publishing house. Particularly since 1979, a large number of editorial firms have entered and left the *fotonovela* business. Even the large, established publishing houses, like Editorial Abril of Argentina, have recently changed hands, often several times. The new owners, even more than the founders, are concerned with profits, not continuity or content.

The depreciation of the *fotonovela* comes not only from its simple presentation aimed primarily at the working class. Comics, too, appeal to that segment of the population but have staunch defenders among literati. In the southern-cone countries, particularly Argentina and Brazil, clubs exist for comic-book aficionados that attract businessmen and intellectuals as well as adolescents. The fans, of course, are primarily male. Women's magazines, likewise, have their defenders among the publishing establishment.

However, a publication aimed at *working-class women* seems not to merit serious consideration. The combination of two negative statuses means that disdain for the readers is translated into disdain for what they read. *Fotonovelas* are published because they are profitable. But, given the assumptions about the low level of the readers, the very fact that they buy *fotonovelas* is evidence that they do not deserve better quality than they are currently receiving. *Fotonovelas* often subsidize the "real" mission publishing houses define for themselves, which tends to be the comics or feature magazines that take a lot of staff to assemble.

SUGGESTIONS FOR FUTURE RESEARCH

Despite the difficulties of acquiring representative samples of *fotonovelas* (which, because the variation among them is relatively minor, is not an insurmountable methodological issue), most of the studies done have analyzed the content of the *fotonovelas* rather than the structures of production or the impact of the *fotonovelas* on the readers. It has been assumed (quite correctly) that they are in general produced by the capitalist class in order to earn money and to reproduce an ideology that maintains that class's superior position in society. It has also been assumed (with much less solid grounding) that the content has the same impact on all readers everywhere. This deduction has been based on the types of quantitative or deep analysis carried out to date.

It is necessary to do much more work with the readers of *fotonovelas* to try to determine who they are and how they respond to the various genres of *fotonovelas* and the various messages they appear to carry. It is quite possible that the type of decoding done by the analyst, given her or his middle-class intellectual background, is quite different from that of a working-class reader. It is conceivable that a decodification of resistance is occurring that subverts rather than supports the current order so comfortable to those on the top.

The *fotonovela* continues to need monitoring in terms of content. New genres are appearing, and themes and messages change. While production of *fotonovelas* is an almost automatic process for many publishers in Latin America, reading and attributing meaning to *fotonovelas* is a complex process for the masses who spend millions of dollars a week in purchasing them. It is to underestimate these masses if we assume they only are gullible dupes simply spending to reinforce their own oppression.

NOTES

1. Portions of this chapter appeared in "The *Fotonovela* in Latin America," *Studies in Latin American Popular Culture* 1 (1982): 15–16. Reprinted by permission.

2. Saint-Michel states that *Grand Hotel* was first published in 1945. Spanish language sources, including Haber and Colomina, give 1947 as the date.

3. Unpublished interviews undertaken by the women's group Centro de Información y Recursos para la Mujer, Bogotá, Colombia, September-October 1980.

BIBLIOGRAPHY

Adorno, T. W. *Prisms* (London: Neville Spearman, 1967).

Aufedeheide, Pat. "Masters, Maids, and Mistresses: A Day Watching Foreign Soaps." *Emmy Magazine* 6 (March-April 1984): 34–35, 48.

Barriga, Patricio y Villacis, Rodrigo. *Fotonovela*. Center for International Education, University of Massachusetts, Amherst, Technical Note No. 13, n.d.

Barthes, Roland. *Mythologies* (London: Paladin, 1973).

Cardona, Elisabeth Fox. "Análisis de las investigaciones sobre la mujer y los medios de comunicación en América Latina." Paper presented at Encuentro de Investigadores en las Areas de Medios Masivos de Comunicación y la Participación de la Mujer en el Desarrollo [Meeting of Researchers in the Areas of Mass Communication and the Participation of Women in Development]. Bogotá, CEDE, Universidad de los Andes, November 1978.

Cardona, Elisabeth y Anzola, Patricia de Morales. "Reseña y discusión sobre las investigaciones de la mujer en los medios en América Latina y en Colombia." Paper presented at Encuentro de Investigadores en las Areas de Medios Masivos de Comunicación y la Participación de la Mujer en el Desarrollo [Meeting of Researchers in the Areas of Mass Communication and the Participation of Women in Development]. Bogotá, CEDE, Universidad de los Andes, November 1978.

Colomina, Marta. *La Celestina mecánica* (Caracas: Monte Avila Editores, 1976).

Curiel, Fernando. *Fotonovela rosa, fotonovela roja*. Cuadernos de Humanidades, No. 9 (México, D.F.: Universidad Nacional Autónoma de México, 1980).

Dorfman, Ariel, and Mattelart, Armand. *How to Read Donald Duck: Imperialist Ideology in the Disney Comic*. Translation and introduction by David Kunzle (New York: International General, 1975).

Erhart, Virginia. "Amor, ideología emascaramiento en Corín Tellado." *Imperialismo y medios masivos de comunicaciones. Casa de las Américas* (Havana) 77 (1973) pp. 93–101.

Flora, Cornelia Butler. "The Passive Female: Her Comparative Image by Class and Culture in Women's Magazine Fiction." *Journal of Marriage and the Family* 33 (August 1971): 435–44.

―――. "The Passive Female and Social Change." In *Female and Male in Latin America: Essays*, edited by Ann Pescatello, 59–85 (Pittsburgh: Pittsburgh University Press, 1973).

―――. "Contradictions of Capitalism: Mass Media in Latin America." In *Studies in Communication*, edited by Thelma McCormack, 19–36 (Greenwich, Conn.: JAI Press, 1980).

―――. "*Fotonovelas*: Message Creation and Reception." *Journal of Popular Culture* 14 (Winter 1980): 534–39.

―――. "Women in Latin American Fotonovelas: From Cinderella to Mata Hari." *Women's Studies: An International Quarterly* I (1980): 95–104.

―――. "La fotonovela en Colombia." *Boletín: Asociación Colombiana de Investigadoes de la Comunicación Social* 3 (February 1980): 3.

―――. "La mujer en las fotonovelas colombianas: Desde la Cenicienta hasta la Mata Hari." In *Debate sobre la mujer en América Latina: Discusión acerca de la unidad de producción-reproducción*. Vol. 1, pp. 164–75. *La realidad Colombiana*. Edited by Magdalena León (Bogotá, ACEP, 1982).

―――. "The *Fotonovela* in Latin America." *Studies in Latin American Popular Culture* 1 (1982): 15–26.

―――. "Roasting Donald Duck: Alternative Comics and Fotonovelas in Latin America." *Journal of Popular Culture* 18, no. 1 (1984): 163–183.

―――. "The *Fotonovela* in Brazil: The First Stage." *Studies in Latin American Popular Culture* 3 (1984): 183–188.

Flora, Cornelia Butler, and Flora, Jan L. "The *Fotonovela* As a Tool for Class and Cultural Domination." *Latin American Perspectives* 5 (Winter 1978): 146–49.

Gubern, Román. *La Literatura de la Imagen* (Barcelona: Editorial Salvat, 1974).

Habert, Angeluccia Bernardes. *Fotonovela e indústria cultural: estudio de uma forma de literatura sentimental fabricada para milhoes* (Petropólis, Brazil: Editora Vozes Ltda., 1974).

Herrera Cuenca de, Gloria. "La prensa femenina, factor deformante de la mujer venezolana." *Orbita* 8 (1974): 7–40.

Hill, Jane H. "Fernando Curiel. *Fotonovela rosa, fotonovela roja: una historia de Fernando Curiel.*" *Studies in Latin American Popular Culture* 1 (1982): 252–57.

Hill, Jane H., and Browner, Carole. "Gender Ambiguity and Class Stereotyping in the Mexican Fotonovela." *Studies in Latin American Popular Culture* 1 (1982): 43–64.

Laverde, María Cristina. "Bibliografía y compendio de la investigación sobre la mujer en los medios masivos en América Latina." Paper presented at Encuentro de Investigadores en las Areas de Medios Masivos de Comunicación y la Participación de la Mujer en el Desarrollo. [Meeting of Researchers in the Areas of Mass Communications and of the Participation of Women in Development]. Bogotá: CEDE, Universidad de los Andes, November 1978.

Merras, Sergio. "Verosímiles destrosados! (O acerca de posibles destrozos en los verosímiles fotonovelescos)." Santiago, Universidad Catolica de Chile, Centro de Comunicaciones Sociales, June 1973.

Marshall, Isabel. "La imagen femenina en la fotonovela amorosa." In *Chile: Mujer y Sociedad*, edited by Paz Covarrubias and Rolando Franco, 590–604 (Santiago de Chile: UNICEF, n.d.).

Mattelart, Michèle. "El nivel mítico de la prensa seudo-amorosa." *Cuadernos de la realidad nacional* 3 (March 1970): 221–80.

———. *La cultura de la opresión femenina* (México, D.F.: Ediciones Era, 1977).

Parlato, Ronald; Parlato, Margaret Burres; and Cain, Bonnie J. *Fotonovelas and Comic Books: The Use of Popular Graphic Media in Development* (Washington, D.C.: Agency for International Development, 1980).

Paz, Ida. *Medios masivos, ideología, y propaganda imperialista* (Havana: Cuadernos de la Revista Unión, 1977).

Saint-Michel, Serge. *Le Roman-Photo* (Paris: Librairie Larousse, 1979).

Torres, Kay. "Colectivo El Ojo y La Fotonovela." *Obscur: Magazines of the Los Angeles Center for Photographic Studies* 2, no. 5 (1983): 18–23.

Vigano, Oscar. *Estudio sobre aceptación y efectividad de las fotonovelas e historietas en la comunicación de conocimientos en áreas rurales de Guatemala* (Basic Village Education Project. Academy for Educational Development, Guatemala, n.d.).

Weaks, Daniel. *The Photonovel: A Tool for Development*. Program and Training Journal Manual Series, No. 4. Action, Peace Corps, Washington, D.C., 1976.

John Mosier

7 Film

Film in Latin America is an area little understood or explored. The best analogy is with Mesoamerican archeology in the early nineteenth century. Until John Lloyd Stephens began to uncover Mayan ruins in the 1830s, virtually nothing was known about the great civilizations of that region. In fact, they were not even presumed to exist; nor was the science of archeology in an exact state. Most of the discoveries were yet to be made, and to be made by amateurs. The same is true of film today. All too little is known about Latin American film, and the study of film is itself not particularly advanced. Almost everything remains to be done, and in no other area is the role of analysis and rigorous methodology so important.

Bearing these caveats in mind, it is well to begin with some practical distinctions about the cinema. The most important differentiation is between fiction films and documentaries. Although it is obvious that the line between these two forms will be perpetually blurred, the evolution of film in this century has been essentially presented as the study of the development of feature-length fiction films. In Latin America documentarists have made important contributions to the growth of the medium, and their work in recent years has justifiably attracted world attention. But it is nonetheless the case that the study of the Latin American cinema is also primarily the study of fiction films.

Another key distinction is the difference between films produced by and for an intellectual or cultural elite and those made for mass consumption. Many Latin American films that are most highly regarded by critics and scholars are works whose impact inside any given country has been minimal. Such films are not, in other words, popular films in the ordinary sense of the word: they are seen by few people, and their influence is essentially limited to the intelligentsia. In fact, in many surprising cases the reputation of the filmmakers derives from the reactions of the intelligentsia outside of Latin America.

On the opposite end of the spectrum are those films that are seen by broad segments of the population. Historically these films have been foreign commodities, and even the most superficial observer of daily life in any country in Latin America will have noticed that the crowds outside of movie theaters are, by and large, waiting to see foreign films, usually films made in the United States. Such films have, during the course of this century, had a profound effect on the popular imagination, although how great it has been and how it could be measured or even understood adequately, is a vexing question that has not yet even been seriously addressed, much less answered.

Unfortunately, the majority of those films made within Latin America since the advent of sound are so highly derivative of foreign films that there is considerable question as to whether they are any more Mexican or Argentine than are the Volkswagens made there. This too is a disturbing question, and one for which there is no easy answer. To what extent has the popular imagination of Latin America been molded by its heavy diet of foreign imports and slavish (although frequently intriguing) imitations?

What is certain, however, is that in recent years a diverse group of artists in the region have accepted that these influences are there, that they are pernicious influences on the population at large, and that the only cure is an authentic regional or national art form. By and large the works of these men and women may be seen as part of a conscious attempt to create an indigenous popular cinema and to ensure that the general public will see them. What is not certain at all is whether the assumptions of these artists are correct or whether their works will endure.

A BRIEF HISTORY

Motion pictures were first produced and exhibited in 1895 when the Lumiere brothers began exhibiting their short films in Paris. Growth was rapid for the new entertainment medium: Latin Americans started making films at virtually the same time that North Americans and Europeans did. One of the earliest, if not the earliest, dates claimed for film exhibition in Latin America is July 9, 1896, when it is alleged that a notice appeared in a newspaper in Rio de Janeiro announcing the showing of a film. Exhibition began in Mexico in August of 1896, and films were being made in Cuba as early as 1896. These dates compare favorably with those elsewhere: December 1895 for the Lumieres in Paris, April 1896 for the United States.

The cinema, then, is not an art form that was introduced into the New World after it had reached maturity in the Old. On the contrary, the development of Latin American film during the silent era paralleled developments outside the region. In both Brazil and Mexico film production was in process by 1898. Unfortunately, most if not all of these early films have disappeared or been destroyed. On the basis of what survives and of contemporary accounts, it appears that the early filmmakers were like their

foreign cousins: they shot travelogues and what we would now call documentaries. Possibly the most famous of these artists was the Mexican en-
gineer Salvadore Toscano, who managed to capture a good deal of the
Mexican Revolution that was then in progress.

The cinema began to develop as an art form, particularly as a popular
one, only after filmmakers began to produce films that were longer than
the contents of one magazine. After the ability to film motion, the second
crucial invention was the ability to edit or join together the developed film
from individual magazines. From the first short travelogues there was a
rapid transition from short melodramas to feature-length films in which
individual scenes were joined together to produce suspense and to tell
stories with multiple plot lines. In North America this took about fifteen
years, and by 1915 the pre-eminence of the feature-length fiction film was
established. Very few of these silent films have survived, regardless of
where they were made. There were three reasons for this: no one thought
there was any reason to save films once audiences had paid to see them;
the films were on a highly flammable stock which blew up, burned, or
otherwise destroyed itself; and stock was routinely run through processors
to reclaim the valuable silver particles.

Nonetheless, it appears that Latin American artists were at this stage
keeping pace with their foreign colleagues. The first Brazilian fiction film
dates from 1906. By the end of World War I Brazilians had made four
hundred feature films. A reasonably vital and successful popular art form
had developed that competed on more or less equal terms with films imported from abroad for a hold on the popular imagination. The advent of
sound and the global depression, together with political events in Europe
(Fascism and the Spanish Civil War), broke the back of the independent
popular film in Latin America, except for Mexico, during World War II.
However, it took all three forces to do this. The advent of sound film
undercut the ability of the artist to produce films that were cheap to make,
easy to show (silent films required neither electricity nor auditoriums), and
exportable all over the world owing to their lack of dialogue. However,
the wealthier film industries of Mexico and Brazil were creating sound films
as early as 1930, that is to say, at the same time that sound films were
being produced in the rest of the world. Sound, by itself, would have simply
meant that Argentina and Mexico would have monopolized the Spanish-
speaking areas and Brazilian film would have developed in isolation. The
depression meant that neither the exhibitors nor the producers of sound
films had access to the capital needed to purchase the equipment to make
and show sound films. This situation was exacerbated by the advent of
color film, which, again, the majors in the industry had the ability to
produce. No country apparently could compete with Hollywood if its films
did not improve upon those of the silent era. The advent of sound raised
linguistic barriers around the region and separated Brazil from its Spanish-

speaking neighbors, while the depression appears to have favored the large at the expense of the small, the foreign at the expense of the local.

Added to these two factors was a third. The Spanish Civil War, and, shortly thereafter, World War II, first sundered many of the contacts between Spanish-speaking Latin America and its closest cultural neighbors, Spain and Italy, and then isolated it from Europe. The unfortunate result was that the new techniques that artists were developing, which would enable them to produce sound (and later color) films with the same power and force as the earlier silent films, came to Latin America quite late. Given the U.S. film industry's own isolation from Europe, and its domination of the Latin American market, it is not surprising that the Latin American cinema of this period, which unfortunately lasted through the 1950s, was aesthetically primitive, exceedingly theatrical in the worst possible sense, and reflective of an alien culture. Ironically, this was at the same time that World War II was causing a tremendous expansion in film production in countries with an advanced production system. This was particularly the case in Mexico, where films were made with great rapidity and in great quantity.

The sound-film era, then, can be divided into two roughly equal parts. In the first part, which corresponds to the 1930s, the smaller indigenous industries die out and are replaced by imports, particularly North American ones. Then, particularly in northern South America and Central America, there is a second period, corresponding roughly to the 1940s and 1950s, during which the market is saturated with a mix of Mexican and North American entertainment films of the crudest sort.

Although these films were popular in the commercial sense, to a remarkable extent they do not reflect as much of the genuine aspirations of the peoples of Latin America as one might suppose. This is because these films, taken as a group, are so derivative of foreign film models. In some cases they are obvious examples of slavish adaptations or remakes, but in the majority of cases it is the acting, the photography, and the editing that is slavishly emulative of foreign models. One could go further and say that many of the aesthetic ideas and ideals of these two-and-one-half decades of sound film are foreign. The leading actress in a film would be chosen for her resemblance to Ingrid Bergman; and the leading actor would look like Clark Gable. There would be nothing in the setting that would give the flavor of the country or the region. Nor would there be anything peculiarly national about the plot. Finally, the music, particularly if there was singing or dancing, would be international or cosmopolitan, that is to say, foreign.

These somewhat harsh general statements must be qualified by the observation that during the second sound period the industries of several countries supported artists of real talent. The first-prize winner at the first

Cannes Film Festival in 1947 was *María Candelaria*, directed by the Mexican Emilio Fernández. The year after, Fernández won the first major film award given to a Latin American: his film *The Pearl* swept the Venice Film Festival. In addition to an award for the film, María Elena Marques was judged best actress, Pedro Armendáriz best actor, and Gabriel Figueroa best cinematographer. At the first Karlovy Vary Film Festival in Czechoslovakia in 1948 the prize went to *Río escondido*, director Fernández, and cinematographer Figueroa. In 1951 at Cannes Luis Buñuel's Mexican film *Los olvidados* [*The Forgotten Ones*] won him the prize as best director, while in 1953 *O cangaçeiro* [*The Bandit*] by the Brazilian Lima Barreto received another award. The next year Alberto Cavalcanti's *O canto do mar* [*Song of the Sea*] won a prize at Karlovy Vary, and the pattern has continued over the years.

The third important period of sound film began at the end of the 1950s and consisted of two separate national film movements that would grow dramatically in the next twenty years and produce that movement which with only minor exaggeration is called the New Latin American Cinema. There are several paradoxes associated with this period. First, although the aim of almost all of the artists working in film from the early 1960s on has been the cultural independence of Latin America from foreign influences, the chief cinematic influences in the region have been foreign. In Brazil, Nelson Pereira dos Santos, working since 1957, adapted many of the ideas of neorealism, while in Cuba the newly founded (1959) Cuban Film Institute, El Instituto Cubano del Arte e Industria Cinematográfica (ICAIC), sponsored the grafting of the socialist filmmaking of Eastern Europe onto native traditions. The second paradox is that although the majority of these artists aimed at producing films that were commercially successful within their own countries and the region, to a remarkable extent their early successes, particularly through the 1960s, were with audiences of intellectuals, mostly foreigners. Films made in Latin America that are original and unquestionably reflect the concerns of the artists of the region—and, to a great extent, those of the general public—have been made only in the last few years. Nonetheless, the films of this period represent some of the most profound and significant shifts in global cinema. Although little understood, this third wave of Latin American sound film is equally as important in the history of global cinema as are its more publicized brothers, neorealism and the French New Wave.

The progenitor is the surprisingly little known artist Nelson Pereira dos Santos, whose 1957 work, *Rio, quarenta graus* [*Rio, Forty Degrees*] is the seminal film of what is customarily known as the Cinema Novo, a shorthand version of the Brazilian expression, *o cinema novo Brasileiro*, or New Brazilian cinema. Other artists associated with this movement are Walter Lima, Jr., Carlos Diegues, David Neves, Glauber Rocha, Rui Guerra,

Joaquim Pedro de Andrade, and Arnaldo Jabor. With the exception of Glauber Rocha, now deceased, all of these men are currently active in Brazil.

The most famous of these directors abroad was Glauber Rocha, whose reputation rests on three difficult and innovative works: *Terra em transe* [*The Troubled Earth*, 1967], *Deus e diabo na terra do sul* [*Black God, White Devil*, 1967], and *O santo guerriero* [known in English as *Antônio das Mortes*, 1972]. Paradoxically, it is difficult to assess Rocha's actual impact on the Latin American public or on Latin American artists. His major works have been little seen in the countries of the region, and it is difficult to imagine that his works will ever attain wide public exposure. Although a seminal figure in Latin American film, the reality of his importance—leaving aside the unquestioned impact of his works as works of art—is that he gained considerable attention in Europe and North America for Latin American film, attention which, although it would surely have come sooner or later, would have, without his efforts, come later.

Meanwhile, in Cuba the 1960s saw the emergence of a small but highly visible and active Cuban cinema. To a remarkable extent the newly organized Cuban cinema is a cinema of documentarists, whose work is aimed primarily at educating the masses to the realities of Cuban and regional history as the socialist government deems them to exist. Paradoxically, however, Cuba has supported one of the region's major artists, Tomás Gutiérrez Alea, whose first major film, *Memorias del subdesarrollo* [*Memories of Underdevelopment*, 1968], is a lucid and complex discussion of the role of the upper-class intellectual in the new Cuban society. At roughly the same time, Humberto Solas directed the important historical feminist melodrama, *Lucía* (1969), and it would appear that this film is a genuinely popular one both within and outside the region. Its blend of popular melodrama, reasonably accurate history, and a persuasive point of view combined to make it a good example of the kind of film that will reach large audiences. It is no coincidence that the remainder of Tomás Gutiérrez Alea's works are essentially historical films: *Una pelea cubana contra los demonios* [*Cuban Struggle Against the Demons*, 1970], *La última cena* [*Last Supper*, 1976], and *Los sobrevivientes* [*The Survivors*, 1979]. The success of this approach, ironically, virtually strangled the industry, which devoted most of its scanty resources to the production of a large and ambitious epic, also directed by Solas, called *Cecilia* (1982). The commercial and critical failure of this film has caused considerable shifts within ICAIC, which, except for the films metioned, has not been particularly successful with fiction films during the 1970s.

Meanwhile, in Brazil Nelson Pereira dos Santos continued making films that were heavily indebted to neorealism, of which the most important was *Vidas secas* [*Barren Lives*, 1962]. Virtually all of the films of this period in Brazil were adaptations of literary classics, which may very well explain their somewhat limited commercial success—as well as the high regard with which they are held by critics in Brazil and elsewhere. By the middle of the 1970s, however, Brazilian artists had turned to historical themes similar to those developed in Cuba, and Carlos Diegues's enormously successful *Xica da Silva* (1976) may well be seen as the prototypical work. At the same time, his colleagues initiated production of films combining elements of popular melodrama as well as elements of the so-called *pornochanchadas*, or erotic comedies, a blending which was both critically and commercially successful. Perhaps the prototypical work was Aranaldo Jabor's *Toda nudez será castigada* [*All Nudity will Be Punished*, 1974], which although in no sense a *pornochanchada*, combines many of the elements, as does Bruno Barreto's immensely successful *Dona Flor* (1978).

Nelson Pereira dos Santos continued his career during the 1970s by directing a set of films whose combination of folk myths, magic, and marginalized protagonists suggests a genuinely popular cinema of a somewhat different sort. Many of his colleagues did likewise, although this in no way suggests a body of films with any great similarities. Outside of high entertainment value and cinematic stimulation, their only common denominator was their relative commercial success, and it has been in this area that Brazilian filmmakers have been most impressive. Increasingly it has been the case in Brazil that audiences are seeing Brazilian films. Although Brazilian filmmakers and the industry are in a far from enviable position, Brazil now clearly dominates the film industries of the region. If the trend continues inside Brazil and in the region as well, it will have the utmost significance for the future of Latin American cinema.

Although Mexico is one of the largest film producers in the region and although there were significant artists at work there, the bulk of the films made were somewhat crude adaptations of foreign genres. In the 1970s, however, a group of younger artists were able to receive funding for their work, and, although none of them has produced enormous commercial successes, they have accomplished a good deal. Perhaps the most important are Jaime Hermosillo, Felipe Casals, Servando Gonzales, Alberto Isaac, Arturo Ripstein, Raúl Araiza, and Marcela Fernández Violante, one of the two established women directors in the region (Ana Carolina Teixeira Soares in Brazil is the other). Closely responsive to the ebb and flow of Mexican politics, the film industry in Mexico has, in recent years, suffered, but it appears that the enormous success of television in Mexico, as in Brazil, has provided a surprising cushion for actors and directors, allowing them to survive as professionals when the prospects for making films are dim.

Artists in other countries have not been so lucky, and in the remainder of Latin America, although we have artists of unquestioned merit, we have all too little of an organized national film industry. The curious exception to this is Argentina, where, although there have been few artists of the stature of those mentioned so far, there has been a steady stream of commercial film production, essentially melodramas and comedies. Many of these are excellently made, and Argentine films have enough penetration of the Latin American market to barely maintain a basic infrastructure.

Elsewhere there is scarcely that, the valiant efforts of filmmakers in Chile, Peru, Colombia, Bolivia, and Venezuela notwithstanding, although the work of Chilean Miguel Littín and Bolivian Jorge Sanjines should be mentioned, hopefully without prejudice to the large numbers of talented artists working in film of which limited space does not allow even a mention.

REFERENCE WORKS

Writings about Latin American cinema, like critical writing about film in general, are of a more irregular quality than the researcher is likely to encounter in other fields. There are three reasons for this. First, much of the writing about film is done by journalists rather than by scholars. Second, previous and present generations of scholars, as a group, are self-taught, since there has been little formal training in film research available in this country. Third, the area is so vast and the logistical problems so formidable that there is a greater opportunity present for error and bias. To these three reasons, which are true of film studies in general, one might add a fourth unique to this particular area of study, which is the fact that the study of Latin American cinema is a recent phenomenon. None of the sorts of standard works that one encounters in other areas of cinema studies have been done, which suggests some intriguing research possibilities discussed briefly in the section on further research. In fact, there is only one book-length study available that deals generally with the field, Burns's *Latin American Cinema: Film and History*. This pioneering work in English, which dates only from 1975, has an unfortunately somewhat misleading title, since half of its pages are devoted to a consideration of film as history. What remains, then, is essentially a brief essay entitled, "A Filmic Approach to Latin America's Past," which is a good, if sometimes factually inaccurate, discussion of filmmakers, primarily of the documentarists in the region, and a thorough bibliography of what has been written about Latin American film through 1974. There is also a current list of the film research centers in Latin America.

Burns's work, useful though it may be, is not a historical overview of film in the area, and there are precious few works in this category. What the field needs is a work such as Jean-Loup Passek's magisterial and comprehensive *Le cinema russe et sovietique* [*Russian and Soviet Cinema*]. What actually exists is Acevedo Latorre's *Historia del cine* [*History of Cinema*], a world history; Torres and Estremera's error-ridden and dated *Nuevo cine latinoamericano* [*New Latin American Cinema*]; and Mosier's short essay "Currents in Latin American Film." Similarly, there is little coverage of

Latin America in the more general studies of global film or in specific aspects of it. The only standard reference texts with substantial and accurate references to the films and artists is Sadoul's *Dictionary*, while the comprehensive *Critical Dictionary* of Roud has only a brief entry on Glauber Rocha. The only study that makes a serious and knowledgeable attempt to incorporate Latin American films into its observations about global film is Hurley's *The Reel Revolution*, although Hochman's *World Cinema since 1945* will, when published, hopefully rectify some of these problems.

However, the situation improves markedly when one considers those works dealing with specific countries. By far the best work has been done on Mexico. Mora's valuable *Mexican Cinema* is the only book by one author in English that attempts to provide the reader with a serious analysis of the subject. Not the least of the book's strengths is its exhaustive bibliography. Since Mora manages to mention, at least in passing, other Latin American filmmakers, his bibliographical researches completely supersede the older *Annotated Bibliography* of Burton, which is currently updated. Although Mora makes heavy use of the many Mexican sources, some of these should still be mentioned, most notably García Ricra's *Historia documental* [*Documentary History*] and Ayala Blanco's *La aventura del cine mexicano* [*The Adventure of Mexican Cinema*]. The compilation of interviews by Reyes Navares, *The Mexican Cinema, Interviews with Thirteen Directors* is also useful, as is Michel's "Mexican Cinema, a Panoramic View," and Treviño's "The New Mexican Cinema" in *Film Quarterly*.

Brazil has seen several studies, of which the pioneering work by Vianey, *Introdução ao cinema brasileiro* [*Introduction to Brazilian Cinema*], remains indispensable for the films through 1955. No one work covers Brazilian cinema as satisfactorily. However, the curiously untitled twenty-fourth issue of *Cultura magazine* [*Culture Magazine*], published by the Brazilian Ministry of Culture, remains the single best collection of writings about Brazilian cinema. There are several excellent studies in Portuguese, of which de Souza's *Trajetórias do cinema moderno* [*The Trajectories of Modern Cinema*] is a model, since it is virtually the only work to compare Brazilian and European filmmakers. Bernadet's *Brasil em tempo de cinema* [*Brazil in the Time of Cinema*] is also a substantial work on the subject. Most researchers will want to make use of Johnson and Stam's *Brazilian Cinema*, which is, despite the authors' protestations to the contrary, essentially an anthology of pronouncements by filmmakers together with a mixed bag of essays on the newer films. There are also some useful pronouncements by the filmmakers themselves. Johnson's *Cinema Novo X Five*, however, offers some of the most comprehensive coverage of Diegues, Rocha, Guerra, Joaquim Pedro de Andrade, and Nelson Pereira dos Santos yet seen. In addition to the article by David Neves, "In Search of the Aesthetics of the Brazilian Cinema" (contained in *Cultura* and reprinted in the *New Orleans Review*), there is the extremely valuable interview done by Rui Nogueria and Nicoletta Zalaffi, "Brasil Ano 1970: Round Table on the Cinema Novo," in *Cinema*. Glauber Rocha, the Latin American director who has received the most critical attention abroad, has been the subject of numerous studies, some of the best of which are contained in *Glauber Rocha*, edited by Salles Gomes. Researchers are also well served by the Brazilian film journal *Filme e cultura* [*Film and Culture*], whose articles in recent years have been indexed by Michael Moulds's (ed.) *Index to International Film Periodicals*, and the earlier years (from 1967) in Burns.

For its size, probably more has been written about film in Cuba than for any other country. Unfortunately, much of what has been written is of dubious value. The best single brief account is Mahieu's "El Cine Cubano" ["Cuban Cinema"], with Johnson's "Report from Cuba" the best overview in English, ably supplemented by Burton's "Revolutionary Cuban Cinema." Myerson's *Memories of Underdevelopment* seems ambiguously titled. Essentially the book contains the screenplays for two important Cuban films (*Lucía* and *Memories*). Unlike Johnson and Stam in their book on Brazil, Myerson spends most of his introduction discussing Watergate and Vietnam, which, fascinating and relevant as these topics may be for Latin Americanists, does not add measurably to their knowledge of Cuban cinema. There is a respected periodical, *Cine cubano* [*Cuban Cinema*], published in Cuba, and its contents are widely indexed, although much of what is contained there must be evaluated carefully. It should be noted that although both of the leading film journals in the region, *Cine cubano* and *Filme Cultura*, do discuss Latin American films, they also treat other topics, and, quite often, the titles of the essays are not reliable indicators as to either the contents or their value.

When one turns to the other countries, the situation deteriorates dramatically. There is an excellent brief history of Argentine cinema by Mahieu, a thorough one on Colombia by Martínez Parda, as well as Coo's book on Chilean film. There have been two other workable histories of Chilean cinema that are both more accessible and more up to date. Chanan's *Chilean Cinema* is, again, somewhat misleadingly titled: the bulk of it consists of interviews with directors, although his discussion of sources is the best extant in English. However, this work should be supplemented by Vega's *Re-visión*, which, although peculiarly organized, is surprisingly comprehensive. Finally, there is an admirable if brief introductory essay on Venezuela by Kenneth Basch. For discussions on the cinema in Uruguay, Bolivia, Argentina, and Colombia, the Pick anthology is worthwhile, although, as its title suggests, its approach is somewhat limited. Unfortunately, many of these sources are somewhat out of date, a problem compounded by the rapid and dramatic growth of Latin American cinema in the past ten years. Much of what has been said—particularly predictions about the demise of the film industries in various countries—appears in retrospect to be woefully inaccurate. For that reason, articles, notices, and film reviews appearing in various journals are of considerable importance. Although such coverage of Latin America is spotty, the situation has both changed and improved in the last decade.

Although the *International Index to Film Periodicals*, edited by Moulds, includes articles about Latin America, it is seriously deficient in the journals it indexes, omitting much that should be included, and including enormous numbers of items written in languages not likely to be accessible to the vast majority of researchers, for example, Czech and Bulgarian. In the 1981 bibliography, one third of the articles dealing with film history in Latin America were in languages that few, if any, researchers are likely to be able to read. In addition, it fails to differentiate what is basically cine-journalism (even if it is in French) from serious film criticism written by critics who can lay some fair claim to being specialists.

There is a surprisingly consistent coverage of the latest films and important events affecting cinema in the weekly *Variety*. Of particular interest is the annual spring issue dealing with Latin America, if for no other reason than that it provides data on the most popular films in the major metropolitan areas. There is regular coverage of current films in *Américas* magazine, published in Washington by the Organization of American States. In Spanish, the journal *Cuadernos hispanoamericanos* offers frequent work. It is important to note that all three of these periodicals have the virtue of consistency, since the work is done by one or two people. In the United States *Cineaste*, *Film Quarterly*, and *Jump Cut* publish serious essays, interviews, and sometimes film reviews, as does the *New Orleans Review*. The coverage of these journals is far superior to that of their Latin American counterparts.

In Latin America itself the situation is somewhat chaotic. The quality of research, particularly in the periodicals *Américas* and *Cuadernos Hispanoamericanos* mentioned earlier, is very high. The chief problem lies in laying hands on them, particularly on back issues. The initial issues of *Filme e cultura*, for example, contain important essays on the concept of *cinema novo* [new cinema], of which Azeredo's essay is perhaps the most crucial. Similarly, it is important to read the barrage of theoretical work published in *Cine Cubano*. The third great source of criticism is the National Autonomous University of Mexico (UNAM), which publishes a sometimes bewildering series of monographs, periodicals, and studies. Fortunately, all of these are cited in Burns and Mora.

In addition to providing updates on what is happening in the cinema, there are works that introduce the researcher to some theories of particular relevance in the study of popular culture and the cinema. None of the three most useful is available in English. Of the group, *Sociología del cine* [*Sociology of the Movies*], by Gomezzara and Selenede Rios, is virtually a model text, while the justly more famous manifesto by Solanas and Getino should be required reading. There is also a model monograph on the influences of foreign movies, *Hollywood na cultura brasileira* [*Hollywood in Brazilian Culture*], by Cicco. All three of these works are far superior to anything in English, although Wohl's work on how Latin Americans appeared in Hollywood films certainly should be mentioned.

For overviews of the contemporary situation of the past few years, there are the articles by Burton ("The Hour of the Embers") and Mosier ("Latin American Cinema in the Seventies"), although, as noted earlier, these essays should be supplemented by some of the other items cited. Finally, it should be noted that in this field it is important to attempt to read everything in order to obtain a balanced perspective. It is also unusually difficult. Many of the books published in Latin America are surprisingly hard to find. Much of what one does find is repetitious: the majority of the film reviews and interviews conducted with artists unfortunately fall into this category. Although the difficulties of working in the field certainly make errors more forgivable than they otherwise might be, all too many of the individual reviews cited in the various bibliographies and indices contain serious errors both of fact and of observation of the films discussed. Burton's annotated bibliography is worth studying simply for her remarks in this regard. Unfortunately the situation has scarcely improved since then.

RESEARCH CENTERS

Every country in Latin America has some type of *cinemateca* [film archive], with a widely assorted set of materials ranging from actual films to printed material, stills, and posters, and Bradford Burns provides a valuable directory of these in his *Latin American Cinema* that is still current. What Burns does not indicate is that no *cinemateca* in the region necessarily has an exhaustive, rigorous, or complete set of anything. It is absolutely useless to plan a project out in advance, because the resources very well may not be there to do the project. Nor is it really possible for the researcher to count on being able to see any great quantity of the films frequently mentioned. These films are either older films that in all too many cases no longer exist, or they are newer films that are commercial properties and are treated accordingly. In other words, there are no real collections in the conventional sense, nor are there research centers.

As far as films go, there are only a few ways in which reasonable quantities of films can be seen. The first is through a prolonged residence in the country itself, although this can be frustrating: except in Brazil, exhibitors are not required to show local films, and they are therefore shown infrequently. This evaluation is perhaps too pessimistic, but it really is true that one has a greater opportunity to see Latin American films at the major European film festivals than one generally does in Latin America.

In recent years the situation has improved dramatically in at least one regard, and the single best exhibition opportunity to see films is the film festival held in Havana by the Cuban Film Institute (ICAIC) in December of each year. The management, since the inception of the festival in 1978, appears to be congenial to visits by scholars and researchers, as is ICAIC itself, although travel to and from Cuba remains both problematic and expensive. Unfortunately the situation within the United States and Great Britain has, if anything, worsened. Within the United States there is no single exhibition series of any great quantity, although the Los Angeles International Film exhibition generally shows a reasonable group of representative films. There are perhaps fifty feature-length films currently handled by North American distributors and the whereabouts of these films is specified in virtually all of the works one runs across.

Access to enough films to form any sort of generalization about any topic is obviously difficult. Fortunately, the situation is somewhat better with regard to the availability of print materials, particularly critical works. These are generally available at the major Latin American Centers in North America, of which UCLA arguably has the best collection. In any case, there are no substantive collections of materials such as stills, scripts, and so forth.

FUTURE RESEARCH

Very little systematic research has been done in English about any aspect of Latin American film. In addition to the modernity of the field and the difficulties involved in doing any research, there are several other problems that are equally important. Fortunately, these last problems are remediable. There is no way that a researcher can solve the problems of geography, of incomplete and in many cases irretrievably lost films, or other similar problems. However, the researcher can maximize his efforts if he is aware of the following factors.

Film production in Latin America is inextricable from governmental control in various ways, and two observations therefore follow: problems of censorship are always present, and virtually all of the films made have a high ideological content. This is as true of the crudest entertainment films as of the most abstract or abstruse pieces of experimental cinema. Although it should be a truism that the two major film movements in the region (the Brazilian and the Cuban) both grew under the aegis of authoritarian governments, this frequently is forgotten, particularly with regard to Chile or Central America. One might add that the openly avowed political orientations of a great many filmmakers (and critics) in the region require one to have a thorough understanding of socialist film theory and practice.

Second, all too much work seems to be based on a somewhat ingenuous acceptance of what the researcher has been told. The old saw that if one wants to find out what radio station a person listens to one looks at the dials on the radios in the parking lot, rather than asking the driver, has a great deal of relevance for the researcher working in this field. There is a lamentable tendency for old, tired ideas to persist, and there is too little critical evaluation of sources, whether they be people, films, or documents.

Third, although the cinema of any one country in the region is too vast a field for any one researcher to learn, it is impossible for a researcher in one country to ignore what has happened somewhere else. Latin American film is a field where the cinema of a country at the other end of the continent—and what has been written about it—may turn out to be more illuminating than additional research in the topic immediately at hand. Essentially this is because there is an utter lack of general studies that would provide the conceptual framework for specialized researchers.

There is no work on Latin American film comparable to Pierre Leprohon's *The Italian Cinema*, and there should be. Although it might be objected that this is because of the geographical and cultural diversity of the region, researchers in other areas of film have managed to surmount this problem: there are several competent surveys of films in Eastern Europe. The Liehms' *The Most Important Art* and Stoil's *Cinema Beyond the Danube*, flawed as those works may very well be, are nonetheless valuable works for the scholar or critic who is pursuing more specialized topics.

One might go further and observe that except for Mora's study on Mexico, none of the works on national cinemas of the region lives up to its title. Again, what is needed are books such as Albert Cervoni's *Les ecrans de sofia* [*The Screens of Sofia*], a concise introduction with perhaps less than one hundred pages of text. One would hope that what Cervoni has done for Bulgarian film could also be done for Argentine, Cuban, Brazilian, or Venezuelan film. There are, in other words, large-scale needs for what are essentially standard critical texts on all of the various aspects of films within the region. For example, nothing of any note has been written about those genres within the region that seem to be a reasonably constant feature from country to country. Films about the frontier, the equivalent to North American Westerns, appear to be present in all of the older national cinemas. To a lesser extent perhaps the same can be said of films dealing with the colonization of the New World and, in what may be a separate category, of films dealing with the relations among the three major racial groups. Such specialized genres, if they can in fact be considered as such, await researchers, as do the more conventional genre films of the regions.

All of these topics are more or less conventional ones. It goes without saying that little or nothing has been done on the whole idea of how films in Latin America have distorted or shaped cultural attitudes or what the reactions of the movie-going public have been to such works. Nor, to conclude on a simpler note, has anyone apparently read all of the extensive interviews with Latin American filmmakers and attempted an evaluation of what they are saying. It is a telling commentary on the state of research that such a logistically simple (although obviously important) piece of work has not yet been done. Although no one should do any serious work in the field without having first been in the field, hardly anything substantive has been done with the relatively little that has been written.

BIBLIOGRAPHY

Ayala Blanco, Jorge. *La aventura del cine mexicano* (México D.F.: Ediciones Era, 1968).

————. *La búsqueda del cine mexicano (1968–1972)*. 2 vols. (México D.F.: UNAM, 1974).

Azevedo, Ely. "O novo cinema Brasiliero." *Filme e Cultura* 1 (1967): 5–14.

Basch, Kenneth, "Cinema Venezuela." *New Orleans Review* 7, no. 2 (1980): 185–89.

Bernadet, Jean-Claude. *Brasil em tempo de cinema* (Rio de Janeiro: Editora Paz e Terra, 1977).

Brazilian Ministry of Culture. "Special Issue on Brazilian Film." Translated by John Stephen Morais. *Cultura Magazine* 24 (n.d.).

Burns, Bradford E. *Latin American Cinema: Film and History* (UCLA Latin American Center: Los Angeles, 1975).

Burton, Julianne. *New Latin American Cinema: An Annotated Bibliography of English Language Sources* (New York: Cineaste, 1976).

————. "The Hour of the Embers." *Film Quarterly* 30, no. 1 (Fall 1976): 33–44.

————. "Revolutionary Cuban Cinema." *Jump Cut* 19 (1978): 17–21.

————. Individual Fulfillment and Collective Achievement." *Cineaste* 4 (1977): 18–26.

Cervoni, Albert. *Les Ecrans de Sofia* (Paris: Filmeditions, 1976).

Chanan, Michael. *Chilean Film* (London: British Film Institute, 1976).

Cicco, Claudio de. *Hollywood na cultura brasileira* (São Paulo: Editions Convivio, 1979).

Coo, Carlos Ossa. *Historia del cine chileno* (Santiago: Quimantú, 1971).

Filme e Cultura (Rio de Janeiro: Instituto Nacional Do Cinema, 1966– to date; publication irregular).

García Riera, Emilio. *Historia documental del cine mexicano*. 10 vols. (México, D.F.: Ediciones Era, 1971).

Gomezzara, Francisco A., and Selene de Rios, Delia. *Sociología del cine* (México D.F.: SepSetentas 110, 1973).

Hochman, Stanley, ed. *World Film since 1945*, 2 vols. (New York: Ungar, 1985).

Hurley, Neil P. *The Reel Revolution* (Maryknoll, N.Y.: Orbis, 1978).

Johnson, Randal. *Cinema Novo X 5* (Austin: University of Texas Press, 1984).

Johnson, Randal and Stam, Robert. *Brazilian Cinema* (East Brunswick, N.J.: Fairleigh Dickinson Press, 1982).

Johnson, William. "Report from Cuba." *Film Quarterly* 19, no. 4 (1966): 31–35.

Kernan, Margot. "Cuban Cinema Today: Tomás Gutiérrez Alea." *Film Quarterly* 39, no. 2 (1975–1976): 45–51.

Latorre, E. Acevedo. *Historia del cine* (México, D.F.: Biblioteca Tema Uteha, 1980).

Leprohon, Pierre. *The Italian Cinema*. Translated by Roger Greaves and Oliver Stallybrass (New York: Praeger Publishers, 1972).

Liehm, Mira, and Liehm, Antonin J. *The Most Important Art: Eastern European Film After 1945* (Berkeley: University of California Press, 1974).

Macotela, Fernando. "Mexican Popular Cinema of the 1970s: How Popular Was It?" *Studies in Latin American Popular Culture* 1 (1982): 27–34.

Mahieu, José Augustín. *Breve historia del cine argentino* (Buenos Aires: Editorial Universitaria de B.A., 1966).

———. "El cine Cubano." *Cuadernos hispanoamericanos* 348 (October 1970): 638–47.

Martínez Parda, Hernando. *Historia del cine colombiana* (Bogotá: Librería y Editorial América Latina, 1978).

Michel, Manuel. "Mexican Cinema, a Panoramic View." *Film Quarterly* 18, no. 4 (Summer 1965): 46–55.

Mora, Carl. *Mexican Cinema: Reflections of a Society, 1896–1980* (Berkeley: University of California Press, 1982).

Mosier, John. "Currents in Latin American Film." *Américas* 30, no. 5 (May 1978): 2–8.

———. "The Importance of Popular Cinema in Latin America." *Studies in Latin American Popular Culture* 1 (1982): 179–86.

———. "Latin American Cinema in the Seventies." *New Orleans Review* 7, no. 3 (1980): 229–36.

Moulds, Michael, ed. *International Index to Film Periodicals* (London: International Federation of Film Archives, 1975 to date).

Murat, Ulyses. *Este cine argentino* (Buenos Aires: Ediciones del Cano de Tespis, 1959).

Myerson, Michael. *Memories of Underdevelopment: The Revolutionary Films of Cuba* (New York: Grossman, 1973).

Neves, David. "In Search of the Aesthetics of the Brazilian Cinema." *New Orleans Review* (Winter 1982; reprinted from *Cultura*).

Nogueira, Rui, and Zalaffi, Nicoletta. "Brasil Ano 170: Round Table on the Cinema Novo." *Cinema* (February 1970): 14–20.

Passek, Jean-Loup, ed. *Le cinema russe et sovietique* (Paris: Centre Georges Pompidou, 1981).

Pick, Zuzana, ed. *Latin American Filmmakers and the Third Cinema* (Ottawa: Carleton University, 1978).

Reyes Navares, Beatriz. *The Mexican Cinema, Interviews with Thirteen Directors*. Translated by Carl Mora and Elizabeth Gard (Albuquerque: University of New Mexico Press, 1976).

de los Reyes, Aurelio. *Los orígenes del cine en México (1896–1900)* (México, D.F.: UNAM, 1973).

Roud, Richard, ed. *Cinema: A Critical Dictionary*. 2 vols. (New York: Viking Press, 1980).

Sadoul, Georges. *Dictionary of Films. Dictionary of Film Makers*. 2 vols. Translated, edited, and updated by Peter Morris (Berkeley: University of California Press, 1972).

————, ed. *Glauber Rocha* (Rio de Janeiro: Editora Paz e Terra, 1977).

Solanas, Fernando, and Getino, Octavio. *Cine, cultura, y descolonización* (Buenos Aires: Siglo Veintiuno Argentina Editores S.A., 1973).

de Souza, Eneas. *Trajetorías do cinema moderno*. 2d ed. (Porto Alegre: Instituto Estadual do Livro, 1974).

Stoil, Michael Jon. *Cinema Beyond the Danube* (Methuen, N.J.: Scarecrow Press, 1974).

Torres, Augusto, and Estremera, Manuel. *Nuevo cine latinoamericano* (Barcelona: Editorial Anagrama, 1973).

Treviño, J.S. "The New Mexican Cinema." *Film Quarterly* 32, no. 3 (1979): 26–37.

Vega, Alicia. *Re-visión del cine chileno* (Santiago: CENECA, 1979).

Vianey, Alex. *Introdução ao Cinema Brasiliero* (Rio de Janeiro: Instituto do Livro, 1959).

Wilson, David. "Aspects of Latin American Political Cinema." *Sight and Sound* 41, no. 1 (Summer 1972): 127–31.

Wohl, Allen. *The Latin Image in American Film*. Rev. ed. (Los Angeles: UCLA Latin American Center, 1980).

Xavier, Ismail. *O discurso cinematografico* (Rio de Janeiro: Editora Paz e Terra, 1977).

Robert H. Lavenda

8 Festivals and Carnivals

Festivals have been part of Latin American life probably for as long as there have been people in Latin America, and it is certainly the case that the first Spanish settlers in the New World brought the celebration of carnival (the three days preceding Ash Wednesday) with them. This chapter will treat one particular aspect of festivals and carnivals in Latin America: their presence in "popular" contexts. By this, we are excluding the purely Indian festivals and carnivals, which have a more limited and local impact and which are not integrated into the national popular culture. However, it should be noted that there is a certain degree of artificiality in this distinction, as there are many connections between the Indian festivals and the "popular" ones (see, for example, Buechler 1980). There is also a significant interpenetration of analytic concerns regarding both kinds of festivals, and this chapter will refer to some of the more important studies of Indian festivals when they are theoretically significant to anyone studying festivals and carnivals in Latin America.

Festivals and carnivals in Latin America have been interpreted in several different ways by the scholars who have studied them. They are variously seen as rites of passage, communication systems, ways of integrating societies, ways of controlling poor Indians or mestizos, and reflections of social organization. To choose one or another of these views to the exclusion of all others seems to be unnecessarily limiting, and it is proposed here that festivals and carnivals are multiplex, multidimensional social performances with many possible functions, some of which include rites of passage, communication of information about the social system, integration of society, and the like. At the same time, it is important to observe that festivals and carnivals also have the potential to disrupt and disintegate societies, a fact which has not been lost on those who hold power in Latin America. From early historic days, there exist decrees banning the celebration of various festivals or carnivals. Thus, in Montevideo in 1788, the *cabildo* [town council] moved to ban public and private dances that involved the *negros*, costumed revelers (Jaúregui, 1944:13). In Caracas, the government took control of the carnival beginning in the 1870s and continues to do so through the present day. In some years, the event was rigidly controlled; in others it was banned completely (Lavenda 1980a, 1980b). The same story is repeated throughout the continent.

Given that this chapter is to cover all Latin America, what (if anything) can be said about the celebration of festivals and carnivals throughout the continent? This is a difficult question, since despite their common Iberian heritage, the countries of Latin America are diverse, indeed. It is, of course, true that all have festivals of one kind or another, and all have in the past celebrated carnival, but beyond that there is not much that can be said to characterize all festivals. On a general level, it is probably the case that all the festivals are somehow involved in the on-going social and political life of the nation in which they occur, and there have been several traditional ways of celebrating festivals, especially carnival. The *juego de agua*— or playing with water—has long been characteristic of carnival, although strenuous efforts have been made to eliminate it, usually without success. It is also probably safe to say that there has always been an opposition, or at least a tension, between the rulers of the society and the poor and dispossessed within the society who have seen these festivals and carnivals as their own.

Most of the festivals, even the "popular" festivals of Latin America, have as their base a religious celebration. Saints' days are particularly important in this regard, and many of the festivals throughout the area begin with homage to the local patron saint. At the same time, it would be a great error to assume that *all* popular festivals in Latin America are religious in nature or even in origin. Many of the popular festivals in Latin America are national holidays, and of these independence days, involving in many countries large military parades and patriotic programs, are the most popular.

The literature on Latin American festivals is surprisingly scanty, particularly when Indian festivals are excluded, and it may well be said that the field of popular festivals in Latin America is wide open for study. As might be expected, the two countries with the largest popular festivals literature are Brazil and Mexico. Bolivia is a close third, and a major analytic work about festivals in Latin America is based on Bolivian materials. This is Hans Buechler's magisterial *The Masked Media*, a study of Aymara Indian fiestas, their extension into the cities of Bolivia, and their articulation with national and popular festivals. This is a most important work, not just for the excellence of the descriptive data, collected over a period of thirteen years, but also for the theoretical position that Buechler presents. For him,

social behavior is to a large extent determined by past interaction in social networks rather than by formal mechanisms of social control. In order to recognize emerging regularities in interpersonal behavior and in order periodically to reassess their position *vis-à-vis* others, individuals require mechanisms which present and process information about social behavior in an orderly and intelligible manner. Periodic public events such as festivals provide such a mechanism (Buechler, 1980: 4–5).

Buechler's points here are important for understanding festivals: social life is never static, people are constantly reassessing their positions in relation to others, and festivals provide a pause, as it were, in social life to allow people to reflect on social interaction. Festivals, then, are metasocial mechanisms that provide information about social behavior and are flexible, supple mechanisms for transmitting information. Migrants from small villages do not relinquish all ties to their home villages; rather, they serve as channels of communication between the urban center to which they have moved and the village left behind—distant, but not forgotten. Indeed, the rise of "folkloric festivals" is associated with this migration from the village to the city. Buechler demonstrates the way in which these new festivals have offered ways of communicating regularities in social interaction that go beyond those which the traditional festivals could offer. The combination of many different local traditions in the urban centers allows for innovation in both local fiestas and urban popular festivals, as well as the emergence of "folkloric festivals." It is important to recognize that the underlying point made by Buechler and supported here is that it is not possible to understand what festivals mean without understanding the social context out of which they emerge. Thus, the traditional manner of studying festivals—arriving the morning of the festival, taking copious notes about the festival, and then leaving—will not provide the kinds of information needed to understand why festivals exist as and where they do. For Buechler, long-term study is essential, given the nature of both festivals and social life: "social life is so complex that we require times, places, and frameworks wherein we can take stock of crucial interaction and thereby lay the foundations for future interpersonal behavior. Aymara festivals are just such public occasions" (357). This notion should inform further research on Latin American festivals, as it provides the potential for understanding festivals in their social and cultural context.

The second major theoretical approach to festivals and carnivals in Latin America comes from the Brazilian anthropologist, Roberto da Matta, who, in a series of important works in the late 1970s, has provided a powerful analysis and comparison of carnival and other secular festivals in mass society. In an early festival article (1973) da Matta describes in considerable detail carnival song-lyrics, texts, behavior (especially between the sexes), and costumes. Upon analyzing them, he notes that they reveal the mechanisms universally revealed in rites of passage, particularly the movement to overturn the structures of everyday life and the movement toward *communitas* [society as an unstructured or scarcely structured and undifferentiated group]. In this, he claims, carnival, as well as other aspects of Brazilian popular culture, deals with the question of the *mestiço*—of race mixture in Brazil and the formation of a national consciousness. He points out that the *mestiço*, as the ambiguous, mediating, middle-term in the Brazilian tripartite race taxonomy, is the perfect symbol for carnival. He concludes by suggesting that the oscillation of Carnival Brazil and Everyday Brazil is also the oscillation at the core of carnival—that of everyone becoming *mestiço*—and as well that of the Brazil of Law and the Brazil of the Rascal. Da Matta has gone on from this beginning to address these same issues as they are reflected in the different aspects of national Brazilian society represented by carnival and football (soccer).

MAJOR REFERENCES BY COUNTRY

With an area as large and diverse as Latin America, it is easiest to provide a schematic outline of the major sources available for each country, but reference should be made to two general works on Latin America as a whole and to two which, although they deal with carnival world-wide, are of particular interest to students of Latin American festivals. The first is Julio Caro Baroja's classic 1965 study of carnival itself in its historico-cultural context. This work is probably the most useful to the student of Latin American festivals, although it is not the only synthetic work on festivals and carnival (the reader may consult, for example, Caradec 1977; Duvignaud 1973, 1977; Fabre 1976; Gaignebet 1974; Jesi 1977; or Mesnil 1974). Caro Baroja provides a detailed consideration of the history of carnival, as well as a functional analysis of its place in the societies in which it has been found over time. The work is particularly strong on the Middle Ages and the Renaissance and provides the reader with an understanding of both the form and function of carnival over time.

The second volume that treats of carnivals world-wide is one of photographs: A. Orloff's *Carnival* (1981). Orloff is a superb photographer, and the volume is an excellent one for achieving an understanding of the particular mix of excitement, sensuality, and festivity that characterizes carnival. For Latin America, the carnivals that are covered include Rio and Mazatlán, and within the Western Hemisphere, New Orleans, Port au Prince, and Trinidad. There is a text, but the magnificent, evocative photographs are the major reason to consult this work.

For Latin America as a whole, there are two volumes of note. The first is *Fiesta Time in Latin America*, by Jean Milne (1965). Despite the title, some ethnocentric comments, and a somewhat unsophisticated approach, this is a valuable book, for it contains an extensive, thorough listing of festivals in Latin America by month and by country. The first part of the work is descriptive—each month is presented, and in each are discussed several festivals from all over the region. Thus, the section on carnival, which is twenty-three pages in length, refers to interesting customs in all the countries in which carnival is celebrated. The second part of the book presents brief listings of festivals by country, each with date, place of celebration, and two or three words on method of celebration. There are two major drawbacks to the book. The first is that the author appears naive and slightly supercilious. The second is more severe. The book has neither bibliography nor preface, so there is no way of knowing how the author has become so expert on so many festivals. Nevertheless, as a starting place, this volume is not bad.

A similar book is that of Félix Coluccio, the Argentine folklorist, whose *Fiestas y costumbres de América* [*Fiestas and Customs of America*, 1954] also reviews the different festivals of the continent. The volume is more scholarly than Milne's.

Argentina

Two particularly important works for studying festivals in Argentina are by Coluccio (1972) and Puccia (1974). The latter is a brief history of carnival in Buenos Aires and is particularly strong on the later nineteenth century and the "heyday" of the Buenos Aires carnival, the period 1900–1915. There are useful photographs. The Coluccio volume is like his earlier work but is a directory of festivals in Argentina. This work, too, follows the calendar: it is arranged by the date of each festival or fair and provides a summary description, vital information (e.g., date, length of celebration, and reason for celebration), and traditions of the event (e.g., songs, costumes, etc.). Other works on Argentine festivals include two detailed analyses of a religious festival in Punta Corral in the province of Jujuy by the archaeologist C. Lafon and several students (Lafon 1965; Aznar, Bilbao, and González, 1960–1965). There are also a series of less detailed but nevertheless useful descriptive works on other Argentine festivals, of which the most salient are Cortázar (1944), Dudán (1952), Kagarov (1931), and Newberry and Rocca (1978).

Bolivia

As already noted, a most significant study of festivals in Latin America is that of Buechler (1980) on Aymara festivals in Bolivia. There are several other valuable works on festivals in Bolivia, including two on carnival in Oruro, one from 1974 (Madrid and Santori), and the other from 1962 (Beltrán Heredia). Other of these works are by Helfritz (1946) on the festival of the Virgin in Copacabana and important works by Paredes Candia (1977) on the popular festivals of Bolivia and R. Smith (1975) on the art of the festival in Bolivia. This last is valuable for the theoretical orientation that it takes.

Brazil

As befitting a country with the world's most famous carnival, there is a considerable amount of information available about festivals in Brazil. First, there are five useful works that do not deal with carnival. Two are by A. M. Araújo: one that deals with São Paulo (1957), and the other, which is a synthetic work, on national folklore (1964). The latter, in particular, is well worth consulting by anyone interested in the folklore of Brazil, as is Mello Moraes (1895), for those interested in a late-nineteenth-century view of festivals and popular traditions in Brazil. Other noncarnival works deal with festivals in Belem (Alves 1980), and the Feast of the Holy Ghost (Willems, 1949).

The remaining works discussed all deal in one way or another with carnival. There are two useful works that do not deal specifically with Rio de Janeiro. They are Verger (1976) on processions and carnival in Brazil in general, and Maranhão (1960) on carnival in Recife. The remaining works to be discussed concern carnival in Rio. Of greatest interest to anthropologists and others concerned with performance is the late Victor Turner's first (and last) article on carnival (1983), in which he applied his traditional breadth of knowledge and insight to this most extraordinary festival. Also by English-speaking anthropologists are Julie Taylor's important work on the politics of the aesthetics of carnival (1982) and Lloyd's study of the samba schools of Rio (1959). It is striking that these seem to be almost all the studies of carnival in Rio written by anglophone scholars. Clearly, the study of carnival in Rio is a field wide open for such scholars.

It is certainly the case, however, that other scholars have studied carnival in Rio, and that pre-eminent among them are Brazilians. The classic history of carnival in Rio, for example, is by the Brazilian, M. de Eneida (1958). Major studies of the modern carnival have come from Brazilian anthropologists, particularly Roberto da Matta and his students. Da Matta has at least four major works that deal with carnival (1973, 1977, 1978, and 1979). Two of these articles have been discussed, and it will suffice here to note that da Matta's studies are among the most analytic studies of such events and that he sets them in contrast to other secular rituals of Brazilian life. He also attempts to see in carnival a key symbol for understanding Brazilian culture and society. These works are provocative and are well worth the efforts of any student of festivals and carnivals.

The student of carnivals should certainly consult Goldwasser (1975) and Leopoldi (1978), both da Matta's students, who have concerned themselves with the social organization of the samba schools characteristic of the Rio carnival. Both of these are solid works, well grounded in theory and providing as well considerable amounts of description of use to other scholars. Both are concerned with the festival in a wider context. For Leopoldi

(p. 15), for example, "the samba school, understood as a social microcosm, reflects in its organization, structural patterns of the global society."

Chile

There seems to be little written about festivals and carnivals in Chile: Pereira Salas's (1947) seems to be the only article specifically about festivals in Chile, although Hoyos Sancho (1970) also refers briefly to historical material about Santiago.

Colombia

The material on Colombia is slightly better than that concerning Chile. There are three articles dealing with festivals and carnivals, one in the central region of the country (Friedemann 1975), and two in the northern part of the country (Castillejo 1957, and Vengoechea 1950). Of these, the Vengoechea deals specifically with *lo popular* [the popular] in the Baranquilla carnival.

Ecuador

There are several good sources for the study of festivals in Ecuador, although much that has been written concerns Indian festivals with little national or "popular" impact. Of these, perhaps the most useful is by Wilgus de Isas (1974), since it provides what appears to be nearly a complete directory of Ecuadorian festivals. It is otherwise highly descriptive of certain Andean festival features. Carvalho-Neto provides some detailed descriptions of festivals in his *Diccionario del folklore ecuatoriano* [*Dictionary of Ecuadorian Folklore*, 1964] and in his study of festivals in Imbabura (1965), particularly the San Juan festival in Otavalo, which receives most of the description in this ninety-page article. Tejada (1965) also devotes a great deal of attention to Otavalo, but it is the celebration of the Day of the Dead that is his topic. Townsend (1978) also discusses many different Ecuadorian festivals.

Guatemala

Much of the work that has been done on festivals in Guatemala concerns the indigenous populations of the country. Of the other material, perhaps the most interesting from both a descriptive and a theoretical point of view comes from the distinguished folklorist Celso Lara, who has written at least two articles on popular festivals in Guatemala (1974 and 1975). Other useful works on festivals in Guatemala include Aguja (1975) and W. Smith (1977).

The latter is a particularly important book on the relation of the fiesta system to economic change. Although the book deals with Indian festivals, it is included here because the theoretical position taken is one that students of festivals and carnivals in Latin America would do well to consider.

Mexico

As might be expected, Mexico provides the largest single entry in the bibliography of Latin American festivals and carnivals. Nevertheless, the Mexican material is not as strong as that of, say, Brazil or Bolivia, since a great deal of it is entirely descriptive and lacking in analysis. It must be recognized, however, that there is a considerable literature, some of it very important for students of popular culture, on indigenous and peasant festivals systems in Mexico. Some of these important works are by Cancian (1965), Greenberg (1981), Ingham (1984), Bricker (1973 and 1981), Vogt (1976), and Crumrine (1970). Important works on popular festivals and carnivals include Wolf (1958) on the Virgin of Guadalupe, Boiles (1971) on the Otomi carnival, Becquelin-Monod and Breton (1973) on carnival in Bachajon, Vogt and Abel (1977) on political rituals, and Nahmad Sitton (1976) on syncretism and cultural identity. Other useful works include Vázquez Santana (1940), on festivals and customs in Mexico, Fay (1960) on the festival days of Mexico, Fisher (1972) on the *quince años* [fifteenth birthday] celebration in upper-middle-class families, Kaplan (1951), a monograph by Vázquez Santana and Dávila Garibi (1931), and a long article by Horcasitas Pimentel (1974) on carnival in Mexico. Striking pictures of carnival masks and costumes are to be found in Cordry (1980). Finally, the remainder of the works on Mexico are of a highly descriptive nature, and include Bejaramo (1970), Fergusson (1934), Gallop (1939), Guerrero (1939), López de los Mozos (1974), Medina Hernández (1964), Montenegro (1929), Pérez Toro (1948), Redfield (1929), Toor (1929), Vargas (1935), and Williams García (1960). The series of articles from 1929 are of some interest; all are from *Mexican Folkways*, a journal whose editor was Frances Toor and whose art editor was Diego Rivera. The issue of January-March, 1929 (volume 5, no. 1) contained four articles, in English and Spanish, about carnival in various villages in the country. These are popular articles and are interesting because the quality of the descriptions is high and because the illustrations are excellent.

Peru

The material on Peru is limited, although for those interested in the hacienda of Vicos and its history, Martínez Arellano (1959) provides an analysis of the role of festivals in cultural integration and disintegration.

Roca (1979) provides an ethnography of a festival in Urubamba, and Qui-
noñes and Tarazona (1977) write of a festival in Quiches.

Uruguay

Although there is little material on festivals and carnivals in Uruguay,
that which exists is of considerable interest. Carvalho-Neto (1967) provides
a superb study of the carnival of Montevideo during the twentieth century,
presenting therein an extraordinary amount of descriptive material on the
celebration of the festival. He is also concerned with the sociological functions of the festival and includes a chapter on changes in the festival un-
derlining the point that such events are highly sensitive to changes in the
socio-political milieu that surround them. Jaúregui's (1944) is an historical
study of the carnival of Montevideo during the nineteenth century and on
into the early years of the twentieth, providing a considerable amount of
useful comparative data.

Venezuela

For Venezuela, too, there is little material in print. Domínguez (1961)
provides a description of traditional festivals in the Venezuelan Andes.
Lavenda (1980a, 1980b) is concerned with the transformation of the Caracas carnival at the end of the nineteenth century and attempts to place
the changes in carnival in a social and political context. This is particularly
the case in Lavenda (1980b), in which changes in the position of Venezuela
within the globalizing world-system are associated with the changes in the
festival.

Indeed, the processes identified in these latter two works may be seen
in carnivals and festivals throughout the region during the late nineteenth
century and is a process that continues into the present. Public events like
carnivals and festivals are ideally situated to be battlegrounds for various
political and social positions within a society, and a glance at the history
of such events reveals that this point has not been lost on those with such
a position to defend or to advance. The history of carnivals and festivals
in Latin America is rife with episodes in which those with power sought
to express that power in the festival and those desiring power sought to
bend the festival to their aims. Thus, the point made at the beginning of
this essay may well be made again: to study festivals as isolated incidents,
as interesting or exotic "folkloric" events occurring only at one particular,
unsituated moment, is to miss the very power and point of these events.
Festivals may have considerable power in a society, and even where they
no longer have the potency they once had, they still may serve as "social
barometers," indicating the positions of those with power, communicating
the social states of a society.

CENTERS FOR THE STUDY OF FESTIVALS

Most universities in Latin America have either departments of anthropology or programs in folklore, or both. These should be the basic starting points for students of Latin American festivals or carnivals seeking research affiliation (usually required and always recommended), assistance, or further information. There are at least four institutions within the region that should be brought to the attention of scholars of festivals and carnivals. Although they are certainly not the only institutions in Latin America that have carried out excellent research on these events, they are known to the author as being interested in such research. The first of these is the Centro de Estudios Folklóricos [Center of Folkloric Studies], associated with the Universidad de San Carlos in Guatemala City, Guatemala. The second is the Instituto Internacional de Estudios Folklóricos [International Institute of Folkloric Studies, INIDEF], in Caracas, Venezuela, an OAS-sponsored research institute. Third is the Instituto Otavaleño de Antropología [Otavalo Institute of Anthropology], in Otavalo, Ecuador, a private research institute that has been carrying out research on Otavalo area festivals for many years. Fourth is the Museo Nacional [National Museum] in Rio de Janeiro, the base of operations for Roberto da Matta and those of his students who have been studying the Rio carnival.

DIRECTIONS FOR FUTURE RESEARCH

Given the present state of research on festivals and carnivals in Latin America, future studies ought to be concerned not only with the festivals and carnivals themselves, but also with situating them in their sociocultural and historical contexts. Although there are numerous descriptions of indigenous and small-town festivals, there are not enough descriptive studies of major popular festivals and carnivals in the cities of Latin America with the possible exception of Rio, where a start has been made. Yet it is here that the popular culture of nation states is being forged, and such studies should be carried out. Festivals and carnivals, it is hardly necessary to point out, are rich in symbolism and metaphor, and the analysis of these symbols and metaphors can provide important understandings of the societies from which the events emerge. Beyond this, the particular symbology chosen for the festival is a sensitive indicator of the state of the surrounding society. For the symbolic anthropologist or other student of human culture and society, the symbolism and metaphors of popular festivals are the stuff of secular rituals and the creation of meaning for human life.

But synchronic description alone is not sufficient; the history of these events must be considered. The late nineteenth century in particular is an important time for carnivals in Latin America. Many were significantly transformed, but the literature on them for this period is not strong. Moreover, the forces that shaped the transformations of the political economies of Latin American nations must be connected with the history of the festivals and carnivals in these nations. From this comes the necessity of at least considering the possibility that popular festivals and carnivals in Latin America are connected with the expression and manipulation of power. This is particularly significant for those who would study some of the most interesting and provocative festivals of all: those festivals and carnivals that have become tourist events, attracting viewers from both home and abroad. What effect does the "touristification" of the festival have on the festival itself, on the people who have been traditionally celebrating it, and on the relationships of power between the tourists and their society and the celebrants and theirs?

Further research on festivals and carnivals ought also to focus on the local aspects of these events, both those regarding the expenses associated with the events and those involved with the interface of the events and the surrounding economy of the locale of the festival, its region, and the nation-state as well.

It is also necessary, following Buechler (1980), to concentrate on the relationship of urban and rural festivals. This is an issue of considerable significance. As Buechler makes clear, the movement between the two different kinds of festivals is not all one way. Just as the urban festivals affect the rural, so too the rural festivals affect the urban ones. Disentangling this connection is necessary, and the results will be of value not only in the study of such popular events as carnivals and festivals, but will also shed considerable light on theoretical issues in migration studies and social urbanization.

In sum, the festival as a thing-in-itself or as an art form presents the scholar with a field open for symbolic, metaphoric, performance, or phenomenological analysis, while the festival as a social and cultural nexus, as a symbol of wider social and cultural processes, or as a way into the study of such processes is also a field for the anthropologist, sociologist, historian, folklorist, political scientist, or general student of popular culture.

BIBLIOGRAPHY

Aguja, Olga María. "El Corpus Christi en Patzún." *Tradiciones de Guatemala* 4 (1975): 221–35.

Alves, Isidro. *O carnaval devote: Um estudio sobre a Festa de Nazaré em Belen* (Petrópolis: Editora Vozes, 1980).

Araújo, Alceu Maynard. *Poranduba paulista* (São Paulo: Escola de Sociologia e Politica de São Paulo, 1957.)

———. *Folclore nacional* (São Paulo: Ed. Melhoramentos, 1964).

Aznar, Pablo; Bilbao, S.; and González, M. "Descripción de los elementos de la fiesta." *Runa* (Buenos Aires) 10, nos. 1/2 (1960–1965): 290–310.

Becquelin-Monod, Aurore, and Breton, Alain. "Le carnaval de Bachajon." *Journal de la Societé des Americanistes* 62 (1973): 89–103.

Bejaramo, Emilio J. "Fiesta de Nuestra Señora de la Luz, en Cañada de Alfaro, Municipio de León." *Boletin del Instituto Nacional de Antropología e Historia* 39 (1970): 34–38.

Beltrán Heredia, B. A. *El carnaval de Oruro y proceso ideológico e historia de grupos folklóricos* (Oruro: Ediciones del Comité del Departamento de Folklore, 1962).

Boiles, Charles L. "Síntesis y sincretismo en el carnaval otomí." *América Indígena* 31, no. 3 (1971): 555–63.

Bricker, Victoria Reifler. *Ritual Humor in Highland Chiapas* (Austin: University of Texas Press, 1973).

———. *The Indian Christ, The Indian King: The Historical Substrata of Maya Myth and Ritual* (Austin: University of Texas Press, 1981).

Buechler, Hans C. *The Masked Media: Aymara Fiestas and Social Interaction in the Bolivian Highlands* (The Hague: Mouton, 1980).

Cancian, Frank. *Economics and Prestige in a Maya Community: The Religious Cargo System in Zinacantan* (Stanford: Stanford University Press, 1965).

Caro Baroja, Julia. *El carnaval: análisis historico-cultural* (Madrid: Taurus, 1965).

Caradec, Francois. *La farce et le sacré: fêtes et farceurs, mythes et mystificateurs* (Paris: Casterman, 1977).

Carvalho-Neto, Paulo. *Diccionario del folklore ecuatoriano* (Quito: Editorial Casa de la Cultura, 1964).

———. "Folklore de Imbabura." *Revista del Folklore Ecuatoriano* 1, no. 1 (1965): 9–93.

———. *El carnaval de Montevideo: folklore, historia, sociología* (Sevilla: Universidad de Sevilla, Facultad de Filosofía y Letras, 1967).

Castillejo, Robert. "El carnaval en el norte de Colombia." *Divulgaciones etnológicas del Instituto de investigación etnológica de la Universidad del Atlántico* (Barranquilla) 6 (1957): 63–71.

Coluccio, Félix. *Fiestas y costumbres de América* (Buenos Aires: Editora Poseidón, 1954).

———. *Fiestas, celebraciones, recordaciones, mercados y ferias populares y/o tradicionales de la República Argentina* (Buenos Aires: Ediciones Culturales Argentinas, 1972).

Cordry, Donald. *Mexican Masks* (Austin: University of Texas Press, 1980).

Cortázar, Augusto Raúl. "La fiesta patronal de Nuestra Señora de la Candelaria en Molinos." *Relaciones de la sociedad argentina de antropología* 4 (1944): 271–86.

Crumrine, N. Ross. "Ritual drama and cultural change." *Comparative Studies in Society and History* 12, no. 4 (1970): 361–72.

DaMatta, Roberto. "Carnaval como um rito de passagem." In *Ensaios de Antropologia Estrutural* (Petrópolis: Editora Vozes, 1973).

———. "Constraint and license: A preliminary study of two Brazilian rituals." In *Secular Ritual*, edited by S. Moore and B. Myerhoff, 244–64 (Assen, Netherlands: Van Gorcum, 1977b).

———. *Carnavais, melandros e herois: Para uma sociologia do dilema Brasileiro* (Rio de Janeiro: Zahar, 1978).

———. "Ritual in complex and tribal societies." *Current Anthropology* 20, no. 3 (1979): 589–90.

Domínguez, Luis Arturo. *Fiestas tradicionales en los estados andinos venezolanos* (Caracas: Ed. del Ejec. Edo. Trujillo, 1961).

Dudán, Lavinia. "Observaciones sobre la orgía en el Carnaval del noroeste argentino." *Revista de Antropología y Ciencias Afines* (Tucumán-Salta) 1 (1952): 43–48.

Dutton, Bertha. "All Saints' Day Ceremonies in Todos Santos, Guatemala." *El Palacio* (Sante Fe) 46 (1939): 205–17.

Duvignaud, Jean. *Fêtes et civilisations* (Paris: Weber, 1973).

———. *Le don du rien: essai d'antropologie de la fête* (Paris: Stock, 1977).

Eneida, M. D. *Historia do Carnaval Carioca* (Rio de Janeiro: Civilização Brasileira, 1958).

Fabre, Daniel. "Le monde du carnaval." *Annales* 31, no. 2 (1976): 389–406.

Fay, George R. "Fiesta Days of Mexico." *Katunob* (miscellaneous series, no. 1, 1960).

Fergusson, Erna. *Fiesta in Mexico* (New York: Knopf, 1934).

Fisher, Janice. "The *quince años* celebration." *Katunob* 8, no. 2 (1972): 85–92.

Friedemann, Nina S. de. "La fiesta del indio en Quibdo: un case de relaciones inter-étnicas en Colombia." *Revista colombiano de antropología* 19 (1975): 65–78.

Gaignebet, Claude. *Le carnaval: essais de mythologie populaire* (Paris: Payot, 1974).

Gallop, Rodney. "The Carnival of Huejotzingo." *Geographical Magazine* 8 (1939): 337–44.

Goldwasser, Julia Maria. *O palacio do samba* (Rio de Janeiro: Editora Zahar, 1975).

Greenberg, James B. *Santiago's Sword: Chatino Peasant Religion and Economics* (Berkeley: University of California Press, 1981).

Guerrero, Raul G. "La fiesta tradicional de Juchitán." *Revista mexicana de estudios antropológicos* 3 (1939): 242–56.

Helfritz, Hans. "La fiesta de la Virgen de Copacabana." *Revista geográfica americana* (Buenos Aires) 25 (1946): 69–74.

Horcasitas Pimentel, Fernando. "Carnaval." In *Lo efímero y eterno del arte popular mexicano*, 635–67 (México: Fondo Editorial de la Plástica Mexicana, 1974).

de Hoyos Sancho. Nieves. "Algo sobre carnavales en Iberoamérica." *Revista de Indias* 30 (1970): 297–314.

Ingham, John. *Mary, Michael, and Lucifer: Folk Catholicism in Central Mexico* (Austin: University of Texas Press, 1984).

Jaúregui, Miguel Angel. *El carnaval de Montevideo en el siglo xix* (Montevideo: Ediciones Ceibo, 1944).

Jesi, Furio, ed. *La Festa, antropologia, etnologia, folklore* (Torino: Rosenberg e Sellier, 1977).

Kagarov, E. "Essai de classification des rites populares." *Revista del Instituto de etnología de la Universidad Nacional de Tucamán* 2 (1931): 49–59.

Kaplan, Bernice. "Changing Functions of the Huanancha Dance at the Corpus Christi Festival en Paracho, Michoacan, Mexico." *Journal of American Folklore* 64 (1951): 383–92.

Lafon, Ciro René. "Fiesta y religión en Punta Corral." *Runa* (Buenos Aires) 10, no. 12 (1965): 256–89.

Lara F., Celso A. "Siete de diciembre: día de la quema del diablo." *Tradiciones de Guatemala* 1 (1974): 115–30.

———. "La quema del diablo en Guatemala." *Journal of Latin American Lore* 1, no. 2 (1975): 199–209.

Lavenda, Robert. "From Festival of Progress to Masque of Degradation: Carnival in Caracas as a Changing Metaphor for Social Relations." In *Play and Culture*, edited by Helen Schwartzman, 19–30 (West Point, N.Y.: Leisure Press, 1980a).

———. "The Festival of Progress: The Globalizing World-System and the Transformation of the Caracas Carnival." *Journal of Popular Culture* 14, no. 3 (1980b): 465–75.

Leopóldi, Jose Savio. *Escola de samba, ritual e sociedade* (Petrópolis: Editora Vozes, 1978).

Lloyd, A. L. "Samba Schools of Rio." *Geographical Magazine* 26 (1959): 382–83.

López de los Mozos, J. R. "La fiesta de la Octava del Corpus en Valverde de los Arroyos." *Revista de dialectología y tradiciones populares* 30, nos. 1–2 (1974): 91–98.

Madrid, L., and Santori, M. E. "Ensayo para un estudio del carnaval en la ciudad de Oruro." *Relaciones de la sociedad argentina de antropología* 8 (1974): 49–62.

Maranhão, Walmyr. "Recife carnival." *Américas* 12, no. 3 (1960): 17–21.

Martínez, Arellano, Héctor. "Vicos, las fiestas en la integración y desintegración cultural." *Revista del Museo Nacional* (Lima) 28 (1959): 189–247.

Medina Hernández, Andrés. "El carnaval de Tenejapa." *Anales del Instituto Nacional de Antropología e Historia* 17, no. 46 (1964): 323–41.

Mello Moraes, Alexandre José de. *Festas e tradições populares do Brazil* (Rio de Janeiro: Fauchon e Cia., 1895).

Mesnil, Marianne. *Trois essais sur la fête: do folklore à l'etnosémiotique* (Bruxelles: Edicions de l'Université de Bruxelles, 1974).

Milne, Jean. *Fiesta Time in Latin America* (Los Angeles: Ward Ritchie Press, 1965).

Montenegro, Roberto. "El carnaval en Záchila, Oaxaca." *Mexican Folkways* 5 (1929): 28–29.

Nahmad Sitton, S. "Mexican Feasts: Syncretism and Cultural Identity." *Cultures* 3, no. 2 (1976): 45–58.

Newberry, Sara, and Rocca, Manuel. "El carnaval chiguano-chané." *Cuadernos del Instituto Nacional de Antropología* (Buenos Aires) 8 (1978): 43–92.

Orloff, Alexander. *Carnival* (Wörgl: Verlag Perlinger, 1981).

Paredes Candia, Antonio, ed. *Fiestas Populares de Bolivia* (La Paz: Ediciones Isla, 1977).

Pereira de Queiroz, María. "Evolution du carnaval latino-americain." *Diogène* 104 (1978): 53–70.

Pereira Salas, Eugenio. *Juegos y alegrías coloniales en Chile* (Santiago: Zig Zag, 1947).

Pérez Toro, Augusto. "Fiesta de mayo en Kimibilá." *Yikal may than* 9 (1948): 94–95.

Puccia, Enrique Horacio. *Breve historia del Carnaval Porteño* (Buenos Aires: Municipalidad de la Ciudad de Buenos Aires, 1974).

Quiñones, Teodor, and Tarazona, Julio. "La fiesta patronal de Quiches." *Apacheta* (Lima) (1977): 26–40.

Redfield, Robert. "The Carnival in Tepoztlán." *Mexican Folkways* 5 (1929): 30–34.

Roca W., Demetrio. "Etnografía de la fiesta del Señor de Torrechayoc en Urubamba." *Wayka* (Cuzco) 6–7 (1979): 115–40.

Smith, Robert J. *The Art of the Festival.* University of Kansas Publications in Anthropology, no. 6 (Lawrence: University of Kansas, 1975).

Smith, Waldemar R. *The Fiesta System and Economic Change* (New York: Columbia University Press, 1977).

Taylor, J. R. "The Politics of Aesthetic Debate: The Case of the Brazilian Carnival." *Ethnology* 21 (1982): 301–11.

Tejada, Leonardo. "Día de difuntos en Otavalo." *Revista del folklore ecuatoriano* 1, no. 1 (1965): 95–113.

Toor, Frances. "Carnivals at the Villages." *Mexican Folkways* 5 (1929): 10–27.

Townsend, Elizabeth Jane. "Festivals of Ecuador." *Américas* 30, no. 4 (1978): 9–16.

Turner, Victor. "*Carnaval* in Rio: Dionysian Drama in an Industrializing Society." In *The Celebration of Society: Perspectives on Contemporary Cultural Performance*, edited by Frank Manning (Bowling Green: Bowling Green University Popular Press, 1983).

Vargas, Alberto. *Guelaguetza: costumbre racial oaxaqueña* (Oaxaca: Imprenta del Gobierno del Estado, 1935).

Vásquez Santana, Higinio. *Fiestas y costumbres mexicanas* (México: Ediciones Botas, 1940).

Vásquez Santana, Higinio, and Dávila Garibi, Ignacio. *El Carnaval* (México: Monografías Históricas y Folklóricas Mexicanas, 1931).

Vengoechea, R., "Lo popular en el Carnaval de Baranquilla." *Divulgaciones del Instituto de Investigación Etnológica de la Universidad del Atlántico* (Barranquilla), 1, no. 2 (1950): 86–105.

Verger, Pierre. "Processiones et carnaval au Brésil." In *L'autre el l'ailleurs: hommage a Roger Bastide* 7, 333–43 (Nice: Institut d'études et de recherches interethniques et interculturelles, 1976).

Vogt, Evon. *Tortillas for the Gods* (Cambridge: Harvard University Press, 1976).

Vogt, Evon, and Abel, Susan. "On Political Rituals in Contemporary Mexico." In *Secular Ritual*, edited by S. Moore and B. Myerhoff (Assen: Van Gorcum, 1977).

Wilgus de Isas, Judith. "Fiestas folklóricas ecuatorianas." *América Indígena* 34, no. 3 (1974): 629–49.

Willems, Emilio. "Acculturative Aspects of the Feast of the Holy Ghost in Brazil." *American Anthropologist* 51 (1949): 400–408.

Williams, García, Roberto. "Carnaval en la Huaxteca Veracruzana." *La Palabra y el hombre* (Xalapa, Veracruz) 15 (1960): 37–45.

Wolf, Eric. "The Virgin of Guadalupe: A Mexican National Symbol." *Journal of American Folklore* 71 (1958): 34–39.

Naomi Lindstrom

9 The Single-Panel Cartoon

Graphic representation has a long-standing place in the history of humorous expression. While the origins of humorous drawing are lost in prehistory, the standardization and popularization of the modern cartoon is a relatively recent phenomenon. The cartoon emerged as a distinct form when it separated from the more general category of popular comical illustration and sketching. While the cartoon had much in common with traditional forms, it distinguished itself by its crucial "gag," punch line, or joke. Other humorous elements, such as the exaggeration of caricature, may be present, but it is the main comic "point" that defines the cartoon as such. Most cartoons rely on language, in the form of captions or balloon dialogue, to convey the essence of the joke. Yet visual wit may predominate even to the point of making language superfluous, as in "mute" humor.

HISTORY

Throughout the last two-thirds of the nineteenth century, the practice of publishing editorializing political caricatures gradually became widespread throughout Latin America. This practice was heavily influenced in style by mass-circulation cartoons in the United States. The press in post-colonial Latin America could only spread the caricature form once the area was sufficiently developed in technology. A second factor was necessary for the success of the cartoon. Political caricature could not become widespread until cartoonists could count on a readership with sufficient interest in the major figures involved in politics and issues of the day.

The independence movements of principally 1810–1830 and the movements of reform that continued to appear throughout the century created a new consciousness of the importance of the principles and questions involved in governance. Liberal notions developed from the Enlightenment provided ideals of democracy and fair procedure, against which the existing practices of real-world politicians could be held to ridicule. A current-day reader, looking back at 1870–1910 cartoons, must be surprised at the extent to which every actor and political issue is labeled. The reader was not required to identify officials, wars, or political struggles. Names appeared printed across a sash worn by an official or simply superimposed on an individual's clothing; in addition, there was extensive use of captions to give basic orienting information. Buildings of emblematic importance and other significant items, such as the constitution (frequently appearing because of the embodiment of liberal reform notions in nineteenth-century constitutions) all were tagged explicitly.

If readers were not trusted to have complete powers of recognition in the area of governmental and other national matters, it was expected that they would have a good traditional education. In particular, allegorical cartoons, relying on classical mythology, presupposed that an educated reader would know the cultural system of classical antiquity. Not only those cultural items that have become part of everyday allusions were included (e.g., the Trojan Horse, Pandora's Box) but also references that would require most modern-day readers to turn to a dictionary of classical mythology. This use of classical allusion suggests the elite nature of the reading audience. It is surprising for one accustomed to current-day cartooning, in which the expanded readership is expected to be well-versed in the details of contemporary events but not necessarily to have a generally broad educational and cultural background.

Noé Jitrik's *La revolución del 90* [*The Revolution of 1890*] contains material that reveals the position taken by contemporary caricaturists vis-à-vis their readership and the figures they satirized. The study, which particularly emphasizes the reflections in popular culture of this Argentine revolution, points to the many linkages between representatives of the press, politicians, military leaders, people hoping to become actors on the political scene, and others involved in public life. Bonds of kinship and marriage existed, supplemented by those provided by a common elite formation, creating such a web of linkages that the leaders of the failed rebellion had to be released unpunished by government leaders. This circumstance, in which virtually no one in public life took the role of pure "outsider," was reflected in the political caricatures of the event. The actors in the drama were all displayed with considerable dignity to their physical persons, even when the cartoon was from a critical perspective. For example, a cartoon of Leandro Alem showed this politician not merely driven by strong ideals but garbed and declaiming as a prophet. It actually presented a flattering physical image of the man's face and body (if not of his zeal). Constraints of decorum and of gentlemanly conduct appear to have prevented the gleeful attack on personal dignity that has animated much successful cartooning.

Up to the twentieth century, subject matter was tightly constrained, containing only "high" events such as affairs of state or the propagation of some well-publicized social, cultural, or esthetic program. The individuals shown remained for the most part politicians, with some attention given to leading cultural figures. Representation of ordinary people was notably lacking except for the occasional Everyman figure signifying some large sector of the population.

This set of conventions was considerably expanded during the next half century as humorous graphic artists began to include material exploiting the comedy inherent in everyday events and people. Some excellent examples of the humorous quotidian scene may be found in the magazine *Caras y caretas* [*Faces and Masks*]. Elegant and modish, it originated in Buenos Aires and was distributed throughout Latin America and features short essays and stories by some of the most fashionable authors of the early twentieth century. It especially favored the *costumbrista* [local-color piece], the type of light, amusing sketch characteristic of sprightly turn-of-the-century writing. This vignette style extended to the graphics of the magazine, which around 1900 began running many witty and light-hearted scenes of everyday life, either as illustrations to written texts or as autonomous features. There was an emphasis on such ordinary activities as beach-going, getting caught in the rain, suffering the discomforts of transportation, or joining a crowd to watch unusual events unfold in public.

More radical and proletarian were turn-of-the century Mexico City street cartoonists, especially Guadalupe José Posada. Posada's etchings, reproduced by the millions, were nothing like the impressionistic clutter of the humorous-sketch artist and were more intrinsically Latin than previous political cartooning. His most notable innovation was the utilization of the skeleton and other folk-form motifs for a variety of satirical, decorative, political, and humorous depictions. Posada was one of many who produced their penny sheets to be sold on street corners to a largely illiterate populace that had to rely on a simple, punchy visualization. While much has been written attempting to specify Posada's importance in the history of Latin American culture, of the democratization of art, and of the development of the visual arts, the strong populist implication of his work remains the central issue. Perhaps most interesting are his works in which the satirized figures who are not precisely identifiable with real-world persons, but rather stand for the various forces exploitative of the working class, for instance, landowners and representatives of the church and other entrenched institutions. Without blatant didacticism, the cartoons point out to the viewer the factors responsible for the nation's inequitable distribution of wealth and power. The tradition of using skeletons, serpents, and vermin as representations continues to be strong in Mexico and parts of Central America.

The young José Clemente Orozco followed Posada's lead. By 1911 his earliest mocking cartoons appeared in radical periodicals. In one populist cartoon, a blond, curly-headed cherub in velvet and lace was heaven's ticket taker: overdressed and overfed bourgeois were given halos, while the poor were forbidden entry. One cannot take seriously the polemical complaint that Orozco's murals constituted cartoons; yet they did spring from the hand of a recognized cartoonist.

Miguel Covarrubias enjoyed international fame immediately upon arriving in New York in 1923 under the auspices of the Mexican government. He melded Mexican forms with the international and advanced the eloquence and playfulness of the cartoon form. He drew from Posada's folk sources and also from knowledge of cubism gained through Diego Rivera. One may see in Covarrubias's cartoon work an anticipation of the Third-World position that holds both United States-style capitalism and the Soviet version of the Marxist state to be equally alienating oversystematizations.

By the 1940s, there was a move away from signs of regionalism, toward Disney-influenced graphics. Conventions for showing dismay or anger, for example, drops of sweat or exclamation marks flying from the head, were introduced. This more stripped-down, less verisimilar manner of popular caricature would predominate. The style was exemplified by Mexico's City's *Siempre* [*Always*] magazine, which came to prominence and was widely distributed in Latin America. Rius (Eduardo del Río) is the most famous artist to emerge from *Siempre*. He currently is best known for his innovative comic- or cartoon-like informative works. However, he has a long-standing reputation as a political cartoonist. Rius is concerned with the modern manifestations of imperialsm. He mocks aggressive "superpower" diplomacy, exploitation of the cheap labor and raw materials of Third World Latin American countries, and United States intervention.

In cartooning the importance of Mexico City and Buenos Aires was disproportionately great prior to the contemporary period. This centralization does not indicate a lack of cartooning talent elsewhere in Latin America: there have been a number of works, such as Pedro Sinzig, *A caricatura na imprensa brasileira* [*Caricature in the Brazilian Press*], 1911; Ricardo Rendón, *Caricaturas* [*Caricatures*] from Bogotá in 1931; Kit, *Caricaturas* [*Caricatures*], 1944, and *Esa bella humanidad* [*That Beautiful Human Race*], 1952, both from Caracas; and Romera, *Apuntes del Olimpo* [*Notes from Olympus*] from Chile, 1949. While artists may have begun their careers either in the provinces or in capitals with lesser publishing industries, however, the tendency was to pursue larger success in the most propitious locations.

An example is the Uruguayan Hermenegildo Sábat, a Buenos Aires resident since 1966. Sábat has the ability to pursue a career with both high-art (gallery expositions of paintings and graphic work) and pop-culture (cartoons and celebrity caricature) dimensions. While this duality has been commented on by analysts of Sábat's work, the artist does not consider it worthy of discussion and discourages attempts to locate him on the cultural spectum. Able to enjoy varying levels of respectability, he is not like the painter required to do cartoons while breaking into the world of "real" art or the celebrated cartoonist who comes to find the form facile and superficial (e.g., Orozco and Covarrubias, respectively).

Clearly, political climate in any country at any one time influences cartoon use and expression. For example, there was an inhibition in Argentina to comment on politics during the régime of General Juan Perón (1946–1955). It became dangerous to create humor with any too-overt political theme, a circumstance that helped to spur the search for an everyday humor. The aggressively nationalist *Rico Tipo* [*Fancy Guy*], launched by Guillermo Divito in 1944, devoted itself exclusively to either brief joke-filled written texts or cartoons that skirted political issues after Perón came to power. The end of Peronism created a climate more open to daring humorous expression. The key figure here is Landrú (Juan Carlos Columbres) who founded the European-influenced magazine *Tía Vicenta* [*Aunt Vicenta*]. Those involved were encouraged to project the image of a gang of cheerful, zany young people through such activities as public hula-hooping near their offices. The leading humorists and even the magazine's secretary became well-known figures, propagating numerous fads, in-jokes, humorous tag-lines, and gimmicks. But the magazine was also able to convey political commentary. It served as the conduit for rumors and underground information the government was reluctant to see expressed. A celebrated example occurred when the magazine began to question a multi-national firm's story that it was buying up tracts of land in Argentina in order to cultivate sugar beets. The magazine did not overtly challenge this unlikely story, but rather hinted at the true basis of the operation by turning the line "uranium-bearing sugar beets" into a running joke.

Post-1959 Cuba had as part of its revolutionary cultural program an attempt to make mass media, including cartoons, serve a consciousness-raising function. The cartoons in *Granma*, the newspaper named after the boat that brought the revolutionaries to the island, have been overtly political; the element of graphic humor, whether visual or conceptual, has been scarce. Most of the work appearing has been of a denunciatory nature, with Uncle Sam, the CIA, international capitalist cartels, and other clearly labeled villains acting unjustly to figures representing the people, Fidel Castro, and the revolution. The style is reminiscent of nineteenth-century political caricature, which was not expected to be especially humorous. The graphic work, however, is often quite contemporary.

In Brazil, the presence of skilled political satirists is traditional; currently a number of artists combine a satirical eye with a visual style that is both sophisticated and accessible to a wide and international audience. The celebrated (Luis Fernando) Veríssimo, based in Porto Alegre, is an artist and an organizer of publications including the iconoclastic *Pato Macho* [*Macho Duck*]. Veríssimo's work is minimalistic, with characters often consisting of little more than a few squiggles signaling their general outline. Veríssimo expands on the new graphic style of the Argentine Quino and others. He often imparts a very undifferentiated Everyman quality to his graphic characters and indeed has expressed himself on the significance of *o popular* (the man on the street). A good deal of the humor has to do with the strategies employed by an expanding middle class with routinized existences, to maintain an element of liveliness, for example, through minor-scale "playboy" behavior and low-budget entertainments. The interaction between these ordinary individuals and power wielders is also a much-examined theme. Veríssimo is interested both in the display of subservience and compliance and in the little man's gesture of defiance. In one recurring situation, a small, meager-looking man takes satisfaction in daring the wrath of God himself by calling the deity insulting names. The resulting thunder and lightning leave the defiant little man with a grin on his face, cheerily boasting to the reader, "That really got him going!" Another cartoon shows the same man insouciantly taking a light from a hurled bolt of lightning.

During the late 1970s, the Bogotá *Alternativa* [*Alternative*], a political commentary magazine distinguished by the presence of Gabriel García Márquez, provided a good selection of topics in its political cartooning. The magazine had an international as well as national focus and, like its most celebrated writer in his reportage work, looked especially at human rights cases, the Cuban government and its troubled relations with the United States, and the development of resistance movements directed against the right-wing dictatorships of Central America. In contrast to García Márquez's reporting, which was characterized by telling anecdotes, humorous touches, and a generally high visibility of style, the cartoons tended to be in a "non-style," without distinguishing features of manner and approach. It was not uncommon for cartoons and other visuals to be unsigned. In line with the magazine's interest in denunciation, the cartoons and miscellaneous visuals tended to show images of extreme squalor and misery including cases of detention and prisoner mistreatment. Recognizable political figures appeared and were in nearly every case shown neglecting or augmenting the lamentable conditions for which they should have assumed responsibility. Typically, political figures were shown interacting with one another or with other powerful individuals. They were intensely engaged in bargaining, dealing, and vying for position—images that agreed with the magazine's overall statement that an alternative must be found to political activity as currently practiced among the representatives of bourgeois interests. Unlike the visual images in the Cuban *Granma*, those in *Alternativa* very seldom represented figures in a heroic light or showed any politician in power as a positive element. In its cartoons, the positive figures were in general underdogs, including those unjustly detained, victims of military and paramilitary violence, as well as guerrillas and underground activists. This fixedly negative portrayal of the standard mode of public life stood in contrast to way things were portrayed in the very popular Bogotá magazine *Cromos* [*Color Photos*].

A contemporary Colombian artist, (Gonzalo) Angarita, stands out for his parodical treatment of those who seek social betterment without due regard for the complexities of the problems at issue. In one cartoon, an allegorical figure of war wears an expression like that of a fighting animal, teeth bared and jaws opened in a ferocious snarl. A small, dapper diplomat, identified as the United Nations, holds up one hand to stop him and deliver to him a written injunction. This cartoon comments not only on the utopian notion of arbitrating war out of existence, but also reflects on the sources of human aggression, as if illustrating the innate aggression theories popularized by Konrad Lorenz and others.

The Venezuelan graphic artist and cartoonist (Pedro León) Zapata has been able to organize a sophisticated, urbane style around topics that are often quite local—even administrative problems at the Universidad Central de Venezuela [Venezuelan Central University], where he is a faculty member. Zapata is not a cartoonist who, like Rius and earlier cartoonists, provides background materials to "fill in" readers who may be unacquainted with the specifics of the matters satirized. He is quite clearly willing to create work that will be specific to a circumscribed place and particular moment and that will hence be a perishable humor. It is notable that when a volume on Zapata was published in the artist's home city of Caracas, the writer of the commentary was obliged to provide information explaining the topical material.

A final example of the widened variety of thematic approaches to the complexity of contemporary Latin American life is from Lima. Giorg, whose work is showcased in the end section of *Marka*, reflects the serious and critical nature of this magazine. He has a special preoccupation with the mania for producing ever more new and improved products. His humorous procedure is to carry this gadgetry fetish to absurdity. Panels consist of pages from an imaginary catalog in which the consumer is offered such inane innovations as a bicycle with power brakes, for power-obsessed executives, and pointless variations on the common household scissors.

BIBLIOGRAPHIC RESOURCES

The most assiduous researcher of pop graphic forms, Maurice Horn, has produced a number of versions of his *World Encyclopedia* compilations. The *World Encyclopedia of Cartoons* is available in recent two- and six-volume versions while the *World Encyclopedia of Comics*, containing considerable material of related interest, is published in a one-volume text and an expanded six-volume (date not set). His *Women in the Comics* reviews pop-graphic history in the light of recent interest in sex-role analysis.

For historical background, and especially for the tracing of the emergence of the modern-day cartoon from such precursor genres as the grotesque or humorous drawing, Colton Waugh's *The Comics* remains a good general informative source. John Chase's *Today's Cartoon* is of particular interest for its preface offering a historical survey of political caricature. Gérard Blanchard's *La bande dessinée: Histoire des histoires en images de la préhistoire à nos jours* [*The Comic Strip: A History of Stories in Images from Prehistoric Times to Our Days*] is principally concerned with the strip but in its capacious scope includes many comments on images that are not in narrative sequence. A much narrower study, focused upon the emergence of the dialogue-bearing balloon, is Robert Benayoun, *Le Ballon dans la bande dessinée: vroum, tchac, zowie* [*The Balloon in the Comics: Vroom, pow, zowie*].

Looking at specifically Latin American bibliographic resources, it is readily apparent that the emphasis is on compiling examples of the work of highly visible, cosmopolitan, and urbane graphic artists—typically those with a unique and identifiable style—for marketing to their admirers. There are many collections by such stars of hip humor with a characteristically innovative and somewhat cerebral approach, for example, the Chilean Arturo Lukas. He exemplifies social cartooning based on linguistic and visual puns and playful juxtapositions. His *Bestiario del reyno de Chile* [*Bestiary of the Kyngdomme of Chile*] presents many known types in bourgeois society while playing with animal metaphors common in Chilean slang. Other imaginative works are Luis Gê, *Os anos 77–80 nas charges* [*The Years 1977–80 in the Press*]; Santiago, *Refandango e outras aventuras do Macanudo Taurino* [*Re-Fandango-ing and other Adventures of the Fantastic Bull-Man*]; Caloi, *Humor libre de Caloi* [*Caloi's Free Humor*]; Armando Santiago (Chago), *El humor otro* [*Humor That's Different*]; Fontanarrosa, *¿Quién es Fontanarrosa?* [*Who is Fontanarrosa?*]; Ildemaro Torres, *Zapata*; Juan Carlos Columbres (Landrú), *Las clases magistrales de Landrú* [*Landrú's Master Classes*] and *Gente paqueta: manual para ser finísimo* [*Fancy People: How to Have True Class*]; Zircaldo, *Jeremias, o bom* [*Jeremiah, the Good*]; Aquiles Nazoa, ed., *Leoncio Martínez genial e ingenioso: la obra literaria y gráfica del gran artista caraqueño* [*Leoncio Martínez, Genius and Wit: The Literary and Graphic Work of the Great Caracas Artist*]; and Hipólito Sánchez, *El caricaturista Miguel Acevedo* [*The Caricaturist Miguel Acevedo*]. Lavado (Quino) collections include *Bien, gracias ¿ y usted?* [*Fine, Thanks, And You?*], *Diez años con Mafalda* [*Ten Years with Mafalda*], *Gente en su sitio* [*People in Place*], *Hombres de bolsillo* [*Pocket Men*], and *Yo que usted* [*If I Were You*].

Along with these recent displays of new talent, stimulated by the infusion of new ideas from underground and hip cartooning, there are a lesser number of compilations of traditional types of caricature. In this case, the emphasis is likely to be not on the unique style of the artist but on the subjects characterized by his grotesque treatment. Morenclavijo certainly presents his work in this light. This Bogotá-based caricaturist has collected his work in such volumes as *El hombre que hacía monitos y otras estampas bogotanas* [*The Man Who Made Doodles and Other Scenes of Bogota Life*], *85 colombianos en el lápiz de Morenclavijo* [*85 Colombians Drawn by Morenclavijo*], and *Mi generación en líneas* [*My Generation in Lines*].

A variant of this approach is to give approximately equal attention to the subject represented in caricature and the special skills of the graphic artist. An example is Herman Lima's *Rui e a caricatura* [*Rui and Caricature*], wherein Lima examines how one famous subject was satirically focused upon. Graphic artists may themselves compile works that stress a theme: Claudius Jaguar e Fortunas, *¿Hay gobierno?* [*Is There a Government?*]; Luis Bello, *Un lápiz contra un régimen: dibujos y textos* [*A Pencil against a Régime: Sketches and Writings*]; Rius, *Caricaturas rechazadas* [*Rejected Caricatures*]; Róger López, *Róger López presenta su exposición de caricaturas: folleto de guía* [*Róger López Presents his Exhibition of Caricatures: A Guide Book*] and *¿Como es quién en Guatemala?* *figuras conocidas* [*What Does Who look Like in Guatemala?*]; and Miguel Covarrubias, *The Prince of Wales and Other Famous Americans* and *Negro Drawings*.

Less deliberately assembled but of strong historical interest are collections such as *Perfiles pacifistas* (*Pacifist Profiles*) and *El Congreso que yo he visto* (*The Congress I Saw*) by Ramón Columba as official caricaturist for the Inter-American Congress for the Maintenance of Peace. The Congress engaged Columba to sketch participants and published his impressions of the speakers over the period 1936–1943. These collections allow the reader to observe developments in caricature, including a move toward a more streamlined and less cluttered visual style and a greater freedom to satirize the features of distinguished people.

Of parallel interest are the collections by the Nicaraguan artist Barahona (Chilo). His *Historia de la caricatura y personajes nicaragüenses* [*History of Caricature and Celebrities in Nicaragua*] and *Reunión de presidentes y personajes* [*A Gathering of Presidents and Celebrities*] are closely coordinated with the development of public events and social history. In this case, though, the possibility of tracing a progression in the conventions and modes of caricature is not present.

As well as one-author collections, there are anthologies that are especially useful in allowing the reader to trace the common lines of thematic or stylistic development of cartoonists. For example, the Brazilian collection by Reinaldo et al., *O novo humor do Pasquim* [*The New-Style Lampoon*], lives up to its title in providing a representative selection of graphic work by recent artists who seek to renovate the caricature and the humorous drawing. Other anthologies are Editora Porto Alegre's compilation *Antología brasileira de humor* [*Brazilian Anthology of Humor*]; Enrique

Lipszyc, *El dibujo a través del temperamento de 150 famosos artistas* [*The Sketch According to 150 Famous Artists*]; Víctor Velarde, ed., *Siete dibujantes con una idea* [*Seven Cartoonists with an Idea*]; and Taller de Gráfica Popular, *Calaveras resurrectas: 16 años de calaveras políticas del Taller de Gráfica Popular* [*Resurrected Skeletons: 16 Years of Political Skeleton Caricatures from the Popular Graphics Workshop*].

Overviews of the topic of caricature and the history of its manifestations in Latin America are more difficult to obtain. José Guadalupe Zuno Hernández, in his *Historia general de la caricatura y la ironía plástica* [*General History of Caricature and Visual Satire*], has a broad and scholarly scope. His *Historia de la caricatura en México* [*History of Caricature in Mexico*] and *Historia de la ironía plástica en Jalisco* [*History of Visual Satire in Jalisco*] are other good sources. Ziraldo, *A última do brasileiro: quatro años de história nos charges do Jornal do Brasil* [*Four Years of History as Issued Forth from the Jornal do Brasil*]; Pedro Sinzig, *A caricatura no imprensa brasileira: contribução para um estudo histórico social* [*Caricature in the Brazilian Press: Toward a Historical-Social Study*]; and Herman Lima, *História da caricatura no Brasil* [*History of Caricature in Brazil*] also provide partial coverage. Groups or organizations concerned with the preservation and recording of local traditions and cultural products have produced useful compilations. For example, the Rio de Janeiro National Library, in cooperation with the newspaper *Jornal do Brasil*, assembled an exhibition on the city's journalism as part of the city's 400th anniversary celebration. A volume on caricatures and cartoons, *O Rio na caricature* [*Rio in Caricature*], was among the results.

The difficulties of researching nineteenth-century political cartooning, as well as the ways in which such investigation may be accomplished, are seen in two useful reference works: Manuel González Ramírez, *La caricatura política, fuentes para la historia de la revolución mexicana* [*Political Caricature: Sources for the History of the Mexican Revolution*], and Salvador Pruneda, *La caricatura come arma política* [*Caricature as a Political Weapon*]. Pruneda was able to share the resources Carrasco Puente assembled and, as well as the resulting overlap of course material, the two volumes have in common an especially good survey of the period from the 1870s to the early twentieth century, notable for disenchantment with the poor record of implementation of reforms. It is clear that, to find telling examples of a critique of the ruling elite, these researchers turned to satirical lampoons, "alternative" newspapers dedicated to mockery of the government, and, in general, sources other than mainstream newspapers and magazines. The greater part of political cartooning in more established and well-distributed periodicals is not sufficiently critical and questioning to qualify as the "political weapon" referred to in Pruneda's title.

Few collections of current-day left-wing political cartoons exist. René de la Nuez, a Cuban whose work appears in the Havana *Granma*, has published drawings that originally appeared in this newspaper in *El humor neuztro de cada día* [*Our Daily Yoomer*]. The content, usually a message of political denunciation, is made to appear the essential factor; the Cuban exile community abroad and representatives of the United States government are typical targets of this critical humor. The movement to focus the public's attention upon transnational coalitions is apparent in a Mexican collection of cartoons by Palomo, originally from *Unomasuno* and reprinted as *El cuarto Reich: es una creación de la ITT, Anaconda, Kennecott, Chase Mahattan Bank . . .* [*The Fourth Reich: It's a Creation of ITT, Anaconda, Kennecott, Chase Manhattan Bank . . .*].

Information may be gleaned from works that are not primarily about cartoons. Cartoons and caricatures by established "fine art" artists can be found in such works as Emily Edwards and Manual A. Bravo, *Painted Walls of Mexico from Prehistoric Times until Today* and Antonio Rodrigues, *A History of Mexican Painting*, as well as exhibition programs, for example, *Orozco! 1883–1949* and *Hermenegildo Sábat*. There are also conference proceedings as seen in Antonio Salomón, *El humor y las historietas que leyó el argentino* [*The Humor and the Comics Read by Argentines*]; Gandin de Fonesa, *Biografia do jornalismo carioca* [*Biography of Rio de Janeiro's Journalism*]; and Fernando Mas, "La historieta en la Argentina" ["The Comics in Argentina"].

Articles provide other sources. The new *Studies in Latin American Popular Culture*, co-edited by Harold E. Hinds, Jr., and Charles M. Tatum, has J. L. Helguera's review essay on Colombian and Venezuelan political cartoons. The *Journal of Popular Culture*, in particular the special Latin American issue co-edited by Hinds and Tatum, has a one-panel cartoon study by Naomi Lindstrom, "Social Commentary in Argentine Cartooning: From Description to Critical Questioning." Other articles are David William Foster, "Disjunctive Strategies in Ziraldo's Cartoons: *Jeremias, o bom*" [*Jeremias, The Good*] and "Hermenegildo Sábat: Caricature as Cultural Dekitschification"; and Rivera, "¡Sonaste, Maneco! historia del humor gráfico argentino I" ["You Really Did It This Time, Maneco! The History of Argentine Graphic Humor, Part I"] and "Una compadrada contra el terror, historia del humor gráfico argentino II" ["Ganging Up On Terror: The History of Argentine Graphic Humor, Part II"]. The chief resource is still the popular press, which in most countries remains unmined.

DIRECTIONS FOR FUTURE RESEARCH

When the question arises of what remains to be done in single-panel Latin American cartoon studies, the first answer to come to mind is "everything." As indicated, little has been attempted in most countries either in surveys or close examinations of particular items. Therefore, it is necessary to look for models of what could be done in closely akin fields of research, such as the study of comic strips and of pulp fiction.

A major gap, and one that presents immediate difficulties to the researcher, is in the area of lesser-known and less cosmopolitan humorous artists. The very urbane, skilled figures, such as Covarrubias, Sábat, or Orozco, who have obtained a position of prominence, have also won the attention of popular-culture commentators. However, those not working in the well-connected and highly visible cultural scenes of the major cities (Mexico City, Buenos Aires, and, for exiles, New York) have, by and large, been neglected. It would be useful to have an investigator produce a work along the lines of C. Sáinz Cidoncha's *Historia de la ciencia-ficción en España* [*History of Science Fiction in Spain*]. Sáinz Cidoncha's survey of Spanish-language science fiction deliberately steers away from the higher-profile figures (in this case, the English- or French-language science-fiction writers or mainstream Spanish writers who occasionally touched upon science-fiction themes) to focus upon more grassroots creators whose fame did not spread to science-fiction circles in other countries or draw the approbation of readers and critics of mainstream literature. Using similar principles for the delimitation of the material to be studied, a student of a particular country or region's popular culture could examine cartoonists whose fame remained geographically limited and who did not find admirers and supporters in the arts community.

Sáinz Cidoncha's remarks concerning his research procedures make it clear that he was obliged to refer to sources other than the customary bibliographic collections, such as book, magazine, and newspaper holdings. The more informal network constituted by "fandom" provided private holdings and informally acquired and transmitted information about the creators, entrepreneurial managers, distributors, and consumers of this largely pulp-level product. It should be mentioned that such research among fans' memorabilia and informal oral historians of a pop genre can be combined with higher-level generalizations, as in the ambitious but uneven *La novela de ciencia-ficción: interpretación de una novela marginal* [*The Science-Fiction Novel: Interpretation of a Marginal Novel*] by Juan Ignacio Ferreras.

Informational collections of cartoons directed at this "fandom" type of readership exist but tend to include more comicstrip than one-panel materials. The team of Carlos Trillo and Guillermo Saccomanno in Argentina edits informative columns about cartoons, strips, and comic books. Their columns appear under the headings *El club de la historieta* [*The Comics Club*] in *Skorpio* and *Introdución a la historieta argentina* [*Introduction to the Argentine Comic*] in *Tit-bits*, both Buenos Aires-based publications of Ediciones Record. Their *Historia de la historieta argentina* [*Story of the Argentine Comic*] and *Y digo yo . . .* [*And I Say . . .*] indicate ways of tapping into informal networks and pools of information that could be utilized in the study of the single-panel cartoon.

A researcher who has especially shown how the fandom network can be utilized is Franco Fossati, the Italian specialist in pulp fiction and pop visuals. In his encyclopedic *Il fumetto argentino* [*The Argentine Comic*], Fossati is skillful in interweaving the anecdotal material he has amassed with a critique of the style and thematic choices of various comic artists. He applies this same auteur-type approach in his *Guida al "giallo"* [*Guide to the Pulps*], co-authored with Roberto DiVanni, while also providing attention to each creator treated. It would be worthwhile to see such a study turned exclusively upon single-panel cartoonists and devoting extensive in-depth coverage to each artist.

An example of sociopolitical analysis of cartoons is John J. Johnson's *Latin America in Caricature*. The cartoons examined are from the United States and refer to Latin American phenomena. Johnson is able to ascertain the tendencies in stereotyping and other types of perception as reflected over an extended period. The same type of analysis could easily be applied to Latin American cartoons with respect to such issues as perceptions of foreign powers, the various social classes and their interests, and changes in the country's status and power. Johnson's emphasis perceptions that cartoonists and caricaturists have in common on what—shared perceptions—obviates a problem in the analysis of the political cartoon, that is, that many political cartoonists are not distinctive or stylish enough to make their graphics worth commenting upon. Indeed, the homogeneous and even monotonous editorial cartoon style helps Johnson spot and highlight significant thematic commonalities. A second United States study on cartoon language is Cheris Kramer, "Folk Linguistics: Wishy-Washy Mommy Talk: Study of Sex Language Differences through Analysis of *New Yorker* Cartoons." Mario T. García's, "Chistes and Caricaturas in the Mexican-American Press, Los Angeles, 1926–1927" is another useful delimited model.

Although aspects of the strip lend themselves more easily to commentary (e.g., the extended sequence makes possible the application of methods of narrative analysis), in many cases what has been examined in the strip may also be examined in the single panel. In this respect Elizabeth K. Baur's *La historieta como experiencia didáctica* [*The Comic Strip as Educational Experience*] gives one useful model. Baur's is an intensive study of a comic strip widely read in West Germany. Baur moves from the study of the strip as a system of signs to convey various meanings (based on notions of semiological analysis developed by Roland Barthes) to the study of ideology and economic interests as they appear in the strip. Perhaps most interesting of all are her suggestions for taking the analysis of particular pop-culture artifacts into the classroom, where young students may learn a more critical and questioning approach to the commercial entertainment products surrounding them. It would be easy to imagine such an approach being fruitful in the examination of such commonplace cartoons as the standard joke cartoons in mainstream magazines from Latin America, for example, *Qué pasa* [*What's Up?*] from Chile. Such cartoons, with their focus on everyday interactions among (predominantly) members of the middle class, lend themselves well to an analysis attentive to questions of economic interests, status maintenance, and concern for material well-being at fairly advanced economic levels.

It should be noted that Baur found herself required to modify the semiological method of analysis to provide for a more direct approach to the reflection to socioeconomic factors in the strip. Nonetheless, a semiological model of analysis could be applied to the cartoon in order to determine the elements that constitute that will be widely recognized and appreciated as a "joke." Clues might be taken from Violette Morín's study of the joke, based upon a study of gag-lines and punch-lines from commercially distributed humorous materials. This study was circulated in Latin America in the volume *Análisis estructural del relato* [*Structural Analysis of the Story*]. Entitled simply "The Joke," Morin's essay has an exceptional relevance to the study of single-panel cartoons. While the principle of studying an extended or developed structure, such as that of narrative or sequences of visual items, has gained much popularity among followers of structuralist models, the isolated and brief item has been less likely to be the object of semiological examination. Morín's emphasis on the conventions that allow the readers of a written joke or of a single-panel cartoon with caption to understand that the quality of jokiness has been duly achieved seems very promising to cartoon research with a Latin American focus.

Several semiological works are worth examining to see how they have been able to approach the analysis of pop graphics, though the applicability to the comic is limited by the reliance on a model of narrative-dominated types of analysis, for example, studies in narrative rhetoric. Here one should cite Umberto Eco, *Apocalittici e integrati: Comunicazioni di massa e teoria della cultura di massa* [*Apocalyptics and Well-Adjusted: Mass Communications and Theory of Mass Culture*], pp. 134–87, on comics, and *Il superuomo di mass* [*Mass Superman*]; Moacy Cirne, *Para ler os quandrinhos; da narrativa cinematográfica a narrativa quadrinhazada* [*How to Read Comics: From Cinema Narrative to Strip Narrative*]; and Román Gubern, *El lenguaje de los cómics* [*The Language of Comics*], and *Literatura de la imagen* [*Literature of Image*]. See also Wolfgang Max Faust and R. Baird Shuman, "Comics and How to Read Them."

As absorbing as the problems of semiological analysis may become, this model has frequently required modification before it can satisfy the needs of a Latin American analysis, where social factors are difficult to set aside. For this reason, it should be recalled, Ariel Dorfman and Armand Mattelart had to adapt considerably Roland Barthe's semiological Marxist critique as developed in the latter's famous *Système de la mode* [*The System of Fashion*]. The result was a ground-breaking study of strips, the 1971 *Para leer al Pato Donald* [*How to Read Donald Duck*]. Since then, the analysis of strips has been continued by several investigators, typically tending to follow more the ideological analysis patterns of Dorfman and Mattelart and less their indications for a semiological study closely focused on a well-delimited corpus. Carlos Montalvo P. et al., *Ensayos marxistas sobre los 'cómics'* [*Marxist Essays on Comics*] is representative. It would be good to see this type of study spread from the strips to which it was initially applied to include the unitary cartoon. The return of the careful reading of particular items of pop culture, the distinguishing feature of Dorfman and Mattelart's analysis, could be resurrected.

The application of newly widespread concepts of sex-role analysis has, again, mostly been the work of comic-narrative investigators. Since the emphasis is often on static, stereotyped images instead of sequential and narrative questions, a transfer of this investigative concern to cartoons is easily feasible. Studies that provide a model include Maurice Horn's *Women in the Comics*; Kramer's "Stereotypes of Women's Speech: The Word from Cartoons"; Stan Lee, *The Superhero Women*; Richard M. Levinson, "From Olive Oyl to Sweet Polly Purebread: Sex Role Stereotypes and Televised Cartoons"; Delores Mitchell, "Women Libeled: Women's Cartoons of Women"; Philippe Perebinosoff, "What Does a Kiss Mean? The Love Comic Formula and the Creation of the Ideal Teenage Girl"; Jack Shadoian, "Yuh Got Pecos! Doggone, Belle, Yuh're As Good as Two Men"; and Helen White Streicher, "The Girls in the Cartoons." Katherine Fishburn provides an overview of the growth of this area of study in her 1982 *Women in Popular Culture: A Reference Guide*.

While denunciatory studies have been relatively plentiful, there is still a good deal of room for intelligent reexaminations of very popular forms that will emphasize their positive aspects. One possible route is that taken by Gloria Steinem, Phyllis Chesler et al. in their *Wonder Woman* (1972). Including both essay material and comic-book examples, this volume seeks to show the modern manifestations of the Amazon myth in a favorable light. Gahan Wilson was in charge of the visuals sections of the group anthology *Bug-Eyed Monsters* (1978), notable for its efforts to arouse in sophisticated readers an appreciation for forms of monster fiction and cartoon humor generally regarded as of low quality and prestige. The special feature of both anthologies is their aim to reach an audience other than the acritical "fandom" and to make a case for the qualities of imagination, myth, and humor in "pulp" magazine fiction and graphic work.

It is also possible to envision works discussing possibilities for a more consciousness-raising form of the cartoon or the political caricature than is presently usually found. The experiment with comic books reported by Ariel Dorfman and Manuel Jofré in their *Superman y sus amigos del alma*

[*Superman and His Bosom Buddies*] might serve as a pattern. Along these same futuristic and experimental lines, Frank Gerace's 1974 *Comunicación horizontal* [*Grassroots Communication*] contains suggestions for bringing all pop forms more into line with actual day-to-day needs of the public affected.

RESEARCH COLLECTIONS

We cannot provide the aspiring researcher with the name of a collection of research materials that focuses on the single-panel cartoon. Wherever Latin American centers exist, however, there are a number of current Latin American newspapers that can be used as a starting point to develop such a specialty. Any file of newspapers affords opportunity; cartoons in *Granma*, for example, contain treatment of the recent emigration from Mariel to the United States. To satirize and deflate the importance of this exodus there is a repertory of conventional visual signs to convey the worthlessness of the emigrés and their actions, which presents an interesting question in content analysis.

More established centers or libraries provide historical primary materials pertinent to the needs of the future cartoon researcher. The evolution of the contemporary cartoon from the humorous sketch, for example, can hardly be considered without taking into account the influence of *Caras y Caretas*.

Alternative publications provide abundant examples of biting social satire. However, they often last for few issues. This circumstance is not surprising when one considers the allegations cartoonists make against those in power. A nation's constitution, for example, may be variously shown as being gnawed by vermin, left to molder, or trod upon by neglectful rulers; recognizable high officials are seen making ignoble deals or practicing deceit. Any files are therefore more limited and scattered, but center or library patrons may donate or loan their private collections for scholarly use.

These obstacles were overcome by *El Ahuizote*, which has been variously subtitled *Semanario Feroz, Aunque de Buenos Instintos* [*A Fierce Weekly, but Good-Hearted*] and *El jacobino* [*The Jacobin*], and retitled *El Hijo de Ahuizote* [*Son of Ahuizote*]. When it first flourished in the middle and late 1870s, this newspaper was collectively edited by Vicente Riva Palacio, Juan M. Mirafuentes, and others. It was an outpost of literate satire and visual wit with a typically liberal critique of institutional corruption, torpor, and short-sightedness. Between 1885 and 1903, Daniel Cabrera revived the paper. The aims were similar though the name frequently changed, and during many periods publication of the periodical was suspended. A satirical newspaper with a similar title appeared during 1913–1914. This publication is a good source of highly skilled political satire revealing a coherent liberal position. Despite its irregular and troubled publishing history, the newspaper has been collected to a considerable extent and is available in the holdings of the Benson Latin American Collection, University of Texas at Austin. Another very interesting satirical paper from Mexico City, Salvador Hernández Chávez's *Yprirange*, appearing during the historically crucial years 1911–1912, has also been collected and made available at the Benson Collection. Also worth mentioning among the exceptionally good runs of periodical holdings in this collection are the elegant *Palante* [*Forward*], published in Havana previous to the current regime and containing some exceptionally skilled examples of caricature drawing, and the Buenos Aires *Cascabel* [*Rattler*] of 1941–1943. The latter is significant in the history of cartooning as a pioneering example of the hard-edged, one-gag type of commercial humor that took over from the more genteel and diffuse humorous vignette.

BIBLIOGRAPHY

Antología brasileira de humor. 2 vols. (Porto Alegre, Brazil: Editora Porto Alegre, 1976).

Barahona, Salomón L. [Chilo]. *Historia de la caricatura y personajes nicaragüenses, por Chilo* (Managua: Editorial San José, 1955).

———. *Literatura de la imagen* (Barcelona: Salvat, 1973).

Barthes, Roland. *Système de la mode* (Paris: Seuil, 1966).

Baur, Elizabeth K. *La historieta como experiencia didáctica* (México: Nueva Imagen, 1978).

Bello, Luis. *Un lápiz contra un régimen: dibujos y textos* (Montevideo: Private Edition, 1946).

Benayoun, Robert. *Le Ballon dans la bande dessinée: vroum, tchac, zowie* (Paris: Ballard, 1968).

Blanchard, Gérard. *La bande dessinée: Histoire des histoires en images de la préhistoire á nos jours* (France: Editions Gérard, 1969).

Caloi. *Humor libre de Caloi* (Buenos Aires: Editorial Nueva Senda, 1972).

Carrasco Puente, Rafael. *La caricatura en México* (México: Imprenta Universitaria, 1953).

Chase, John. *Today's Cartoon* (New Orleans: Hauser Press, 1962).

Chesler, Phyllis. "The Amazon Legacy." In *Wonder Woman: A Ms. Book* (New York: Holt, Rinehart and Winston/Warner Books. 1972).

———. *Reunión de presidentes y personajes* (Managua: Editorial San José, 1957).

Chilo [Salomón L. Barahona]. *Historia de la caricatura y personajes Nicaragüenses* (Managua: Editorial San José, 1955).

Cirne, Moacy. *Para ler os quadrinhos: da narrativa cinematográfica a narrativa quadrinhazada* (Petrópolis: Editorial Vozes, 1972).

Columba, Ramón. *El Congreso que yo he visto* (Buenos Aires: Inter-American Congress for the Maintenance of Peace, 1948).

———. *Perfiles pacifistas* (Buenos Aires: Inter-American Congress for the Maintenance of Peace, 1936).

Columbres, Juan Carlos (Landrú). *Las clases magistrales de Landrú* (Buenos Aires: Merlín, 1972).

———. *Gente paqueta: manual para ser finísimo* (Buenos Aires: Merlín, 1977).

Covarrubias, Miguel. *Negro Drawings* (New York: Knopf, 1927).

———. *The Prince of Wales and Other Famous Americans* (New York: Knopf, 1925).

Dorfman, Ariel, and Mattelart, Armand. *How to Read Donald Duck*. Translated by David Kunzle (New York: International General, 1975).

———. *Para leer al Pato Donald* (México: Siglo XXI, 1971).

Dorfman, Ariel, and Jofré, Manuel. *Superman y sus amigos del alma* (Buenos Aires: Galerna: 1974).

Eco, Umberto. *Apocalittici e intergrati: Comunicazioni di massa e teoria della cultura di massa* (Milan: Bompiani, 1965).

———. *Il superuomo di massa* (Milan: Bompiani, 1978).

Edwards, Emily, and Bravo, Manuel A. *Painted Walls of Mexico from Prehistoric Times until Today* (Austin: Texas, 1966).

Faust, Wolfgang Max, and Baird Shuman, R. "Comics and How to Read Them." *Journal of Popular Culture* 5 (1971): 194–202.

Ferreras, Juan Ignacio. *La novela de ciencia-ficción: interpretación de una novela marginal* (Madrid: Siglo Veinte de España, 1972).

Fishburn, Katherine. *Women in Popular Culture: A Reference Guide* (Westport, Conn.: Greenwood Press, 1982).

Fonseco, Gandin da. *Biografia do jornalismo carioca* (Rio de Janeiro: Livia Quaresma, 1944).

Fontanarrosa, [Roberto]. *¿Quién es Fontanarrosa?* (Buenos Aires: Ediciones de la Flor, 1974).

Fossati, Franco. *Il fumetto argentino* (Turin: Pirella, 1980).

Fossati, Franco, and DiVanni, Roberto. *Guida al "giallo"* (Milan: Gammalibri, 1979).

Foster, David William. "Disjunctive Strategies in Ziraldo's Cartoons: *Jeremias, o bom*." Unpublished paper.

———. "Hermenegildo Sábat: Caricature as Cultural Dekitschification." *Latin American Digest* 15, nos. 3–4 (1981): 1–3, 27.

García, Mario T. "Chistes and Caricaturas in the Mexican-American Press. Los Angeles, 1926–1927." *Studies in Latin American Popular Culture* 1 (1982): 74–90.

Gê, Luiz. *Os anos 77–80 nas charges* (São Paulo: T. A. Queiroz, 1981).

Gerace, Frank. *Comunicación horizontal* (Lima: Stadium, 1971).

González Ramírez, Manuel. *La caricatura política, fuentes para la historia de la revolución mexicana* (México: Fondo de Cultura Económica, 1955).

Gubern, Román. *El lenguaje de los cómics* (Barcelona: Península, 1972).

———. *Literatura de la imagen* (Barcelona: Salvat, 1973).

Helguera, J. León. "Nineteenth Century Cartoons: Colombian and Venezuelan Examples." *Studies in Latin American Popular Culture* 2 (1982): 219–25.

Horn, Maurice. *Women in the Comics* (New York: Chelsea House, 1981).

———. *World Encyclopedia of Cartoons* (New York: Chelsea House, 1980, 1981).

———. *World Encyclopedia of Comics* (New York: Chelsea House, 1976).

Jaguar y Fortunas, Claudius. *¿Hay gobierno?* (Rio de Janeiro: Civilização Brasileira, 1964).

Jitrik, Noé. *La revolución del 90* (Buenos Aires: Centro Editor de América Latina, 1971).

Johnson, John J. *Latin America in Caricature* (Austin: University of Texas Press, 1980).

Kit. *Caricaturas* (Caracas: Editorial Elite, 1944).

———. *Esa bella humanidad* (Caracas, 1952).

Kramer, Cheris. "Folk Linguistics: Wishy-Washy Mommy Talk: Study of Sex Language Differences through Analysis of *New Yorker* Cartoons." *Psychology Today* 8, no. 1 (1974): 82–85.

———. "Stereotypes of Woman's Speech: The Word from Cartoons." *Journal of Popular Culture* 8 (1974): 624–30.

Lavado, Joaquín S. [Quino]. *Bien, gracias, ¿y usted?* (México: Imagen/Lumen, 1980).

———. *Diez años con Mafalda* (Barcelona: Lumen, 1973).

———. *Gente en su sitio* (México: Nueva Imagen, 1978).

———. *Hombres de bolsillo* (Barcelona: Lumen, 1977).

———. *Yo que usted* (Buenos Aires: Siglo Veintiuno, 1974).

Lee, Stan. *The Superhero Women* (New York: Simon and Schuster, 1977).

Levinson, Richard M. "From Olive Oyl to Sweet Polly Purebread: Sex Role Stereotypes and Televised Cartoons." *Journal of Popular Culture*, 9 (1975): 561–72.

Lima, Herman. *História da caricatura no Brasil*. 4 vols. (Rio de Janeiro: José Olympio, 1963).

———. *Rui e a caricatura* (Rio de Janeiro: Barbosa, 1949).

Lindstrom, Naomi. "Latin American Cartooning: Between Lovers and Critics." *Studies in Latin American Popular Culture* 1 (1982): 246–51.

———. "Social Commentary in Argentine Cartooning: From Description to Critical Questioning."*Journal of Popular Culture* 14 (1980): 117–21.

Lipszyc, David, and Masotta, Oscar. "Argentina." In *La historieta mundial*, edited by World Congress of Comics (Buenos Aires: Escuela Panamericana de Arte, 1968).

Lipszyc, Enrique. *El dibujo a través del temperamento de 150 famosos artistas* (Buenos Aires: Editorial Lipszyc, 1961).

López, Róger. *¿Cómo es quién en Gautemala? figuras conocidas* (Guatemala: Artes Gráficas, 1945).

———. *Róger López presenta su exposición de caricaturas: folleto de guía* (Guatemala: Artes Gráficas, 1945).

Lukas, [Arturo]. *Bestiario del reyno de Chile* (Valparaíso: Ediciones Universitarias de Valparaíso, 1972).

Mas, Fernando. "La historieta en la Argentina." *LINEA* (Buenos Aires) 2 (1969).

Mitchel, Delores. "Women Libeled: Women's Cartoons of Women." *Journal of Popular Culture* 14 (1981): 97–610.

Montalvo P., Carlos, ed. *Ensayos marxistas sobre los cómics* (Bogotá: Los Comuneros, 1978).

Moreno Clavijo (Morenclavijo). *Mi generación en líneas* (Bogotá: Kelly, 1951).

————. *El hombre que hacía monitos y otras estampas bogotanas* (Bogotá: Ediciones Tercer Mundo, 1969).

————. *85 colombianos en el lápiz de Morenclavijo* (Bogotá: O.K., 1946).

Morin, Violette. "El chiste." In *Análisis estructural del relato*, edited by Roland Barthes et al. (Buenos Aires: Tiempo Contemporáneo, 1969). pp. 121–145.

Nazoa, Aquiles, ed. *Leoncio Martínez, genial e ingenioso: la obra literaria y gráfica del gran artista caraqueño* (Caracas: Consejo Municipal, 1976).

Nuez, René de la. *El humor nueztro de cada día* (Havana: Orbe, 1976).

O Rio na caricatura (Rio de Janeiro: Biblioteca Nacional/Jornal do Brasil, 1965).

Orozco, José Clemente. *Orozco! 1883–1949*. Book accompanying exhibition organized by the Ministry of Foreign Affairs and Institute of Fine Arts, Mexico (Oxford: Museum of Modern Art, 1980).

Palomo. *El cuarto Reich: es una creación de la ITT, Anaconda, Kennecott, Chase Manhattan Bank*. . . 2d ed. (México: Nueva Imagen, 1980).

Perebinosoff, Philippe. "What Does a Kiss Mean? The Love Comic Formula and the Creation of the Ideal Teen-Age Girl." *Journal of Popular Culture* 8, no. 4 (1975): 825–35.

Pruneda, Salvador. *La caricatura como arma política* (México: Instituto Nacional de Estudios Históricos de la Revolución Méxicana, 1958).

Reinaldo, editor. *O novo humor pasquim* (Rio de Janeiro: Codecri, 1977).

Rendón, Ricardo. *Caricaturas* (Bogotá: Cromos, 1931).

Río, Eduardo del (Rius). *Caricaturas rechazadas* (México: Fondo de Cultura Popular, 1968).

Rivera, Jorge. "¡Sonaste, Maneco! historia del humor gráfico argentino I." *Crisis* (Buenos Aires) 34 (1976): 16–24. Continued as "Una compadrada contra el terror, historia del humor gráfico argentino II." 35 (1976): 57–73.

Rodrigues, Antonio. *A History of Mexican Mural Painting* (London: Thames and Hudson, 1969).

Romera. *Apuntes del Olimpo* (Santiago de Chile: Nascimento, 1949).

Sáinz Cidoncha, C. *Historia de la ciencia-ficción en España* (Madrid: Sala Editorial, 1976).

Sábat, Hermenegildo. *Hermenegildo Sábat* (Quilmes, Argentina: Museo Municipal de Artes Visuales, 1980). Exposition Program.

Salomón, Antonio. *El humor y las historietas que leyó el argentino* (Córdoba, Argentina: Congreso Bianual de la Historieta de Córdoba; 1972, 1974, 1976, 1979 editions of conference proceedings).

Sánchez Quell, Hipólito. *El caricaturista Miguel Acevedo* (Asunción: Casa América, 1974).

Santiago. *Refandango e outras aventuras do Macanudo Taurino* (Porto Alegre: L&PM editores, 1977).

Santiano, Armando [Chago]. *El humor otro* (Havana: Ediciones Revolucionarias, 1973).

Shadoian, Jack. "Yuh Got Pecos! Doggone, Belle, Yuh're As Good As Two Men." *Journal of Popular Culture* 12 (1979): 721–36.

Sinzig, Pedro. *A caricatura na imprensa brasileira: contribução para um estudo histórico-social* (Petrópolis: Vozes de Petrópolis, 1911).

Streicher, Helen White. "The Girls in the Cartoons." *Journal of Communication* 24, no. 2 (1974): 125–29.

Steinem, Gloria. Introduction to *Wonder Woman: A Ms. Book* (New York: Holt, Rinehart and Winston/Warner Books, 1972).

Taller de Gráfica Popular, *Calaveras resurrectas: 16 años de calaveras políticas del Taller da Gráfica Popular (México: Beltrán, 1954)*.

Torres, Ildemaro. *Zapata* (Caracas: Concejo Municipal del Distrito Federal, 1979).

Trillo, Carlos, and Saccomanno, Guillermo. *Historia de la historieta argentina* (Buenos Aires: Ediciones Récord, 1980).

———. *Y digo yo . . .* (Buenos Aires: Ediciones de la Flor, 1971).

Velarde, Víctor, ed. *Siete dibujantes con una idea* (México: Editorial Libros y Revistas, 1954).

Waugh, Colton. *The Comics* (New York: MacMillan, 1947).

Wilson, Gahan, editor. *Bug-Eyed Monsters* (New York: Harcourt Brace Jovanovich, 1978).

Ziraldo, [Alves Pinto]. *A última do brasileiro: quatro años de história nos charges do Jornal do Brasil* (Rio de Janeiro: Codecri, 1975).

———. *Jeremias, o bom* (Rio de Janeiro/São Paulo: Expressão e Cultura, 1969).

Zuno Hernández, José Guadalupe. *Historia de la caricatura en México* (Guadalajara: Biblioteca de Autores Jaliscienses Modernos, 1967).

———. *Historia de la ironía plástica en Jalisco* (Guadalajara: Biblioteca de Autores Jaliscienses Modernos, 1972).

———. *Historia general de la caricatura y la ironía plástica* (Guadalajara: Biblioteca de Autores Jaliscienses Modernos, 1972).

Robert N. Pierce and Kurt Kent

10 Newspapers

HISTORY OF THE PRESS

In any newspaper office in Latin America a visitor can find dusty volumes of back issues, perhaps reaching back a century or more. Unlike the electronic filing systems of a typical American newspaper library with everything on microfilm, it still is common for a researcher to be given the originals themselves, cracking with age and exhaling mildew as one turns the pages.

The most remarkable discovery for anyone familiar with North American newspaper archives is that the counterparts in Latin America look uncannily similar. The names and the language are different, of course, but there are the same kinds of photographs of self-important politicians, the same polemical interviews with newsmakers, and the same kind of editorials pointing with pride and viewing with alarm.

This comes as a shock to anyone looking for other-worldly oddity, for a revelation of how underdeveloped nations fashioned a journalism that marked them as "non-westerners." The simple truth is that the press has always been both a vehicle for and evidence of Latin America's linkage to Europe and the United States. In varying degrees, the nations of Latin America have always contained nuclei of literates who were aware of western journalistic standards and demanded newspapers and magazines roughly resembling those of New York, London, Paris, and Madrid.

The press in Latin America has taken a different path from that of the United States and Europe. It is a path mandated by a different society and different economy, by tastes that were not supported by resources to satisfy them. But because this path has crossed the same ideological territory as has that of the other press systems, it would be a handicap to overlook the similarities while searching out the divergences.

Just as the international context is necessary in viewing the Latin American press, so is the cultural matrix within the region and, in varying degrees, within each country. Only in the twentieth century did the press begin to develop an identity of its own, separate from political, religious, and economic institutions. This is not to say that it had no importance before 1900, but rather that the press was primarily an instrument by which other institutions achieved their ends, as it is today in Communist countries.

Newspapers have gone through definite changes in general character over the centuries in Latin America, and it is useful to isolate some important stages. These could be called Pre-Journalism, roughly running from 1539 to 1790; Founding Period, 1790–1820; Factional Press, 1820–1900; Transition to Modernism, 1900–1960; and the Modern Period, since 1960.

Columbus's landfall on an Antillean island in 1492 was followed by a frenzied search for riches that could fuel the ambitions of Ferdinand and Isabella, the "Catholic Kings" of newly unified Spain. The first substantial settlements were in what are now the Dominican Republic and Cuba, but these towns were too crude and tentative to justify such luxuries as reading material. When Cortés conquered Mexico in 1521, he had at his feet an Indian empire that could fill the treasure ships and also support a leisure class in the colonial capital. Thus, encouraged by the government, an Italian immigrant, whom the Spanish called Juan Pablos, in about 1539 set up a printing press, an invention that had appeared less than a century before in Germany and had flourished in northern Italy as well as other areas. In Europe the church had produced most of the handwritten books for centuries; it continued to influence heavily this automated output. The bishops had at least as much control in the New World as in Spain, so it was natural for the titles to be largely religious tracts.

Thus it was that, as a few presses were set up in important Spanish colonies over the next 250 years, little of journalistic consequence came from them. Aside from the religious material, government-sanctioned chronicles of discovery formed the bulk of what was printed. In Mexico, the first periodical newspaper was founded in 1722 by Juan Ignacio de Castoreña; it was called *La gaceta de México* [*The Mexican Gazette*]. Seven years later, Mexico's most important colonial offshoot, Guatemala, was provided its own newspaper, *La gaceta de Guatemala* [*The Guatemalan Gazette*]. The names of these pioneering publications indicate their nature—court gazettes. As John Spicer Nichols has commented, "All Guatemalan colonial newspapers were licensed and under the watchful eye of local governors and, by extension, the Spanish crown. The contents of the newspapers usually was confined to official announcements, information on religious festivals and other local news or news from Spain, approved by the local government and religious leaders" (Kurian 1982: 410). Ironically, the country that now has the most rudimentary press in Latin America was perhaps the most active center of journalism in colonial times. This was Haiti, which was well endowed with French intellectuals in the period just before the revolution in the home country. Between 1750 and 1775, about fifty publications operated at one time or another (Kurian 1982: 430). Even Colombia, a relatively important Spanish colony, did not get its first press until 1737, and it did not produce a newspaper for another fifty-four years (Kurian 1982: 234).

Thus the press almost to the end of the colonial period had little to do with the transmission of popular culture, for various reasons:

1. The product was too expensive, as the laborious printing processes had scarcely changed since Gutenberg's invention.
2. The masses had neither the literacy nor the tastes for such sober fare.
3. The printed material was largely an imitation of European forms and thus had little to do with the indigenous customs emerging in the colonies.

Sparks from the American and French revolutions ignited the first journalistic tinder in Latin America. Restless intellectuals, usually the sons of the rich settlers, were eager to bring the best of the Enlightenment to their homelands and build a consciousness that the New World was something more than a weak shadow of Europe. In the time-honored manner of revolutionaries, they passed around handwritten treatises, partly because of the paucity of printing facilities. But the fervor was too much for a quill pen, and the polemicists turned to the press. In the three decades following 1790, all the larger countries saw the birth of newspapers. In Peru, *El mercurio peruano* [*The Peruvian Mercury*] started in 1791, the same year as *El papel periódico de la ciudad de Santa Fe de Bogotá* [*The City of Santa Fe de Bogota's Periodical Paper*] in Colombia.

It was clear from the first that these publications did not have information as their primary function, but rather political agitation. The semantics of the matter must be remembered. From its beginning (as indicated in the name of the pacesetter in Bogota) the phenomenon was labeled only as something that appeared periodically, whereas almost from its origins the counterpart in Britain and the United States has been called a newspaper. The two labels have remained until today and still reflect differences in norms.

Despite the involvement of tens of thousands of poor people in the wars of independence, the newspaper press remained out of their hands. Since the content was nearly all political, it could not be related to popular culture in the modern sense. However, this obsession with adversarial political content could perhaps be related to the highly personal and familial view that the great majority of Latin Americans have always had toward politics. In that sense it could be argued that political journalism, from its beginnings in the excitement over separation from European rule, was a truly popular expression.

The press in Brazil got off to a slightly different start, although the result was the same. The Portuguese royal court fled to Brazil in 1808 because of the Napoleonic Wars. These eminent exiles set up the first newspaper that year, soon followed by an opposition publication printed in England and smuggled into Brazil. After the king returned to Portugal in 1820, the Brazilian independence movement crystallized around his son and later the grandson, who each became emperor of a relatively progressive and liberal government. A substantial degree of press freedom ensued.

The rest of the nineteenth century witnessed an explosion in the numbers of newspaper titles published in Latin America, although their circulations were generally small and their lives short. They reflected three essential movements in their societies. First there was the necessity to forge truly national governments from the fragments of personal cliques and regional rivalries. It was an era of *caudillismo* [political bossism], opportunism, and corruption, all lightly disguised by the labels and rhetoric of ideology. Newspapers were instruments for the ambitions of individuals advancing their own careers, and the common good had little to do with it. The typical man of affairs was one who darted from one vocation to another—politics, diplomacy, literature, law, and ranching. Journalism, even founding one's own paper, was a favorite way station between these various fields, because it often propelled the editor into success elsewhere. The weakness of the book publishing industry led many persons to seek out newspapers as vehicles for their literary efforts.

Another trend was the development of commercialism. A new middle class was slowly emerging, and its members based their claims to attention not on birth or military exploits but rather on their ability to buy and sell. Their interests lay primarily in importing consumer goods, as opposed to the aristocratic landowners' need to export raw materials. Thus they wanted some medium of advertising their goods, and none served better than the newspaper. Furthermore, like their counterparts in Europe, they created a demand for news that was not political ammunition but rather information that would help them in their business—stock market reports, economic policies of governments, wars, disasters, and the like. This did not mean that politics no longer dominated journalism, but it was slowly receding.

A third tendency had to do with the development of cultural norms as reflected in journalism. This development was largely one of rushing to catch up with Europe in matters such as education, styles of behavior and dress, architecture, technology, and the arts. Native customs were shunned as regressive or were overromanticized. The practice of news-oriented journalism itself was a foreign curiosity, an ill-fitting garment that nevertheless the Latin Americans tried on. News of the world was funneled through the distorting influences of London and Paris, as were mechanical improvements, supplies, styles of writing and editing, and illustrations.

Most of today's leading newspapers were founded in this period. These include *La prensa* [*The Press*] and *La nación* [*The Nation*] of Buenos Aires,

El mercurio [*The Mercury*] of Santiago de Chile, *El día* [*The Day*] of Montevideo, *O estado de São Paulo* [*The State of São Paulo*], *Jornal do Brasil* [*The Brazilian Journal*] of Rio de Janeiro, *El comercio* [*Commerce*] of Lima, *El espectador* [*The Spectator*] of Bogotá and *Listin Díario* [*Listin Daily*] of Santo Domingo.

The turn of the century brought with it a wave of change throughout Latin America, and in general the common man now had some political relevance and received a fair amount of justice. In many places he, for the first time, was able to vote, get social security, go to school, and join a union. This, of course, entailed an upsurge in demand for newspapers, and a vast number were founded in the first two decades of this century to take advantage of the bounty of news and the suddenly expanded sense of public participation. Having escaped World War I, the area counted hundreds of fortunes made from the boom in raw materials; in Cuba this phenomenon was called "The Dance of the Millions." Some of this trickled down to the laborer, and carrying a newspaper under his arm was his badge of respectability.

Latin American newspapers also underwent a technological revolution in this period. Almost simultaneously the printing industry went through a wide variety of basic changes. Presses progressed from steam to electricity; type was set by machine instead of hand; relatively cheap wood-pulp paper replaced rag bond; and the telephone, telegraph, and cable opened up a world of news. These allowed newspapers to be produced at ten times the speed as before and at a fifth of the price. Thus mass-appeal publications became commercially feasible, although the market for them was by no means as extensive as in the industrialized countries of the West.

Economic hardship cast a shadow over Latin America in the 1930s, even if the slump was less severe because of the scarcity of industry. Nevertheless, the wave of dictatorships that afflicted Europe also swept across this region, and the consequent press controls hindered newspaper development.

Again, the fact that Latin America had little involvement in a world war meant that the aftermath was different for it. The outburst of political idealism that swept away dictatorships in most of Western Europe was delayed, Rojas Pinilla in Colombia, Pérez Jiménez in Venezuela, Perón in Argentina, Batista in Cuba and others stayed on into the middle or late 1950s before being overthrown, and the press meanwhile remained on a leash.

Just as Woodrow Wilson had symbolized to the world the idealism of democracy a generation earlier, so John F. Kennedy infected Latin America with a frenzy of optimism starting in 1960. His Alliance for Progress stimulated the non-Communist left throughout the region to achieve victory after victory in politics, and the press was ready to grow with it. Journalism education took hold in a serious way; correspondents were sent abroad, new buildings were put up, and contents were modernized. For the first time editors began to give sustained attention to some nonpolitical aspects of society, other than to sports news, which had long been popular. Now they began sending reporters out to the slums to get "the other side" of life. Brazilian newspapers, for example, gave massive coverage to the black woman of the slums of São Paulo who wrote a primitive but eloquent diary of the misery around her (María Carolina de Jesús 1962). The arts papers also began recognizing artists who dealt with themes of mass culture.

The changes set afoot in the 1960s were braked somewhat by the return of military autocracy in the 1970s. In one aspect, however, the populist trends were augmented. Recent rulers have firmly resolved to restrict what they call cultural imperialism in all the media, including newspapers, and to encourage cultural nationalism. Evidence of such a trend has ranged from attempts to reduce the quota of foreign news, as in Argentina, to regulations on advertising. Peru's leftist generals outlawed Santa Claus as a Yankee usurper for a while and also clamped down on foreign-produced advertising copy and illustrations, a move also promoted by more democratic governments.

Latin America has been fertile ground for the ideas associated with the New World Information Order, a move put forward by Third World and other countries within the United Nations Educational, Scientific, and Cultural Organization (UNESCO). Its purpose is to make the mass media, often by government coercion, cast away the influences of the western press and more faithfully reflect the aspirations and traditions of their own peoples. While there is doubt over how deeply this debate has affected the Latin American newspaper, there is no doubt that the residue will be permanent.

REFERENCE WORKS

The diversity of approaches to studying newspapers and popular culture in Latin America indicates that a variety of reference tools will be useful. For those just beginning research on a particular topic involving newspapers, the first place to turn may be basic guides to the study of newspapers in general. Fortunately, a 1981 number of *Journalism Monographs* by M. Gilbert Dunn and Douglas W. Cooper may serve as a guide for the novice through the forest of resources available. Though focusing on United States media (including broadcasting and film as well as newspapers), many of the works discussed would prove helpful in studying newspapers in Latin America. Only the most relevant will be mentioned here.

Bibliographies

For several specific topics relating to newspapers in Latin America, a helpful first reference will be the extensive "Bibliography of Bibliographies" compiled by Heinz-Dietrich Fischer and John C. Merrill and published in their 1976 book, *International and Intercultural Communication*. Earlier, but exhaustively covering its field of books (1950–1970) and periodicals (1960–1969) dealing with the use of mass media in the developing countries, is the annotated 1971 bibliography from Belgium by Jean-Marie van Bol and Abdelfattah Fakhfakh. Other bibliographies in the broad field of international communication that may prove useful include works by Hamid Mowlana, Delbert T. Myren, Hassan Rafi-Zadeh, and UNESCO.

Researchers considering a new approach to newspapers and popular culture in Latin America may wish to consult a general mass communication bibliography for works dealing with other parts of the world. The standard in the field is Eleanor Blum's 1980 *Basic Books in the Mass Media*, which carries well-considered annotations. Coverage includes directories and other sources of information. Additional bibliographies are discussed in Blum and in other sources already mentioned. Bibliographies that focus on particular topics from a global or North American perspective include the series from the International Association from Mass Communication Research, for example the socialization bibliography edited by James D. Halloran, and the Thomas F. Gordon and Mary Ellen Berna bibliography on mass communication effects and processes. Most generally, the *Bibliographic Index* provides a continuing bibliography of bibliographies.

Turning to bibliographies concerning Latin American newspapers (and usually other mass media in addition), first mention must go to the excellent program of the Centro Internacional de Estudios Superiores de Comunicación para América Latina [International Center of Higher Studies on Communication for Latin America]. The organization's acronym, CIESPAL, reflects an earlier title with Periodismo [Journalism] in the place now held by Comunicación. A list of publications and a description of the bibliographic program are available from CIESPAL, one of the global network of UNESCO bibliographic centers for mass communication.[1] Another center of bibliographic excellence, especially active in Portuguese, is the Sociedade Brasileira de Estudos Interdisciplinares de Comunicação [Brazilian Society for Interdisciplinary Study of Communication (INTERCOM)].[2] That association publishes the highly regarded annual *Bibliografía brasileira de comunicação* [*Brazilian Bibliography of Communication*], in addition to its *Boletím INTERCOM* [*INTERCOM Bulletin*], which carries a regular bibliography. INTERCOM includes among its "study groups" one dealing with communication and popular culture; coordinator of the group is Carlos Eduardo Lins da Silva. A third organization providing useful bibliographic service on the mass media of Latin America is the International Communication Division of the Association for Education in Journalism and Mass Communication (AEJMC). The Division's *ICB: International Communication Bulletin*, published quarterly, regularly carries a section of references to works on Latin America. The section supplements rather than duplicates the "Articles on Mass Communication in United States and Foreign Journals" in AEJMC's *Journalism Quarterly*. In that journal also may be found book reviews and the regular feature "Other Books and Pamphlets on Journalistic Subjects." Items concerning Latin American newspapers are published from time to time in each of these sections. Another journal with a regular bibliography is *Gazette*, published in the Netherlands. The young organization Centro de Cultura Transnacional [Center for Transnational Culture] in Lima, Peru, which has as one of its concerns the topic of popular culture, also offers bibliographic services. See its quarterly, *Materiales para la comunicación popular* [*Materials for Popular Communication*].

A small number of bibliographies published in the United States deal specifically with the press of Latin America. The most recent takes the form of "A Selected List of Useful Books on Journalism and Communication for School Libraries in Latin American Universities," Appendix B to Raymond B. Nixon's *Education for Journalism in Latin America: A Report of Progress*. The 1981 publication lists 340 books, in Spanish, Portuguese, or English, carefully selected through extensive consultation with Latin American scholars to be of the most use to three types of schools: small, medium-sized, and highly research-oriented. Works are not annotated. Most are in the first two of the languages listed. Another bibliography, Mary A. Gardner's "Central and South America Mass Communication: Selected Information Sources," is followed directly in the same 1978 issue of *The Journal of Broadcasting* by Daniel Appelman's "The Mass Media of Latin America: Selected Information Sources." Gardner concentrates on newspapers and Appelman on electronic media, though Appelman does include some sources omitted by Gardner that are helpful in studying the printed media. Both bibliographies carry some annotation. Gardner also compiled a 1973 bibliography of carefully selected works, *The Press of Latin America: A Tentative and Selected Bibliography in Spanish and Portuguese*. It deals primarily with the history and law of the press of individual countries. Earlier bibliographies by Alisky and Swindler also may be useful. Finally, an extensive bibliography of histories, directories, and other works, listed country by country, forms the final portion of Steven M. Charno's union list of Latin American newspapers in United States libraries.

Indicative of the rapidly advancing state of bibliographic efforts on mass communication in Latin America is publication of a bibliography dealing solely with the works of one scholar. That bibliography, prepared by Guillermo Isaza V. and Nohora Olaya B., covers the efforts of the prolific Colombian, Luis Ramiro Beltrán S.

Bibliographies concerning the social sciences or humanities in Latin America often list materials absent from other types of works. Among such bibliographies, the *Handbook of Latin American Studies*, published annually since 1935, provides perhaps the most detailed references to books and articles. Author and subject indexes facilitate access to the material. Brief annotations are given. Since 1964 the publication has been divided into two sections printed in alternate years, one dealing with the humanities and the other with the social sciences. Both contain references to the press. Bibliographic essays heading each section put the references in a useful context.

Probably the most extensive listing of current books and monographs on Latin America now published is the *Bibliographic Guide to Latin American Studies*, which updates the publication of the complete University of Texas Latin American Collection card catalog with new accessions from both that university and the Library of Congress. Martin H. Sable's 1967 *Guide to Latin American Studies* gives in its 5,024 annotated entries an excellent basic bibliography with author and subject indexes. S. A. Bayitch's 1967 *Latin America and the Caribbean: A Bibliographic Guide to Works in English*, though annotated, is particularly strong in the law and the Caribbean. The 1965 compilation of reference works from Abel Rodolfo Geoghegan includes not only bibliographies, but also dictionaries, guides, and annuals for all of Latin America. They are listed country by country.

Because one major approach to the study of popular culture in Latin America is from a Marxist perspective, four specialized bibliographies may be of particular interest. Martin H. Sable, with M. Wayne Dennis, compiled *Communism in Latin America, An International Bibliography: 1900–1945, 1960–1967*. It extended Ludwig Lauerhass, Jr.'s *Communism in Latin America, A Bibliography: The Post-War Years (1945–1960)*. Third, Leo Okinshevich and Robert G. Carleton prepared *Latin America in Soviet Writings, A Bibliography* in two volumes covering 1917 through 1964. Finally, the series *Marxism and the Mass Media: Towards A Basic Bibliography*, has been collected in two volumes, published in 1976 and 1978. Coverage is global and multilingual.

National bibliographic annuals or bibliographies of bibliographies frequently contain sections dealing with newspapers. See, for example, the bibliography of Argentine bibliographies by Abel Rodolfo Geoghegan. National bibliographies themselves are identified and analyzed in Irene Zimmerman's 1971 *Current National Bibliographies of Latin America: A State of the Art Study*. For later developments see the discussions and listings under "Bibliography and General Works" in the *Handbook of Latin American Studies*.

Periodical literature

The *Handbook of Latin American Studies* indexes articles and provides annotations by authorities in the fields covered. For coverage before its

1935 starting date, the *Index to Latin American Periodical Literature* may be useful. It consists of reproductions of the card index at the Columbus Memorial Library of the Pan American Union and thus reflects the shifting interests of that organization. It was continued in supplements to 1971. Extensive coverage, organized by subject (including newspapers), is found in the annual *Hispanic-American Periodicals Index*. An accompanying tool is the *HAPI Thesarus and Name Authority, 1975–1977*, compiled by Barbara G. Valk. A drawback of the *HAPI* for studying newspapers is that it fails to index the leading periodicals focusing on the press.

For description of periodicals, including some defunct titles, see Irene Zimmerman's 1961 *A Guide to Current Latin American Periodicals*. A partial updating is provided in Martin H. Sable's 1965 *Master Directory for Latin America*. For identification or location of periodicals from the time of a Latin American country's independence or formation, the most helpful source may be Rosa Quintero Mesa's *Latin American Serial Documents: A Holdings List*, in twelve volumes. Broader coverage in geographic origin of periodicals concerning Latin America is provided in the *Liste mondiale des périodiques spécialisés: Amérique latine* [*World List of Specialized Periodicals: Latin America*], from the Service d'Echange d'Informations Scientifiques of the Maison des sciences de l'Homme [Service for the Exchange of Scientific Information of the House of the Sciences of Man]. For publications of Latin American universities, the guide compiled by Nadia Levi et al. may be of assistance. An introduction to mostly North American sources is provided by Frances Goins Wilhoit and D. Craig Mitchell in *Mass Media Periodicals: An Annotated Bibliography*. The 1978 publication discusses some 125 periodicals, indexes, and statistical yearbooks; a particularly useful feature may be that it tells where each periodical is indexed. Finally, scholars who wish to place an article for publication might check the 1971 work by Alexander S. Birkos and Lewis A. Tambs, *Academic Writer's Guide to Periodicals*: Vol. 1, *Latini American Studies*.

Theses and Dissertations

Carl W. Deal provides a guide, organized by subject and indexed by author, to more than 7,200 dissertations in his 1978 *Latin America and the Caribbean: A Dissertation Bibliography*. It includes only works available from Xerox University Microfilms. Both theses and dissertations are indexed in *Journalism Abstracts*, published annually since 1963 by the Association for Education in Journalism and Mass Communication. The serial provides good coverage of United States programs granting advanced degrees in the association's field of interest. For theses and dissertations from Latin American schools, inquire of CIESPAL. Historical coverage of dissertations, primarily from United States universities, is provided by *Comprehensive Dissertation Index 1861–1972*. Current works from United States universities are covered in *Dissertation Abstracts International. A: The Humanities and Social Sciences*, with annual indexes.

Newspapers

The leading collection of Latin American newspapers in the United States is held by the Library of Congress. As described by Georgette Magassy Dorn in a 1983 article, the collection is strongest from 1930 to date, but it includes many titles from before that time. The basic guide to holdings in seventy United States libraries is Steven M. Charno's 1968 *Latin American Newspapers in United States Libraries: A Union List*, which gives about 5,500 titles. Newspapers from thirteen Latin American countries are listed in *Newspapers in Microform: Foreign Countries, 1948–1972*, which has become a continuing serial. In addition to these North American sources, several Latin American countries have published catalogs of library holdings of periodicals.

A number of directories, often compiled for advertising purposes, list newspapers. Some are serials. From Latin America, publications were located that cover Brazil in *Anuário de imprensa . . . [Press Directory]*, Central America and the Caribbean in *Directorio de medios publicitarios . . . [Directory of Publicity Media]*, and Mexico in *Directorio de medios [Media Directory]*. Guides with global coverage, including Latin America, are *Benn's Guide . . .* (from 1846) and *Editor & Publisher International Yearbook* (from 1920). If both fail to list a publication of interest, it might be found in the 1970 *Handbuch der Weltpresse [Handbook of the World Press]*.

Descriptive summaries of the press situation country by country are provided in George T. Kurian's 1982 *World Press Encyclopedia*. Earlier overviews are given in John C. Merrill et al., *The Foreign Press*. Greater depth is found in the United States Department of the Army *Area Handbooks*, researched by the Foreign Area Studies Division of American University. The *Handbooks* are updated periodically. The UNESCO series *Communication Policies in . . .* (name of country), starting in the mid-1970s, gives a broad context for analyzing a nation's press.

The fifth edition of UNESCO's *World Communications*, published in 1975, covered 200 countries. It provides brief histories and descriptions of the situation of the press, compiled from official statistics. The official statistical information is updated in UNESCO's *Statistical Yearbook*. Historical information on the press is found in UNESCO's *Press, Film, Radio: Reports on the Facilities of Mass Communication*, which reported on a post-World War II survey carried out to aid reconstruction efforts. That report was followed up with another one from UNESCO, *The Daily Press: A Survey of the World Situation in 1952*.

Two specialized press directories are the 1971 *International Guide to the*

Student Press and Dennis L. Wilcox's 1967 *English Language Newspapers Abroad: A Guide to Daily Newspapers in 56 Non-English-Speaking Countries*. Wilcox reports briefly on newspapers in seven Latin American countries.

Two services aid in locating coverage of Latin America in the daily press. *ISLA: Information Services on Latin America* has since October 1, 1970, indexed clippings about Latin America from *The Christian Science Monitor, Financial Times* (London), *Journal of Commerce, Los Angeles Times, Miami Herald, Manchester Guardian, Le Monde, New York Times, Washington Post*, and *Wall Street Journal*. The other service, *Bell & Howell Transdex*, provides translations made by the Joint Publications Research Service, a United States government agency, of documents and of articles from newspapers and other publications. The translations included are those requested by the government itself, and articles tend heavily toward technology and politics. Few pieces directly concern newspapers. Many items do come from Latin American newspapers.

The monthly magazine *World Press Review* also carries many translations of articles from Latin American newspapers. Some deal with newspapers.

Twenty years ago political scientists Karl M. Schmitt and David D. Burks described the newspapers they considered especially useful in studying Latin America: *The Christian Science Monitor, Correio da manha* [*Morning Courier*] and *Ultima hora* [*Latest Hour*] of Rio de Janeiro, *O Estado de São Paulo, Ecélsior* of Mexico City, *Miami Herald, New York Times, La Prensa* of Buenos Aires, *El siglo* [*The Century*] and *El tiempo* [*Time*] of Bogotá, *Wall Street Journal, Washington Post*, and *Washington Times Herald*. Some have since ceased publication. To this list might well be added *Uno más Uno* [*One-Plus-One*] of Mexico City. Finally, a list of sixty-one "Newspapers with Latin American Coverage and Interest Published in United States of America" was printed in Martin H. Sable's 1965 *Master Directory for Latin America*.

Book Reviews

Summaries of reviews are provided in Matos's annual *Guide to Reviews from and about Hispanic America*. About 580 of the principal review media are covered. Also useful might be the monthly publication, cumulated annually, *Book Review Digest*, and its companion, Dunmore-Leiber's *Book Review Digest: Author/Title Index, 1905/1974*.

Annual Reviews

Scholarly articles and reviews, some of which have involved newspapers, are published in *Studies in Latin American Popular Culture*. Annual reviews in communication include *International & Intercultural Communication An-*

nual, Mass Communication Review Yearbook, Communication Yearbook, and *Sage Annual Review of Communication Research*. While primarily useful for theoretical overviews, some provide pieces focusing on Latin American mass communication from time to time.

Miscellaneous Research Aids

Only a few of the many directories, handbooks, and other aids to research for Latin Americanists can be mentioned. Martin H. Sable's *The Latin American Studies Directory*, published in 1981, provides a recent guide to research centers and libraries. The Library of Congress gave information on 2,695 Latin Americanists in the social sciences and humanities in its 1971 directory. Latin American countries also publish national directories such as the ones for the United States; see, for example, the work of Guadelupe Salas Ortega.

Working Press of the Nation is broader in scope than its title suggests, including among its international coverage a newspaper and allied service directory and a directory of feature writers and syndicates. Martin H. Sable's 1965 *Master Directory for Latin America*, though dated, does contain valuable listings of national and international organizations, research centers, and training programs.

Several sources provide information about training for journalists in Latin America. In addition to CIESPAL, the recently formed Federación Latinoamericana de Asociaciones de Facultades de Comunicaión Social (FELAFALS) [Latin American Federation of Associations of Social Communication Faculties] has listed schools and discussed their programs in works by Joaquín Sánchez García. The previously mentioned 1981 publication by Raymond B. Nixon updates a 1970 study. William M. Pepper, Jr.'s, *Practical Translator. A Dictionary for Journalism and the Graphic Arts*, an English/Spanish, Spanish/English dictionary will enable one to understand the trade jargon of journalists.

RESEARCH ASSESSMENT AND FUTURE RESEARCH

Study of Latin American newspapers as popular culture has surged forward in the past few decades, though the term "popular culture" seldom has been used. The phrase "popular communication" is sometimes found, as in the 1983 special issue of *Chasqui* devoted to that topic.

Many of the studies have dealt with several media or media other than newspapers, not newspapers alone. The ideas from these studies may be applicable, nonetheless. Examples would include works by Luis Ramiro Beltrán S. and Elizabeth Fox de Cardona, Armand Mattelart, Antonio Pasquali, Ludovico Silva, Herbert I. Schiller, and others on "cultural imperialism." Historical studies have assumed a new depth, starting to move away from the mere listings that so dominated the historical study of the press at the time Gardner prepared her 1973 bibliography. See, for example, Alfredo Albuja Galindo's study of Ecuadorian journalism and Eduardo Ocampo Moscoso's history of journalism in Bolivia.

Part of the reason for the change may have been the growth of schools of "social communication" in Latin America, often replacing earlier educational programs directed at a narrower occupational purpose. The change was documented by Raymond B. Nixon in his 1981 study. The vital role of the training of journalists has been recognized in a book by José Baldivia Urdininea and others.

As students of the press in Latin America soon realize, newspapers of the area are strongly affected by their national governments. The ties reverberate throughout the content of the press, playing a crucial role in newspapers' impact on popular culture. Two recent books, by Marvin Alisky and Robert N. Pierce, have examined these relationships in detail.

Semiotic analysis, as shown, for example, in the work of Eliseo Verón, has contributed to understanding of the part played by newspapers.

Shortcomings of mass communication theory as developed primarily in North America also may have contributed to the rise of concern for the place of newspapers in popular culture. Two critical aspects in which the theory fell short seem to have been the focus on the individual and accompanying lesser attention to societal-level concerns, and a reluctance on the part of some scholars to address implications of their work for national policy. One result has been an increasing volume of writing on what has been termed "administrative versus critical research." A useful compilation on the issues may be found in the summer 1983 special issue of the *Journal of Communication*, "Ferment in the Field." Many authors stray far from the concerns of Paul Lazarsfeld, an early expositor of the distinction. The focus has been shifted by Everett Rogers to "empirical and critical schools of communication research." An acquaintance with recent thinking about the ideas involved will enhance appreciation of research on newspapers and popular culture.

Many areas on the research map remain only sparsely populated, however. Even basic descriptive studies are lacking for some smaller countries, as well as for the provincial press and for the alternative press, encompassing fringe, minority, and protest press. The role of women in the press has received little attention, as has the impact of the images of women conveyed by the press on society.

NOTES

1. Centro Internacional de Estudios Superiores de Comunicación para América Latina (CIESPAL), Avenida Amazonas 1521, Apartado 584, Quito, Ecuador.

2. Sociedade Brasileira de Estudos Interdisciplinares de Comunicação (INTER-
COM), Caixa Postal 20793, São Paulo, S.P., CEP 01000, Brasil.

PERIODICALS

Bell & Howell Transdex. Wooster, Ohio.
Boletím INTERCOM. São Paulo, Brazil.
Boletín Felafacs. Lima, Peru.
Cadernos de Jornalismo e Comunicação. Rio de Janeiro, Brazil.
Cadernos INTERCOM. São Paulo, Brazil.
Chasqui. Quito, Ecuador.
Columbia Journalism Review. New York.
Comunicación Integral. Medellín, Colombia.
Comunicación y Cultura. Buenos Aires, Argentina.
Cuadernos del Tercer Mundo. México, D.F.
The Democratic Journalist. Prague, Czechoslovakia.
Editor & Publisher. New York.
Freedom at Issue. New York.
Gazette. Amsterdam, The Netherlands.
IAPA News. Miami, Fla.
IAPA Report of the Committee on Freedom of the Press. Miami, Fla.
Index on Censorship. London.
ININCO. Caracas, Venezuela.
International Communications Bulletin (ICB). College Park, Md.
IPI Report. London.
ISLA: Information Services on Latin America. Oakland, Calif.
Jounalism Monographs. Columbia, S.C.
Journalism Quarterly. Columbia, S.C.
Journal of Communication. Philadelphia.
Latin American Perspectives. Riverside, Calif.
Materiales para la comunicación popular. Lima, Peru.
NACLA Report on the Americas. New York.
Overseas Press Club Bulletin. New York.
Periodismo Colombiano. Medellín, Colombia.
Periodista. Caracas, Venezuela.
World Press Review. New York.

BIBLIOGRAPHY

Albuja Galindo, Alfredo. *El periodismo en la dialéctica ecuatoriana* (Quito: Talleres
Gráficos Minerva, 1979).
Alisky, Marvin. *Latin American Journalism Bibliography* (México, D.F.: Fondo
de Publicidad Interamericana, 1958).
———. *Latin American Media—Guidance and Censorship* (Ames: Iowa State Uni-
versity Press, 1981).
Amiana, Manuel A. *El periodismo en la República Dominicana* (Santo Domingo:
La Nación, 1933).

Anuário de imprensa, rádio, & television (Rio de Janeiro: Impresa Jornalística, annual).

Appelman, Daniel. "The Mass Media of Latin America: Selected Information Sources." *Journal of Broadcasting* 22 (Spring 1978): 217–40.

Baldivia Urdininea, José; Planet, Mario; Solís, Javier; and Guerra, Tomás. *La formación de los periodistas en América Latina (México, Chile y Costa Rica)* (México, D.F.: Editorial Nueva Imagen, with Centro de Estudios Económicos y Sociales del Tercer Mundo, 1981).

Bayitch, S. A. *Latin America and the Caribbean: A Bibliography Guide to Works in English* (Coral Gables, Fla.: University of Miami Press, 1967).

Behrendt, Richard F. *Modern Latin America in Social Science Literature.* 3d rev. ed. (Albuquerque, N.M.: University of New Mexico Press, 1949).

———. *Modern Latin America in Social Science Literature. Supplement I, Part I* (Washington, D.C.: Pan American Union, Social Science Section, Department of Cultural Affairs, 1950).

———. *Modern Latin America in Social Science Literature. Supplement I, Part II* (Washington, D.C.: Pan American Union, Social Science Section, Department of Cultural Affairs, 1950).

Beltrán, Oscar Rafael. *Historia del periodismo argentino* (Buenos Aires: Editorial Sopena Argentina, 1943).

Beltrán S., Luis Ramiro, and Cardona, Elizabeth Fox de. *Comunicación dominada: Estados Unidos en los medios de América Latina* (México, D.F.: Instituto Latinoamericano de Estudios Transnacionales with Editorial Nueva Imagen, 1980).

Benn's Guide to Newspapers and Periodicals of the World (London: Benn Brothers Ltd., annual).

Bibliografía Brasileira de Comunicação (São Paulo: Sociedade Brasileira de Estudos Interdisciplinares de Comunicação, annual).

Bibliographic Guide to Latin American Studies (Boston: G. K. Hall, annual).

Bibliographic Index: A Cumulative Bibliography of Bibliographies (New York: H. W. Wilson, quarterly. Cumulated annually).

Birkos, Alexander S., and Tambs, Lewis A., comps. and eds. *Academic Writer's Guide to Periodicals.* Vol. 1, *Latin American Studies* (Kent, Ohio: Kent State University Press, 1971).

Blanco, Desiderio, and Bueno, Raúl. *Metodología del análisis semiótico* (Lima, Perú: Ed. Universidad de Lima, 1980).

Blum, Eleanor. *Basic Books in the Mass Media.* 2d ed. (Urbana: University of Illinois Press, 1980).

Book Review Digest (Bronx, New York: H. W. Wilson, monthly. 1905–date. Cumulated annually).

Bosi, Ecléa. *Cultura de massa e cultura popular—leituras operárias* (Petrópolis, Brazil: Editorial Vozes, 1972).

Cacua Prada, Antonio. *Historia del periodismo colombiano* (Bogotá: Imprenta Fondo Rotatorio Policía Nacional, 1968).

Carolina de Jesus, María. *Child of the Dark* (New York: E. P. Dutton & Co., 1962).

Charno, Steven M., comp. *Latin American Newspapers in United States Libraries: A Union List* (Austin: University of Texas Press, 1968).

Communication Yearbook (New Brunswick, N.J.: Transaction Books, annual).
Comprehensive Dissertation Index 1861–1972. 37 vols. (Ann Arbor, Mich.: Xerox University Microfilms, 1973).
Costa Lima, Luiz, ed. *Teoria da cultura de massa* (Rio de Janeiro, Brazil: Saga, 1969).
Deal, Carl W. *Latin America and the Caribbean: A Dissertation Bibliography* (Ann Arbor, Mich.: University Microfilms International, 1978).
Díaz Bordenave, Juan, and Arce, Antonio M. *Three Preliminary Bibliographies of Works Related to the Social Sciences in Latin America* (San José, Costa Rica: Programa Interamericano de Información Popular, 1962).
Directorio de medios: Información y tarifas (México, D.F.: Medios Publicitarios Mexicanos, quarterly).
Directorio de medios publicitarios de Centroamérica y el Caribe (Tegucigalpa, Honduras: Ediciones Técnicas Centroamericanas, 1972/73).
Dissertation Abstracts International. A: The Humanities and Social Sciences (Ann Arbor, Mich.: Xerox University Microfilms, monthly. Annual index).
Dorn, Georgette Magassy. "The Library of Congress and Other Latin American Resources in the Washington Area." *The Americas* 39 (April 1983): 537–47.
Dunmore-Leiber, Leslie, ed. *Book Review Digest: Author/Title Index, 1905–1974* 4 vols. (Bronx, New York: H. W. Wilson, 1976).
Dunn, M. Gilbert, and Cooper, Douglas W. "A Guide to Mass Communication Sources." *Journalism Monographs* 74 (November 1981).
Editor & Publisher International Yearbook (New York: Editor & Publisher, annual).
Faraone, Roque. *La prensa de Montevideo* (Montevideo: Universidad de la República, 1960).
Fernández y Medina, Benjamín. *La imprenta y la prensa en Uruguay desde 1807 a 1900* (Montevideo: Imprenta de Dornaleche y Reyes, 1960).
Fischer, Heinz-Dietrich, and Merrill, John C. *International and Intercultural Communication*. 2d ed. (New York: Hastings House, 1976).
Foreign Newspaper Report (Washington, D.C.: Library of Congress, 1973). Continued by *Foreign Newspaper and Gazette Report*.
Gálvez, María Albertina. *Historia de la imprenta* (Guatemala City: Editorial del Ministerio de Educación Pública, 1960).
Gardner, Mary A. "Central and South America Mass Communication: Selected Information Sources." *Journal of Broadcasting* 22 (Spring 1978): 196–216.
———. *The Inter American Press Association and Its Fight for Freedom of the Press, 1926–1960* (Austin: University of Texas Press, 1967).
———. *The Press of Latin America: A Tentative and Selected Bibliography in Spanish and Portuguese* (Austin: University of Texas, Institute of Latin American Studies, 1973).
Geoghegan, Abel Rodolfo. *Bibliografía de bibliografías argentinas, 1807–1970* (Buenos Aires: Casa Pardo, 1970).
———. *Obras de referencia de América Latina: Repertorio selectivo y anotado* (Buenos Aires: Impresa Crisol, 1965).
Gerbner, George, ed. "Ferment in the Field." *Journal of Communication* 33, no. 3 (Summer 1983).
Gordon, Thomas F., and Berna, Mary Ellen. *Mass Communication Effects and*

Processes: A Comprehensive Bibliography, 1950–1975 (Beverly Hills, Calif.: Sage, 1978).

Gropp, Arthur E., comp. *A Bibliography of Latin American Bibliographies* (Metuchen, N.J.: Scarecrow Press, 1968).

————. *A Bibliography of Latin American Bibliographies: Supplement* (Metuchen, N.J.: Scarecrow Press, 1971).

————. *A Bibliography of Latin American Bibliographies Published in Periodicals* (Metuchen, N.J.: Scarecrow Press, 1976).

Halloran, James D., ed. *Mass Media and Socialization: International Bibliography and Different Perspectives* (Leicester, England: International Association for Mass Communication Research, 1976).

Handbook of Latin American Studies (Washington, D.C.: Library of Congress, Hispanic Foundation, annual).

Handbuch der Weltpresse. 2 vols. (Cologne: Westdeutscher Verlag, 1970).

Henestrosa, Andrés, and Fernández de Castro, José Antonio. *Periodismo y periodistas de Hispanoamérica* (México, D.F.: Secretaría de Educación Pública, 1947).

Hispanic-American Periodicals Index (Tempe: Arizona State University, Center for Latin American Studies, annual).

Index to Latin American Periodical Literature (Boston: G. K. Hall, quarterly. Cumulated annually).

Index to Latin American Periodical Literature 1929–1960. Vols. 1 to 9 cumulative (Boston: G. K. Hall, 1962).

International and Intercultural Communication Annual (Chicago: Intercultural Press, annual).

International Guide to the Student Press (Leiden, The Netherlands: National Unions of Students, Coordinating Secretariat, 1971).

Isaza V., Guillermo, and Olaya B., Nohora. "Bibliografía de trabajos técnicos y científicos de Luis Ramiro Beltrán." (Bogotá, Colombia, 1980).

Journalism Abstracts (Columbia, S.C.: Association for Education in Journalism and Mass Communication, annual).

Kurian, George T., ed. *World Press Encyclopedia*. 2 vols. (New York: Facts on File, 1982).

Lauerhass, Ludwig, Jr., comp. *Communism in Latin America, A Bibliography: The Post-War Years (1945–1960)* (Los Angeles: University of California, Latin American Center, 1962).

Lazarsfeld, Paul F. "Remarks on Administrative and Critical Communications Research." *Studies in Philosophy and Social Sciences* 9, no. 1 (1941): 2–16.

Levi, Nadia; Basso, María Luisa; Morales, Josefina; and Vilar, Angela, compilers. *Guía de publicaciones periódicas de universidades latinoamericanas* (México, D.F.: Universidad Nacional Autónoma de México, 1967).

Llaverías y Martínez, Joaquín. *Contribución a la historia de la prensa periodística* (Havana: Publicaciones del Archivo Nacional de Cuba, 1957).

López Vallecillos, Italo. *El periodismo en El Salvador* (San Salvador: Editorial Universitaria, 1964).

Maison des Sciences de l'Homme, Service d'Echange d'Informations Scientifiques. *Liste mondiale des periodiques spécialisés: Amérique latine* (Paris: Mouton, 1974).

Mantilla, Jorge, ed. "Comunicación Popular." *Chasqui* (Quito) 8 (October–December 1983).

Marxism and the Mass Media: Towards a Basic Bibliography. 5 vols. in 2 (New York: International General, 1976, 1978).

Mass Communication Review Yearbook (Beverly Hills, Calif.: Sage, annual).

Matos, Antonio, comp. and ed. *A Guide to Reviews of Books From and About Hispanic America* (Detroit: Blaine Ethridge Books, annual).

Mattelart, Armand. *La comunicación masiva en el proceso de liberación* (México, D.F.: Siglo Veintiuno Editores, 1973).

———. *La cultura como empresa multinacional.* 2d ed. (México, D.F.: Ediciones Era, 1976).

———. *La industria cultural* (Bogotá, Colombia: Ed. Círculo Rojo, n.d.).

———. *Mito burgués vs. lucha de clases* (Bogotá, Colombia: Ed. Aquelarre, 1973).

———. *Multinacionales y sistemas de comunicación: Los apartos ideológicos del imperialismo* (México, D.F.: Siglo Veintiuno Editores, 1977).

Mattelart, Armand; Biedma, Patricio; and Funes, Santiago. *Comunicación masiva y revolución socialista* (Santiago, Chile: Ediciones Prensa Lationoamericana, 1971).

Mattelart, Armand; Piccini, Mabel; and Mattelart, Michèle. *Los medios de comunicación de masas: La ideología de la prensa liberal en Chile.* 3d ed. (Buenos Aires: Schapire-El Cid, 1976).

Merrill, John C.; Bryan, Carter R.; and Alisky, Marvin. *The Foreign Press* (Baton Rouge: Louisiana State University Press, 1964; 2d ed., 1970).

Mesa, Rosa Quintero, comp. *Latin American Serial Documents: A Holdings List.* 12 vols. (Ann Arbor, Mich.: University Microfilms, Xerox Education Group, 1968–1977).

Millares Carlo, Agustín. *La imprenta y el periodismo en Venezuela* (Caracas: Monte Avila Editores, 1969).

Montalván, José H. *Breves apuntes para la historia del periodismo nicaragüense* (León: Universidad Nacional de Nicaragua, 1958).

Mowlana, Hamid. *International Communication: A Selected Bibliography* (Dubuque, Iowa: Kendall/Hunt, 1971).

Myren, Delbert T. *Bibliography: Communications in Agricultural Development* (México, D.F.: Rockefeller Foundation, Mexican Agricultural Program, 1965).

Nixon, Raymond B. *Education for Journalism in Latin America* (New York: Council on Higher Education in the American Republics, 1970).

———. *Education for Journalism in Latin America: A Report of Progress* (Minneapolis: University of Minnesota, Minnesota Journalism Center, 1981).

Núñez, Francisco María. *La evolución del periodismo en Costa Rica* (San José: Imprenta Minerva, 1921).

Ocampo Moscoso, Eduardo. *Historia del periodismo boliviano* (La Paz: Librería Editorial Juventud, 1970, 1978).

———. *Orígenes de la imprenta en España y su desarrollo en América* (Buenos Aires: Institución Cultural Española, 1940).

Ochoa Campos, Moisés. *Reseña histórica del periodismo mexicano* (México, D.F.: Editorial Porrúa, 1960, 1968).

Okinshevich, Leo, and Carleton, Robert G. *Latin America in Soviet Writings: A*

Bibliography. Vol. 1, 1917–1958; Vol. 2, 1959–1964 (Baltimore, Maryland: Johns Hopkins University Press, 1966).

Olivos, Luis. "Publicaciones que contienen datos bibliográficos sobre las ciencias sociales en América Latina." *Revista Interamericana de Ciencias Sociales* 1 (1962).

Otero Muñoz, Gustavo Adolfo. *El periodismo en América, esquema de su historia a través de la cultura latino-americana (1492–1946)* (Lima: Editorial PTCM, 1946).

———. *Historia del periodismo en Colombia* (Bogotá: Editorial Minerva, 1936).

Pasquali, Antonio. *Comunicación y cultura de masas* (Caracas, Venezuela: Monte Avila, 1972).

Pepper, William M., Jr. *Practical Translator. A Dictionary for Journalism and the Graphic Arts* (New York: Inter American Press Association, 1971).

Pereyra, Miguel Carlos. *Acción de influencia del periodismo argentino en la cultura popular* (Rosario de Santa Fé, Argentina: Fenner, 1918).

Peruzzolo, Adair Caetano. *Comunicação e cultura* (Porto Alegre, Brazil: Sulina, 1972).

Picón-Salas, Mariano. *A Cultural History of Spanish America* (Berkeley: University of California Press, 1965).

Pierce, Robert N. *Keeping the Flame: Media and Government in Latin America* (New York: Hastings House, 1979).

Porras Barrenechea, Raúl. *El periodismo en el Perú* (Lima: Instituto Raúl Porras Barrenechea, 1970).

Rafi-Zadeh, Hassan. *International Mass Communications: Computerized Annotated Bibliography* (Carbondale, Ill.: Southern Illinois University, International Understanding Series, Honorary Relations Zone, 1972).

Recuero, María T. *Breve historia del periodismo en Panamá* (Panama City, 1935).

Reyes Matta, Fernando. *La comunicación masiva como escuela paralela* (México, D.F.: Instituto Latinoamericano de Estudios Transnacionales with Editorial Nueva Imagen, 1980).

Rocío Guadarrama, María del. *Bibliografía de América Latina: economía, política, sociología* (México, D.F.: Universidad Nacional Autónoma de México, Facultad de Ciencias Políticas y Sociales, 1976).

Rogers, Everett M. "The Empirical and the Critical Schools of Communication Research." In *Communication Yearbooks*, edited by Michael Burgoon (New Brunswick, N.J.: Transaction Books, 1982).

Sable, Martin H. *A Guide to Latin American Studies*. 2 vols. (Los Angeles: University of California, Latin American Center, 1967).

———. *The Latin American Studies Directory* (Detroit: Blaine Ethridge Books, 1981).

———. *Master Directory for Latin America* (Los Angeles: University of California, Latin American Center, 1965).

Sable, Martin H., with Dennis, M. Wayne, comps. *Communism in Latin America, An International Bibliography: 1900–1945, 1960–1967* (Los Angeles: University of California, Latin American Center, 1968).

Sage Annual Review of Communication Research (Beverly Hills, Calif.: Sage, annual).

Salas Ortega, Guadelupe, ed. *Directorio de asociaciones e institutos científicos y culturales de la República Mexicana* (México, D.F.: Dirección General de Publicaciones, 1959).

Sánchez, Carlos Enrique. *La imprenta en al Ecuador* (Quito: Talleres Gráficos Nacionales, 1935).

Sánchez, García, Joaquín. "Criterios para la formación de comunicadores sociales en América Latina." Paper presented at I Foro Internacional de Comunicación y Poder, Bogotá, Colombia, June 7–11, 1982.

――――. *Federación Lationamericana de Asociaciones de Facultades de Comunicación Social: Plan de Trabajo para Dos Años: 1982–1983: Proyecto* (Melgar, Colombia: Felafacs, 1981).

Schiller, Herbert I. *Mass Communications and American Empire* (New York: A. M. Kelley, 1969).

――――. *The Mind Managers* (Boston: Beacon Press, 1973).

――――. *Who Knows: Information in the Age of the Fortune 500* (Norwood, N.J.: Ablex, 1981).

Schmitt, Karl M., and Burks, David D. *Evolution or Chaos: Dynamics of Latin American Government and Politics* (New York: Praeger, 1963).

Silva, Ludovico. *La plusvalía ideológica* (México, D.F.: Nuestro Tiempo, 1971).

――――. *Teoría y práctica de la ideología* (México, D.F.: Nuestro Tiempo, 1971).

Smith, T. Lynn. "Bibliografía comentada sobre la sociología rural en Latino-américa." *Revista Mexicana de Sociología* 19 (January–April 1957): 175–83; (May–August 1957): 560–72; (September–December 1957): 946–50.

Sodre, Nelson Werneck. *Historia da imprensa do Brasil*. Retratos do Brasil, vol. 51 (Rio de Janiero: Editora Civilicação Brasileira, 1966).

Studies in Latin American Popular Culture (Las Cruces, New Mexico: Studies in Latin American Popular Culture, annual).

Swindler, William F., ed. *Latin American Journalism*. Contributions to Bibliography in Journalism, no. 4 (Lincoln: University of Nebraska, School of Journalism, 1944).

Swingewood, Alan. *O mito da cultura de massa* (Rio de Janeiro, Brazil: Ed. Interciéncia, 1978).

Thompson, Lawrence S. *Printing in Colonial Spanish America* (Hamden, Conn.: Archon Books, 1962).

Toribio Medina, José. *Historia de la imprenta en los antiguos dominios españoles de América y Oceania* (Santiago de Chile: Fondo Histórico y Bibliográfico José Toribio Medina, 1958).

Torre Revello, José. *El libro, la imprenta y el periodismo en América durante la dominación española* (Buenos Aires: Talleres, S.A., Casa Jacobo Pueser, 1940).

――――. *Orígenes de la imprenta en España y su desarrollo en América* (Buenos Aires: Institución Cultural Española, 1940).

UNESCO. *The Daily Press: A Survey of the World Situation in 1952*. Reports and Papers on Mass Communication, no. 7 (Paris: UNESCO, , 1953).

――――. *Press, Film, Radio: Reports on the Facilities of Mass Communication*. 5 vols. and supplements 1 and 2 (Paris: UNESCO, 1947–1951).

――――. *Statistical Yearbook* (Paris: UNESCO, annual).

――――. *Tentative International Bibliography of Works Dealing With Press Problems*

1900–1952. Reports and Papers on Mass Communication, no. 14 (Paris: UNESCO, 1954).

———. *World Communications: A 200-Country Survey of Press, Radio, Television, and Film*. 5th ed. (Paris: UNESCO, 1975).

U.S. Department of the Army. *Area Handbook* . . . (Washington, D.C.: U.S. Government Printing Office, irregular issuance).

U.S. Library of Congress, Catalog Publication Division. *Newspapers in Microform: Foreign Countries, 1948–1972* (Washington, D.C.: Library of Congress, 1973). Continued in the periodical *Newspapers in Microform*.

———. *Newspapers in Microform: Foreign Countries, 1973–1977* (Washington, D.C.: Library of Congress, 1978).

U.S. Library of Congress, Hispanic Foundation. *National Directory of Latin Americanists: Biobibliographies of 2,695 Specialists in the Social Sciences and Humanities*. 2d ed. (Washington, D.C.: U.S. Government Printing Office, 1971).

Valdebenito, Alfonso. *Historia del periodismo chileno, 1812–1955*. 2d ed. (Santiago: Imprenta Fantasía, 1965).

Valle, Rafael Heliodoro. *El periodismo en Honduras: Notas para su historia* (Mexico City, 1960).

Valk, Barbara G., comp. *HAPI Thesaurus and Name Authority, 1975–1977* (Los Angeles: University of California, Latin American Center, 1979)

———. *Hispanic American Periodicals Index* (Los Angeles: University of California, Latin American Center, annual).

Van Bol, Jean-Marie, and Fakhfakh, Abdelfattah. *L'emploi des moyens de communication de masse dans les pays en voie de developement* (Brussels, Belgium: Centre International de Documentation Economique et Sociale Africaine, 1971).

Verón, Eliseo, comp. *Lenguaje y comunicación social*. 2d ed. (Buenos Aires: Nueva Visión, 1971).

Verón, Eliseo. *Conducta, estructura, y comunicación* (Buenos Aires: Ed. Tiempo Contemporáneo, 1972).

Wilcox, Dennis L. *English Language Newspapers Abroad: A Guide to Daily Newspapers in 56 Non-English-Speaking Countries* (Detroit: Gale Research Co., 1967).

Wilhoit, Frances Goins, and Mitchell, D. Craig. *Mass Media Periodicals: An Annotated Bibliography* (Bloomington: Indiana University, School of Journalism, Center for New Communications, 1978).

Working Press of the Nation (New York: Farrell Publications, annual).

Zimmerman, Irene. *Current National Bibliographies of Latin America: A State of the Art Study* (Gainesville: University of Florida, Center for Latin American Studies, 1971).

———. *A Guide to Current Latin American Periodicals: Humanities and Social Sciences* (Gainesville, Fla.: Kallman Publishing Co., 1961).

Index

Contributors

GERARD BÉHAGUE is professor of musicology and ethnomusicology and chairman of the Department of Music at the University of Texas at Austin. He specializes in Latin American ethnomusicology, specifically in Afro-Brazilian religious musics and Brazilian urban popular music. His publications include *Music in Latin America: An Introduction* (Prentice-Hall), which has been translated into Spanish by Monte Avila Editores; *Performance Practice: Ethnomusicological Perspectives* (Greenwood Press); 121 entries in *The New Grove Dictionary of Music and Musicians*; and 120 entries in *Dizionario Enciclopedico Universale Della Musica E Dei Musicisti* on Latin America and Latin American musicians. Professor Béhague is past president of the Society for Ethnomusicology, has served on the Board of Directors of the College Music Society and the American Musicological Society, and is chairman of the Discipline Screening Committee in Music and Musicology of the Council for International Exchange of Scholars.

KENT MAYNARD is assistant professor of sociology/anthropology at Denison University. He has been engaged in ethnographic research in both Ecuador and Cameroon, with interests in the study of religious movements, proselytization, therapy systems, and social theory. Published articles include work on theories of social change and on models of society in the ethnographies of E. E. Evans-Pritchard. He is working presently on a monograph concerning the social identity and organization of Protestant groups in urban Ecuador.

HAROLD E. HINDS, JR., is associate professor of Latin American history and coordinator of Latin American Area Studies at the University of Minnesota, Morris. He has published numerous articles on Mexican popular culture, one of which won the Russell B. Nye Award. Along with Charles Tatum, he is co-editor of the annual journal, *Studies in Latin*

American Popular Culture and is preparing a book-length study of Mexican comic books.

JOSEPH STRAUBHAAR is assistant professor of telecommunication at Michigan State University. His research and teaching interests are in international telecommunication, the impact of new technologies in the Third World, and Latin American media. He has published articles on *telenovelas* and TV variety shows in Brazil, on American influence on Brazilian TV, and on cross-border program flows and their impact. He is currently editing a book on broadcasting in Latin American and researching another on the impact of videocassette recorders in the Third World. He has a Ph.D. in International Relations from the Fletcher School of Law and Diplomacy, Tufts University.

ERIC A. WAGNER is professor of sociology at Ohio University and previously chaired the Department of Sociology and Anthropology. His research interests center around the social aspects of Latin American sport. Recent publications include studies of baseball in Cuba, sport and revolution in Nicaragua, a comparative study of Cuba and Nicaragua, and sport participation in Cuba, Belize, and Nicaragua. He offers courses on the sociology of sport, Third World development, and urban sociology.

CORNELIA BUTLER FLORA has studied and written about *fotonovelas* in Latin America for the last fifteen years. She is professor of sociology at Kansas State University, where she is involved in a variety of projects on agricultural development in Latin America and Africa. Her current research focuses on the changing role of women and the myths that surround that change in the United States and Latin America.

JOHN MOSIER is associate director of the Film Buffs Institute at Loyola University in New Orleans. He is editor of *The New Orleans Review* and a contributing editor for *Américas* magazine. He was a member of the Camera d'Or Jury at the Cannes Film Festival from 1978 to 1982. He is co-editor of *Women and Men Together*, an anthology of short fiction. His articles on Latin American and Eastern European film have been published in Europe, North America, Brazil, and Mexico.

ROBERT H. LAVENDA is associate professor of anthropology at St. Cloud (Minn.) State University. He has carried out research on festivals and carnivals in Venezuela and Ecuador and has most recently been studying community festivals in Minnesota. He has published articles on carnival in Caracas during the late nineteenth century, the process of social urbanization in Caracas, and small town festivals in Minnesota, as well as a review article on the study of Latin American festivals. He is on the editorial board of *Studies in Latin American Popular Culture* and served on the Executive Council of the Association for the Anthropological Study of Play.

NAOMI LINDSTROM is associate professor of Spanish and Portuguese and student advisor at the Institute for Latin American Studies at the University of Texas at Austin. Her area of specialization is innovative writing of the 1920s and 1930s. She is the author of *Literary Expressionism in Argentina, Macedonio Fernández*, and the forthcoming *Woman's Voice in Latin American Literature*. She teaches literary theory and a comparative survey of avant garde movements.

ROBERT N. PIERCE is professor of journalism at the University of Florida. His principal fields are Latin American mass communications and journalism as literature. He has traveled in thirty-seven countries, taught and lived in several, and gathered data in most. He is the author of *Keeping the Flame: Media and Government in Latin America*. He has worked for the *Miami Herald* and the *Associated Press* and now is translating and editing the early journalism of Gabriel García Márquez.

KURT KENT is professor of journalism and Director of Graduate Studies in the College of Journalism and Communications, University of Florida. He has served as director of the College's Communication Research Center and director of the Latin American Data Bank of the Center for Latin American Studies, University of Florida. He teaches courses in mass communication theory and research methods and in international communication.